RAZZLE DAZZLE

THE BATTLE FOR BROADWAY

MICHAEL RIEDEL

SIMON & SCHUSTER

New York London Toronto Sydney New Delhi

Simon & Schuster
1230 Avenue of the Americas
New York, NY 10020

First Simon & Schuster hardcover edition October 2015

SIMON & SCHUSTER and colophon are registered trademarks
of Simon & Schuster, Inc.

For information about special discounts for bulk purchases,
please contact Simon & Schuster Special Sales at 1-866-506-1949 or
business@simonandschuster.com.

The Simon & Schuster Speakers Bureau can bring authors to your live event.
For more information or to book an event contact the
Simon & Schuster Speakers Bureau at 1-866-248-3049 or
visit our website at www.simonspeakers.com.

Interior design by Joy O'Meara

Manufactured in the United States of America

10   9   8   7   6   5   4   3

Library of Congress Cataloging-in-Publication Data is available.

ISBN 978-1-4516-7216-9
ISBN 978-1-4516-7218-3 (ebook)

For my parents,
and for my friends
Mike Kuchwara, Jacques le Sourd, and Martin Gottfried

CONTENTS

AUTHOR'S NOTE

The first time I ever heard the names "Shubert" and "Nederlander" would have been in the spring of 1987, when I had an internship in the office of Broadway producer Elizabeth I. McCann. I was nineteen and studying history at Columbia. I liked Broadway and knew something about its famous shows, writers, and performers. But I couldn't have told you what a producer did, let alone a theater owner like the Shuberts or the Nederlanders.

As it so happened, McCann was coproducing *Les Liaisons Dangereuses* that spring with both companies. One of my first jobs was to deliver the opening night guest list to their offices.

I went to the Nederlander headquarters above the Palace Theatre first. I rode up in a rickety old cage of an elevator operated by an ancient black man who opened his Bible and prayed for me. I stepped out of the elevator into a dusty office full of shabby furniture. I handed the envelope to the receptionist, who was on the phone and barely looked at me. Everybody else in the office was on the phone as well. You could take your pick of at least a half dozen conversations. As I left, I caught sight of a man in another office. His feet were on the desk, and he was yelling into his phone. All that was missing was a cigar in his mouth. He looked like the boss.

I crossed Times Square to Shubert Alley and walked through a discreet doorway next to the Shubert Theatre. Another small, though not rickety, elevator took me up to the executive offices of the Shubert

Organization. The doors opened on to what looked to me like a suite from the Palace of Versailles. The furniture was plush and elegant. Sunlight streamed in from a skylight. Tapestries like something you'd find in the Cloisters hung from the walls. There were bookcases full of leather-bound books. I had no idea such luxury existed in the heart of seedy Times Square. The place was silent. The receptionist sat behind an enormous desk. I handed her the envelope. "Thank you," she whispered.

I didn't know it at the time, but what I had seen that day was power. At the Nederlanders, the power was scrappy and energetic. At the Shuberts, it was quiet, rich, abiding, and intimidating.

I never met the people who wielded that power during my internship. I barely met my boss, Liz McCann. She never bothered to learn my name—I was "the kid"—and to this day she has no memory of my having worked for her. Years later I told her she gave me my start in the theater. "I have that to add to my sins?" she said.

But I never forgot my brief glimpses of where the Shuberts and the Nederlanders conducted their affairs.

In 1989, just a few days after graduation, I landed a job as the managing editor of *TheaterWeek,* a tiny magazine run out of an old storage room at 28 West Twenty-Fifth Street. I started hearing the names Shubert and Nederlander all the time, and now that I had a perch in the theater world (on the lowest branch), I was determined to meet them.

I first saw Bernard B. Jacobs, the president of the Shubert Organization, in 1992 at a benefit for the United Jewish Appeal. He was being honored, and everybody in the room lined up to pay their respects. It was like the wedding scene in *The Godfather.* I introduced myself as the managing editor of *TheaterWeek*—and made no discernable impression.

I made a little more headway with Gerald Schoenfeld, the chairman of the Shubert Organization. He was voluble and engaging. Afterward, whenever I ran into him at an event, he was always happy to talk. But I didn't get to know him well until after Jacobs's death in 1996. By then I was the theater reporter for the *New York Daily News* and often called him for a quote. He was an excellent source. He didn't leak stories, but he confirmed what I'd heard, and provided background and perspective.

I lunched with him at Frankie & Johnnie's Steakhouse and spent afternoons in his office watching him at work. I was privy to everything, with the stipulation that my visits were off the record. He delighted in showing me around the executive offices, and regaled me with tales of working for J. J. Shubert, the youngest of the three brothers who founded the empire. I had a glimmer back then that there was a story to be told about the Shuberts and Broadway, but I had no idea I'd be the one to tell it.

I also got to know Philip J. Smith, who became second-in-command after Jacobs died. His knowledge of the Shuberts was vast, and he was a superb storyteller. He could remember who was in the room during a crucial meeting, where everybody sat, and what they said. He was close to Jacobs, and he impressed upon me how important Bernie and Jerry were to the Shubert Organization and Broadway in the 1970s, when Times Square was a mess, the theater business was in trouble, and New York City was careening toward bankruptcy.

I developed a friendship with Jacobs's widow, Betty, and spent several summer weekends with her at her house on Shelter Island. One afternoon she showed me an interview Jacobs had done for the League of American Theaters and Producers shortly before he died. He gave a candid, funny, and insightful account of how he and Schoenfeld fought their way to the top of the Shubert empire and to the top of the American theater. Once again, I had a sense that there was a story to be told here.

I got to know James M. Nederlander, the man I saw with his feet up on his desk that day in 1987, through my friendship with his son Jimmy Jr. and Jimmy Jr.'s wife, Margo. Over a couple of dinners, Jimmy Sr. told me about the family theater business in Detroit and his early years in New York. "Senior loves talking to you," Margo said. About five years ago, she asked if I would do some taped interviews with him for a possible memoir. I lunched with him once a week for about a year, enjoying colorful tales of his father's rivalry with the Shubert brothers, and his own battles with Schoenfeld and Jacobs. For the third time, I remember thinking there was a story there.

As I got to know the Shuberts and the Nederlanders, I was covering—first for the *News* and then, starting in 1998, the *New York Post*—a Broadway that was emerging from the backwaters of the entertainment industry to become the multibillion-dollar global empire it is today.

In 1989, the first year I attended the Tony Awards, Broadway was so thin that only three shows were nominated for Best Musical—*Starmites* (a musical about the guardian angels of "Innerspace"), *Black and Blue* (a revue of songs by Fats Waller, Eubie Blake, and Duke Ellington), and *Jerome Robbins' Broadway* (a revue of scenes and dances from the director's famous musicals). Since then, I've covered Tony Awards that featured such musicals as *Beauty and the Beast, Rent, The Lion King, Ragtime, The Producers, Hairspray, Chicago, Mamma Mia!, Wicked, Billy Elliot,* and *The Book of Mormon*—productions that have played all over the world and made hundreds of millions of dollars.

I've also seen the neighborhood I've worked in for twenty-five years, Times Square, go from a squalid place people avoided to the shiny tourist attraction it is today. The Times Square of the 1980s never bothered me. It was rough but fun, and it felt like nowhere else in America. But I don't deride the Times Square of 2015, which detractors bemoan as "Disneyfied." The throngs of gaping tourists you have to thread your way through to get to the theater on a summer night can be exasperating. But cities change, and I'd rather a thriving, if touristy, Times Square than a sad, derelict one.

Physically, the Times Square of today has changed enormously from that of the seventies and eighties, except for West Forty-Fourth and Forty-Fifth Streets, which are still lined with Broadway theaters that were built in the early part of the twentieth century. Most of the businesses in Times Square have come and gone, but Broadway and its theaters have always been there.

"There's only one Broadway, and it's in New York," said the narrator of the famous I Love New York TV commercials I watched as a kid in upstate New York in the seventies and eighties.

The connection between the fortunes of Broadway and New York was the key to pulling together all the stories I'd heard from Jerry Schoenfeld, Phil Smith, Betty Jacobs, and Jimmy Nederlander. Like the city itself, Broadway nearly collapsed in the 1970s. But a handful of people—the Shuberts, the Nederlanders, and some others you'll meet in these pages—stood by it and shored it up. In so doing, they helped lift the fortunes of Times Square and, I think, New York City itself.

This book is about their struggle, and if it makes any impression at all I hope it's that Broadway and its fractious band of colorful characters were as important to the survival of this city as any Wall Street titan, real estate magnate, civic leader, or politician.

RAZZLE
DAZZLE

CHAPTER ONE

The Ice Age

This is a very weird way to begin an investigation, David Clurman thought as he listened to the anonymous caller on the other end of the line.

A special assistant to the powerful New York State attorney general, Louis J. Lefkowitz, Clurman knew nothing about the economics of the Broadway theater. His speciality was real estate and securities. At thirty-five, he'd already made a name for himself as a tough investigator of the city's powerful real estate magnates, authoring the first law in New York state history regulating the sales of co-ops and condominiums.

Important, to be sure; glamorous, hardly.

But here he was, sitting in his office at 80 Centre Street in the spring of 1963, listening to a fast-talking, agitated, self-described "angel," which, as the caller explained to Clurman, was showbiz slang for backers of Broadway shows.

"I'm not going to give you my name," the angel said. "But you should look into what goes on with the money on Broadway."

Clurman asked why the angel was concerned.

"Well, I made an investment in a play, and the producer used the money to buy a lobster boat in Montauk."

"A lobster boat?" Clurman said. This was indeed a strange way to begin an investigation.

But Clurman, who could smell flimflam down to the paperclips,

was interested. He spent nearly an hour on the phone with the tip-
ster, getting a crash course in the murky world of Broadway financing.
Investors, it seemed, were in the dark about everything—production
costs, weekly running costs, where the money they invested went,
whether the shows were fully capitalized or not, how much they lost
when they closed. Sometimes their money went into the productions
they wanted to support; sometimes it wound up in shows they didn't
even know about. And sometimes it went to buy lobster boats in
Montauk.

Producers wanted to take an angel's money, give him a hug on
opening night, give him some money if the show worked, and if it
didn't, well, that's Broadway—it's a crap shoot. Move on to the next
show, next season. It's going to be a surefire hit. Stick with me, the
producers seemed to say, because I have a script on my desk right now
that's a winner.

"What about accountants?" Clurman asked. "Don't you get a complete accounting of the production after it closes?"

"Accountants?" the caller responded, laughing. They just accept
whatever documents the producers give them. Ledgers, balance
sheets, profit and loss statements—they don't exist on Broadway. Angels were like slot machine players. Bewitched by the twinkling lights,
they put in quarter after quarter, hoping to hit the jackpot. And if
they did—if they backed *The Music Man*, *My Fair Lady*, *Oliver!*—the
quarters come so fast, who thought about where all those other quarters went?

Broadway's a casino, New York City's very own Las Vegas.

"Everything he told me was so antithetical to the whole idea of
disclosure that it amazed me," Clurman said, remembering the phone
call nearly fifty years later.

Clurman thanked the caller and hung up. Something was going
on here, he thought, something worth investigating. You can't have a
business in New York City—a business as high profile and as important
to the life of the city as Broadway—that doesn't abide by basic rules
of accounting.

Financially, it sounded like the Wild, Wild West—with tap shoes.

Clurman left his office on the way to lunch, passing the room for "the boys," as Attorney General Lefkowitz called the reporters who covered him. Lefkowitz, popular, charming, a politician who loved to be in the papers, liked the boys and had given them a room of their own near his office in the state office building. As Clurman walked by, he ran into Lawrence O'Kane, a reporter for the *New York Times*. Clurman liked O'Kane. He was smart, curious, fair. They'd talked about a number of cases Clurman had investigated, and he found O'Kane to be a good sounding board.

Clurman asked O'Kane if he knew anything about the theater. The *Times*, after all, was located on West Forty-Third Street, right in the heart of Broadway. It covered the theater aggressively and its critics and theater reporters—Brooks Atkinson, Sam Zolotow, Louis Funke—were, to *Times* readers, household names.

Not really, O'Kane said. Why?

Clurman recounted his conversation with the angel. He was talking to O'Kane as a friend, telling him about this odd call. There were no names mentioned, no talk of an investigation, just a general discussion about some funny business on Broadway.

O'Kane was interested. Clurman said he'd tell him if anything came of it.

The next morning, on his way to the subway, Clurman bought a copy of the *New York Times*. Standing on the platform, he glanced at the headlines above the fold—KENNEDY MEETING WITH MACMILLAN LIKELY JUNE 29–30; RISE IN TEEN-AGE JOBLESS PUSHES U.S. RATE TO 5.9%. Then he looked at the stories below the fold. One caught his eye. FINANCING PRACTICES IN THEATER UNDER BROADWAY INQUIRY BY STATE.

"A 'far-reaching' investigation of theatrical practices—both on and Off-Broadway—is under way in the office of the State Attorney General," the article began. Lefkowitz, O'Kane wrote, "decided to make the investigation after a preliminary study had given indications of 'peculiar' financing methods in the industry and a possible need for corrective legislation."

Clurman was stunned. Holy God, he thought. What is going on? He'd never dreamed that a casual conversation with one of the boys would wind up as front-page news in the *New York Times*. His preliminary study consisted of a few notes he'd scribbled on a yellow legal pad during the phone call.

When he arrived at 80 Centre Street, Lefkowitz summoned him to his office. "How come you didn't tell me about this?" Lefkowitz demanded.

Clurman explained that he thought his conversation with O'Kane had been casual. It was not in any way, he said, an official announcement. Still, he added, it might be worth looking into the financial practices of Broadway. And, as this morning's *Times* proved, it would get headlines.

"Can I conduct an inquiry into this to see what's going on?" he asked.

Lefkowitz, enticed by headlines, gave him the go ahead.

Underneath his quiet, scholarly demeanor, Clurman had the investigating zeal of Inspector Javert. Let the hunt begin, he thought.

That morning, in Shubert Alley, the town square of Broadway, everybody was on edge. There had been investigations in the past about money flying around the theater. They always seemed to coincide with the election of the attorney general. But they never amounted to much. This one, however, made the front page of the *New York Times*, which meant that it was serious. Emanuel "Manny" Azenberg, then a young company manager, recalled, "Everybody that day was walking around with a little brown spot on the back of their pants."

Clurman didn't know where to begin. He was now in charge of a "far-reaching" investigation into the financial practices of Broadway about which, aside from being a casual theatergoer who had enjoyed *My Fair Lady*, he knew nothing.

And then he got another call.

If you were a lawyer in 1963, Morris Ernst was a name you knew. A founder of the American Civil Liberties Union, Ernst represented Random House in its fight to get James Joyce's *Ulysses* published in the United States despite state-by-state laws against obscenity. A fixture of New York society, he had been close to Franklin Roosevelt, Harry Truman, and several Supreme Court justices. He loved the theater, and numbered among his friends Edna Ferber, Groucho Marx, E. B. White, and Charles Addams.

Ernst told Clurman he knew some people who were interested in his investigation. He invited Clurman to his apartment at Two Fifth Avenue that night for an informal meeting. Nothing official, he stressed. He just wanted to introduce Clurman to some theater people who, he thought, might be able to help him. "They think your investigation needs to be amplified," Ernst said.

When Clurman arrived at Two Fifth Avenue, just north of Washington Square Park, he was introduced to an impressive array of theater people. Leland Hayward, tall, patrician, elegant, the son of a United States senator, seemed to be the leader. His productions included *South Pacific*, *Mister Roberts*, and *Gypsy*.

Gilbert Miller, son of the legendary producer Henry Miller, was there, too. Gilbert specialized in high-class plays—Shaw's *Candida*, Anouilh's *Ring Around the Moon*, Eliot's *The Cocktail Party*.

Another impressive figure was Roger Stevens, one of the founders of the Kennedy Center for the Performing Arts and the National Endowment for the Arts. Dickie Moore, one-time child actor who starred in the *Our Gang* series, was there representing the Actors' Equity Association, for which he was the public relations director. Representing the Dramatists Guild was Russel Crouse, coauthor of the book to *The Sound of Music*.

"This was not a bunch of little guys who invest in the theater," Clurman recalled. "These were some very notable people."

Hayward took the floor. Clurman's investigation into the financial practices on Broadway was essential, he said. Clurman remembered thinking how unusual it was "for the people I was talking to to want to be investigated." But Hayward said too many of his colleagues were "kidnapping" investors' money, and the investors were getting fed up. Money was becoming harder and harder to raise, and Broadway itself was in a precarious position. Its so-called golden age—from 1940 to 1960—was winding down. There had only been seventeen new shows in the 1962–63 season, many of them flops.

When Hayward finished speaking, somebody called out from the back of the room, "What about the ice?"

"Ice." Other than being something you put in your drink, Clurman did not know the term. The room fell silent, and then Clurman's education began.

Ice—ticket corruption—went as far back as Jenny Lind's sold-out performances in 1850.[1] "It has been a thriving fungus ever since," William Goldman noted in his classic theater book, *The Season*.

Other theater historians say ticket corruption goes back much further, to ancient Athens, where you had to bribe someone to get a ticket for a sold-out run of *Medea* at the Theater of Dionysus.

Whatever its murky history, ice is a function of supply and demand. Broadway theaters seat, at most, eighteen hundred people. If a show's a hit, a lot more than eighteen hundred people want to see it, and they want to see it from the best seat possible. The show is, of course, sold out, but somebody, usually a ticket broker, can help—for a price considerably higher than the face value of the ticket. To get that ticket, the broker has to bribe someone, usually someone in the box office. And that bribe—the difference between the face value of the ticket and the amount the broker paid to get his hands on it—is the ice.

The producers explained to Clurman how this black market worked. The top ticket price for a musical at the time was about ten dollars. This was, of course, before computers, so the tickets were hard tickets, kept in racks in the box offices. The men who ran the box offices controlled the tickets. Arthur Cantor, a producer and publicist in the early sixties, was desperate to get a pair of seats for a client to Neil Simon's hit play *Barefoot in the Park* at the Biltmore Theatre. He called in a lot of favors, but to no avail. And then one afternoon, walking through Shubert Alley, he ran into the box office treasurer at the Biltmore. He asked if he could help. The treasurer smiled and said, "Let me see what the Rabbi has." He pulled out a fistful of tickets—that weekend's best orchestra locations.

A broker might pay a box office man five, ten, fifteen dollars above face value, depending on the popularity of the show, to get a ticket. The broker would then resell that ticket for as much as fifty dollars. The box office man pocketed the bribe, which because it was cash, was untraceable. It melted away, just like ice.

For years, the box office treasurers never asked for a raise. They didn't need to. They were running, as one producer said, "their very own concession stand."

There was a law on the books for years governing the reselling of tickets in New York. It restricted the broker markup to just a dollar fifty plus a fifteen-cent tax. The producers said nobody ever paid any attention to the law.

How much ice was there? Clurman wondered. No one could say for certain, but it flowed down Broadway as if a giant iceberg up in Washington Heights had melted. And, of course, no one ever paid taxes on ice.

Hayward and the others were upset that the ice was going to box office people (and others) who had nothing to do with creating the show. Money was being made off the work of producers, writers, directors. Many weren't seeing any of it. Investors, too, were getting screwed.

And so was the public. Tickets were not available to hit shows because brokers had scooped them up. Brokers' offices lined the side streets of Times Square. (Some were legitimate, but many were just hole-in-the-wall scalpers.) You had to have connections—or be willing to pay astronomical prices—to get into, say, *Stop the World—I Want to Get Off!* Hayward himself had once called the box office of one of his shows and been told the performance that night was sold out. But when he arrived at the theater he was dismayed to see rows of empty seats. The brokers had not been able to unload all their tickets.[2]

The regular theatergoer, Hayward said, was getting fed up with being told the show was sold out when brokers had tickets.

Clurman told the group, "If this relates to the use of funds that are coming in from investors, I suppose I could say I have jurisdiction to go into it."

A solemn man with dark eyes whom Clurman had not noticed jumped up from his seat in the corner of the room and said, "This man knows the jokes!" The solemn man began to smile. Clurman recognized him—Richard Rodgers, composer of *Oklahoma!*, *Carousel*, and *The King and I*.

Rodgers, a producer as well as composer, hated ice. People were pocketing huge amounts of money from his hit shows, and neither he nor his investors ever saw a penny of it. He'd had fights with theater owners about ticket corruption.

In 1946, Rodgers and Oscar Hammerstein produced Irving Berlin's *Annie Get Your Gun*, starring Ethel Merman. Its out-of-town tryout was in Philadelphia at a Shubert theater. A local reporter went to the box office the day tickets went on sale and was told nothing in the orchestra was available for the run of the show. She was suspicious since the musical hadn't even been advertised in the papers yet. So she called Oscar Hammerstein. He was flabbergasted. "Richard Rodgers and I have nothing to do with the distributions of tickets," he said.[3] Rodgers and Hammerstein were furious. They called Lee Shubert, the head of the company. Lee called the box office manager in Philadelphia and bellowed, "Get those goddamned tickets back, you hear me? I don't want to know anything except you get those tickets!"

Orchestra seats to *Annie Get Your Gun* in Philadelphia became available. And Dick Rodgers became interested in what went on in the box offices of his shows.

Clurman left the meeting after nearly three hours determined to investigate Broadway. From what he'd heard, ticket scalping and misuse of investor money was out of control. Over the next six months, he interviewed, and in some cases subpoenaed, nearly three hundred people in the theater, from producers to theater owners, box office staffers to employees of companies that serviced Broadway productions. Some cooperated, but many took the Fifth Amendment.

But Clurman got hold of hotel records, which revealed that hundreds and hundreds of tickets had been directed to hotel concierges. He subpoenaed records from major New York corporations—banks and several textile companies—that paid huge amounts to brokers to secure seats to hit shows for their clients. He also found informants— "some pretty horrible little people," he would say years later—who agreed to cooperate with his investigation.

As he nosed around Broadway he began to get some strange phone calls. One person told him, "Don't stand too close to the edge of the subway platform." Another caller asked if "he liked chorus girls." When he said he wasn't interested, the caller replied, "Oh, you're that kind. Do you want some chorus boys?"

What Clurman uncovered during his six-month examination of Broadway stunned even so seasoned an investigator as himself. It wasn't just that money was flying around, unaccounted for. Or that bribes were being paid under the table. He discovered a "train of aggravated corruption. Everybody," he recalled, "was having a ball—and nobody was watching."

There were scams of all sorts, about which angels knew nothing. For instance, if three trucks were required to bring scenery down from the shop to the theater, the trucking company might make out a bill for four—and the producer could pocket the money for the fourth, nonexistent, truck.

Suppliers of scenery, costumes, and lights admitted to giving kickbacks to producers and general managers (the people who run the day-to-day operations of a production) in exchange for contracts. On any one show, the kickbacks could amount to several thousand dollars.

Clurman, an expert in accounting, was shocked to discover such clauses in investment papers as this: "Our audit was conducted in accordance with generally accepted theatrical accounting principles. Such statements as to the operations and cash position of theatrical ventures do not customarily require the rendering of an opinion. No direct verification of assets or liabilities was undertaken."

In plain English: "We have no idea if these statements are true."

Clurman subpoenaed records from some productions, and discovered that on one show, which had been produced for $500,000, the books were kept in pencil. The numbers were smudged.

But the real money was in the ice. Clurman discovered that it wasn't limited to box office personnel. Many people—theater owners, general managers, producers—were taking their cut. Anybody with access to tickets could flip them to brokers, including writers, directors, designers, and stars, who, in their contracts, were guaranteed at least two prime orchestra seats—"house seats"—a night.

Rudy Vallee, one of the stars of *How to Succeed in Business Without Really Trying*, openly shopped his house seats around Times Square to the highest bidder, usually the Hollywood Ticket Office.

It was said that Frederick Loewe, the composer of *Brigadoon* and *My Fair Lady*, traded his house seats for fur coats from friends in the garment business. Many a chorus girl in a Frederick Loewe show was known to keep warm in the winter with one of Freddie's furs. Clur-man discovered that a Broadway leading lady—whose name he would not give up even fifty years after the fact—had a deal with a broker who paid her $10,000 a year for her house seats. A well-known Broadway producer had bags of cash delivered to his East Side town house every night.

The bigger the hit, the more the ice. And at that point, the longest-running show in Broadway history was *My Fair Lady*, which opened March 15, 1956, at the Mark Hellinger Theatre and closed September 29, 1962, after 2,717 performances. A few months after *My Fair Lady* opened, a Russian submarine, the *Myest*, disappeared in the Baltic Sea. The day news of the sinking appeared in the papers, Bernie Hart, general manager of *My Fair Lady* (and the brother of the director Moss Hart) told his staff that the Russians had located the sub. "It broke through the ice," he said, laughing, "at the Hellinger!" *

Stanley Stahl, a Times Square real estate magnate, bought the Hellinger during the run of *My Fair Lady*. He did so, according to his friend Arthur Rubin, so he could get a cut of the ice from the box office.

My Fair Lady was produced by CBS, which put up $360,000. But even executives at CBS couldn't get tickets to the show without going through brokers. Marion Branch, a secretary at CBS, told Clurman that she bought as many as five pairs of seats a week from brokers. She paid $50 a ticket—$500 a week, she said ($3,500 today)—and gave them to CBS clients.

During the course of his investigation, Clurman discovered that the distribution of tickets and bribes wasn't limited to Broadway box offices. He discovered that one theater chain had centralized the black market in tickets. The Shubert Organization controlled seventeen of Broadway's best theaters. The company also owned the Sardi Build-

---

* Bernie Hart was thought to be one of the funniest men on Broadway, much funnier than Moss, who with George S. Kaufman wrote the classic comedies *You Can't Take It with You* and *The Man Who Came to Dinner*. After Moss's play *The Climate of Eden* got slaughtered by the critics in Philadephia, Moss and Bernie took the train back to New York. As soon as they arrived, they headed to the Little Bar at Sardi's. "Did you see those reviews, Bernie?" Moss said. "How are we ever going to get out of Philadelphia with those reviews? There is no way we can get out of Philadelphia with those reviews." Bernie replied, "Moss, relax. We got out of Egypt. We'll get out of Philadelphia."

ing on West Forty-Fourth Street, named after the famed Broadway restaurant housed on the ground floor. Four floors above Sardi's was a room—504—set aside for a special purpose. Here brokers or their runners went to buy tickets for shows in Shubert theaters. Sometimes there was a line out the door. Clurman found a former runner—Melvin D. Hecht, a twenty-six-year-old "freelance writer" from Philadelphia—who told him that, every Monday, he would deliver an envelope stuffed with cash to a man in 504.[4] The man was Murray Helwitz, a distant cousin of the three Shubert Brothers—Sam, Lee, and J. J.—who had founded the mighty theatrical empire.

The money was divided up in room 504 and distributed up and down the chain of command. A company manager who worked at a Shubert show at the time said, "I was going on vacation once, and the box office treasurer came up to me, handed me an envelope and said, 'Have fun, kid.' There was a hundred dollars in cash in the envelope."

Manny Azenberg recalled, "Everybody knew about the ice. You couldn't wait to become important so that you got your envelope."*

The ticketing scandal reached right into the heart of Broadway's biggest landlord—the Shubert Organization. Clurman spoke to many Shubert employees, many of whom took the Fifth Amendment. But two employees, he would later say, were "very helpful to my investigation." They were J. J. Shubert's lawyers and advisors—Gerald Schoenfeld and Bernard B. Jacobs. Middle-aged, low-key, always in the background, they seemed, Clurman would later say, to understand that the company was in peril. Several people in the organization were collecting hundreds of thousands of dollars—perhaps millions—every year without reporting any of it to the Internal Revenue Service.

"Along came these two guys, these two lawyers, and I got to know them," Clurman said. "They were not stupid people. They were helpful. It was hard to figure out what their motivation was, but they were very helpful."

---

* Five years later, Azenberg was offered his envelope. He was the general manager of *Two Gentlemen of Verona*, and it came by way of the box office. He met with his business partner, Eugene Wolsk, and they decided not to take it. "After the '63 investigation, it was a felony," Azenberg said.

In 2005, when the Shubert Organization renamed the Plymouth Theatre after Gerald Schoenfeld, then chairman of the board, Clurman sent him a note. "I want to congratulate you," he wrote. "And I really believe that you're one of the people who helped save the theater in 1963."

Clurman had to make a decision. He had enough evidence—kickbacks, bribes, diverted funds—to bring down Broadway, not least its most powerful entity, the Shubert Organization. He believed that the ice flowed to the top of the company, right into the executive offices of Lawrence Shubert Lawrence Jr., the president and chief operating officer. But if Clurman brought the Shuberts down he might decimate Broadway itself. Who, after all, would look after those seventeen theaters, especially as Times Square was getting seedier and seedier and the theater business itself was losing ground to television? He went to his boss to talk it over. Lefkowitz agreed. We'll hold hearings, he said, put them on notice, pass some laws governing theater investing and ticket distribution. But Broadway was vital to New York. It could not be wiped out.

"It would have been easy to indict a multitude of people," Clurman said. "I knew some of these guys hated me, but I don't think they realized that I saved their necks."

Clurman opened his public hearings on Broadway's financial practices on December 10, 1963. He began with a headline-grabbing number. Based on the evidence collected, the attorney general estimated that at least $10 million ($75 million today) in ice was collected each year on Broadway. All of it was in cash and tax-free. Most Broadway productions failed, Clurman pointed out. In the 1961–62 season, investors lost nearly $6 million, he calculated. But the well connected were hauling in millions—at the expense of other people's money.

Broadway producers, general managers, box office personnel, and other theater people gathered at 80 Centre Street, and were called on to testify. One of the first to speak was David Merrick, then the most powerful producer on Broadway. Merrick's string of hit shows included *Fanny, Look Back in Anger, Irma La Douce,* and *Carnival!.*

Merrick took the stand and said he knew little about ice. What he did know, he said, was rumor and conjecture. The term itself, he believed, was a turn-of-the-century political expression meaning "incidental campaign expenses."

Clurman and just about everybody else in the room had to stifle laughs. David Merrick didn't know about ice? His right-hand man was Jack Schlissel, as tough a general manager as they came on Broadway. Schlissel was Merrick's enforcer. He did the negotiating, the hiring, and often, the firing. "He was a worm," Richard Seff, a veteran agent, says. "Slimy." His name, in Yiddish, meant "key" (*shlisl*), and the joke around Broadway was that if you wanted to get at the ice on a Merrick show, you had to have the key. Schlissel and Merrick made hundreds of thousands of dollars from ice.

Informants told Clurman that Merrick's offices above the St. James were almost as busy in the black market for tickets as room 504 in the Sardi Building. What Clurman didn't know was that as soon as news of his investigation broke, Merrick contacted his longtime property man and ordered him to remove filing cabinets from his office in the middle of the night and dump them into the Hudson River. The cabinets contained Merrick's secret accounts of the cash flowing in from the ice, the kickbacks, and the various other schemes he was running. And here was David Merrick claiming he only knew the term as incidental campaign expenses.

Merrick's other schemes—of which his investors and Clurman were unaware—included a little side business with the souvenir program. Merrick and Schlissel had a deal with a small-time printer named Abe Zamachansky. He printed the souvenir programs for Merrick's shows. They were sold in the lobby for a dollar. It doesn't sound like much, but on a hit show, playing a fifteen-hundred-seat theater eight times a week, packed with theatergoers who might want to take something home to remember their night on Broadway, those dollars added up. At the end of the week, Zamachansky would split the profits with Merrick and Schlissel. "No one got a piece of that but the three of them," said an old associate of Merrick's. "No one. No investors. No creative people. Nobody. It was a very profitable business. And when the creative people started demanding their share, Merrick stopped doing the book!"

As Clurman had discovered, financial documentation for Broadway shows was sketchy, at best. If Merrick's investors had any idea how to read their contracts, they might—*might*—have discovered that a certain company was entitled to buy, at minimal cost, all the lighting and electrical equipment from Merrick's shows when they closed. Merrick owned the company. He shipped the equipment to a warehouse in upstate New York and then rented it out to other shows in New York and around the country. The original investors in the show that had closed paid for lighting equipment. But only Merrick pocketed the money from its subsequent rental. Another small fortune was being made off Broadway's oblivious angels.

Clurman called others to the stand. Every box office treasurer, he recalled, took the Fifth Amendment. But the CBS secretary, Marion Branch, testified, and so, too, did Melvin D. Hecht, the runner. He told about the payoffs he made every Monday morning to box office treasurers. He also said he carried two envelopes. One contained checks for the regular box office price of the tickets. The other contained cash. He distributed the checks to the box office.

"What did you do with the cash?" Clurman asked.

"I delivered it in person to an individual in an office building."

Clurman had instructed Hecht not to name the person or the building, but everybody in the room knew he was talking about Murray Helwitz, the Shubert iceman, who worked out of room 504 in the Sardi Building.

After Hecht was done, Alvin Cooperman, a Shubert executive, took the stand and announced that the Shubert Organization "deplores any unethical practices in ticket selling and production investing." Any Shubert employee who accepted ice "would be summarily dismissed."[5]

Again, much of the room had to stifle a laugh.

At the end of the day, Merrick asked if he could return to the stand. He said he was "appalled" at what he'd learned that day, and he was "happy and delighted" that the attorney general was exposing such practices and "cleaning out the vermin." He congratulated Lefkowitz and called the hearing "the best show of the season."[6]

On December 26, 1963—just two weeks after the hearings that engulfed the Shubert Organization in scandal—J. J. Shubert, the last of the three brothers who built the empire, died of a cerebral hemorrhage in his penthouse apartment on the eleventh floor of the Sardi Building. He was eighty-six. On Broadway they called him the "Phantom," as no one had seen him in years. It was an ironic nickname, though no one knew it at the time. Twenty-five years later, another phantom, the one with the mask, would make more money for the Shubert Organization than any other show in its one-hundred-year history.

J. J.'s dementia had set in around 1958, and by 1960 his mind was gone. He was bedridden in his apartment, surrounded by Louis XIV furniture he'd collected on long-ago trips to Europe. He was attended to by nurses and by his second wife, who let few people into the apartment. Those old confidants who were allowed to see this belligerent, brutal old despot said his face seemed fixed in a scowl.

Above a massive fireplace in his living room hung a painting of his only son, John, at the age of eight dressed like Little Lord Fauntleroy. J. J. had trained John to take over the Shubert empire. But in November 1962, John had died from a heart attack on a train to Clearwater, Florida. He was fifty-three.

The Shubert lawyers, Gerald Schoenfeld and Bernard B. Jacobs, fearing the news would kill the old man—or perhaps that he would not have grasped it at all—never told J. J. that his only direct heir, the only direct heir to his empire, was dead.

CHAPTER TWO

The Phantom

By 1958 Henry Speckman had worked as a maintenance man for the Shubert Organization for forty-one years. Short and stocky, he was suffering from severe emphysema. He didn't talk—he wheezed. His doctor told him he didn't have much time left, even less if he kept working. He requested a meeting with Mr. J. J., as everyone called J. J. Shubert.

J. J. rarely met with anyone unless his two lawyers, Gerald Schoenfeld and Bernard Jacobs, were present. J. J. received people from behind a large desk in his sixth-floor office in the Sardi Building. The lawyers sat on either side of the desk, close to J. J. The "victim," as the visitor was called, sat opposite J. J. The lawyers had their backs to the "victim" so he could not make out what they were whispering. Speckman was the victim that day. He came in, wheezing as usual.

"Mr. J. J.," he began, "I've been with Shubert for forty-one years, but I can no longer work. I've got emphysema, and I've checked on my insurance and it's not enough. I can't live on it. Even with the social security, it's just not enough. I was wondering, Would you give me something to help supplement it? Something more in my pension, maybe. . . ."

J. J. glared at him. "How long did you say you were here?"

"Forty-one years."

"I've taken care of you for forty-one years," J. J. replied. "Now go and find someone else to take care of you."

"That's the way he was," Jacobs would recall nearly forty years later. "He was not conscious of the fact he was cruel or mean. After all, he grew up in a world in which he and his brothers came out of nothing. And they clawed their way to become the dominant force in the American theater."

Short, thick, rumpled, and prone to titanic rages, J. J. ran his empire, which at one point included twenty theaters in New York and another fifty or so around the country, with an imperious hand. Since 1953, when his only partner, his brother Lee, died, he answered to no one. He was surrounded by courtiers who every day at six vied to take up the box of papers for Mr. J. J. to sign in his penthouse. He who had the box had the king's ear, at least for the night.

J. J. was grooming his son, John, to take over one day. But he was not ready to relinquish control yet, and John often feared his father would never do so. In fact, there were times when John feared his father might throw him out of the company. If he made a bad decision, J. J. would explode and scream, "You're fired." [1]

J. J. told his underlings, "My son has no more authority here than the porters in my theaters." [2]

Once, when John refused to ride in a car with one of J. J.'s mistresses, his father punched him in the face. When, in a divorce case in 1916, his first wife, Catherine Mary, accused him of having caught syphilis from hookers, he struck back by denying John was even his son. John's real father, J. J. swore under oath, was one of Catherine Mary's many lovers.

J. J.'s brutal treatment of actors, directors, chorus girls, even his own family, was legendary. He screamed, he bullied, and sometimes he lashed out physically at those who displeased him. A notorious incident occurred in 1911 involving a showgirl named Peggy Forbes. A grandniece of President Zachary Taylor, Forbes was confident, even a bit arrogant. J. J. didn't like her attitude. He preferred chorus girls who were subservient in every way. One day after a matinee at the Winter Garden Theatre, he fired her. As she later recounted in court, she marched up to him and said, "Mr. Shubert, are you a man or are you a monkey?" and then turned to walk away. Enraged, J. J. spun her around and smacked her twice in the face. She sued him, claiming the assault left her with a swollen eye and a bleeding lip. The suit made the papers, and everybody had a good laugh at J. J.'s expense. He hit Miss Forbes, he said, only after she'd stuck him with a hatpin. J. J. produced several witnesses, all Shubert employees, who backed up the hatpin story and added another detail—Miss Forbes brought whiskey backstage! Willie Klein, the longtime Shubert lawyer who cleaned up many a mess after a J. J. temper tantrum, settled the case out of court.

J. J. had no sense of humor, but his outbursts could be funny, even if he wasn't in on the joke. "There is only one captain of this ship," he once bellowed. "The director and me!"

One day, while inspecting the Majestic Theatre, one of his finest musical houses, he was told that the seats at the rear of the orchestra were fraying and needed to be re-covered.

"The only thing I want covering my seats are asses!" he responded.

J. J.'s employees—there were over twelve hundred at one point— were always falling in and out of favor with the boss. J. J. kept a mental list of where they stood when it came time to pass out Christmas bonuses. He sat at his desk with stacks of one-, five-, ten-, and twenty-dollar bills in front of him. His secretary would hand him an envelope with an employee's name on it, and J. J. would select bills from the various piles. If he liked the person, he'd take, perhaps, two from the five-dollar pile and one from the twenty-dollar pile. But then he might remember that the employee had not been deferential enough to him at the last opening night. So he'd retrieve the envelope and take out one of the fives. Or perhaps the employee had said a cheery good afternoon to him last summer in Shubert Alley, and he'd add another five. Bernie Jacobs once joked that passing out Christmas bonuses at the Shubert Organization took until February.

J. J.'s kingdom extended from West Forty-Fourth Street, where he owned the Shubert, the Broadhurst, and the Majestic Theatres as well as the Sardi Building, to West Fifty-Fourth Street, where he controlled the George Abbott Theatre (torn down in 1970—a Hilton Hotel occupies the site today). He prowled his ten-block domain at all hours of the day, often popping into a theater unannounced to observe his employees. The only person who ever seemed to know where he was at all times was Kitty Hall, the gravelly-voiced chief telephone operator who worked at a switchboard above the Shubert Theatre. If she thought a conversation was going to be interesting, she'd plug in. If it was boring, she'd click off. Kitty had her favorites among the army of Shubert employees. Whenever she got wind that J. J. was coming around for a surprise inspection, she'd ring them up with the alert, recalled Philip J. Smith, who today is chairman of the Shubert Organization. (Smith joined the Shuberts in 1957.)

"He's coming, kid," she said. "He's on his way over."

"If she didn't like you, she'd let you suffer the results when J. J. showed up," Smith said. "And then J. J. would wander in and scowl at everybody."

J. J. ruled his empire from his sumptuous penthouse on the eleventh floor of the Sardi Building. The lighting fixtures in the vast living room had been obtained from the old Knickerbocker Hotel in Times Square, and there was a glass ceiling, fashioned by Tiffany's, above the dining room table. The most prominent feature of the apartment was a three-ton, intricately carved wrought-iron door J. J. picked up from a palazzo in Venice. In the center of the door was a bas-relief of a woman with six breasts. J. J. acquired two such doors, but installing the first one was such trouble—it took ten men to haul it up to his apartment—he consigned the other to the basement of the Cort Theatre, where it languished in a crate for decades. (That second door seems to have vanished; nobody at the Shubert Organization today has any idea where it is.)

J. J. lived in his penthouse with his second wife, Muriel. They met in 1921. She was a chorus girl in one of his shows at the Winter Garden. They'd been companions for years, marrying in 1951. Muriel was on the Shubert payroll. Every week, she was issued a check for $546.38. As soon as she got her hands on the check, she'd call one of the Shubert box office treasurers to see if he could cash it for her. Once she had the money in hand, her chauffeur, Pablo, would drive her to the Empire Bank where she'd put the cash in a safety deposit box. "No one ever knew what Muriel did with her money," said an old Shubert employee. "Maybe she was planning on making a fast getaway."

J. J. was the youngest of the three Shubert brothers. They were born in Eastern Europe, though no one knows where exactly. Foster Hirsch, in *The Boys from Syracuse*, writes that they probably came from a small town on the border of Poland and Germany. Their father, David, was a peddler and a smuggler—he smuggled tea across the border into Germany, which had levied a steep tax on tea. He married their mother, Katrina Helwitz, in 1870. In 1881, like millions of other Jews fleeing pogroms and starvation, David and Katrina packed up their family—their three sons, Levi (the oldest), Sam, Jacob, and their three daughters, Fanny, Sarah, and Lisa—and emigrated to America.

David was a difficult man. He showed no interest in working, preferring instead to spend his days praying. He was also a secret drinker. He would eventually become a full-blown alcoholic, and it may well have been his failure as a provider—and his unquenchable thirst for a drop—that turned his sons into workaholics and fueled their enormous ambition. Though alcohol has always been the social lubricant of choice in the theater, Sam, Lee, and J. J. were noted for their abstinence.

David, Katrina, and their children lived for a time in Queens with Katrina's relatives, the Helwitzes. But the Helwitzes soon became fed up with David's freeloading, so they kicked the family out. The Shuberts headed to Syracuse, New York, where one of David's sisters had emigrated a few years before. They moved into a dilapidated house next to the railroad tracks in the Seventh Ward, the Jewish ghetto. That first winter, they had almost nothing to eat, and Lisa, the youngest and frailest child, died of starvation. David had no choice but to work. He managed to get hold of some dry goods, strapped a sack on his back, and sold his wares throughout upstate New York. But, as always, he was a failure, blaming his misfortune not on the real culprit—whiskey—but what he said were debilitating bouts of rheumatism.

It fell to Levi, the oldest child, to help the old man earn a living. He became a peddler, too, at the age of ten. But Levi, who could barely read, had a knack for business, and soon was outstripping his father in earnings. Levi, whose jet-black hair and eyebrows, unsmiling lips, and slightly slanted eyes gave him the whiff of the "inscrutable Oriental," as a phrase of the time had it, also ran bets for a bookie on baseball games and prize fights. After a stint in a cigar store, and with the backing of a rich Jewish merchant, he went into business for himself. He opened a haberdashery shop in downtown Syracuse. But as Shubert biographer

Hirsch writes, "he found the work tedious" and spent most of his time staring "at the bustling main street of downtown Syracuse." [3]

While Levi stared out his shop window, dreaming perhaps of bigger, more exciting things to do, J. J. started hawking newspapers. Sam went to work as a shoeshine boy. Delicate, thin, and often ill, Sam was a pretty boy with a sensuous mouth and a faraway look in his black eyes. Katrina fretted over him all the time, but he was not a mama's boy. He turned out to be tougher and even more ambitious than Levi. Sam envisioned the empire he and his brothers would create.

It all began one frigid winter afternoon outside the Grand Opera House in downtown Syracuse. Sam was there with his shoeshine kit, bereft of customers and shivering in the cold. The manager of the opera house, Charles Plummer, noticed the frail boy standing out in the snow and invited him in to see the show—*The Black Crook*, generally thought to be the first American musical. Sam was entranced. The world of songs, sets, actors, and makeup—the world of make-believe—must have been a tremendous escape from the harsh world of poverty and hunger in that dilapidated house by the railroad tracks.

Plummer, a well-known figure about town, took an instant liking to Sam, and offered him a job at a dollar fifty a week selling programs, according to Foster Hirsch in *The Boys from Syracuse*. Sam learned everything he could about the theater business. Within a few months, Plummer put him in the box office, the "sanctum sanctorum in the Shubert saga," Hirsch writes. Sam had a talent for figures and could tally up the day's receipts in his head. He was the first Shubert—and there would be a long line of them—to obsess over weekly grosses.

Sam proved so adept a ticket seller at the Grand that he came to the attention of the manager of Syracuse's leading theater, the Wieting. The manager offered him a job as box office treasurer and within a few months—the year was 1891—he was promoted to house manager. His first hire was his brother Levi, whom he put in charge of the ushers.

While working at the Wieting, Sam met the man who would instill in him the dream of one day becoming a theatrical impresario himself. The theater attracts some odd characters, but few as odd as David Belasco. Born in San Francisco in 1853, he wrote his first successful play when he was nineteen and moved to New York. He churned out a play a season, mostly melodramatic twaddle with titles such as *Polly with a Past* and *The Harem*. Of the seven hundred plays he wrote or directed, only two have endured—*Madame Butterfly* and *The Girl of the Golden West*—and that's only because Puccini turned them into operas. The critic George Jean Nathan called Belasco the "Rasputin of Broadway" because his plays were such hokum. He retaliated by having a mural painted in his theater—the Belasco on West Forty-Fourth Street—depicting the beheading of a knight. The knight resembled Nathan, the executioner Belasco.

Belasco was obsessed with realism on stage. One of his plays was set in a boarding house, so he scoured New York for an actual boarding house, bought it, took it apart, and reassembled it on stage. To get the type of scream he wanted from a leading lady, he snuck up behind her at rehearsal and stuck her with a hatpin. When a show wasn't going well, he'd take out his pocket watch, throw it on the stage, and stamp it to bits in front of the cast. He had a trunk full of pocket watches for just such a display of temper.

But his greatest eccentricity was his dress. He strutted around Broadway in priestly garb, right down to the white collar and rosary beads. No one knew why. Some said that as a teenager he contemplated entering a monastery. Others said he once played a priest and, believing it to have been his finest performance, decided to spend the rest of his life in costume. Cynics said he was an egomaniac who just wanted to draw attention to himself. Another of Belasco's nicknames was the "Bishop of Broadway."

Which is not to say he practiced celibacy. He bedded most of his leading ladies. He enticed them to his penthouse above the theater, which was designed like a gothic cathedral, complete with crosses, gargoyles, and a confessional in the front hall. The actress would have to "confess" her sins, removing an article of clothing for each offense.

Belasco was still an up-and-comer when he arrived in Syracuse with a play called *May Blossoms*. He needed four local boys to fill out the cast. He selected three from a nearby elementary school and found the fourth, little Sam Shubert, working at the Wieting. Sam fell under Belasco's spell. The acting bug never bit Sam, but watching the charismatic Belasco at work, the producing bug did. With Belasco's encouragement, Sam went around to some rich Jewish businessmen in Syracuse and raised the money for his very first production, a farce from New York called *A Texas Steer* by Charles Hoyt. Sam produced it at the Wieting and then toured it in upstate New York and New England.

He had the bit in his mouth now. He brought J. J. to the Wieting as an assistant manager. He produced a couple of long-forgotten plays by Hoyt, but realized that a producer had only so much power. A producer was at the mercy of theater owners. They decided what to book and what to evict. Real estate. That's where the authority—and the money—were. So Sam, with money from those Jewish merchants who had invested in his first play, took a lease on the Bastable, a second-class theater in Syracuse. He fixed it up and trumpeted his productions as "direct from New York." The Shubert appetite for theaters was born, and a year later, 1899, he got control of the Grand Opera House, where he'd begun his career twelve years earlier.

Sam installed Lee and J. J. at the Bastable and the Grand, and then, with the backing of many of his original investors in *A Texas Steer*, snapped up second-rate theaters in Rochester, Utica, Troy, and Albany.

The theaters were second-rate—that is, small and shabby—because the large, sparkling playhouses were already under the control of the Syndicate.

One of the most powerful monopolies in the history of show business, the Syndicate, at the turn of the century, controlled almost every major theater in every major city across the country. It was formed over lunch in 1896 at the Holland House in New York. Five of the most powerful managers in the theater—Abe Erlanger, Charles Frohman, Al Hayman, Marc Klaw, and Sam Nixon—gathered that afternoon and brought order to the chaos of booking theaters in America.

The Syndicate could impose order because its five founders each controlled the best theaters in all the big cities. Together, they had a chain of playhouses stretching from one end of the continent to the other. They could now pick and choose which shows would play where and when. Producers, playwrights, and actors found themselves at their mercy. If they did not abide by the Syndicate's terms—and they grew more onerous with each new theatrical season—they would be locked out of the best theaters in America.

Abe Erlanger was the dominant force in the Syndicate, which had its headquarters above the New Amsterdam Theatre on West Forty-Second Street. He was a vicious tyrant, who revelled in crushing anyone who defied him. Brooks Atkinson, the gentle, scholarly *New York Times* critic who never said a bad word about anyone, described Erlanger as a "fat, squat, greedy, crude egotist who had no interest in the theater as an art or as a social institution. He was a dangerous enemy." [4]

Erlanger revered Napoleon and stocked his office with actual guns, drums, and swords from Napoleon's battles. He posed for his official portrait with his right hand thrust into his shirt at his breast.

Erlanger was only vaguely aware of the Shuberts as Sam was building up his little circuit in upstate New York, which by now included the small Baker Theater in Rochester. But when the owner of the Lyceum, Rochester's best theater, bristled at Erlanger's terms (the Syndicate wanted 50 percent of the profits from every show that played at the theater), Erlanger decided to anoint the Shuberts' little Baker Theater as the official Syndicate house in Rochester. Sam agreed to the terms because it meant he'd get all the best attractions from New York. But then the owner of the Lyceum, fearing his theater would end up with second-rate shows, relented. Erlanger preferred the Lyceum and rerouted his productions there. The Shuberts would now get the second-rate goods. They were in no position to fight the double cross—yet. But they never forgot it. And within one year they marched on to Erlanger's turf—New York City.

It was inevitable that a producer as restless and ambitious as Sam Shubert would make a run at New York. With at least fifty productions—farces, melodramas, operettas, revues—opening every year in theaters stretching from Union Square to Longacre Square (soon to be renamed Times Square when the *New York Times* opened its headquarters there), New York was the engine of the American theater. Sam had to be there to see what the latest hits were and bargain for shows to fill his upstate theaters. Because of his connection to Belasco, he met all the major theatrical personalities of the era. He became especially close to a group of powerful actors who had begun to chafe under the dominance of the Syndicate.

Sam arrived in New York in 1900 set on finding his own theater. But the Syndicate controlled the best houses. So, just as he'd done in Syracuse, Sam had to settle for a second-rate house, the Herald Square, which stood directly across from what today is Macy's department store. His backers were those same Jewish merchants from Syracuse who'd been with him from the start.

Theaters, then as now, had reputations. If something was booked at, say, Charles Frohman's Empire on Forty-Second Street, audiences knew it would be first-class. The Herald was low-rent. But the truth is there's no such thing as a bad house—just a bad show. To come up in the world, all a theater needs is a production people want to see. Sam needed a star attraction for the Herald, and that, he decided, would be the great actor Richard Mansfield. Using all his youthful charm as well as generous terms, Sam convinced Mansfield to appear as a supercilious dandy in Booth Tarkington's *Monsieur Beaucaire*. Mansfield was delightful in the role, and suddenly the down-at-the-heels Herald shot up in the world. Mansfield returned a year later, and scored another triumph as Brutus in *Julius Caesar*.

Sam now went on another buying spree, acquiring leases on the Princess, a burlesque house at Broadway and Twenty-Ninth Street, and the Casino, a Moorish palace ten blocks north. And then, once again following in the footsteps of Belasco, he decided to build a theater of his own. He opened the Lyric Theatre on West Forty-Second Street on October 12, 1903. His premiere attraction was his favorite headliner, Richard Mansfield, who starred in the play *Old Heidelberg*.

Across the street from the Lyric, Klaw and Erlanger had just moved into their new headquarters, the New Amsterdam. From his office above the theater, Erlanger could see little Sam Shubert from Syracuse moving up in the world, Erlanger's world. Erlanger vowed to destroy Sam Shubert. He summoned Sam and Lee (J. J. was in Syracuse running the theaters upstate) to his office one day and told them, "Go back to Syracuse. There is no place for you in the theatrical business. It belongs to us." [5]

Erlanger always made good on his threats. He put out the word to everyone connected to the Syndicate—producers, playwrights, theater managers, and stars—that if they did business with the Shuberts, they would be cast out of his kingdom. This edict meant, effectively, that the Shuberts would be denied first-class attractions to fill their theaters, and that any show they produced would be barred from playing first-class Syndicate theaters around the country.

But Sam did not flinch. There was only one way to battle Erlanger—acquire more theaters (build them, if necessary) and produce first-rate attractions of his own. Sam spearheaded the strategy with the quiet counsel of Belasco. He had in Lee and J. J. the loyalest of foot soldiers. There were plans to construct Shubert theaters in New York and up and down the East Coast. Sam also headed to London, where the Syndicate had no power, and built the Waldorf Theatre. As Erlanger tightened the noose—some Shubert theaters were sitting dark for lack of product—Sam lined up major stars who'd had enough of Erlanger's bullying. The actress Minnie Maddern Fiske, who chafed under Syndicate control, inspired Sam. Barred from playing Syndicate houses, she performed in tents. Her shows were sold out. To pry stars away from the Syndicate, Sam offered generous contracts, which sometimes meant the Shuberts might just break even on an attraction—but they would have it in their theater. Fay Templeton and Lillian Russell joined Mansfield in the Shubert stable. Sam also lined up the great Sarah Bernhardt for a farewell tour of America. He offered her the astronomical sum of $1,800 a day for the two-hundred-performance tour. She insisted on being paid in gold before each show. The Syndicate struck back by refusing to book Bernhardt in cities where Sam didn't have theaters. But Sam had the example of Mrs. Fiske to follow, and he put Bernhardt in tents, town halls, ice-skating rinks, and, in one case, on the side of a hill.

By 1905, the Shuberts had theaters in Boston, Cleveland, Chicago, Buffalo, and St. Louis. Sam had his eye on the Duquesne in Pittsburgh. The Syndicate pressured its owners not to give Sam a lease, and Sam hit back with a restraint of free trade suit. The night before a court appearance, he took the train from New York to Pittsburgh with his lawyer, William Klein, and another associate, Abe Thalheimer. Belasco had planned to join them but canceled at the last minute. Outside Harrisburg, in the dead of night, the speeding passenger train approached a work train parked on a curve in the track. The passenger train nicked one of the cars of the work train. There was a huge explosion. The car was packed with dynamite. The passenger train flew off the tracks, engulfed in flames.

Thalheimer, who was thrown from the train, ran back to the car where Sam and Klein had berths. He found Sam stuck in his berth, which was on fire. Thalheimer pulled him out and saw that Sam's legs were black and smoking. He then rescued an unconscious Klein. Sam was taken to the Commonwealth Hotel. Third-degree burns covered the lower half of his body. But he was conscious and managed to give a couple of phone interviews to newspaper reporters in New York. "I could feel the flame curling up the side of my berth, and it was eating into my legs," he said.[6]

Lee was in London, so J. J. raced to Harrisburg with his mother, sisters, and the family's personal doctor. When they arrived at the hotel, Sam was in a coma. He died at 9:30 a.m. on May 12, 1905. He was thirty years old. "The serious nature of his injuries was not known here," the *New York Times* reported, "and his death was unexpected."

Sam S. Shubert was buried on May 14, 1905, at Salem Fields Cemetery in Brooklyn, New York. At the start of every new theater season in the fall, Lee and J. J. "reverentially visited the grave of their genius brother," the *Times* noted three years later.

In the final year of his life, J. J., the Phantom of the Sardi Building, rarely uttered a word. But every now and then, he would open his eyes and whisper, "Sammy."

CHAPTER THREE

Mr. Lee and Mr. J. J.

After Sam's funeral, the question in New York theater circles—and certainly in the Syndicate's head offices in the New Amsterdam Theatre—was: Would Lee and J. J. carry on? Sam's death shattered Lee. J. J., who hadn't strayed too far from Shubert operations in upstate New York, was unknown around Broadway. Erlanger did not press his advantage in the wake of Sam's death. Despite their battles, he and Sam had still managed to do some business together. The theater was a small world and they were bound to become involved with each other one way or another. A few months after Sam's death, Lee asked to meet with Erlanger. He told Erlanger neither he nor J. J. had any desire to keep the war going, according to Jerry Stagg, author of *The Brothers Shubert.* They didn't even want to expand the empire anymore and would consider selling some of their theaters to Erlanger. Without Sam at the helm, Lee and J. J. were adrift.

The white flag waving across his desk, Erlanger could have reached out and grabbed it. There were just a couple of details to hammer out. Sam had a contract with his beloved friend Belasco stipulating that in some cities Shubert theaters would book upcoming Belasco productions. Lee asked Erlanger to honor the contract.

"I don't honor contracts with dead men," Erlanger said.

Lee "turned pale with rage and stalked out," Stagg writes. Lee told J. J. what Erlanger had said. J. J. replied, "We'll kill the son of a bitch." [1]

And they did, the only way they knew how. They started acquiring and building more theaters—and producing more attractions—with which to crush the Syndicate. Lee had a knack for real estate. He liked to buy whole blocks, so that the only theaters that could be built on them were Shubert theaters. He acquired land between Forty-Fourth and Forty-Fifth Streets behind the Astor Hotel and built the Booth Theatre and the Sam S. Shubert Memorial Theatre ("Memorial" eventually would be dropped because it made the place sound more like a tomb than a theater). A little thoroughfare ran between the hotel and the theaters. The Astor owned one half, the Shuberts the other. In time, the thoroughfare would become known as Shubert Alley, the heart of the Broadway theater district. The Shuberts still own half of it. The other half once belonged to real estate magnate Jerome Minskoff, who tore down the Astor Hotel in 1968 and built One Astor Plaza, which contains the Minskoff Theatre. Shubert Alley is a private street. The Shubert Organization allows pedestrians to cut through the alley, and limousines that ferry Shubert executives around town are parked there.

In addition to building the Booth and the Shubert, Lee also acquired the gigantic Hippodrome on Forty-Third Street and Sixth Avenue. He installed an enormous water tank onstage in which more than a dozen chorus girls swam around dressed as mermaids in a watery spectacle called *Neptune's Daughter*.

J. J., meanwhile, wanted a theater of his own. One day he walked past the American Horse Exchange, which had been built by William K. Vanderbilt, on Broadway between Fiftieth and Fifty-First Streets. As horses trotted about the arena, J. J. imagined a theater to house lavish Shubert spectacles. He struck a deal with Vanderbilt—$40,000 a year for forty years, according to Shubert biographer Foster Hirsch—and transformed the horse arena into the Winter Garden Theatre. (Trusses from the horse exchange can still be seen on the roof of the Seventh Avenue side of the theater.) The Winter Garden became home to *The Passing Show*, the Shuberts' lucrative response to Florenz Ziegfeld's *Follies*. *The Passing Show*, which ran from 1912 to 1924, was, of course, over the top. Each show featured what was always called "a bevy" of scantily clad showgirls who paraded up and down a runway that stretched into the audience. The runway was dubbed "the Bridge of Thighs." Writers of *The Passing Show* revues included George Gershwin, Jerome Kern, Irving Caesar, and Sigmund Romberg, who would become something of a Shubert in-house composer.

But J. J.'s most significant discovery was Al Jolson, who appeared in the first *Passing Show* in blackface singing "Paris Is a Paradise for Coons." Jolson became a star attraction at the Winter Garden, appearing there (at an ever increasing salary) until 1926, when he left to make movie history singing "My Mammy" in *The Jazz Singer*.

Lee and J. J. also acquired or built theaters in Chicago, Philadelphia, New Haven, and Boston, where the brothers would eventually control most of the land around Boston Common. Against the backdrop of this real estate spree, the war with Erlanger raged on. Much of it was fought in newspapers controlled or heavily influenced by the Syndicate, which was a major advertiser. Erlanger's ink-drenched weapon of choice was the *Morning Telegraph*, which hounded the Shuberts. *Telegraph* critics, who were on Erlanger's payroll, ripped into any production under the Shubert banner. Editorials blasted the Shuberts for putting on smutty shows. Gossip columnists insinuated Lee and J. J. were running their brother Sam's business into the ground. Fashion writers mocked them for their taste in clothes—Lee, drab and conservative; J. J., an unmade bed.

But as always, the Shuberts gave as good as they got. They started their own newspaper—the *New York Review*—in 1909 and returned volley for volley. The man who did most of the shooting was the Shuberts' publicity chief, the fantastically named A. Toxen Worm. Born in Denmark, he was called the "Great Dane" by Shubert Alley wags. He wrote article after article attacking the Syndicate for being a corrupt monopoly. He always referred to Erlanger as "Little Abie." Aided by Worm's gift for invective, the Shuberts, as historian Foster Hirsch notes, positioned themselves as Davids against the Syndicate's Goliath. Increasingly, producers and stars supported them as welcome competition for the Syndicate. They also had youth on their side. Lee and J. J. were only in their twenties; Erlanger and his henchmen were in their fifties. Their time was running out, and by the 1920s the Syndicate was beginning to fray. Charles Frohman went down with the *Lusitania* in 1915, and three other members—Samuel Nixon, Fred Zimmerman, and Al Hayman—retired. Marc Klaw, Erlanger's closest crony, turned on him. He accused Erlanger in several lawsuits of financial shenanigans.

The Syndicate was falling apart, historian Peter A. Davis writes in *Inventing Times Square*, because it was organized as an "informal pool" that allowed its original members to go their own way whenever they wished. As a result, in the face of competition from the Shuberts and the burgeoning movie business, the Syndicate eroded as its associates scrambled to save their own businesses.

The Shuberts were a highly centralized company. Though they frequently raised money from outside investors, Lee and J. J. made all the decisions.

The stock market crash of 1929 ruined Erlanger. He died, broke, on March 7, 1930. The Shuberts had won the battle, and in a final gesture of contempt they bought Erlanger's Theatre on West Forty-Fourth Street and renamed it the St. James.

Lee and J. J. were now the most powerful theater owners and producers in America. On the eve of the Great Depression they owned thirty theaters in New York and another thirty around the country. Having become something of a Syndicate themselves, they also controlled the booking of productions at seven hundred and fifty other theaters. Historian Ken Bloom notes that at the time they were pulling in $1 million a week at the box office ($14 million today). They wielded enormous power but, having watched the imperious Syndicate rack up so many enemies, they did so quietly. The Shuberts, it was said, were tough—but they wouldn't kill you. Lee could be downright generous to producers he liked. Toward the end of his life, Lee took a liking to a young ticket agent turned producer named Michael Abbott. Abbott produced his first Broadway play, *Late Love* with Arlene Francis, at the Booth Theatre. Reviews were lukewarm and the show struggled. Lee waived the rent and the show ran for six months.

Lee and J. J. conducted business from opposite sides of West Forty-Fourth Street. J. J. was ensconced in the Sardi Building, while Lee operated out of a small, circular office above the Sam S. Shubert Theatre. The office was right next to a walk-in safe. "Lee liked to be right near the money," an old Shubert employee once said. Lee's office was part of a spacious penthouse above the theater. He lived "above the store." His living room, painted burgundy, overlooked West Forty-Fourth Street. Its outstanding feature was a massive, hand-crafted grandfather clock from London. His bedroom looked down on the Broadhurst Theatre. He also had a library, stocked with leather-bound first editions of the classics. They remain unread today, some of the pages still uncut. Lee read contracts and scripts, not books.

Lee worked through the night and never got up before noon. At four o'clock every afternoon, his barber came up to the apartment to give him a shave. When the barber was finished, Lee often entertained one of the chorus girls in his shows. "He didn't only get a shave in that chair," a longtime Shubert employee said, "he also got blowjobs from the 'Five O'Clock Girls,' as they were called."

Lee and J. J. were notorious around Broadway for their sexual prowess. Chorus girls regularly paraded up to their offices. And sometimes they didn't even get that far. J. J. often enjoyed his girls in the stairwell of the Shubert Theatre.

Lee fathered at least one child out of wedlock—Barry Bond—whose mother, Frederica, had been a showgirl. A few years after Lee's death, John Shubert, J. J.'s son who was being groomed to take over, called Phil Smith, an assistant box office treasurer, into his office. "You'll understand, Phil, that we'll have to look out for Barry," he said. Smith replied, "I understand, Mr. John." Nothing more was said. "He didn't have to draw a picture for me," Smith recalled.*

Lee acquired the nickname the "Wooden Indian" because he was always tan. A. J. Liebling, who profiled the brothers for the *New Yorker* in 1939, reported that on summer mornings, Lee could be found in Central Park asleep in the open tonneau of his Isotta Fraschini "with

---

* Smith installed Bond into the box office of the Plymouth Theatre, one of the smaller Shubert houses. Bond earned the reputation for being "the dumbest box office treasurer on Broadway," said producer Elizabeth I. McCann, whose many hit plays included the Tony Award–winning *The Elephant Man*. In 1994, Stephen Sondheim's *Passion* played the Plymouth. The show was about an ugly woman with warts on her face named Fosca who becomes obsessed with a handsome soldier. Donna Murphy played Fosca, and her face, warts and all, was prominently displayed on posters in front of the theater. One day as McCann was walking past the Plymouth, Bond dashed out of the box office. "Liz!" he shouted. Pointing to the picture of the hideous Fosca, he said, "Every time I look at that I think of you." McCann gasped. "Barry," she said, "I know I'm no beauty, but really?" "No, no," he said. "I don't mean that. I mean, I think you should revive *The Elephant Man*. It was about an ugly person, too!"

his face turned towards the sun." [2] Richard Seff, a young agent in the 1950s, would sometimes see Lee in Shubert Alley. "He seemed like a mummy," Seff said. "He was very prune-faced."

Lee and J. J.—or Mr. Lee and Mr. J. J. as employees called them— divided up the running of their empire. Lee favored nonmusical plays, booking them into the smaller Shubert theaters. J. J. preferred musical revues and operettas, especially by his favorite composer, Sigmund Romberg. The Shuberts produced countless revivals of Romberg's treacly *The Student Prince*, and had a warehouse in Fort Lee, New Jersey, where they kept the sets. Some of the furniture from *The Student Prince* wound up in offices in the Sardi Building and above the Shubert Theatre.

Most nights after the curtains came down at their theaters, Lee and J. J. held court at separate tables in the bar of the Astor Hotel. They were accessible—managers, agents, directors, anyone with a question or a problem could approach them. They would listen and then confer privately. That night or, at the latest, the next morning, they had the answer. Lee and J. J. did not agonize over decisions.

They weathered the Great Depression, though their empire went into receivership in 1931 after losing $3 million. The Irving Trust Company held the theaters for two years—in close consultation with Lee. On April 7, 1933, the bank put them up for auction. Broadway was nearly bust then, so nobody was rushing to buy theaters. There was only one bidder—Lee Shubert. He paid $400,000 to regain his empire. And then it was back to business. Lee and J. J. aided producers during the Depression by not charging rent, a significant savings that helped boost the number of productions on Broadway. Instead of rent, the Shuberts took a cut of the box office. As the Depression wore on, they acquired more theaters at rock-bottom prices.

There is no question that Lee and J. J. saved Broadway during the Great Depression. Had they lost their theaters, many would have been torn down to make way for more lucrative real estate. The Shubert, the St. James, the Broadhurst, the Booth, the Royale, the Plymouth— to say nothing of Shubert houses around the country—could have met the wrecking ball. Broadway's geography could have been wiped out. "If Lee Shubert had walked away from his business, the basic hardware of the American theater might well have been demolished," concludes biographer Foster Hirsch.[3]

Their empire intact, Lee and J. J. were poised to make more money than ever as Broadway entered its golden age after World War II. *Oklahoma!* opened at the St. James in 1943, and for the next twenty years, Shubert theaters would house such celebrated productions as *Annie Get Your Gun, The King and I, Gypsy, The Skin of Our Teeth, A Streetcar Named Desire, The Cradle Will Rock, Fiorello!*, and *Kiss Me, Kate*.

As the New York economy boomed after the war, producers were awash in investment money. The Shuberts no longer had to supply their own product. They withdrew from producing and became landlords, though they often made investments in shows that played their theaters. Lee, always aloof, grew more and more remote. He rarely attended first nights, preferring to stay up in his aerie above the Shubert Theatre playing pinochle with old cronies. J. J. could still be volatile—he once punched out his chauffeur—but even he wasn't the force he'd been while overseeing the productions of *The Passing Show* at his Winter Garden Theatre twenty years earlier.

But Lee and J. J. had one more fight on their hands. And this time the enemy was the United States government.

The Shuberts dominated Broadway in the 1940s. And they were not averse to using their power. They could move shows in and out of their theaters at will. Legally, a show had to fall below a certain weekly box office gross, called the "stop clause," before they could kick it out. But if they wanted something else in the theater, they ordered the box office treasurer to tell customers the show was sold out. If they wanted to prop a show up, they bought their own tickets. They had their own booking arm, United Booking Office (UBO), which demanded a percentage of every show booked into a Shubert house. Lee and J. J. were getting money two ways—as theater owners and bookers. And they could invest in whatever they liked—on their terms, since producers needed, if not their money, their theaters.

Producers began to resent the Shuberts' grip on the theater business. One producer complained to *Variety* in 1941: "Ninety percent of all scripts are said to go through the Brothers Shubert for appraisal.

If a play doesn't appeal to the company, out it goes. If it clicks, the Shuberts take either a piece of the investment or a house percentage—whichever looks more profitable."

The Shuberts also controlled the best seats in their theaters. House seats had always been part of the theater business. But they were kept at a minimum, a pair for the creator, a pair for the producer, a pair for the house. The Shuberts jacked up their allotment. By the time *South Pacific* opened in 1949 at the Majestic Theatre, they had their hands on fifty prime orchestra seats at every performance.[4]

The ice was flowing. The *Annie Get Your Gun* ticket scandal in Philadelphia drew unwelcome attention to Shubert practices, and Richard Rodgers, that implacable foe of ice, heard tales of shenanigans at his hit show, *South Pacific*, at the Majestic Theatre.

In Washington, D.C., Congressman Emanuel Celler, a Democrat who represented parts of Brooklyn and Queens, was gaining a reputation as a trust buster. He and Estes Kefauver (D-Tennessee) coauthored a law in 1950 that strengthened the federal government's hand in busting up monopolies. Right across the river from his district was a tempting target—the Shubert Organization. He held hearings, accusing the Shuberts of having a stranglehold on the theater business in America. The U.S. attorney general was also interested in Shubert business practices and opened up his own investigation. Suddenly, the Shuberts were facing a pincer attack—Celler, denouncing them in the House of Representatives; the U.S. attorney general, interviewing witnesses about Shubert business practices.

In 1950, the U.S. attorney general said Lee and J. J. dominated the theater business in America to such an extent that competition did not exist. The government demanded that the Shuberts get out of the booking business and divest themselves of some of their theaters.

Lee and J. J. balked. They had built their business up from nothing, they felt they were honorable, if tough men, and they had stuck by the theater during the Great Depression, when it all could have gone under. They instructed their lawyers to fight back, and they turned to their friends at the newspapers. The powerful critic George Jean Nathan wrote, "Play shortage has been so acute that, in order to fill their theaters, the Shuberts have now and then been forced to put money into outside producers' productions, and then demand the producers book them in their theaters. And why shouldn't they?"

The battle was in full tilt when, on December 21, 1953, Lee Shubert collapsed in his small circular office next to the safe. He'd had a stroke. The brain damage was irreparable. He died, still sporting a tan from a recent trip to Miami, on December 25, 1953.

J. J. was left to battle the U.S. government—and run the Shubert empire—alone. Soon, though, he would acquire the services of two bright young lawyers. So bright, in fact, they would one day take control of his company for themselves.

CHAPTER FOUR

While There Is Death
There Is Hope

In the fall of 1996 Gerald S. Schoenfeld, the chairman of the board of the Shubert Organization, was lunching at Sardi's with his old friend, producer Elizabeth I. (Liz) McCann. She was having her chopped salad, Schoenfeld his club sandwich. The most powerful man in the American theater, Schoenfeld was in a reflective mood that day. His long-time business partner and great friend, Bernard B. Jacobs, had died in August. They'd known each other since they'd been teenagers on the Upper West Side of Manhattan and, together, they'd taken control of the Shubert Organization and turned it into one of the most powerful and lucrative entertainment companies in the country. Promotions had just been announced at the organization. Philip J. Smith, Jacobs's right-hand man for years, was named president. Robert Wankel, an accountant who worked directly under Schoenfeld, was made executive vice president. Both men were Catholic, in a company that had always been run by Jews.

"Liz," Schoenfeld said in his resonant, authoritative, and at times ridiculously pompous voice, "now that Bernie's gone, I'm the only Jew left at Shubert."

McCann, an Irish Catholic, said, "You know, Jerry, there's something you can do about that."

"What?" Schoenfeld asked.

"Hire more Jews!"

"No, no," Schoenfeld said. "J. J. always said, 'Don't hire any bright Jewish boys. They'll take the business away from you someday.'"

McCann smiled. "Well, Jerry—isn't that what you and Bernie did?"

Schoenfeld raised his eyebrows above his thick glasses and laughed.

On September 22, 1924, as Lee and J. J. were expanding the Shubert empire, Sam and Fanny Schoenfeld welcomed a new addition to the household, a chubby boy with dark, rather tentative eyes. They named him Gerald. The Schoenfelds were comfortably middle-class. Sam sold fur coats, enough of them to keep his wife and two sons in an elegant apartment at 400 West End Avenue. Joe DiMaggio lived in the penthouse. Gerald was a good student at P.S. 87, displaying at an early age an interest in the law—and power. In his charming but score-settling memoir *Mr. Broadway*, he writes about being active in student government. One student was mayor, another district attorney, a third, the cop on the beat. If a student misbehaved he was brought to trial. "I was the judge," Schoenfeld writes, proudly.

Schoenfeld discovered he had a gift for oratory. He could recite poetry, Shakespeare, and the Gettysburg Address. At twelve years old, he won a speaking prize from the Child Welfare League of America. The award meant a great deal to him all his life. The prize was a speaking engagement at the Waldorf Astoria hotel. It didn't take much prodding to get him to reminisce about how he held such celebrities as comedian Joe E. Brown and Mayor Fiorello La Guardia "in the palm of my hand with my spellbinding oratorical skills!" It was a pompous claim, but he always said it with a twinkle. His love of the spotlight, though, did not lead him to the theater. He seldom attended a Broadway show and he had never heard of the Shubert brothers. An early draft of his memoir—which he loved to read aloud to visitors in his elegant office above the Shubert Theatre (the office had once been Lee's bedroom)—contained a chapter that opened, "When I was a boy, the name Schubert meant one thing—a Trout Quintet!" (That line never made it into the published *Mr. Broadway*.)

In 1941, Jerry enrolled at the University of Illinois at Urbana-Champaign. He was only seventeen, but everyone who knew him as a boy said he always looked and acted older than his years. He was a serious student, though as he himself admitted he lacked direction. He studied business and engineering and became a great reader, especially of history. When World War II broke out, he joined the army air corps and was sent to MIT to learn physics, calculus, and meteorology. None appealed to him, and because he couldn't draw maps he flunked the course. He also had trouble assembling machine guns, and the thought of flying terrified him.

"I had visions of a plane door falling off and me tumbling out into space with nothing to save me," he wrote in his memoir.

Fortunately, he was never called upon to jump out of a B-17 bomber—or fire one of those machine guns he had so much trouble assembling. He got through the war at various technical training schools in the South. After being discharged in 1946, he returned to New York with the vague idea of following his father into the garment business. But there was another option—law. His brother Irving's best friend from the neighborhood, Bernie Jacobs, recently graduated from Columbia Law School. Jacobs encouraged Schoenfeld to try law, and in 1947 Schoenfeld entered New York University Law School. But his best teacher wasn't on the NYU faculty. "Jerry used to call Bernie every night for advice about his classes," Betty Jacobs, Bernie's widow, said decades later. "That's how they became close."

Bernard B. Jacobs was born in Manhattan in 1916. His father was also in the garment industry, though he was not as successful as Sam Schoenfeld. He ran a woolen waste business, reselling scraps of left-over material. Bernie grew up in an apartment building on Broadway and 102nd Street. It wasn't the ghetto, but it was not as upscale an address as the Schoenfelds' on West End Avenue. Bernie Jacobs was not, at first blush, gregarious, or even friendly. He had a long face, dark eyes, and a large, slightly crooked nose. His lips drooped at the edges. He always seemed to be frowning. But he had a cutting sense of humor and a quick mind. He could do complicated math in his head and, though just a teenager, seemed wiser than his years. If you had a problem, you went to Bernie for advice. After graduating from DeWitt Clinton High School, he shot through NYU and then Columbia Law School, earning his degree just before he was drafted into the army.

He would be sent to the Pacific, but not before meeting Betty Shulman. Her sorority sister was Bernie's cousin. "She gave him my number and he called. That's how everybody got dates in those days. He called and we talked on the phone for about six weeks before he asked me for a date," Betty said.

When he showed up at Betty Shulman's apartment, he brought with him his best friend, Irving Schoenfeld. "I didn't know which one was my date and which one wasn't," Betty recalled. "And what happened was we went for a ride. We went up to Westchester to an inn that had a parking lot, and Irving gave Bernie a driving lesson. That was our first date. Not a big romantic afternoon!"

They dated for a few months, and then Bernie went into the army and was sent to the Pacific. While there, he met up for a drink one day with Betty's brother, who was a navigator in the navy. Several weeks later, Betty got a letter from her brother. "I caught up with Bernie," he wrote. "Marry him. He's the only man in the South Pacific who can get fresh eggs."

After the war, Bernie returned to New York and asked Betty on a date. He took her to a Broadway show—which one she's not sure of anymore. But the tickets were three dollars each, and they sat in the balcony—"I could hear in those days," she said, "and see!"

Bernie Jacobs married Betty Shulman on June 13, 1946, and then went to work with his brother, who was also a lawyer, representing clients in the jewelry business. It was not, he would tell his young wife, interesting work.

Jerry Schoenfeld met Pat Miller in the winter of 1947, while he was in law school. A pretty NYU undergraduate who wanted to be a teacher, Pat looked like the actress Poupée Bocar, who in the sixties and seventies would become a familiar face from guest appearances on TV shows such as *Get Smart*, *Ironside*, and *Columbo*. Jerry had a date with Pat's older sister, and Pat tagged along with a boy she was seeing at the time. Pat lived around the corner from Jerry on the Upper West Side. They often ran into each other on the subway on their way to NYU. A friendship sprang up, and they began to date casually. Pat saw other boys as well, but she often went to Jerry for advice. And she appreciated his sense of humor. But, working hard at law school and then landing his first job in 1949 for a mere forty dollars a week, he was in no rush to get married. And then in 1950, Pat told him another boy she was seeing, a boy from a rich family, was getting serious about her. Jerry made his decision. They became engaged, officially, on her birthday—April 4. They were married in October, lived with her parents for six months, and then, when they'd saved enough money, rented a one-bedroom apartment in Peter Cooper Village, a partially subsidized apartment complex on the East River in lower Manhattan.

As Pat was finishing her degree at NYU, Jerry worked as a clerk at a law firm called Klein & Weir. The "Klein" was William Klein, who had been the Shubert brothers' lawyer for years, and who had been with Sam in that fatal train crash. By 1949, he was old and ailing. His partner, Milton Weir, and their junior associate, Adolph Lund, handled most of the firm's work. They had two clients, the Shuberts and a coat hanger manufacturer. Every afternoon Weir would visit Lee in his office above the Shubert Theatre and J. J. at his in the Sardi Building. By this point, the brothers were estranged. Their personalities never did mesh—J. J. volcanic, Lee inscrutable. In addition, J. J. wanted his son, John, to take over the business; Lee, who didn't think John had the brains or strength to run the empire, was grooming a nephew, Milton. The legend is that Lee and J. J. no longer even spoke to each other, communicating through memos dictated to their secretaries. Yet it's hard to believe those two brothers, who plotted and clawed their way to the top, who defeated powerful enemies, who buried their beloved brother Sam, had little interaction at the end of their lives. When they were under attack, Lee and J. J. put aside whatever differences they had and joined forces, an old Shubert employee said. In the end, they trusted no one but each other, and though face-to-face meetings were infrequent, they could sometimes be seen late at night huddled at a corner table in the Astor Hotel.

In 1950, as Schoenfeld was beginning his career, they huddled together to discuss the antitrust suit brought against them by the United States government. The Justice Department demanded that the Shuberts divest themselves of some of their theaters in New York and other cities, and close down their booking office, which gave them the power to place shows around the country in any theater they wanted. Milton Weir studied the government's antitrust action and then handed it to his forty-dollar-a-week clerk, Jerry Schoenfeld, to prepare a response.

As he recounts in his memoir, Schoenfeld was "stunned." He knew little about antitrust laws and had never prepared a response to the United States government. But he couldn't duck the assignment, so he hit the books, studying not only antitrust cases but also the history of the American theater and of the Shubert brothers. He developed a unique argument. Schoenfeld pointed out that the Shubert Organization had gone bankrupt during the Great Depression. Its theaters were put up for auction, but there was only one bidder—Lee. "The Shuberts had not purchased the theaters to drive competitors out of business," Schoenfeld wrote in his memoir. They had, in fact, few competitors during the Great Depression. Whatever monopoly they acquired "had been thrust upon them as a result of their original company's bankruptcy," Schoenfeld argued. They had not created a monopoly deliberately.

"Some are born great, some achieve greatness and some have greatness thrust upon them," Shakespeare wrote in *Twelfth Night*. Lee and J. J. Shubert had achieved greatness, but they had monopoly "thrust upon them," Schoenfeld argued.

It was a clever riposte, and it bought the Shubert Organization time in its fight against the government.

Lee's death in 1953 thrust Schoenfeld into yet another battle—this one a bitter family feud. In his will, Lee attempted to block J. J.'s son, John, from taking over the company by naming his nephew Milton Shubert as his successor. By all accounts a mild-mannered junior executive with little flair for a fight, Milton moved into Lee's office above the Shubert Theatre, while J. J. fumed across the street. J. J. insisted Milton had no authority in an empire that was now his, and his alone. Milton Weir, who had been close to Lee, disagreed, citing Lee's will, which specifically delegated his duties to Milton Shubert. J. J. turned to his other lawyer, Adolph Lund, and Lund's associate, Schoenfeld, for help. According to Schoenfeld, J. J. produced a copy of an agreement, drawn up decades earlier, that laid out the partnership between him and Lee. It was a fifty-fifty split. Neither could overrule the other; decisions were made together. Lund advised J. J. that the Shubert business was indeed his. J. J. could annihilate his nephew Milton—and he did. When Milton left his office (Lee's old office) above the Shubert Theatre one afternoon for an appointment, J. J. dashed across Forty-Fourth Street with Lund, Schoenfeld, and a locksmith. He ordered all the locks in his brother's former office changed. Then, according to biographer Foster Hirsch, he waited for Milton to return, seated behind his brother's old desk. But Milton heard what had happened—the Shubert grapevine must have been buzzing that day—and stormed in, accompanied by the other Shubert lawyer, Milton Weir. J. J. ordered his nephew out on the street. When Weir protested, J. J. tried to punch him in the face. Schoenfeld reports that J. J. then asked Lund if he could call the police and have his adversaries arrested for trespassing. Lund said, "You can do whatever you want."[1]

In the end, Milton Shubert backed down. Few people could withstand J. J.'s tirades, and his agreement with his brother was ironclad. Milton left the office that day, never to return to the Shubert Organization. Then J. J. turned on Milton Weir, fired him, and demanded that Lund break up the firm of Klein & Weir. The new firm became Klein & Lund, and Schoenfeld moved up a rung on the ladder.

A few days after J. J. annihilated the two Miltons, United States District Court Judge John C. Knox threw out the government's suit against the Shuberts, arguing that "theatrical bookings, like organized baseball, are not subject to antitrust laws."[2] He cited *Toolson v. New York Yankees*, which had exempted Major League Baseball from the Sherman Antitrust Act. The U.S. government appealed. The case would drag on for another three years. Lund and Schoenfeld enlisted the aid of more lawyers, including Alfred McCormack, a renowned antitrust specialist. J. J. raged and raged, threatening at one point to sell all his theaters just to spite the government. The battle finally reached the Supreme Court, which overturned Knox's decision and reinstated the antitrust suit. J. J. had a choice: cut a deal or risk a trial, which McCormack feared he would lose.

On February 17, 1956, perhaps worn down by one too many battles, J. J. buckled. He signed a consent decree with the U.S. government, agreeing to sell off twelve theaters. J. J. lost a few prime houses—the St. James in New York, the Colonial in Boston, the Shubert in Philadelphia—but he cleverly used the consent decree to dispose of smaller, less profitable theaters ("the junk," as producer Liz McCann would call them) such as the Ritz and the Maxine Elliott in New York. The Shuberts' powerful booking office was disbanded, and J. J. also agreed to dissolve partnerships with theater owners across the country. The consent decree also banned the Shuberts from buying any more theaters.

An antitrust battle, a family feud, a consent decree, dismantling an empire—Jerry Schoenfeld was thrust into the theater business. All along his guide was Adolph Lund, "my friend and mentor," he wrote. Lund taught him the ins and outs of the Shubert Organization and shielded him from J. J.'s rages. In the spring of 1956, Lund, complaining of an ulcer, had surgery, rendering him absent for a month. Schoenfeld had to handle J. J.'s business. Lund warned him, "You're entering a lion's den. Be prepared for the worst." But as Schoenfeld writes in his memoir, "To my surprise . . . J. J. and I got along fairly well." Lund laughed. "You'll learn," he told his protégé, "that with the Shuberts, familiarity breeds contempt."[3]

Lund returned to work, but was not the same. He was tired all the time, and his stomach continued to bother him. On December 31, 1956, he checked into Mount Sinai Hospital. He was dead the next day, from colon cancer. Schoenfeld, thirty-two, was devastated. Klein had retired; Lund was dead. Klein & Lund—Schoenfeld's employer— existed in name only.

Harold Laski, the English Marxist and Labour Party politician, liked to say that in British politics "while there is death there is hope."[4] Such was the case in Shubert Alley. A few days after Lund died, J. J. asked another lawyer, James Vaughan, to replace Lund. Vaughan, a respected estates litigation lawyer well connected at the New York State Surrogate Court, had drawn up J. J.'s will. But Vaughan turned down the job of Shubert in-house counsel. "My father did not want to be beholden to one person," Edward Foley Vaughan recalled. James Vaughan told J. J. he should consider hiring young Schoenfeld. Jerry was bright, energetic, and he was getting to know the Shubert business first-hand. "My father loved Jerry," Foley Vaughan said. "And Jerry looked up to him as a kind of father figure." J. J. took Vaughan's advice and offered Schoenfeld the job. "You'll need some help," he said. "Go out and find someone." [5]

Schoenfeld called his friend and informal law school tutor, Bernie Jacobs. Over lunch, Schoenfeld asked Jacobs if he'd like to be his partner. Jacobs went home that night to discuss the offer with his wife. He decided to take the job. "I don't know much about theater law," he told Betty, "but anything I need to know I can probably learn in two weeks."

Jacobs joined the Shubert Organization in 1957, working alongside Schoenfeld. The pay wasn't much—about $150 week, Betty Jacobs remembers. (Schoenfeld, in his memoir, claims it was $300.) The first time she ever attended a Broadway opening, she had to borrow her mother's fur coat. But J. J. gave his lawyers free office space above the Shubert Theatre. Jacobs moved into what had once been Lee Shubert's living room, Schoenfeld into Lee's bedroom. J. J. also let them do legal work for other clients. But, J. J. warned, "If you're working for me, it's a twenty-four-hour job." Which meant if he was up and about in the middle of the night—as he often was—they could expect a call. And it wasn't just a call. It was a summons. "Be at my office in half an hour," J. J. would say. Since Jerry and Pat lived in Manhattan and Bernie and Betty lived in Roslyn, Long Island, it usually fell to Jerry to answer the summons. "That's why Bernie never wanted to move into the city," Betty Jacobs recalled.

Now in his seventies, J. J. was beginning to fade. But his hold on his empire could be extended through his son, John. "John Shubert," Bernie Jacobs once said, "was one of the kindest, most decent men I ever met. But he was dominated, completely, by his father." The son of warring parents—J. J. despised John's mother, Catherine Mary, and she returned the animosity—he hated confrontation. He didn't have much of a passion for the theater, producing only a handful of plays, all flops. He liked carpentry. He was tall and gentle looking, with his father's plump face and his uncle Sammy's soft, sad eyes. He drank a great deal, usually at seedy bars in Times Square. But he was not a belligerent drunk. Just a sad one. He seemed content, Schoenfeld and Jacobs thought, to preside over a business that was, in many ways, winding down.

The Shuberts, by the late 1950s and early sixties, had all but ceased to produce. Why bother? There were plenty of producers around to take the risk for them. David Merrick was at his height, cranking out show after show every season. Cy Feuer and Ernie Martin were producing such shows as *How to Succeed in Business Without Really Trying*, *Silk Stockings*, *Little Me*, and *The Boy Friend*. Kermit Bloomgarden, a tough former accountant with taste (he backed *Death of a Salesman* after other producers turned it down because they thought it too depressing), offered up *The Most Happy Fella*, *A View from the Bridge*, and *The Diary of Anne Frank*. Alexander H. Cohen, a splashy, free-spending promoter-turned-impresario, produced a show every season. Most were flops, but it didn't deter him. "Kid," he once said, "I've had a million and I've owed a million—and my lifestyle has never changed." Among his flops, though, were gems—*An Evening with Mike Nichols and Elaine May*, *Beyond the Fringe*, and *The School for Scandal*, starring John Gielgud and Ralph Richardson. Richard Rodgers and Oscar Hammerstein were still at it, and in 1959 would come up with one of their biggest hits ever, *The Sound of Music*. Robert Whitehead and Roger Stevens—rich, gentleman producers—presented plays by Arthur Miller, Tennessee Williams, Terence Rattigan, Eugene O'Neill, Shaw, and Shakespeare. Harold (Hal) Prince, who had begun his career as a stage manager for director George Abbott, was now emerging as a musical theater producer of the first order with *The Pajama Game*, *Damn Yankees*, *West Side Story*, and *Fiorello!*

"We did a show a year," said Hal Prince. "We were as important as the theater owners. Do you know we negotiated our terms for every theater? We had power."

If John Shubert wasn't interested in developing plays or musicals himself, there was one aspect of the theater business about which he wanted some measure of control—ice. John must have heard his father rail against box office personnel—"thieves," he called them. J. J. often told the story of the time he was sailing back from Europe and, in first class, ran into one of his box office treasurers. "They should be paying me for their jobs," he would say. "I've given them the concession stands!"

John Shubert, with the help of two distant cousins, Lawrence Shubert Lawrence Jr. and Murray Helwitz, centralized the flow of ice from room 504 of the Sardi Building. Before 504, ice was collected and distributed by box office treasurers on an informal basis. But by 1960, John had set up the ice "bank," as producer Alexander H. Cohen called room 504. "John made the absurd mistake of formalizing the arrangements for ice."[6]

As Assistant Attorney General David Clurman discovered in 1963, ice flowed to employees throughout the Shubert chain. Did J. J.'s lawyers, Jerry Schoenfeld and Bernie Jacobs, get their cut? In his memoir, Schoenfeld writes that when he and Jacobs learned about ice, they told John Shubert to end it. "It is fraught with peril," Schoenfeld wrote. "It would be hard to deny illegal activities one floor below your own office."[7] Jacobs rarely spoke about the ice scandal. But in a 1979 interview with John Corry of the *New York Times*—a reporter he liked and trusted—he said, "Jerry and I have been on the street a long time. We know you'll hear people saying things we wouldn't like, but you'll never hear anyone say we touched anything dishonest."

As J. J.'s lawyers, Schoenfeld and Jacobs each had a pair of house seats (row G, 2–8) for every performance of a show in a Shubert theater. Jack Small, who booked shows for Shubert, told them he could sell their house seats to a broker. "Give me your seats and I'll give you five dollars for each one," he said. Jacobs replied, "Thanks very much, but I have use for those seats. I have friends and family to take care of." Schoenfeld turned him down as well.

People who were—or became—close to Schoenfeld and Jacobs do not believe they were on the take. "They were lawyers, and they were very proud of being lawyers, especially Jerry," said producer Elizabeth I. McCann. "They would not have done anything that might have gotten them disbarred." James Vaughan, the respected estate lawyer who handled J. J.'s will, "believed in their rectitude," his son Foley Vaughan said. "I worked alongside my father in the sixties and I never had any sense that they participated in the ice scandal."

Another prominent New York attorney, John Wharton, cofounder of the powerful law firm Paul, Weiss, Rifkind, Wharton & Garrison, also thought Schoenfeld and Jacobs were free of ice. "John Wharton believed the two of them would never do anything to threaten their standing in the legal community," McCann said. "He had faith in them, and that carried a lot of weight because John Wharton was like the pope in legal circles." Wharton, who represented such prominent theater people as Cole Porter, Maxwell Anderson, S. N. Berhman, and Robert E. Sherwood, deplored ice. "The people who create the entertainment and the people who supply the capital for production are all excluded," he wrote in his book, *Life Among the Playwrights*. "That is the tragic part."

When Schoenfeld and Jacobs warned John Shubert about ice, he responded that room 504 had been set up to prevent brokers from getting their hands on the best tickets. "That, of course, was sheer nonsense," said Phil Smith. "Either John Shubert was naive or a criminal."

John Shubert did not live to see the family empire rattled by a ticket scandal he helped create. On November 16, 1962, he died of a heart attack on a train to Clearwater, Florida. Though they didn't know it at the time, John's death was the opening that would one day allow Schoenfeld and Jacobs to ascend to the top of the American theater. "While there is death there is hope." Or, as Bernie Jacobs once put it, "Gerald and I got where we are because the right people died at the right time."

CHAPTER FIVE

Bastards, Criminals, and Drunks

Betty and Bernie Jacobs flew to Clearwater, Florida, to claim John Shubert's body. He had gone to Florida to celebrate Thanksgiving with his mistress, Nancy Mae Eyerman, a tall, slender, attractive brunette. John's wife, Kerttu Helene Eklund Shubert—"Eckie," as everyone called her—lived in New York in an apartment on West Fifty-Fourth Street and in a palatial white colonial house in Byram, Connecticut. John and Eckie, a former showgirl, had been married since 1937. But they had been estranged for years at the time of his death, and he had told those close to him that the love of his life was Nancy, whom he'd met on a transatlantic ocean liner in 1958. He had two children with Nancy, Sarah Catherine and John Jason—J. J. Jr. John had no children with Eckie—it was rumored that he forced her to have at least two abortions—and few people knew about his second family in Clearwater. Betty and Bernie Jacobs knew about it, however. And they knew something else. Nancy Eyerman wasn't just John's mistress; she was his second wife. In 1961, John and Nancy traveled to El Paso, Texas. They slipped across the border to Juarez, Mexico, where John got a divorce from Eckie. (In the 1960s, Mexico did not require spouses to be present at divorce hearings. Many celebrities of the era, including Marilyn Monroe, Katharine Hepburn, and Johnny Carson, were also granted Mexican or "quickie" divorces.) A few days later he married Nancy.

Eckie knew about John's second marriage, too. The day he filed for the Mexican divorce, he wrote her a letter of apology, telling her the divorce was worthless and that he still loved her. "I think she took John to the train when he went down to see Nancy before he died," recalled Betty Jacobs. In Clearwater, Bernie and Betty met with Nancy and asked her not to come to the funeral in New York. It would be awkward. The Shubert family didn't need another scandal.

John Shubert's funeral was held on November 21, 1962, on the stage of the Majestic Theatre, where *Camelot* was playing. In his will, John stipulated that no one but Eckie be onstage during the service. She sat in a chair next to his coffin. And where was Wife Number Two? Accounts differ. Shubert biographer Foster Hirsch reports that people who knew Nancy were stationed at the doors of the Majestic to bar her from entering if she turned up. He says Nancy did not attend the service. But Betty Jacobs has a different recollection. "She was there. I saw her. She sat in the back of the theater. Eckie was up there with the coffin. Nancy was at the back. We asked her not to come, but she came. What were we going to do? She was a wife, too."

Schoenfeld and Jacobs sorted out John Shubert's affairs. He had, they discovered, safe deposit boxes in banks all over town. Squirreled away was about $500,000 in cash. Crisp, clean bills. Some people were quick to suspect that this was John's share of the ice from room 504. The IRS eventually examined the bills and discovered that the serial numbers were from the 1920s. "Those bills hadn't seen the daylight for a long time," said Phil Smith. "They were out of circulation for so long, they weren't even taxable."

In the end, the newspapers reported that John's estate amounted to $600,000, though many on Broadway thought it was at least $1 million or more. Whatever the figure, it was dwarfed by the value of the Shubert empire. The real money—$15 million, if not more, according to estimates at the time—still belonged to J. J. Shubert. But he was bedridden in his Sardi's penthouse apartment, lost in the fog of dementia.

With John dead and J. J. enfeebled, who would run the Shubert empire? Bernie Jacobs thought Schoenfeld should step forward. Schoenfeld had been dealing with Shubert business for more than ten years. He knew as much about the business as anybody else working on West Forty-Fourth Street. He had the respect and support of influential lawyers like John Wharton and Jim Vaughan. He didn't know much about reading scripts and hiring directors, but that didn't matter. The Shuberts had been out of the producing business for several years. The empire was, for the most part, a real estate business. But Schoenfeld wasn't ready. "Jerry was cautious," said Phil Smith. "I don't think he thought it would look right. Shubert was a family business."

Milton Shubert was in Florida, still recovering from the evisceration he'd suffered at J. J.'s hands in 1954. Murray Helwitz was a distant Shubert cousin, but "Stuttering M-M-Murray," as they called him because he stuttered when he got nervous, was running 504. Not exactly the Harvard Business School. The best candidate appeared to be Lawrence Shubert Lawrence Jr. His father, Lawrence Shubert Lawrence Sr., was Lee and J. J.'s nephew and ran their theaters in Philadelphia. Lawrence Jr. had attended the right schools—Lawrenceville prep in New Jersey, the University of Pennsylvania. He'd worked under J. J. and John for thirty-six years as manager of various theaters in New York. He also had the Shubert name. He was appointed head of the Shubert Organization after John's funeral "to provide the illusion of continuity" and calm fears around Broadway that the company might be disbanded and the theaters sold off.[1] After his appointment was announced, he celebrated at the second-floor bar at Sardi's. And that is where you could find him for most of his tenure as head of the Shubert empire.

This is what Bernie Jacobs had to say about Lawrence Shubert Lawrence Jr. in 1996: "Lawrence had alcohol in his system twenty-four hours a day. He woke up in the morning drinking, and he went to sleep drinking. He was an egomaniac, incompetent, and terrible to work with. And still we lived with him for ten years. They were terrible times. The business was going to the devil. Everything was out of control."

Sam, Lee, and J. J. were not afflicted by the alcoholism that ruined their father. But their nephew, Lawrence Sr., and his son, Lawrence Jr., certainly were.

In 1956, Harvey Sabinson, then a young press agent, landed his first Broadway-bound show, Eduardo de Filippo's *The Best House in Naples*. The tryout was in Philadelphia at the Shubert-owned Walnut Street

Theatre. "Opening night in Philadelphia—I'll never forget this—in front of the theater, Lawrence Shubert Lawrence Sr. pukes all over the sidewalk as the audience is coming in," Sabinson recalled. "I thought, How do these guys wind up with these jobs? Well, it's because they're named Shubert!" Larry Sr. would sometimes drive up to New York from Philadelphia to see a show. He'd park his Bentley in Shubert Alley and then head straight to the Piccadilly Circus Bar in the Piccadilly Hotel on West Forty-Fifth Street. He'd get so drunk, he'd miss the show and have to sleep it off in the hotel.

Larry Jr.'s drink of choice was Dewar's. "Let's have a blast," he'd say. After downing several Scotches, he'd relieve himself in the men's room and say, "I'm just the middleman—it goes right through me!" "That was his favorite joke," said an old Shubert hand. "He thought it was hilarious."

Larry Shubert was at the second-floor bar in Sardi's so often, he had a phone installed at one end of the bar in case he had to conduct business. One afternoon someone else was in his usual seat by the phone. The next day he had another phone installed at the other end of the bar. If he wasn't at Sardi's, you could find him at the Piccadilly Circus Bar. Or at the Playbill Bar in the Hotel Manhattan (now the Row NYC). You'd seldom find him in a theater. He wasn't interested in shows. Bernie Jacobs once accompanied him to London to see some plays headed for New York. As soon as they got to the Savoy Hotel, Larry headed for the bar. They were supposed to see a play of the Royal Shakespeare Company's that night, but Larry didn't want to go. "Why bother? It's not worth it," he said. Jacobs returned to the hotel after the show and found Larry still at the bar. "Well, how was it?" he asked. "*Much Ado About Nothing*," Jacobs said. "I thought so!" Larry replied, triumphantly.

"He was considered that branch of the family where the brains had gone bad," said Bernard Gersten, who was then working alongside Joe Papp at the New York Shakespeare Festival. "He was disregarded by Bernie and Jerry."

When Larry did turn up at the theater, it was usually to leer at the chorus girls during auditions or rehearsals. Betty Jacobs said, "Larry's mother once told me, 'Watch out for my son. He's after you.' I didn't pay much attention to that, but I remember she said it."

Larry's girlfriend was Oona White, the choreographer of shows such as *The Music Man* and *Take Me Along*. But he favored pretty young blondes. One afternoon he was invited to a reading of a new play at a fancy apartment on Fifth Avenue. He wanted Phil Smith, who had recently joined the company, to drive up from Shubert Alley with him. But first he wanted a drink.

"Wait for me," he said.

"Larry, I want to go now," Smith replied.

"You wait for me, you hear?" he said.

Smith recalled, "He'd always give you the 'Hear me!' And that meant, 'I'm the boss.'"

They took Larry's limousine up to the apartment, but before they went in, the boss said, "I want to have a blast. Where can we go?" The Stanhope Hotel on Fifth Avenue across the street from the Metropolitan Museum was nearby. So Larry had "a blast." And then, said Smith, "He had himself another blast. He was a fast drinker."

Smith finally got Larry out of the Stanhope and up to the apartment. A young, beautiful blond actress named Blythe Danner had a small part in the reading. Larry, who by now was tipsy, stared at her and started saying, "Weee! Weee!" throughout the reading.

The ice scandal hit Broadway and the Shuberts not long after Larry succeeded John Shubert. Even in his alcoholic haze he must have realized that the company was in jeopardy. Assistant Attorney General Clurman had enough evidence to indict Stuttering M-M-Murray Helwitz. He pressed Helwitz to finger some higher-ups. Lawrence Shubert Lawrence Jr. was in his sights. But Helwitz wouldn't talk. "Murray Helwitz took the fall for the industry," says producer Manny Azenberg. Helwitz pled guilty to taking more than $70,000 from nine ticket brokers in 1963. Clurman said the figure was conservative, believing it was at least $250,000. The criminal court judge who heard the case added, "I suspect somebody above you got some of the money. There's a well-known rumor that the money trickles upward, not downward. There's a strong indication that whoever gets the gravy sends it upstairs, not downstairs."

Helwitz was sentenced to eight months in jail and fined $4,600. When he got out, he went back to work for the Shubert Organization, now under the direction of Lawrence Shubert Lawrence Jr.

•   •   •

As the ice scandal was unfolding, another scandal hit the Shubert family. In May 1963, Nancy Mae Eyerman Shubert filed a claim in Surrogate Court that she was the real Mrs. John Shubert and that her two children were entitled to his estate. Eckie filed her own claim. The ruling would be crucial to the fate of the Shubert empire. If Nancy won, the Shubert estate would probably have to be broken up. Theaters and other pieces of real estate would be sold to settle accounts. But if Eckie won, it would be business as usual. The case went to court in August 1963, with Surrogate Judge Samuel DiFalco presiding. A product of Tammany Hall, DiFalco and his court were famously corrupt. DiFalco was indicted on misconduct charges in 1976 but died before the case went to trial. One of his schemes was to pass out "guardianships" to cronies. These were practically no-show jobs that came with hefty fees. DiFalco appointed Arthur N. Field as guardian to John Shubert's children. Field was DiFalco's former law partner, and he was paid $15,000 to "sit down with us for fifteen minutes," Nancy would recall ten years later.[2]

Eckie attended the trial in a wheelchair, as she'd broken her leg. She wore a short-sleeved black dress, two strands of pearls, and a diamond cross. Both Nancy and Eckie wore wedding rings.[3] They sat in the courtroom listening to testimony about the Mexican divorce and marriage; John's letter to Eckie telling her the divorce was worthless; charges of John having a "divided life" and a "dual personality," according to Nancy's attorney. Nancy's father, Edward Eyerman, said John had told him his life with Eckie was "unbearable" because she drank and cheated on him. The next day the tabloids ran sordid stories about the Shubert family. A young reporter at the *New York Post* with a stylish pen—Nora Ephron—had fun with John's letter to Eckie. "It's a rare man who will take the trouble to write loving and consoling letters to his first wife while clearing the way to acquire a new one," Ephron wrote. "Nobody, it appears, was more thoughtful about such matters than John Shubert."[4]

It was all too much for both Eckie and Nancy, neither of whom had ever sought publicity. Edward Eyerman, a prosperous banker from Kingston, Pennsylvania, was disgusted with the spectacle. He was battling cancer and wanted to go home. He had no use for the Shuberts and their messy lives. "You don't need their money," he told his daughter. "Let's go home."[5]

The next day, Nancy settled out of court. She did not want to embarrass herself or her children anymore. DiFalco helped draw up the settlement. It could not have been more favorable to the Shuberts. Nancy agreed to give up the name Shubert and never again claim to have been married to John. The Mexican divorce and marriage were invalidated. Eckie was deemed the real Mrs. John Shubert. Nancy's children were declared legitimate and each received $12,500. But they gave up all claims to the estate of their father or grandfather. Once again, the empire was saved. It would be business as usual.*

Was the decision fair? Foley Vaughan, who with his father represented many clients in Surrogate Court, said, "It was a horrible result. Now, there was not as much tender feeling toward out-of-wedlock children as there is today. Illegitimacy was a real barrier. But it was a terrible result for those kids and an advantageous result for the Shuberts. But I never heard anyone say the wire was in."

"The wire was in"—this was an old expression whispered often around the Surrogate Court. It meant the fix was in. It meant somebody had gotten to DiFalco and secured a favorable decision. It was around the time of the Shubert settlement that a Runyonesque figure named Irving Goldman emerged from the back rooms of New York politics to play a role in Shubert affairs. "Irving Goldman was in the 'favors business,'" said veteran producer Albert Poland. "He had the charm of a guy who sells you used Chevrolet upholstery. And I mean used!"

Goldman's background is murky. He was, he would say, born into grinding poverty in Brooklyn. He claimed he wore cardboard shoes to school. As a teenager he got a job in a paint company and would later claim that, while delivering paint to a Shubert theater, he met J. J. Shubert. Goldman said J. J. took a liking to him immediately. "You won't be an errand boy for long," J. J. predicted. J. J. took to calling him "son"

* Decades later, Ephron, now a celebrated screenwriter, became friendly with Jerry and Pat Schoenfeld. "Jerry told me nobody really understood how important that case was," she said at a luncheon in 2012 at the Four Seasons Restaurant for the creators of *The Book of Mormon*. "He said if it hadn't gone their way, the company would have been broken up."

and gave him a few thousand dollars to start his own paint business. By 1960, according to Shubert biographer Foster Hirsch, Goldman had a thriving business called Gothic Color that supplied paint to Broadway theaters and set shops. He always boasted of his friendship with J. J., but nobody believed him. J. J. barely felt paternal to his own son. Why would he take kindly to a little paint salesman?[6]

"I think he made the whole thing up," said Phil Smith. "Because I talked to guys back then who knew J. J., and nobody remembers him. One guy said to me, 'I spent a lot of time with J. J. I think I would have remembered Irving Goldman. I don't remember him.'"

When he wasn't selling paint, Goldman was cultivating powerful friends, including Abe Beame, who would become mayor in 1974, and Surrogate Court Judge Samuel DiFalco.

"He called DiFalco 'Speedy,'" Smith remembered. "We were at an event once and he dragged me into the bar at the Bull and the Bear restaurant and said, 'I want you to come in and have a drink with Speedy and myself!'"

Was Goldman "the wire"? In 1974, *New York Post* reporter Joseph Berger examined Goldman's connection to the Shubert settlement. By then, Goldman had become a Shubert executive. Quoting unnamed sources, Berger reported that Goldman boasted of his influence in the case with DiFalco. "It was a tough task I had to do," Goldman allegedly said. One of Berger's sources added, "Goldman never let [the Shuberts] forget it was a difficult case." Berger also interviewed Nancy Eyerman, who recalled that a Shubert secretary named Violet Fisch told her, "DiFalco and a man named Goldman had it all set up. DiFalco wasn't going to sit there and be impartial the way you'd hope a judge would be." But Fisch herself said in the same article that she couldn't remember the incident. And DiFalco told the *Post*, "No third party has ever influenced me."[7]

Whether or not Goldman had anything to do with the Shubert settlement will probably never be known. But after the decision came down, he became a regular visitor to the Shubert executive offices, and a good deal of business from the company came his way. In *Playbills* from the 1960s, his paint company is credited with doing interiors of Shubert theaters. He also cultivated a relationship with Lawrence Shubert Lawrence Jr., hanging out with him in bars and introducing him to politicians. In 1971, Lawrence appointed him to the Shubert board of directors. He also got to know Jerry Schoenfeld and Bernie Jacobs. It was an association both men would come to regret.

On December 26, 1963—four months after John Shubert's bigamy case was settled out of court—J. J. Shubert, age eighty-six, died of a cerebral hemorrhage in his penthouse. Around three hundred people attended the old tyrant's funeral at Temple Emanu-El on Fifth Avenue, including producer Max Gordon and actress Jane Manners. Nobody spoke but the rabbi, who hadn't even known J. J., and his eulogy was enigmatic. "He was a warm and princely generous man, but he was as reticent in his public benefactions as he was in his private life." [8]

J. J.'s death profoundly altered the Shubert empire. Up until then, it had been a family business. But in his will, J. J. left most of his money—and all of his theaters—to a little-known charitable organization called the Sam S. Shubert Foundation. J. J. and Lee had set up the foundation in 1945 in honor of their brother. Its mission, broadly defined, was to give away money to scientific, literary, and educational causes. Its other mission was to squirrel away as much money as possible from the United States government. There was no law (as there is now) requiring foundations to give away at least 5 percent of their assets annually. "It was a wonderful way of putting money into limbo," said Lee Seidler, an accountant who joined the board of the Shubert Foundation in the 1990s. [9]

And now the foundation controlled the theaters, which meant it controlled the Shubert empire. No one could ever own the theaters again. There would never be any equity in the Shubert Organization. From now on, anybody who ran the Shubert Organization would be an employee of the foundation and its board of directors. But a seat on that board would be a very nice plum indeed. And one day, Irving Goldman—"He had the charm of a guy who sells you used Chevrolet upholstery!"—would become the head of the Shubert Foundation.

For now, though, Larry Shubert presided. Though he knew he would never own the company, he strutted around as if he did. He surrounded himself with drinking buddies who encouraged him to behave as if

the empire belonged to him. One of his drinking buddies was Irving
"Hickey" Katz, who owned a ticket agency called Hickey's. Hickey was
available anytime, day or night, to meet Lawrence for a drink. Another
crony was Walter Kaiser, an insurance broker who had an office in the
Sardi Building. He'd had J. J.'s ear and John's—and now he had Larry's.
His currency was gossip, the coin of the Broadway realm. "He was
really good," said Phil Smith. "He heard everything; he carried tales
to Larry. He was known as the 'Tale Carrier.' " Bernard Friedman, the
comptroller at Shubert, also propped Larry up at the bar and began
to feed him stories about how Schoenfeld and Jacobs were plotting
against him.

A classier crony was Howard Teichmann—"Tyke," as everyone
called him. A graduate of the University of Wisconsin, he worked under Orson Welles at the legendary Mercury Theatre in the 1930s. He'd
written plays—his most famous, *The Solid Gold Cadillac*, was a collaboration with George S. Kaufman—and would go on to write popular
biographies of Kaufman, Alexander Woollcott, and Alice Roosevelt
Longworth. A charming and gifted storyteller, he came into the Shubert orbit in 1962 with a proposal to write a book about the company.
John Shubert liked him and put him in charge of selecting plays. Under
Larry, he became an unofficial PR man, writing Larry's speeches and
the occasional article that would appear under Larry's byline in *Variety* or the *New York Times*. Larry also put him in charge of dispensing
grants from the foundation to up-and-coming playwrights. But his job
description was vague, at best. "Nobody really knew what Teichmann
did," said Jerry Leichtling, who worked as Schoenfeld's office boy in
the late sixties. "He read plays, but it was a very genteel, nonfocused
operation. There was no sense of going out and searching for and finding new shows." Tyke was not a championship drinker like Larry or
Hickey. After three drinks, he'd be smashed, Smith recalled. But he
was available to hang out at the bar, and he entertained Larry with old
showbiz stories.

The one sycophant who could match Larry drink for drink was his
cousin Norman Light. He booked the theaters—and what a booker
he was! He never pursued a show, wooed a producer, courted a playwright. He didn't much care for theater people. His attitude toward

producers—his clients, in effect—was, "We'll get them before they get us." He read stop clauses to find out what shows he could evict from Shubert theaters. "There was an attitude, fostered by Lawrence and Norman, that it was us against them—Shubert against the producers," said Phil Smith. On the hour every hour, no matter what he was doing, Light would say, "I'll be right back," then head over to the Piccadilly Bar and knock back a drink. He didn't even have to order one. As soon as the bartenders saw him come through the door, they'd pour him a glass and leave it on the bar.

Larry Shubert and his cronies worked (when they worked) out of the Sardi Building on West Forty-Fourth Street. Across the street in Lee's old apartment were Schoenfeld and Jacobs, "the lawyers," as Larry's gang called them. Neither was a drinker; both hard workers. Since Larry didn't come to work until late in the day, Schoenfeld and Jacobs increasingly handled most of the company's affairs. They got to know the producers because they drew up the contracts, though Larry always insisted on initialling the paperwork. They also began to handle contract negotiations with the unions—stagehands, musicians, actors. Both were adept negotiators, something which was not lost on union officials. The most powerful union was Local One, which represented stagehands. It was run by tough, street-smart men with no education—"dees, dems, and dose guys," said Robert McDonald, a young stagehand in the early sixties who would eventually become its president. Their leader was Solly Pernick. Since Local One also represented television workers, Pernick negotiated with William S. Paley, who built CBS. Pernick would walk into Paley's elegant offices at "Black Rock" (CBS's headquarters), take a drag on his cigar, and then spit on Paley's plush carpet. "These guys came from the streets," said McDonald. "And they never let you forget it."

Before Schoenfeld and Jacobs took over negotiations, the stagehands cut deals with independent producers in a catch-as-catch-can fashion. "There was no leadership on their side," McDonald said, "which was advantageous to us. The Shuberts were powerful, but they were content to be landlords." Schoenfeld and Jacobs turned out to be far more sophisticated negotiators—tough but fair, was their reputation—than most of the producers. As the two lawyers became more and more influential, the old guard at the stagehand union realized they needed "some college boys" on their side. "That's why they started grooming guys like me," said McDonald, who, rare for a stagehand, had a college degree. McDonald got to know Bernie Jacobs in the mid-sixties over a contract negotiation. What solidified their relationship was a blowup McDonald had one day with Larry Shubert. Larry didn't respect the young union leader and told him he would only deal with "some of my friends" at Local One. McDonald held his ground. If Larry Shubert negotiated behind his back, he would examine every contract for every show in a Shubert theater and enforce every detail, no matter how petty or insignficiant. "And if you have a problem," McDonald told Larry, "call your 'friends' at my union and see if they can bail you out."

Jacobs and Phil Smith, who were in the room, enjoyed watching McDonald give Larry Shubert a dressing down. Shortly after the confrontation, McDonald began dealing only with them.

As Schoenfeld and Jacobs began shouldering more and more of the work at the Shubert Organization they acquired a few allies of their own, Shubert employees who realized the company was not functioning well under Larry and his drinking buddies. Phil Smith became their most important supporter. Born and raised in Brooklyn, Smith was the eldest son of Irish immigrants. His father worked as a mechanic for the Brooklyn Union Gas Company; his mother raised him and his three brothers. His career in the theater began in 1949, when he was seventeen, in the balcony of the RKO Orpheum Theatre in Brooklyn. Smith and a friend had gone to see a movie. Back then, before the movie started, there was a live act, usually some holdover from vaudeville telling old jokes or singing old songs. On this particular afternoon, there were some "vulgar characters" in the balcony, Smith recalled, and they began throwing pennies at the performer. An usher appeared and told them to knock it off. One of them lunged at the usher, and a fight broke out. The usher was knocked out. Smith turned to his friend and said, "You know, I'm going to see if I can get a job here for a couple of weeks. It looks like fun." He went downstairs and knocked on the manager's office.

"Mr. Feldman?" he said.

"What do you want, kid?" Feldman replied.

"Do you have any jobs open here for ushers."

"Where do you go to school?" Feldman asked.

"Bishop Loughlin High School, down the street."

"OK, a job has opened up," he said. Feldman had heard one of his ushers had been decked. "When can you start?"

"I can start tomorrow," the teenager said.

"And that's exactly what happened," Smith recalled years later. "I put the uniform on after school the next day and went to work."

Within a few months, Smith became the head usher, overseeing a staff of twenty-eight. "I took my job seriously," he said. "I made the ushers adhere to rules and regulations that the company wanted enforced." He was promoted to assistant manager of the theater and soon caught the attention of higher-ups at RKO, which owned and operated over a hundred movie palaces in New York City. They gave him a sensitive assignment. The men's room of the RKO theater on Third Avenue and Fifty-Eighth Street had become a gay cruising spot, especially at lunch. "The company needed someone to handle things with sensitivity and discretion," Smith said. "You didn't want it to become an issue." Smith had an idea. If a man was caught with his pants down (so to speak), he was brought to the manager's office, where Smith was waiting. Smith would tell the gentleman, politely but firmly, that RKO would not tolerate such behavior in its theater. If the gentleman appeared at the theater again, RKO would have no choice but to notify the police. "We then asked for some identification," Smith said. "It was enough to scare them away. Most of them were family men—they didn't want any trouble. And they never came back."

Smith would eventually be rewarded with a plum job—assistant manager of RKO's flagship house, the legendary Palace Theatre on Forty-Seventh Street and Broadway. Here, Smith got to know some of the great stage performers—Danny Kaye, Jerry Lewis, and, his favorite, Judy Garland, whose nineteen-week run at the Palace in 1951–52 was, according to UPI critic Jack Garver, "one of the greatest personal triumphs in show business history."

"Judy was a sweetheart," Smith recalled. "She was twenty-eight years old, and wonderful. But she had her problems, and when she

missed a performance you had to intervene. You had to talk to her, get
her to come to the theater." Smith learned how to attend to a star's
needs. One Sunday night, Garland called him into her dressing room.
"Phil," she said, "I just realized that I only have a few bottles of Canadian Club left. And if I'm going to have guests come back here and visit
me after the show, what am I going to serve?"

"Judy, I'll get you some," Smith said. "We'll make sure your guests
have something to drink." Since it was a Sunday night, all the liquor
stores were closed. But there was a bar across the street from the theater that was open. Smith went in and introduced himself to the bartender. "We need some whiskey, and it's Sunday, so we can't buy it.
But if you loan some to me, I'll replace it tomorrow." The bartender
obliged, and Smith went back to Garland's dressing room armed with
several bottles of Canadian Club. "Oh thank you, Phil," she said, and
then lined the bottles up along her windowsill and brought down the
venetian blind to hide them.

Smith worked at the Palace for a couple of years and, to earn more
money, took jobs as an admissions manager at race tracks in Yonkers
and Long Island. After the racing season, he had four weeks off and
decided he might pick up some more money as a stagehand. At a retirement party for an old box office man at Gallagher's Steakhouse,
Smith ran into a friend, Abe Baranoff, who was a box office treasurer.
He told Baranoff his plan. Baranoff said, "Phil, you're crazy. You're a
good box office man. Why do you want to work as a stagehand? Let
me introduce you to Larry Shubert. He's over there at the bar. He'll
give you a job."

The next day Smith, twenty-six, was in the box office of the Imperial Theatre selling tickets to Frank Loesser's hit musical *The Most
Happy Fella*. With his sharp mind for figures and his affability, he was
soon moved to the company's flagship theater, the Sam S. Shubert.
And one Saturday afternoon in 1963 an incident occurred that brought
him to the attention of Bernie Jacobs. *Stop the World—I Want to Get
Off!*, written by and starring Anthony Newley, was at the Shubert. David Merrick was the producer. The show had started off strong but
was beginning to weaken at the box office, coming close to its stop
clause of $28,000. That afternoon, a little man showed up at the box

office and bought fifty tickets. Smith was suspicious. "Nobody bought fifty tickets, especially in those days." He waited a minute or so and then followed the little man down the street. The man darted into a small door next to the St. James Theatre. Smith knew what was up. Merrick's office was above the St. James. The little man had been dispatched by Merrick—or, more likely, by Merrick's general manager, Jack Schlissel—to buy enough tickets to keep *Stop the World* above its stop clause. Smith called Schlissel and confronted him.

"Philip, are you crazy? I'd never do that," Schlissel said.

"Jack, I followed your man back to your office. I don't know what you're trying to achieve here, but it's not right."

Schlissel hung up the phone. Smith tried to reach a Shubert executive, but he wasn't home. Then he remembered the lawyers—Jerry Schoenfeld and Bernie Jacobs. He rang up Jacobs at his house in Roslyn, Long Island, and told him what had happened. "Very good, Phil," Jacobs said. "We'll meet with Merrick on Monday, and I would like you to be there."

On Monday, Jacobs confronted Merrick with Smith's story. "I'm appalled," Merrick said. "I'm appalled at Jack. I'm appalled at my friend Jack!"

It was classic Merrick. When he left, Jacobs and Smith had a good laugh. They became friends. Both had a head for numbers—Jacobs would say Smith was the only man who could add up the figures faster than he could—and they both had a sense of honesty and fairness in a business that did not lack for shady characters. They would deal with Merrick many times in the years to come, but it wasn't always such fun. "David Merrick is the only person in this business who gives me a stomach ache," Jacobs would say.

CHAPTER SIX

Changing of the Guard

amelot, Alan Jay Lerner and Frederick Loewe's melodious tour through King Arthur's Court, is generally thought to be the last show of the golden age of musical theater. That period began in 1943 with Rodgers and Hammerstein's *Oklahoma!*—an intoxicating blend of musical comedy, romance, and darker themes about American life. Rodgers and Hammerstein were the pioneers of the era, creating such landmarks as *Carousel,* about a carnival barker in Maine; *South Pacific,* which dealt forthrightly with racism; and *The King and I,* an opulent depiction of the differences between the East and the West.

During the golden age all the elements of the musical—score, book, dance, design—served character and narrative. In *On the Town,* Leonard Bernstein, Betty Comden, Adolph Green, and Jerome Robbins created a vivid snapshot of New York during World War II as seen by three navy men on twenty-four-hour shore leave. Though the show was played mainly for laughs, it featured Robbins's breathtaking *Fancy Free* (now a staple of the ballet repertoire) and the poignant song "Some Other Time," sung by young men who may not survive their next tour of duty.

A year after the war ended, Irving Berlin, who mastered songwriting during the revue craze of the early twentieth century, wrote a beautifully integrated musical comedy—*Annie Get Your Gun*—for Ethel Merman. Cole Porter, also schooled in revues, came up with *Kiss Me, Kate,* the first show he ever wrote in which his score was anchored to plot and character. And Frank Loesser fashioned Damon Runyan's short stories about gangsters and molls into that immortal evocation of Times Square, *Guys and Dolls.* The golden age reached its zenith (at least for me) in Lerner and Loewe's *My Fair Lady*, the perfect musical romance. Not a song, a scene, or a dance was out of step with the story and characters.

By the early sixties, the writers who had made their mark in the golden age were winding down. Rodgers and Hammerstein wrote their last show, *The Sound of Music*, in 1959. A few months after it opened, they met for lunch at the Plaza Hotel and Hammerstein, who had been ill for nearly a year, told Rodgers he had cancer. "I'm just going down to Doylestown [where he had an estate], and stay on the farm until I die," he said.[1] He went and died there, on August 23, 1960. Rodgers tried his hand at lyrics, writing some lovely ones for *No Strings* in 1962. And he experimented with new collaborators—Stephen Sondheim (*Do I Hear a Waltz?*), Martin Charnin (*Two By Two*), and Sheldon Harnick (*Rex*). But none of those shows ever matched the power and beauty of his collaborations with Hammerstein.

At age seventy-four, Irving Berlin wrote the score to *Mr. President*, a merry romp with the First Family in the White House. It has its retro charms today—"The Secret Service makes me nervous . . ."!— but in 1962, coming on the heels of Elvis Presley, it sounded hopelessly square. The show was a flop, and Berlin retired from show business. The man who had changed American popular music with "Alexander's Ragtime Band" in 1911 could make no sense of rock 'n' roll. "You don't have to stop yourself [from writing songs]," he said shortly before *Mr. President* closed. "The people who have to listen to your songs tell you to stop."[2]

Berlin withdrew not only from show business but also the world. For the last two decades of his life, he shunned publicity, seldom leaving his elegant Beekman Place mansion.

He lived to be 101, long enough to see his first hit, "Alexander's Ragtime Band," enter public domain. "That was a dark day in the house," his daughter Mary Ellin Barrett recalled. Berlin died in his small bedroom at the top of No. 17 Beekman Place in 1989.

•   •   •

After *Kiss Me, Kate*, Cole Porter wrote two more hits, *Can-Can* and *Silk Stockings*, but neither had the impact of *Kiss Me, Kate*. He was in constant pain due to a riding accident in 1937 that left him nearly crippled, and in 1958 one of his legs had to be amputated. He never wrote another song after the operation and died in 1964.

Camelot was the last Broadway show Lerner and Loewe wrote. Loewe drifted into retirement. Lerner found a new partner, Burton Lane, and wrote the gorgeous score to *On a Clear Day You Can See Forever*. But Lerner's script, about a woman with ESP, was a disaster. Lerner wrote it while receiving daily injections of amphetamines from Max Jacobson, the infamous "Dr. Feelgood" whose patients included Marilyn Monroe, Yul Brynner, Nelson Rockefeller, and John F. Kennedy. *On a Clear Day* flopped, as did every other show Lerner wrote after that until his death in 1986.

Frank Loesser wrote two wonderful shows after *Guys and Dolls*—the operatic *The Most Happy Fella* in 1956 and the sharp corporate satire *How to Succeed in Business Without Really Trying* in 1961. But his 1965 show *Pleasures and Palaces* closed out of town. He died of cancer in 1969.

By the 1960s, Leonard Bernstein, who'd written *West Side Story* and *Wonderful Town*, had left Broadway for the New York Philharmonic. He wrote one more original musical—*1600 Pennsylvania Avenue*, with Alan Jay Lerner—but it flopped. Betty Comden and Adolph Green were still at it in the 1960s, but shows such as *Do Re Mi* and *Subways Are for Sleeping* were no match for *On the Town* or even *Bells Are Ringing*, which they wrote with composer Jule Styne in 1956.

Though its golden age was passing, Broadway, in the early to mid-sixties, was still vigorous. New talents that had grown up with the shows of Rodgers and Hammerstein were emerging. In 1959, a couple of cabaret writers, Charles Strouse and Lee Adams, wrote the hit *Bye Bye Birdie*, a satire of the Elvis Presley craze. Its rock numbers were parodies of Presley songs, while its pop hit—"Put on a Happy Face"—was an old-fashioned showtune.

Jerry Bock and Sheldon Harnick wrote the delightful *Fiorello!* to-

ward the end of the golden age, but they created their masterpiece—
Fiddler on the Roof—in 1964. Based on the short stories of Sholem
Aleichem, it was set in the waning days of the shtetls of Russia as
life for the Jews was becoming increasingly unbearable under the czar.
Fiddler on the Roof was the perfect show for a Broadway whose audience was predominantly Jewish. Many theatergoers would have heard
stories of shtetl life from their parents or grandparents. And the protagonist Tevye's struggle to preserve Jewish traditions in the face of a
changing and often dangerous world would have resonated with theatergoers grappling with images of Auschwitz and Dachau. *Fiddler* ran
3,242 performances, making it at that point the longest-running show
in Broadway history.

Jerry Herman, a composer and lyricist, wrote two of the biggest
hits of the 1960s—*Hello, Dolly!*, starring Carol Channing, and *Mame*,
starring Angela Lansbury. Herman's parents worked in summer camps
in the Catskills and the Berkshires. His father was a gym teacher, his
mother an English teacher and part-time performer. Herman directed
musicals at the summer camps. By the time he was fifteen, he had
learned the entire American popular songbook. A self-taught musician, he also composed little tunes of his own. One of his mother's
bridge partners knew Frank Loesser, so Mrs. Herman arranged for
her sixteen-year-old son to meet the celebrated composer. Herman
showed up at Loesser's office in the Brill Building wearing a neatly
pressed suit and "carrying my little briefcase full of my ditties," he recalled. The meeting, originally scheduled for half an hour, turned into
a lengthy musical audition. Loesser wanted to hear every one of Herman's songs. "Suddenly," Herman said, "he turned to me and said, 'Do
you mind if I call your parents?' I gave him their number, and he told
them that even though this is a very tough business, he believed I had
something worth pursuing. The course of my life changed that day."[3]

Harvey Schmidt and Tom Jones caught Broadway's attention with
a little Off-Broadway show called *The Fantasticks* in 1960. It featured
the popular song "Try To Remember." Schmidt, who came to New
York from Dallas, wrote the melody in about five minutes. He rented
a rehearsal room in the Steinway Building—"I couldn't afford a piano
back then," he said—and spent most of the hour composing a com-

plicated melody that was going nowhere. "It was a hot day, there was no air conditioning, and I was tired," he recalled. "I had a few minutes rehearsal time left, and I didn't want to waste them. So I just put my hands on the piano and thought, I'll just play a simple song. I played 'Try To Remember' from start to finish without changing a note. But I didn't know it was my song. I'd been to Europe that summer and I just assumed it was a folk song I'd heard along the way." A few days later he played it for Jones, who thought, folk song or not, it would work well in *The Fantasticks*. Jones wrote the lyrics aboard the Staten Island ferry on his way to visit his girlfriend.

The Fantasticks would eventually become the longest-running musical of all time (for every dollar invested the backers received $700). Producer David Merrick liked it, and hired Schmidt and Jones to write two modest Broadway hits in the sixties—*110 in the Shade*, based on the N. Richard Nash play *The Rainmaker*, and a charming two-character revue about marriage called *I Do! I Do!* It starred Mary Martin and Robert Preston, both at the peak of their box office drawing powers.

Another songwriting team that sprang up in the early 1960s became known as Kander and Ebb.

John Kander, who came from a rich Jewish family in Kansas City, had been the rehearsal pianist for *Gypsy* in 1959. He wrote his first musical, *A Family Affair*, with James and William Goldman. Rehearsals were chaotic and two weeks before the show opened on Broadway, Kander begged his friend, producer Hal Prince, to take over the direction. *A Family Affair* was Hal Prince's directorial debut.

Born and raised in New York, Fred Ebb studied English literature at Columbia University. Whenever he had a few dollars in his pocket, he bought a ticket to a Broadway show, usually a musical. He wrote lyrics and special material for nightclub performer Kaye Ballard. He realized a good song needed a few things. The first was a catchy title. Frank Loesser, he thought, always came up with good titles—"On a Slow Boat to China," "Baby, It's Cold Outside." [4] The second was an unexpected twist at the end. One of Ebb's early songs was called "I Never Loved Him Anyhow." A woman sings about breaking up with a man she says she never really loved in the first place. "I never loved him anyhow," she says at the end of the song. There's a beat. "Well, not much."

Tommy Valando, the music publisher, introduced Kander and Ebb. The first song they wrote was "My Coloring Book," which became a modest hit for Barbra Streisand, who had become a Broadway star in *Funny Girl*. Hal Prince asked them to write the score for his new show, *Flora the Red Menace*, in which a nineteen-year-old Liza Minnelli made her Broadway debut.

Kander and Ebb's next show solidified their partnership and made them one of the most famous songwriting teams of the 1960s and seventies. Hal Prince acquired the rights to *I Am a Camera*, a 1951 play based on Christopher Isherwood's novel *Goodbye to Berlin*. The setting was a seedy nightclub in Berlin in the early thirties as the Nazis were coming to power. The protagonists were Sally Bowles, a second-rate singer but first-rate party girl, and an American writer named Cliff Bradshaw. Given the cabaret setting, Prince thought the material could be adapted as a musical. He hired Joe Masteroff to write the book, and Kander and Ebb to do the score. *Cabaret* opened November 20, 1966, at the Broadhurst Theatre and shocked audiences. A show called *Cabaret*, they assumed, would be a lighthearted romp in a nightclub. The songs were catchy, but the seediness of the cabaret, the creepiness of the Master of Ceremonies (a brilliant Joel Grey), and the backdrop of National Socialism on the rise were unsettling. And Ebb came up with a sensational lyric twist. At the end of the song "If You Could See Her," Joel Grey, who had been dancing with the love of his life, a gorilla, sang, "If you could see her through my eyes," and then whispered, "she wouldn't look Jewish at all." It was a brutal expression of the anti-Semitism coursing through Germany in the 1930s. But Jewish theatergoers were offended. Some Jewish groups boycotted the musical during its Boston tryout because of the song. Ebb changed the last line to "She isn't a *Mieskeit* at all," taking some of the sting out of the song. (Bob Fosse, who directed the Oscar-winning 1972 movie, reinstated the original lyric, and it's been used in revivals ever since.)

Stephen Sondheim, who wrote the lyrics to *West Side Story* and *Gypsy*, had a hit in the 1960s with *A Funny Thing Happened on the Way to the Forum* for which he wrote both lyrics and music. But his next two shows—*Anyone Can Whistle* and *Do I Hear a Waltz?*—were flops. A third show, *Company*, was a modest hit, but a fourth, *Follies*, was a flop. First directed by Hal Prince, *Company* and *Follies* today are considered classics of the American musical theater. Only a few critics praised them at the time, however, and their brittle, cynical tone left audiences cold.

Hal Prince wasn't the only influential director who worked regularly on Broadway in the 1960s. Though he was spending more and more time creating dances for the New York City Ballet, Jerome Robbins, probably the greatest director-choreographer in the American musical theater, pitched in (uncredited) and helped save two shows floundering in tryouts, *A Funny Thing Happened on the Way to the Forum* and *Funny Girl*. And he directed and choreographed the biggest hit of the sixties—*Fiddler on the Roof*.

Robbins was every producer's number one choice to stage a new musical. If he wasn't available—and he was very difficult to get—Gower Champion was usually the second choice. Tall, handsome, suave, Champion and his wife Marge were popular dancers in Hollywood musicals. But Champion, who'd danced in Broadway shows in the 1940s, wanted to be more than a performer. He got his chance to direct a little show called *Lend an Ear* in 1948, and cast a young, oddball performer with a high-pitched but gravelly voice named Carol Channing. Champion's first hit was *Bye Bye Birdie*. Then came *Carnival!*, a lovely, gentle show produced by David Merrick. Champion and Merrick's next show—*Hello, Dolly!*—cemented the partnership, which continued to flourish with *I Do! I Do!*

The fourth major Broadway director of the sixties was Bob Fosse. The inventor of jazz dancing ("jazz hands!") on Broadway, Fosse choreographed *The Pajama Game* and *Damn Yankees* in the 1950s, and *How to Succeed in Business Without Really Trying* in 1961. He codirected the hit musical comedy *Little Me* in 1962. It had a delightful score by composer Cy Coleman and lyricist Carolyn Leigh. During the out-of-town tryout, Fosse, exercising total control over the show, altered some of Leigh's lyrics. When she found out, she called the police and ordered them to arrest him as well as book writer Neil Simon and producer Cy Feuer. Turning to Coleman, she said, "Him, you can leave to me." [5]

Fosse had another hit with *Sweet Charity* in 1966. Based on the Fellini movie *Nights of Cabiria*, it softens the subject matter—prostitution—

by turning the title character into a dancer for hire in a Times Square dance hall. Charity was played by Fosse's wife, Gwen Verdon, who delivered her customary quirky, stylish, and, in the end, heartbreaking performance. The score, by Coleman and Dorothy Fields, was a winner, too. *Sweet Charity* ran nearly two years at the Palace Theatre.

Musicals have always been the financial engine of Broadway. But nonmusical plays were in good supply in the sixties as well. The most successful writer of the era was Neil Simon. His plays performed like musicals at the box office. Simon honed his skill for gags and jokes in television, most famously in the legendary writers' room on Sid Caesar's *Your Show of Shows.* Eager to get out of television, Simon wrote his first play, *Come Blow Your Horn,* in 1960. It ran more than six hundred performances. His next comedy, *Barefoot in the Park,* was an even bigger hit. A charming comedy about newlyweds living in a walk-up apartment in Greenwich Village—Robert Redford and Elizabeth Ashley—it ran 1,530 performances. And then came the gold mines—*The Odd Couple, Plaza Suite, The Last of the Red Hot Lovers.* Collectively, these plays ran more than three thousand performances in the 1960s. Simon was a Broadway superstar. All his producer, Saint Subber, had to do back then was take out an ad in the *New York Times* announcing "A new play by Neil Simon . . ." and there would be lines at the box office. No writer in the history of the theater made as much money as Simon in the sixties and seventies. One estimate in 1974 put his weekly income, from Broadway alone, at nearly $50,000. In 1968, he bought his own theater, the Eugene O'Neill on West Forty-Ninth Street. He was the first playwright since David Belasco to become his own landlord.

With Neil Simon and Jerry Herman cranking out hits; David Merrick producing a show a year (sometimes two or three); and Hal Prince, Gower Champion, Jerome Robbins, and Bob Fosse all working at the top of their game, Broadway was a good investment in the 1960s. Ten years before, during Broadway's golden age, attendance averaged seven million a year. But in the 1967–68 season, with *The Odd Couple, Hello, Dolly!, I Do! I Do!, Fiddler on the Roof,* and many other shows on the boards, nearly 10 million people went to Broadway. The Shuberts' seventeen theaters were always booked. There was no reason for the head of the company, Larry Shubert, to abandon his spot at the Sardi's bar.

But just four years later, the Broadway audience would be cut in half. Shubert theaters would be dark. And Larry Shubert didn't get off his bar stool. He ordered another "blast" as an empire crumbled.

CHAPTER SEVEN

New York, New York, a Helluva Mess

William Goldman, a journalist and playwright who would go on to write Oscar-winning screenplays, spent a year—1967 to 1968—studying the Broadway theater. The book that resulted, *The Season*, is still devoured by theater lovers. It's a sharp, candid, witty tour of the Great White Way, and although much has changed in the theater business in forty-five years, many of Goldman's observations are still timely. Broadway, he noted, was a high-risk business. But if you have a smash, you earn set-for-life money. Citing *Variety*, Goldman noted the 1967–68 season was lucrative, with gross receipts totalling $60 million. He didn't ignore Broadway's problems—escalating costs, a paucity of good American playwrights, lack of young, vibrant producers, hot young actors such as Robert Redford running off to Hollywood—but he concluded Broadway was far from dead. There was still plenty of money to be scooped up in Shubert Alley.

But on the last page of *The Season*, Goldman reports on a class he taught at a college just outside New York. The students were aspiring screenwriters, and they discussed the key movies of the day—*Dr. Strangelove*, *The Pawnbroker*, *Blow-Up*, *Tom Jones*. Then he asked this class of bright young writers what their memorable Broadway experiences were. "And no one raised a hand," he writes.

Goldman caught the tail end of Broadway's robust run in the six-

ties. In 1968, 9.5 million people took in a Broadway show, according to
Variety. After that, the numbers began to slide, precipitously. In 1970,
attendance dropped to 7.4 million. A year later, it dipped to 6.5 million.
The bottom fell out in 1972. Only 5.4 million tickets were sold, the
fewest in Broadway history. How, within just four years, did the theater
industry lose nearly half its audience?

Broadway weathered competition from the movies in the thirties
and forties and television in the fifties. What it nearly didn't survive,
toward the end of the sixties, was rock music. Once the Beatles hit
town, Broadway became something to take your grandmother to on
a Sunday afternoon. The change in popular culture played out on *The
Ed Sullivan Show*. Sullivan began his career as a sports columnist for the
New York Evening Graphic and then took over the Broadway beat when
Walter Winchell left the *Graphic* for the *Daily Mirror*. Sullivan eventually took his Broadway column to the *New York Daily News*. He loved
the theater, especially musicals. One of his best friends was Richard
Rodgers who, along with his writing partner Oscar Hammerstein II,
appeared on the very first episode of Sullivan's show, then called *Toast
of the Town*. In 1960, Julie Andrews and Richard Burton appeared on
Sullivan's program to sing songs from *Camelot*, which had just opened
to mixed reviews. Nearly 12 million people watched the episode and
the exposure helped *Camelot* overcome the reviews and rack up a run
of nearly nine hundred performances. But by the late sixties, Broadway shows were not cropping up as often on Sullivan's program. The
acts he booked instead were the Beach Boys, the Rolling Stones, Are-
tha Franklin, Dionne Warwick, the Jackson 5, the Supremes, Sly and
the Family Stone, and the Doors. Sullivan still loved "Some Enchanted
Evening"—but he could not afford to ignore popular music's new stars.
How square, suddenly, does Ethel Merman look singing "There's No
Business Like Show Business" next to Jim Morrison singing "Light My
Fire"?

Broadway did little to keep up with changing tastes in music. One
exception, *Hair*, appeared in 1968, but it did not originate on Broadway.
It began at the Public Theater, Joseph Papp's dynamic Off-Broadway
theater down on Lafayette Street. Few people thought *Hair* could
make it on Broadway. None of the big producers of the day—Merrick,

Prince, Bloomgarden—would touch it. Michael Butler, a rich Chicago businessman who campaigned against the Vietnam War, produced it. The Shuberts wouldn't give him a theater—the show featured three seconds of nudity, for heaven's sake!—so Butler wound up going to the small Biltmore Theatre on West Forty-Seventh Street, owned by a family friend. *Hair* was a sensation. It ran 1,750 performances. But it hardly caused a revolution on Broadway. The next rock musical, playing Off-Broadway, was *Your Own Thing*, which no one remembers today. Another show called *Soon* lasted three performances.

In London, Tim Rice and Andrew Lloyd Webber wrote *Jesus Christ Superstar*, which was originally conceived as a rock album. It opened on Broadway in 1971, and though neither Lloyd Webber nor Rice cared for the production, it managed to run over a year. "Andrew and I thought we opened up the way for rock music in the theater," Rice said. "But nobody followed us." It's telling that almost none of the great songwriters of the sixties—Paul Simon, Bob Dylan, Carole King, Brian Wilson, John Lennon—attempted a Broadway show at the height of their careers (though Lennon did contribute a song to the revue *Oh, Calcutta!* and Simon would write *The Capeman*, a notorious flop, in 1998). An art form that once produced the greatest of American songwriters no longer attracted them.*

Rock music would never really take hold on Broadway until *Rent* opened in 1996.

One popular songwriting team of the 1960s—Burt Bacharach and Hal David—did write a show, the snappy *Promises, Promises*, produced by David Merrick in 1968. The score is still as bracing as a martini in August, but Bacharach hated that, theater being live, his music sounded different every night. He preferred the recording studio, where he could control the sound. He never returned to Broadway.

After their groundbreaking 1966 musical *Cabaret*, John Kander and Fred Ebb wrote two conventional shows, *The Happy Time*, starring Robert Goulet as a French-Canadian photographer with an accent thicker

---

* Many years later, Bono and the Edge decided to write a rock score to *Spider-Man: Turn off the Dark* after attending a dinner party at which Andrew Lloyd Webber joked, "I want to thank rock musicians for leaving me alone for twenty-five years—I've had the theater all to myself!" Considering the fate of *Spider-Man: Turn off the Dark*, Bono and the Edge should never have taken the bait.

than Inspector Clouseau's, and *Zorba*, which has its earthy charms but can only be revived today with a big star in the lead (Anthony Quinn made a fortune touring it in the 1980s).

Jerry Herman wrote two major hits of the 1960s—*Hello, Dolly!* and *Mame*. But he stumbled with his next show, *Dear World*. Though the score is a delight, the book, based on the play *The Madwoman of Chaillot*, is, theater historian Ken Mandelbaum notes, "virtually plotless."[1] Herman would write two more flops—*Mack & Mabel* and *The Grand Tour*—before roaring back in 1983 with *La Cage aux Folles*.

Jerry Bock and Sheldon Harnick's *Fiddler on the Roof* ran 3,242 performances from 1964 to 1972. But their partnership ended in 1970 with a flop called *The Rothschilds*, starring Hal Linden. They split up over the director, the overrated Derek Godby. Harnick wanted him fired; Bock backed him. (He was eventually replaced by Michael Kidd.) Bock and Harnick split but agreed never to speak publicly about the feud.

By 1970, as attendance began to slide, Broadway offered little excitement. The hit musical was the Lauren Bacall vehicle *Applause*, adapted from the movie *All About Eve*. Right at the end of the turbulent sixties—Woodstock, Kent State, Vietnam, the deaths of Bobby Kennedy and Martin Luther King Jr.—Broadway's big offering was a musical whose show-stopping number included the lyrics: "What is it that we're living for? Applause, applause!"—sung by Bonnie Franklin and a bunch of chorus boys.

Is it any wonder no one raised a hand in Goldman's class?

Another strike against Broadway was the unraveling of New York City itself. The seeds of New York's troubles were planted during the New Deal. No city embraced the cornerstones of the New Deal—government expansion, redistribution of wealth through welfare programs, unionization, municipal works projects—as fervently as New York. Mayor Fiorello La Guardia paid for the ever-expanding city government in the 1930s through tax hike after tax hike, a cycle that would be repeated by his successors until so many businesses and middle-class residents had fled that New York had to be rescued from bankruptcy in the 1970s. As urban historian Fred Siegel wrote of La Guardia's legacy, "except for boom times, New York would never again be able to afford its government."[2]

There were warning signs of the city's impending disaster in the 1950s under Mayor Robert F. Wagner Jr. Three recessions hammered New York's manufacturing base, a key economic engine of the city during and after World War II. By the late fifties, manufacturing was also under assault by automation, high taxes, and traffic congestion that made it difficult to move goods out of the city. "From 1958 to 1964, metropolitan factory employment fell by eighty-seven thousand jobs," writes George J. Lankevich in *New York City: A Short History.* A prescient series in the *Herald Tribune* in 1965 chronicled the city's growing economic problems. One article headlined BUSINESSES COME—BUT MOSTLY GO noted that between 1958 and 1964, thirty thousand manufacturing jobs evaporated from the garment industry alone.[3]

The steady, unstoppable decline of the garment industry was a serious setback for Broadway. Garment executives were among the city's most devoted playgoers ever since their business district migrated, in the 1920s, from the south end of Manhattan to the West Side between Thirty-Fourth and Fortieth Streets. The garment district was at the doorstep of Times Square and the Broadway theater. It was also an industry run mainly by Jews, a significant portion of the Broadway audience. (A 1980 study by the Broadway League—then known as the League of New York Theatres and Producers—showed that 40 percent of the Broadway audience was Jewish.)

The garment industry also provided lucrative jobs for Broadway writers, directors, and performers in the form of industrial shows—musical revues tailored to a textile company's clients. The most lavish of all was the Milliken Breakfast Show, sponsored by Milliken & Company, which made fabrics. It ran annually—for twelve consecutive performances—at the Waldorf Astoria beginning in 1956. Some two thousand textiles executives attended each performance. The company hired such stars as Angela Lansbury, Ann Miller, Robert Morse, and Carol Channing to perform material written by Charles Strouse or Jerry Herman or Sheldon Harnick. Michael Bennett, an up-and-coming choreographer in the sixties, staged several Milliken shows, hiring friends such as Donna McKechnie and Tommy Tune.

The Milliken shows became less and less lavish in the late seventies when investors in the company complained how much money they cost. The last splashy Milliken show was in 1980. After that, fashion buyers weren't interested in "Millikiddies," or Broadway for that matter. As Howard Kissel, then the drama critic for *Women's Wear Daily*, noted, "They wanted to know where they could get the best cocaine."

The Broadway audience has always been white, middle-aged, and upper-middle class. New Yorkers, in the fifties and sixties, made up the majority of that audience. The great white flight from cities in the mid-twentieth century took a huge toll on the theater. During Mayor Wagner's tenure, eight hundred thousand white people left the city for the suburbs.[4] As crime rates soared in the 1960s, schools decayed and city services such as garbage collection and policing frayed, white flight in New York became an exodus. At the same time, the city's ranks swelled with Puerto Ricans, who were fleeing economic collapse on their island, and blacks, who could not find work in the rural South. White residents "were replaced in the city by various minorities with lesser skills who did not qualify for jobs but required a greater amount of public service than did the exiting whites."[5] Even if Puerto Ricans coming to the city had money to spend on a Broadway show—which they certainly did not—it's hard to imagine they would have flocked to see a Russian-Jewish milkman fretting about one of his daughters marrying a goy.

Though the clouds of economic collapse were gathering, New Yorkers had reason to hope for the future with the election of John Lindsay in 1965. A liberal Republican, he had defeated the Democratic nominee, Abe Beame, an old-line machine politician. Lindsay was New York's JFK. Handsome, rich, well educated, but not stuffy, he promised to look out for the downtrodden and mend the growing racial divide.[6] It was the era of the great liberal experiment—the belief that the power of government, a good and true government, not one run by Tammany Hall, could raise the fortunes of those in need. Where would the resources come from? From the prosperous, of course. Tax, tax, tax, and then spend, spend, spend, and—voilà!—Utopia.

Broadway has always leaned left—BROADWAY REDDER THAN FILMS! screamed a *New York Post* headline in 1947—but Lindsay was a Republican theater people could embrace. For starters, he looked fabulous in a tuxedo. And he loved the theater. He was a regular at opening nights, and a fixture at Sardi's (his caricature still hangs in the main dining room). He went to the opening of *On a Clear Day You Can See Forever* with his friend Alan Jay Lerner. He was as Broadway saw itself—rich, sophisticated, elegant, white, but compassionate. He was also, arguably, one of the worst mayors in the history of the city. The damage he did to New York—and Broadway—would not be repaired until the city elected Ed Koch in 1978 (he shored up the city's finances) and Rudolph Giuliani in 1992 (he shored up its quality of life).

Lindsay's disastrous tenure is chronicled, definitively, in Vincent J. Cannato's *The Ungovernable City: John Lindsay and His Struggle to Save New York*. Lindsay presided over strikes that paralyzed the city—a transit workers' strike, a sanitation workers' strike, a teachers' strike. Race riots set Harlem and the Bronx on fire. Whites fought blacks over control of public schools. College students rioted against the Vietnam War, most famously at Columbia University, which was shut down for several days in 1968 because of a violent, student-led insurrection. Crime exploded. The murder rate alone soared 137 percent between 1966 and 1973.[7] Police morale plummeted. The police were considered the enemy, and not without reason. This was, after all, an era of profound police corruption, the most famous whistle-blower being Frank Serpico. By the early 1970s, New York City, the great melting pot, had turned into a seething cauldron.

For Broadway, the most pressing problem was the disintegration of its neighborhood—the area around Times Square. In the late sixties, the "Crossroads of the World" became a twenty-four-hour carnival of sex, drugs, and crime. The 1969 movie *Midnight Cowboy*, about a male hustler (Jon Voight), captures the area and all its sleaze. A series of Supreme Court decisions in the 1950s and sixties granted First Amendment protection to pornography, which by the late 1960s was being sold openly in Times Square. Peep shows and dirty bookstores flourished. Prostitutes (along Eighth Avenue) and male hustlers (on Forty-Second Street between Seventh and Eighth Avenues) sold their wares openly as well. Drugs could be scored in broad daylight. Live sex shows, which were also protected by the First Amendment—provided there was no penetration—drew more customers than Angela Lansbury in *Dear World*. Dilapidated "grocery stores" along side streets sold beer, knives, condoms, and fake photo IDs. "Those 'grocery stores' became the support system for the criminals who would then conduct their activities throughout Times Square," said Carl Weisbrod, who ran New York State's 42nd Street Development Project during Ed Koch's administration.[8] Muggings and stabbings occurred daily. And there were plenty of murders, many unreported. "When people would argue that we shouldn't be spending manpower and money on prostitution because it's a 'victimless crime,' I would tell them about the prostitutes we found cut up in little pieces in plastic bags," said Sidney J. Baumgarten, a lawyer who ran the mayor's Midtown Enforcement Project in the mid-seventies. "And what about the johns, the out-of-towners, who get picked up and then mutilated by prostitutes? Many of them don't even report the crimes because they're so ashamed to go back to Podunk and tell their families."[9] The neighborhood became so dangerous by the early seventies that Vincent Sardi Jr., owner of Broadway's most famous restaurant, hired a private security team to escort his employees to and from their cars every night.

Times Square had always had a seedy side. Originally called Longacre Square, it was once the center of New York's horse-trading and carriage industries. Full of smelly stables, saloons, pickpockets, and prostitutes, it was a rough part of town. It began to gussy up a bit when producer Oscar Hammerstein I (grandfather of the lyricist) built a splendid theater called the Olympia on the corner of Seventh Avenue and Forty-Second Street. Modeled on a French Renaissance palace, it had three auditoriums and an air-conditioning system, which Hammerstein patented. He also built the Theatre Republic and the Victoria. When other producers followed, New York's theater district migrated along Broadway from Union Square to Forty-Second Street. In 1904, Adolph Ochs, the publisher of the *New York Times*, joined his friend Hammerstein in the neighborhood, relocating his newspaper from Park Row near City Hall to a brand-new tower, modeled on the Campanile in Florence, on a patch of land in the middle of Longacre Square. A few months later, a major subway station opened on Forty-Second Street and Seventh Avenue. Pedestrians packed the streets. Ochs lobbied to have the neighborhood renamed Times Square. Longacre

Square became Times Square by proclamation of Mayor George B. McClellan in April 1904.[10]

Impresarios built more splendid theaters in the neighborhood, many with roof gardens where patrons could see late-night shows featuring chorus girls wearing fewer clothes than they had during performances earlier in the evening. (The most famous roof garden was atop the original Madison Square Garden, where Harry Thaw shot the architect Stanford White in 1906.) Spectacular productions featured real chariot races and gigantic water tanks in which chorus girls decked out like mermaids frolicked. Around the theaters, lobster palaces such as Rector's flourished. Here, the city's newly prosperous merchant classes could gorge on oysters, steaks, and vast quantities of champagne.

Gambling was rampant around Times Square and so, too, was prostitution. The Tenderloin district—New York's cluster of brothels, saloons, and gambling joints—migrated up Eighth Avenue to the west side of mid-Manhattan. By 1901, Forty-Third Street between Broadway and Eighth Avenue was known as "Soubrette Row" because of all its French brothels. Once prostitution took hold on Eighth Avenue in the West Forties and Fifties, it would thrive there for another eighty years, until the area was cleaned up during the Giuliani administration.

The Times Square of lobster palaces and Ziegfeld's *Follies* was wiped out by Prohibition. That great, disastrous experiment brought a new criminal element to Times Square—mobsters, who controlled most of the speakeasies that sprang up throughout the neighborhood. Meanwhile, the great theaters of yesterday's showmen—Hammerstein's Victoria, Belasco's Republic, Klaw and Erlanger's New Amsterdam—were in trouble, ironically as a result of increasing land values in the Times Square they helped create. Being single-use properties, open only eight or nine times a week, legitimate theaters "found it difficult to generate sufficient revenues to retain command over the street," writes Lynne B. Sagalyn in *Times Square Roulette*. Most would be converted into movie houses. In the 1930s, they faced crushing competition from the great movie palaces the studios built along Broadway. By 1940, most of the theaters on Forty-Second Street had been converted into burlesque houses or "grinders," which showed reruns of old movies. Grinders were not places to take the family, and Forty-Second Street quickly became a male bastion of sleaze. "The grinders brought a new kind of commercial promotion to the street: garish marquees, sexually suggestive posters, bizarre devices to lure crowds," Sagalyn writes.[11] The grinders would become the porn houses of the sixties and seventies.

When Times Square became the theatrical capital of the world, gay men, who had clustered around the waterfronts of lower Manhattan ("Hello, sailor!"), began moving uptown as well. The theater would be nothing without gay men. They are its creators, and much of its audience. Gay culture flourished in New York during World War I. As George Chauncey notes in *Gay New York: Gender, Urban Culture, and the Making of the Gay Male World 1890–1940*, the war disgorged hordes of single young men from all over the country into the city, which was a clearinghouse for soldiers on their way to Europe. In the 1920s, as Prohibition loosened Victorian-era morals, there was even a "pansy craze" in Times Square. So-called queer balls were staged at Madison Square Garden and the Astor Hotel. Nightclubs featuring gay emcees became fashionable.

The repeal of Prohibition drove Times Square's thriving gay culture into the shadows. The sale of alcohol was regulated by the powerful New York State Liquor Authority, which, at the urging of La Guardia, cracked down on bars that served "lewd and dissolute people" such as homosexuals.[12] The Mafia could offer protection from the State Liquor Authority to gay bars, and by the end of the thirties, mobsters owned many of those bars. The Great Depression ushered in what, in the 1970s, would become an emblem of Forty-Second Street: the male hustler. With the unemployment rate at nearly 30 percent in the city, many young men were forced to sell their bodies in and around the grinders. By the 1970s, Forty-Second Street between Seventh and Eighth Avenues was almost exclusively a male domain. "A major indicator of the perception of the safety of an area is the percentage of women to men," said Carl Weisbrod. "One study done in the late 1970s revealed that for every one woman who spent time on Forty-Second Street, there were nine men." On average, five felonies a day occurred along the "Deuce," as the street is sometimes called. Skyscrapers were rising on the east side of Midtown Manhattan in the 1960s as global conglomerates planted their flags in New York City. But along West

Forty-Second Street not a single new building had been constructed since 1939. "For a Midtown block, that is unbelievable," said Weisbrod.

Adding to Times Square's slide into sleaze was the neighborhood in the West Forties and Fifties. Hell's Kitchen was its name. It had always been a tough place, dominated by the Westies, the Irish mob. The side streets were lined with single-room occupancy buildings (SROs), which could be rented by the hour. They became de facto whorehouses. Many of these SROs stood right alongside Broadway theaters. In the summer of 1972, Gail Sheehy, writing in *New York* magazine, profiled Jimmy Della Bella, the manager of Hotel Raymona, an SRO brothel on the corner of Eighth Avenue and West Forty-Ninth Street. As she was interviewing Della Bella, his brother Phil was keeping an eye out for cops. Suddenly, Phil yelled to the women in the lobby, "Get baaaack!" He'd spotted a squad car coming down the street. Sheehy reported that she couldn't see anything but an empty street. "Spotted him way up at the corner," Phil said. "See, I got very special eyes. I can see reflections in the Eugene O'Neill Theater."

During the 1940s and 1950s, Broadway shows and first-run movies were the main attractions in Times Square. But by the end of the sixties, the neighborhood's unsavory elements began to overwhelm legitimate entertainments. "It sort of flipped," said Weisbrod. Theater people with long memories are still haunted by a *60 Minutes* report in the 1970s that showed a group of tourists from the South getting off their bus to see a Broadway show—and then getting right back on again because Times Square was so dangerous. "They were so scared, they wouldn't walk one block," recalled George Wachtel, who headed up audience research and development for the Broadway League, then known as the League of New York Theatres and Producers.

As Times Square slid into the gutter, Mayor Lindsay shrugged. "I don't think that it's gotten worse," he said, adding that as a congressman in the 1950s he'd heard the same complaints. Theater people, many his friends, were appalled. If things continued this way, Broadway might unravel as well.[13] A few theater people made an effort to brighten up Times Square. Producer Joseph "Kippy" Kipness bought several potted trees one day and put them at the corner of Broadway and West Forty-Seventh Street. "It was his way of cleaning up the place," recalled his press agent, Shirley Herz. Under pressure, Lindsay created the Times Square Law Enforcement Coordination Committee in 1972. It made some headway but wouldn't become a force in the area until the aggressive Sidney Baumgarten ran it during the Beame administration. As Sheehy reported in *New York* magazine, all of the massage parlors the police had closed down in the fall of 1971 had reopened by the summer of 1972.

As if Broadway didn't have enough trouble by 1970, the great bull market that had begun in 1963—and created many backers of Broadway shows—came crashing down. In May 1969, the Dow Jones Industrial Average peaked at 970. A year later, it fell to 631. Money that could have been risked for a flutter on a Broadway show vanished. There were just fifty-nine productions (nearly a third revivals) in the 1969–70 Broadway season. Most were flops. "We went off the cliff," recalled producer Manny Azenberg.

Broadway was facing its worst crisis since the Great Depression. But back then, it had two saviors, Lee and J. J. Shubert, who preserved their theaters and kept the industry afloat. This time around, Lawrence Shubert Lawrence Jr. was at the helm, running the business from his barstool at Sardi's. If the Shubert empire was to survive—if Broadway was to survive—he could not.

CHAPTER EIGHT

The Coup

By 1972, a civil war was raging within the Shubert empire. On one side, in the Sardi Building, were Lawrence Shubert Lawrence Jr. and his sycophants—Howard Teichmann, Hickey Katz, Bernard Friedman (Norman Light, who could match Larry drink for drink, had died in 1970). On the other side—across the street on West Forty-Fourth above the Shubert Theatre—were Gerald Schoenfeld and Bernard Jacobs. "You didn't have to be around here too long to recognize that Bernie and Jerry were the guys that were good for the company, and this other group was bad," their strongest ally, Phil Smith, said.

As Schoenfeld and Jacobs gained more influence due to Larry's heavy drinking and lax work habits (he usually didn't show up to the office until well after noon), the sycophants warned him that the lawyers were trying to take over. "You can't trust them, they're looking to do you in," was a constant refrain in the Sardi Building. Booze exacerbated Larry's paranoia and erratic behavior. He once interviewed a stagehand for a job. The stagehand announced, "I don't drink, Mr. Lawrence." Larry exploded. "What's wrong with a guy who drinks?!" "He almost challenged the guy to a fight over that remark," Smith recalled. The sycophants also encouraged Larry in the belief that he owned the company, when in fact, according to J. J.'s will, the Shubert Foundation did. Schoenfeld and Jacobs, he believed, could be fired at his whim.

The lawyers, meanwhile, were frustrated that, as the theater business was crumbling, Larry Shubert had no interest in trying to save it. By 1972, the Shuberts had lost many of their longtime tenants. *Mame* and *Cabaret* both closed in 1970. *Fiddler on the Roof,* which had earned the company a fortune in rent, played its final performance July 2, 1972. Not much had come along to replace them, and since the Shuberts had not invested in these hits, the company reaped nothing from touring productions.

Larry Shubert never had a nose for hits in any case. He had the chance to put *Hello, Dolly!* into one of his theaters in 1964, but didn't go after it. David Merrick had another show that year—*110 in the Shade.* The Shuberts took that instead. Schoenfeld and Jacobs, having attended backers' auditions for both shows, urged Larry to take *Hello, Dolly!* He overruled them. One Merrick show was just like another, he said. *110 in the Shade* ran a little over a year; *Hello, Dolly!* was a blockbuster.

Larry Shubert cultivated few relationships with producers and creators. When a producer wanted to book a theater for a stage adaptation of *The Selling of the President,* Joe McGinniss's account of the marketing of Richard Nixon in the 1968 campaign, Larry balked. "We'll get sued—Nixon will sue us!" he yelled. Never mind that Nixon was a public figure, or that the producer, John Flaxman, would have cleared the text with his own lawyers. Larry Shubert worried instead that the president of the United States would sue him. (The show eventually wound up at a Shubert theater, but it was a flop.) There were other kinds of shows Larry didn't want in his theaters—black shows. The Shuberts had an unexpected hit in 1971 at the Ambassador Theatre with *Ain't Supposed to Die a Natural Death,* Melvin Van Peebles's musical about life in the ghetto. Peebles had a new show—*Don't Play Us Cheap*—and wanted to put it in a Shubert theater, many of which were empty in 1972. Schoenfeld, Jacobs, and Smith wanted the booking. But when they brought it up with Larry, he resisted. "Wait a minute, wait a minute. My mother went to see *Ain't Supposed to Die a Natural Death* the other day and she was scared for her life!" he said. "Those blacks talk to the stage!" When the lawyers suggested that it would not be helpful if the company were seen as discriminating against black shows, Larry barked, "Well, I'm voting for Lester Maddox—twice!"

Although Larry Shubert could barely understand the terms of his own theater contracts—"numbers went over his head," said Smith—he insisted on signing everything. Which meant tracking him down at one of his haunts and attempting to explain the deal. His usual, drunken response was, "Are these Merrick terms? I don't want Merrick terms!" He was convinced that David Merrick was always getting the better of him, even though he never negotiated with Merrick or even bothered to learn the basics of tenant-landlord agreements. And he remained suspicious of "the lawyers." When they drew up a contract, they would go over to his office and talk him through the terms. After he signed the contract, he'd go drinking with his buddies, who would fuel his paranoia and convince him that his lawyers had given him a raw deal. Then he'd return to the office, summon Schoenfeld and Jacobs, and demand that contracts be renegotiated. When they tried to explain that the deal was fair—and that it had been signed—he would snap, "I went to the University of Pennsylvania. I was an English major. Don't talk down to me!" Jerry Leichtling, Schoenfeld's assistant, recalled, "Every time Bernie and Jerry would come back from their journeys across the street, they would be absolutely flaring. The whole place was thick with tension. There were factions everywhere."

Above the Shubert Theatre, the lawyers, aided by a small but loyal team, did what they could to keep the company from falling apart. Despite the intrigue and backstabbing over at the Sardi Building, Schoenfeld and Jacobs tried to keep the atmosphere in their offices jolly. "It was an utterly wonderful place to work," said Leichtling, "as sweet and competent and generous a place as you could want. There was a real sense of family above the Shubert Theatre—that this was a family business. It wasn't their family, but that was the climate they created." The two men were a study in contrasts. Schoenfeld was always well dressed, courtly, and gregarious. Jacobs "dressed like a guy who gets his suits off the rack," said Leichtling, and could be awkward and taciturn, though he had a sly wit. He liked Sinatra at Madison Square Garden, while Schoenfeld preferred Vladimir Horowitz at Carnegie Hall.

Though Larry Shubert came to despise the lawyers, he must have known he could not function without them. He never tried to throw them out. But he struck at them in petty ways, such as taking away their house seats or banishing them from opening nights. Meanwhile, producers were reluctant to deal with the Shuberts. "You didn't want to bother with Larry," said producer Manny Azenberg. "If you went up to audition a show for him, he'd be drunk and fall asleep. It was embarrassing. You could talk to Bernie and Jerry, but they weren't the boss. Larry was. And he was a disaster. It was easier to deal with other theater owners—and there were a lot more back then."

The company was in trouble. In the 1971–72 season, the theaters lost $2 million. The nontheatrical properties earned $1.5 million, but that still meant an overall loss of $500,000 for the company. "Shubert officials believe this is the first time since the Depression that the over-all operation of the Shubert businesses has suffered a loss," the *New York Times* reported.[1]

From their offices above the Shubert Theatre, Schoenfeld and Jacobs began planning a coup. The power in the empire rested not with Larry Shubert but, as per J. J.'s will, with the board of directors of the Shubert Foundation. There were, in 1972, six directors—Larry Shubert, Eckie Shubert (John's widow), Irving "Rocky" Wall (Larry's lawyer), Jerry Schoenfeld, Bernie Jacobs, and the mysterious Irving Goldman, who had been appointed by Larry for, as some whispered, services rendered during the Surrogate Court battle for John Shubert's estate. After her husband's death, Eckie, like Larry, was suspicious of the lawyers. But over the years they courted her. "They were extremely solicitous of her," said Leichtling. Schoenfeld was a frequent visitor to her large white house in Byram, Connecticut, taking up papers for her to sign and keeping her up to date on the goings-on at the company. It is likely that during those visits, Schoenfeld informed her of Larry Shubert's manifest shortcomings. By 1972, Eckie Shubert was on the side of the lawyers. Rocky Wall was coming around to their point of view as well. Wall wound up on the Shubert board because he represented the choreographer Oona White, who was Larry Shubert's girlfriend. Though recruited by Larry, he, too, recognized that an incompetent was running the company and began to throw his support to the lawyers.

The lone holdout was Irving Goldman. He supported Larry Shubert, not much caring, it seemed, about his drinking or the company's growing financial concerns. Goldman wasn't around the Shubert offices much. When he did show up there was a "sense of sleaziness" about him, Leichtling recalled. He was running his paint company as well as the Jola Candy Company, which operated candy vending machines throughout the New York City subway system. Schoenfeld, who was guarded about Goldman's connection to the Shubert empire, would often whisper how his fellow board member was raking in a lot of "nickels and dimes" from all those vending machines. Goldman also had an interest in Shubert ticketing. Leichtling delivered theater tickets to Goldman's good friend, Surrogate Court Judge Samuel Di-Falco, exchanging them for envelopes he'd then drop off at Goldman's office. "I never knew what was in those envelopes," he said, "but my deep suspicion—cash."

Goldman's other area of expertise was backroom politics, primarily getting his close friend Abe Beame elected mayor in 1974. John Lindsay, who by now had switched from the Republican Party to the Democratic Party, had decided to run for the Democratic presidential nomination in 1972. Lindsay had defeated Beame in 1965, but with the city careening to bankruptcy, Beame, plodding and uninspiring, began to have some appeal. An accountant by training, he had served as city comptroller from 1961 to 1969. His financial expertise was desperately needed (or so it was believed at the time).

Though Schoenfeld and Jacobs were beginning to have concerns about Goldman's reputation, they needed his vote to oust Lawrence Shubert Lawrence Jr. from the board. And they'd begun to sense his relationship with Larry Shubert was fraying. When Larry got drunk, he was capable of insulting anyone. One night he got into a fight with Goldman (nobody knows about what), and the next day, a fuming Goldman told Schoenfeld, "He'll never talk to me like that again and get away with it. Ever." Goldman was turning on his friend. But the support of someone like Irving Goldman always comes with a price. And so a deal was stuck. If Goldman agreed to vote against Lawrence Shubert Lawrence Jr., he could rule over the Shubert empire alongside Schoenfeld and Jacobs. The company would be run by a three-man executive committee, with Schoenfeld overseeing nontheatrical real estate operations and public relations, Jacobs running and booking Shubert theaters, and Goldman controlling vendors and concessions.

Goldman held out for another plum: president of the Shubert Foundation, which would give him control over millions of dollars to be doled out in the form of grants to organizations of his choosing.

The fox was angling to guard the hen house.

"Bernie and Jerry recognized that in order to survive, they needed Irving," said Phil Smith. "So that meant they had to give him more power."

Bernie Jacobs put it this way: "The price of getting rid of Lawrence was Goldman. We didn't know how high the price would be." [2]

Albert Poland, a young producer, had a sense something was wrong at the Shubert offices one summer day in 1972. Jerry was "wound up tighter than a drum" and his secretary, Betty Spitz, "looked like she was on the verge of running to the nearest exit," Poland remembered. Schoenfeld and Jacobs were fond of Poland, and did legal work for him on the side. Their main client was, of course, Shubert, but as they were not highly paid corporate lawyers, J. J. had always allowed them to freelance—provided they drop everything when he called. In addition to Poland, they also represented a young producer named Bruce Paltrow, who would go on to create some of television's most popular shows, including *The White Shadow* and *St. Elsewhere*. Poland was a frequent visitor to the offices above the Shubert Theatre. He liked to wear a cape, much to Schoenfeld's delight. "Here comes David Belasco!" he'd say whenever Poland swept in.

Poland met the lawyers in the mid-sixties, when he produced his first show, a touring production of *The Fantasticks*. His little show was orchestrated for four musicians, but many of the theaters he booked had contracts with the musicians' union that required many more players. With his youthful charm and quick humor, Poland could get the union to waive the requirement. Except in Philadelphia. The Forrest Theatre required a minimum of twenty musicians. The union would not budge. The theater manager told Poland to call Gerald Schoenfeld, who negotiated contracts with the musicians. Schoenfeld agreed to look into the matter. But he wasn't much help. "Look," he told Poland. "The musicians are ready and willing to play. And if you don't have orchestrations for twenty of them, that's your problem."

Poland was furious. He went over to G. Schirmer's music store in New York and got an orchestration for "The Star-Spangled Banner" for twenty musicians. He told his stage manager to put folding chairs on the stage of the Forrest and order the musicians to play "The Star-Spangled Banner" at every performance. After that, he planned to lock them in their dressing room until the show was over. The press loved the stunt. The *Wall Street Journal* cheered him on. Poland called Schoenfeld and told him what he had done. Schoenfeld was amused. "Well, Albert," he said, "you won the first round. Let's see what we can do together." From then on, Schoenfeld and Jacobs represented Poland and his burgeoning Off-Broadway career.

But Poland had noticed some strange goings-on lately. For one thing, Schoenfeld had summoned him to his office and told him to take his and Jacobs's names out of the *Playbills* for his shows. Schoenfeld also wanted to scrutinize the finances of an Off-Broadway show Poland was producing, *The Dirtiest Show in Town*, a raunchy revue with a witty script by Tom Eyen (who would go on to create *Dreamgirls*). Off Broadway, an umbrella term for small theaters outside of Times Square, was doing a tidy business in the late sixties and early seventies just as Broadway was spiraling downward. There was energy and excitement in New York's smaller theaters. The *New York Times* was heralding such writers as Lanford Wilson, Sam Shepard, David Rabe, and Charles Ludlam. Tickets were also cheap. The Broadway establishment had taken notice—and was not happy. The League of New York Theatres and Producers began suggesting that its mortal enemies, the theater unions, close in on Off Broadway. When Poland told Schoenfeld that *The Dirtiest Show in Town* was making a profit of $6,500 a week on a gross of $12,000, Schoenfeld said, "That's too much profit. You need some union stagehands down there."

The unions went after Off Broadway in 1971 with a three-month strike by Actors' Equity that nearly killed off many small theater companies. Shortly before the strike, Schoenfeld offered Poland a job as a house manager at a Broadway theater. Poland turned him down. Looking back, Poland thinks Schoenfeld was part of the League's conspiracy to destroy Off Broadway. Since he and Jacobs were planning to take over the floundering Shubert empire, the last thing they needed was competition from non-union theaters. But Schoenfeld was also looking out for Poland by offering him a job on Broadway. "I think Jerry was trying to be a friend while destroying my turf," said Poland. "And shortly after he and Bernie took over, he began referring to Off Broadway as 'the sewer.' I'd run into him on the street and he'd say, 'How are things in the sewer, Albert?' "

But all of that would become clear much later. In the summer of 1972, sitting in Schoenfeld's office, all Poland saw was a distracted, agitated man. "I'm finding you impossible today," he told Schoenfeld. "I'll come back another time." The next day Poland picked up the *New York Times* and read SHUBERT NO LONGER A FAMILY AFFAIR.

The day of the coup—Friday, July 7, 1972—Schoenfeld showed up at Phil Smith's office on the sixth floor of the Sardi Building. "Phil, don't go to lunch today," he said. "Don't leave this floor. Send out for lunch—whatever you have to do. But do not leave this building. Important things are about to happen." Smith huddled with a couple of other employees who sided with Schoenfeld and Jacobs against Larry Shubert. "I guess they're going to dump him," one of them said. "So the three of us just sat there, waiting for the bomb to go off," Smith recalled.

At 11:00 a.m., Larry Shubert threw open the door of his sixth-floor office in the Sardi Building and staggered out, ashen faced. He'd been deposed. A few minutes later, Jacobs summoned Smith into the room. Schoenfeld looked tense, Jacobs calm and businesslike. Irving Goldman was smiling. Jacobs issued orders. The most pressing problem was the company's new theater, the Shubert, in Century City, Los Angeles. Hal Prince's *Follies* was due to open there at the end of the month, but the theater wasn't finished. Larry Shubert had deferred decisions about the new theater for months. If it wasn't ready by the time *Follies* played its first preview in a couple of weeks, the Shuberts would have to pay Prince tens of thousands of dollars in penalties.

"From all appearances, it does not look like this theater is going to open," Jacobs said. "So, Phil, you're going to have to take that on as your responsibility. That theater has to be ready." As Smith was leaving the office to pack a bag and get on a plane, he had a thought. "Bernie," he said, "I have to take you over to the precinct and have you finger-printed."

"Why?" Jacobs wondered.

"Because we have a liquor license in Los Angeles, and they want the president of the company to be fingerprinted," Smith replied. He made a phone call to the Forty-Seventh Street precinct and took Jacobs, the new president of the Shubert Organization, over to have him fingerprinted. "That was my first official act under the new regime," Smith said.

Smith flew out that night to Los Angeles and checked into the Beverly Hills Hotel. The next morning he had a two-hour phone conversation with Jacobs. The new president told his right-hand man to call him, day or night, at the office or at home, if he needed to run something by him. But, he added, "If you don't think it's necessary to check with me, don't call. Just get it done."

Meanwhile, Schoenfeld took charge of announcing the change at the Shubert Organization. He called an old friend, Harvey Sabinson, who had been David Merrick's publicist, for advice. Schoenfeld handed him a piece of paper on which he'd written eight lines stating that Lawrence Shubert Lawrence Jr. had been made chairman of the board but that Schoenfeld and Jacobs were now the chief executive officers of the Shubert Organization. Irving Goldman had been handed more power as well. It was a bland announcement that would probably merit scant attention even in *Variety*. But Sabinson knew a good story when he saw one and told Schoenfeld, "This is history in the making. Not since 1900, when this company was founded, has a Shubert not been in charge of it. I think this is a front page story for the *New York Times*." Sabinson went round the corner to the Times building on West Forty-Third Street and explained the situation to his old friend, Arthur Gelb, a rising editor at the *Times* who had once been the paper's theater reporter. "You're right. It's a front page story," said Gelb.

Memories can be hazy forty years after the fact. The *Times* story ran on page twenty-four, not page one. But it conveyed the significance of the coup. "For the first time since its founding 72 years ago," it read, "the Shubert organization, the largest theatrical empire in the world, will be operated by men not in the Shubert family. In a drastic reorgani-

zation, this cluster of 23 corporations was put in charge of a troika. . . .
The shift in control of 17 of the city's 30 Broadway theaters touched
off intensive speculation in show business about what this might mean
in booking shows and how it might affect the artistic standards the new
executives might impose. . . . Those in show business did not know the
answer. But all agreed this was one of the major developments in the
legitimate theater in recent years."

Schoenfeld and Jacobs gave the *Times* a brief interview, denying
reports that they planned to sell any theaters. Schoenfeld said the company would increase pressure on the city to rid Times Square of prostitutes, drug dealers, and pornographers.

Variety, whose coverage was led by its tenacious editor, Abel Green,
did a racier job of capturing the intrigue. Describing the announcement of the new ruling troika as "cryptic," Green wrote: "Whether
this restructuring of duties, whereby two lawyers and a scenic paint
tycoon are officially placed in charge of virtually all of the day-to-day
operations, augurs a power struggle is conjectural at the moment."
But, he noted, the "omission of Lawrence's trademark Shubert middle-
name [the press release referred to him as Lawrence S. Lawrence] may
be deliberate. . . ." Green also noted the announcement was not made
by Howard Teichmann, the Shubert's official spokesman, but by an
outside press agent, Sabinson. Green managed to get Larry Shubert
on the phone. The deposed king said he might have something to say
in the future, but when Green told him that Schoenfeld and Jacobs had
announced they'd been with the company eighteen years, he cracked,
"So? I've been with the Shuberts for thirty-two years!"[3]

Around the office there were no wisecracks. "Every time I walked
into the office, for weeks after the announcement, Lawrence Shubert
Lawrence would yell at me and say, 'You know what those traitors did
to me?'" recalls Sabinson, laughing.

Schoenfeld and Jacobs solidified their power. They dispensed with
the sycophants, cutting them loose or stripping them of authority.
They hated Teichmann most of all because he was always "winding
Larry up about them," said Smith. Teichmann was out of a job by
the end of July 1972. But, with his connections in the press, he would
prove a formidable enemy. Over the next six months, he leaked stories

suggesting that Schoenfeld and Jacobs had been plotting their coup for years and that they intended to sell off the Shubert theaters and focus on nontheatrical real estate. Schoenfeld and Jacobs denied the reports, which cropped up in *Variety* and the *New York Post*. Teichmann also struck back with a blistering letter to his friend, Robert M. Morgenthau, who was angling to become Manhattan District Attorney (which he did in 1975). Teichmann believed the lawyers had been planning their coup ever since John Shubert's death in 1962. They began to wield, he wrote, power well outside the scope of their duties as in-house lawyers. (He neglected to mention that they had to do so, since the head of the company was usually drunk at the Sardi's bar by lunchtime.) He went after Goldman, too, saying he'd been appointed to the board because he fixed the Surrogate Court case in the Shubert's favor. Teichmann ended his jeremiad with a ringing charge of corruption. "I believe that what Schoenfeld, Jacobs, and Goldman are running is not the Shubert theaters but a partnership in which each man shares in everything from house seats to concessions to real estate ventures to maintenance contracts and who knows what else. It is my opinion they have been milking the theaters with the same brashness they have used as trustees of the Foundation."[4]

Evelyn Teichmann gave her husband's letter to writer Foster Hirsch, who made extensive use of it in his 1998 book, *The Boys from Syracuse*. Teichmann died in 1987, but his widow carried on the war against Schoenfeld and Jacobs, telling Hirsch that they were out to do in her husband and get control of the company for themselves.

Schoenfeld, who loathed Hirsch's book, denied all the charges in his memoir—and to this writer during the course of several conversations over many years. Irving Goldman, Schoenfeld maintained, was a friend of Larry Shubert's, not his or Jacobs's. Jacobs never had any illusions about Goldman. "He was not someone you could admire," he said. But they needed him to oust Larry. Phil Smith, who worked alongside everyone at the time, said, "Teichmann hated Goldman. They were always fighting. He wanted Bernie and Jerry to intercede, but what could they do? Irving was on the board, appointed by Lawrence. Tyke really didn't do anything at the company. He was just Larry's buddy. As for house seats, nobody wanted more house seats than Tyke. He used them to ingratiate himself with his friends in the press. He loved being able to pass them out."

Schoenfeld and Jacobs did not, as Teichmann charged, sell off the theaters or "milk them for their own personal gain." In 1972, the seventeen Shubert theaters were not that valuable. Jacobs discovered this shortly after the coup as he tried to stem the company's cash flow problem. "When we were given the power to run the business the first thing we discovered was that the business was close to being bankrupt," he said. "There were assets but they were not liquid. There was not sufficient cash around to pay our bills." Jacobs went to Morgan Guaranty, which oversaw J. J. Shubert's estate, and asked for a $1 million line of credit. For collateral, he put up the seventeen Broadway theaters. The bank turned him down. The theaters were, the bank said, "specialized properties" in a deteriorating neighborhood. They were not worth $1 million. Had Schoenfeld and Jacobs wanted to milk the theaters they would have sold them off (theaters were not landmarked then as they are today) to developers who would have turned them into something far more valuable than theaters—parking lots. As the impresario Dimitri Weismann says in Stephen Sondheim's *Follies*, "It is 1971 . . . every year between the Great Wars, I produced the *Follies* in this theater. Since then this house has been home to ballet, movies, blue movies, and, now, in a final burst of glory, it's to be a parking lot." But the lawyers didn't sell. Just as Lee and J. J. Shubert kept their theaters during the Great Depression, Schoenfeld and Jacobs held the chain together during the company's—and the city's—financial catastrophe of the 1970s.

Phil Smith had no doubt his new bosses would keep the theaters. "They had worked at Shubert most of their adult lives," said Smith. "It's what they knew. Many of us had been there a long time. If the company had been broken up—if the theaters were sold—all those years would have been for nothing. We had to try to save it. And don't forget—Bernie and Jerry loved the business. They were not theater people in the beginning but they took to it right away."

Jerry Leichtling, Schoenfeld's office assistant, also believed the lawyers would keep the Shubert empire intact. "Jerry lived by something called the 'Prudent Man Rule'—he talked about it all the time," Leichtling said. A legal term that goes back to 1830, the Prudent Man Rule applies to trustees of estates, who are urged to look after the estate as if it were their own—"with prudence, intelligence, and discretion." One of its key tenets is to preserve the estate. J. J. Shubert's estate was made up in large part of his theaters—and his will stipulated that they remain theaters. As J. J.'s former lawyer, and an executor of his estate, Schoenfeld felt duty-bound to keep Shubert going as a theatrical force. The Prudent Man would act on J. J.'s wishes and keep the theaters as theaters. They were, in many ways, J. J.'s children. And in 1972 they needed looking after.

But Schoenfeld and Jacobs were also ambitious men. They saw an opportunity to depose a weak king, and they took it. They would go on to reap the rewards of running the Shubert empire—power, perks, money, and stature. But since the Shubert Foundation controlled the Shubert Organization, they knew they would never own the company. They would never make the kind of money theater owners and producers who owned their properties and shows would. As powerful as Schoenfeld and Jacobs became, they remained, as they often said, employees of the Shubert Foundation.

If Howard Teichmann misjudged Schoenfeld and Jacobs's intentions, he was right about Irving Goldman's. Phil Smith had been in Los Angeles for a week trying to get the new Shubert Theatre ready for the opening of *Follies* when Goldman arrived. Over lunch at a Chinese restaurant in Century City, Goldman began quizzing Smith on preparations for opening night. You have a red carpet, he wanted to know. Yes, said Smith. Who'd you get it from? Goldman asked. Smith gave the name of a company that had done the red carpet for years for the Oscars. Goldman was silent for a moment and then asked, "You have klieg lights?" Yes, Smith said, adding that he'd also lined up Army Archerd, the top columnist at *Variety*, to cover the opening on the red carpet under the klieg lights. Goldman seemed pleased.

But the next day he rang up Smith and said, "Cancel the red carpet." Smith was taken aback. "I've got a better place," Goldman said. Smith had put down a substantial deposit which would have to be forfeited. "Well, whatever it is, pay it," Goldman said. He then gave Smith the

name of another lighting company he wanted to use for the opening
night. Then he wanted the list of VIPs who were going to attend the
opening. He asked Smith if such and such a person had picked up his
tickets. "I foolishly said, 'No,'" Smith recalled.

"Good. Give them to me. I'll make sure he gets them," Goldman
would respond.

"And then I recognized what was going on," said Smith. "It took me
three or four names, but then I started saying, 'Yes! He picked up his
tickets.' I gave Irving a lot of yeses. I exhausted his list."

That afternoon, Smith called Bernie Jacobs in New York and told
him about Irving's interest in red carpets, klieg lights, and VIP tickets.

"Phil, we'll be out there in two days," Jacobs said. "Jerry and I are
coming out. Just hold on until we get there."

A few weeks later, back in New York after the opening of *Follies* (which
flopped in Los Angeles as it had on Broadway), Phil Smith had lunch
with Abe Margulies, an old friend who'd become a successful businessman. Abe had read about the takeover of the Shubert empire in the
Times.

"Philly," he said. "Have Bernie and Jerry gone crazy?"

"What do you mean, Abe?" Smith asked.

"Irving Goldman! He's a thief!"

"Where?"

"Anywhere, Philly. Everywhere."

Smith looked at his friend and said, "Thanks, Abe. I'll pass on the
word."

CHAPTER NINE

Rotten to the Core

A few months after the coup, the *New York Times* ran a lengthy profile of the new triumvirate under the headline SHUBERT EMPIRE FIGHTING A FINANCIAL CRISIS. The article was accompanied by a photograph of Schoenfeld, Jacobs, and Goldman standing under the Shubert Theatre, whose marquee read, ARTHUR MILLER'S THE CREATION OF THE WORLD AND OTHER BUSINESS—a flop that would close five days after the article appeared. Goldman, grinning, stood in the center, flanked by a pudgy Schoenfeld in a fedora and a smiling (for once) Jacobs in a raincoat. Jacobs summed up their situation, saying, "We are fighting for more than just the survival of the Shubert theaters. We are fighting for the survival of the American legitimate theater. If the Shubert business does not survive, there won't be any American theater."

There were just fifty-six productions in the 1971–72 Broadway season. With few exceptions—Neil Simon's *The Prisoner of Second Avenue*, Van Peebles's *Ain't Supposed to Die a Natural Death*—most were duds. The Shuberts seemed to have a knack for picking the worst of the lot. In addition to *Creation of the World*, they had booked such gems as *The Sign in Sidney Brustein's Window* (five performances), *The Incomparable Max* (ten performances), *There's One in Every Marriage* (sixteen performances), and *Solitaire/Double Solitaire* (a hit at thirty-six performances!).

"There was a point where we only had five theaters open," Phil Smith recalled. "The Broadhurst was dark for almost a year. The Broadhurst! One of our best theaters. It was pretty sad."

As the *Times* reported, this was the worst Shubert season since the Depression. The paper noted that during the post–World War II boom on Broadway, the Shubert empire was valued at more than $400 million. By 1972, its value had fallen to between $60 million and $100 million.

The most pressing problem was cash flow. Stymied by Morgan Guaranty's refusal of a $1 million line of credit, Schoenfeld and Jacobs had to do something the Shubert brothers never did—sell some real estate. But contrary to their enemies' whispers, they did not sell theaters. Instead they sold off a parcel of land on Broadway between Sixty-Second and Sixty-Third Streets for $3.5 million.

But for the Shubert empire to thrive, it needed shows. So Schoenfeld and Jacobs made what would turn out to be one of the most important decisions of their reign. They would begin investing Shubert money in new productions. They would also start meeting with writers, directors, and performers to discuss new projects. After more than a decade of acting solely as a landlord, the Shubert Organization would start producing again. Jacobs took over the company's booking department. He began reading scripts instead of just contracts. Here he had another ally, his wife, Betty, who, it turned out, was a good script reader herself. On Friday nights, he'd take a pile of scripts out to his house in Roslyn, Long Island, where he and Betty read them over the weekend. Their kitchen table became the Shubert booking office.

The first show the new management invested in was *Pippin*, which they booked into the Imperial Theatre. Stephen Schwartz, a young songwriter fresh out of Carnegie Mellon University, had fashioned a freewheeling musical loosely based on the life of Charlemagne's eldest son. The show was of its time—more a "happening" than a traditional musical. But the score was tuneful and contemporary. In his memoir, *Present at the Creation, Leaping in the Dark, and Going Against the Grain*, producer Stuart Ostrow wrote, "From the moment he played 'Corner of the Sky,' I knew Stephen was the new voice I was looking for." Ostrow worked with Schwartz on the script for over a year. In the meantime, Schwartz had an unexpected Off-Broadway smash called *Godspell*, which produced the hit tune "Day by Day." Ostrow asked Bob Fosse, with whom he played poker, to direct *Pippin*. Fosse transformed

Schwartz's "sincere, naive morality play," as Ostrow called it, into a cynical burlesque narrated by a character called the Leading Player.[1] For that role, Fosse cast his friend Ben Vereen. Schwartz was aghast at what Fosse was doing to his show, but Fosse ignored him. He told a reporter that Schwartz was "talented but not as talented as he thinks he is." There were flare-ups during rehearsals on a daily basis. At one point Schwartz said, "I'm getting out of here." Fosse replied icily, "You can get out, and you can stay out"—and banned him from rehearsals.[2]

Though he had Fosse as his director, Ostrow had difficulty raising the money for *Pippin*. It was an expensive show, and the country was still in the grip of recession. Schoenfeld and Jacobs decided to help. But to do so they had to ignore a stipulation in J. J. Shubert's will that limited investments in shows to no more than $25,000. Ostrow needed more, so they gave him $50,000. "We did so timorously," Jacobs recalled. The day before *Pippin* opened, Jacobs asked Ostrow if they could sell off their investment. "So much for faithfulness," Ostrow wrote.

It was a mistake. *Pippin* was a smash, made even more so by a pioneering TV commercial, directed by Fosse, that, for the first time, featured performers doing an actual dance from a show. The announcer said, "Here's a free minute from *Pippin*"—as Ben Vereen began to dance. At the end of the commercial, the announcer said, "You can see the other 119 minutes of *Pippin* live at the Imperial Theatre. Without commercial interruption." (*Pippin* detractors said the only thing you needed to see of the show was Fosse's one-minute commercial.)

Pippin ran four and a half years on Broadway and earned $3.5 million. Had the Shuberts held on to their investment, they would have made a nice profit. Still, they got the rent from a hit show in one of their largest theaters. They got something else as well: a lesson in producing. Schoenfeld and, especially, Jacobs spent a lot of time at the theater watching Fosse work. What Jacobs grasped was that a director-choreographer of Fosse's stature is essential to a musical's success. He had no illusions about the script to *Pippin*. The music was fine but the show was not built with the precision of *My Fair Lady*. Fosse took what many of the newspaper critics dismissed as second-rate material and turned it into first-rate entertainment. If the material was the horse, Jacobs was looking for the jockey who could ride it to the finish

line. As his friend Manny Azenberg would say, "Bernie Jacobs learned
to bet on the jockeys."

Another decision the new regime made was to change Shubert
curtain times. For years, Broadway shows opened at 8:30, which gave
people time to have a couple of martinis and dinner. But that was a
tradition from a safer Times Square. By 1972, "the neighborhood became unsafe after seven thirty," Jacobs recalled. "We realized we were
chasing our customers away." The new curtain time would be 7:30.
Producer David Merrick, however, set his curtain times at 8:00, so he
could scoop up whatever business remained after the other shows had
started. Eventually, everybody else followed and the curtain time was
established at 8:00 p.m.

During the run of *Pippin*, Schoenfeld and Jacobs discovered that
the booking deal was more favorable to the producer than the theater
owner. As long as anyone could remember, the basic deal was that the
producer took 70 percent of the box office receipts and the theater
owner took 30 percent. The costs were split the same way: 70 percent
on the producer's back, 30 percent on the theater owner's. The theater
owner paid for some of the stagehands as well as the doormen, porters
and ushers, and other theater personnel. This meant, in effect, that the
theater owner was the producer's partner. Their interests dovetailed.
But during the run of *Pippin*, the new Shubert management noticed
that, with all their expenses (plus taxes on their theaters), they were
getting just 10 percent of the revenues. And sometimes less. Or nothing at all. "There came a time when we were losing $2,500 a week on
Pippin, and Stuart Ostrow was making $25,000 a week," Jacobs said.
"So we changed the agreement."

From the late seventies onward, the Shuberts took a smaller percentage of the box office receipts—originally 10 percent, but when
business conditions worsened, dipping to 7 percent—but paid none of
the costs. Everything—stagehands, doormen, ushers, insurance, light-
bulbs, even toilet paper—was billed to the producer. "We thought we
had invented the wheel," Jacobs said. "Then we went to London and
discovered they'd been doing it forever." Nobody objected at the time.
After all, 10 percent was less than 30 percent. But the new agreement
altered the relationship between the producer and the theater owner.

They were no longer partners. And their interests began to diverge. As Schoenfeld and Jacobs solidified their position as Broadway's chief labor negotiators, producers began to complain that they were "giving away the store" to the unions. They negotiated the contracts—and then passed on the expenses to the producers. "They never wanted a strike because that would mean dark theaters," said a veteran producer. "So they gave too much away. And as the costs escalated over the years, we were left with the bills."

Schoenfeld and Jacobs scoffed at such charges—were they not becoming producers as well?—but in time, the new arrangement would alienate the Shuberts from many producers. The seeds of resentment and bitterness had been planted.

As they scrambled on all fronts to shore up the Shubert Organization, Schoenfeld and Jacobs had one more round to go with Larry Shubert. The deposed king stewed for five months and then in December 1972 struck back. Murray Schumach of the *New York Times* called the Shubert executive offices on December 20. He wanted a comment from Schoenfeld and Jacobs about a complaint Larry Shubert had filed with attorney general Louis Lefkowitz charging his adversaries with illegal seizure of power, conflicts of interest, and excessive disbursements of Shubert Foundation funds to pet charities. Though Schoenfeld and Jacobs had not seen the complaint, they dismissed it as "utterly groundless." In his article the next day, Schumach wrote that Larry Shubert's complaint amounted to a "virtual declaration of war."[3]

When Schoenfeld and Jacobs got hold of the complaint, it must have scorched their hands. "Free this great business from the Schoenfeld and Jacobs vice," it thundered, "through which they have perpetuated themselves as directors and principal officers of the subsidiaries, as attorneys for the subsidiaries, as member-directors and officers of the foundation and thereby ensconced themselves and their cohort [Irving] Goldman as dictators of each and every charitable bequest which the multi-million-dollar Foundation makes in their lifetime."[4]

Larry Shubert was charging his assassins with activities bordering on the criminal. "I, my family, the Shubert business and charitable beneficiaries have all been betrayed," he said. "Schoenfeld, Jacobs, and Goldman are using this public interest for their private interest." [5] He claimed Schoenfeld and Jacobs, while each making $150,000 a year from the Shubert Organization, were doing outside legal work that netted them another $250,000 to $500,000. (Betty Jacobs, in an interview in 2013, laughed at that figure. So did Phil Smith, who said, "Nobody at Shubert ever made that kind of money!") Larry Shubert claimed Goldman gave a $1 million contract to a paint company. He noted Goldman was in the paint business, but conceded he could not prove Goldman had profited from the contract. He accused Schoenfeld and Jacobs of double-dealing, representing both the Shuberts and producers who wanted to book Shubert theaters. And he claimed that a handwritten note found in J. J. Shubert's desk a few days after he died expressed his wish that "there should always be a blood member in the Shuberts in charge."

Jacobs responded to the charges, telling the *Times*, "For selfish reasons and out of personal pique, [Larry Shubert] has leveled unjustified and untruthful charges against his fellow directors in the foundation. . . . His charges are baseless . . . the foundation's affairs are being conducted [in] the best interests of the American theater."

Attorney General Lefkowitz told the paper, "I will look into every point raised. . . . If we find any evidence of crime, we will turn it over to the office of the District Attorney."

In the end, Larry Shubert's "virtual declaration of war" didn't even amount to a skirmish. Three months after it was filed, a state supreme court judge threw it out, partly on a technicality (it had not been filed in time to meet a four-month statute of limitations on corporate elections) but also because the charges against the new Shubert leaders were vague. The judge could find little evidence to support Larry's allegations of "pay-offs," "manipulation," "undue influence," and "self-aggrandizement." Schoenfeld, Jacobs, and Goldman were safe— for now. [6]

That was the end, in the Shubert universe, of Larry Shubert. He slipped away, eventually retiring to Boca Raton, Florida, where, according to Shubert biographer Foster Hirsch, he kept a book titled *The Terrible Truth About Lawyers* on his coffee table.

Larry Shubert died of cancer on July 18, 1992. But in true Shubert fashion, there was a battle for his estate, pitting his sons, Larry and Lee, against his companion, Gloria Anderson. Gary Pearlman of the *Palm Beach Times* attended his funeral. "No one cried," he noted. He overheard two women discussing the battle for Larry's estate. Speaking of his sons, one woman said, "They are ruthless. I hope they choke on the money."[7]

Lawrence Shubert Lawrence Jr., an incompetent drunk, was never much of a threat to Schoenfeld and Jacobs. But his complaint against them pricked the attention of Attorney General Louis Lefkowitz. Using the power of his office, which regulated charitable foundations, Lefkowitz began investigating the Shubert Foundation and its new leaders. A real enemy was on the march.

Up at the Shubert offices, the search was on for shows to fill empty theaters. A manager representing Neil Diamond came to see Phil Smith about booking the Winter Garden Theatre. "Quite frankly, we'd never heard of him," Smith said. "I knew 'Sweet Caroline,' but that was about it." The manager took Smith over to Colony Records on Broadway and Forty-Ninth and bought him three Neil Diamond albums. "Listen to them, and get back to me," he said. The Shuberts booked Diamond for a sold-out, month-long concert at the Winter Garden in October 1972.

Schoenfeld and Jacobs began looking around for something they could produce. They decided they needed some help. Bill Liberman, a young general manager who had overseen many Broadway shows for the producer Hillard Elkins, impressed them. Jacobs invited Liberman up to his office one morning and told him that because of the consent decree against the Shubert Organization stemming back to the 1950s the company had been discouraged from producing on Broadway. "We're looking to test that consent decree," Jacobs said. "We want to produce something with our name above the title. But we're lawyers. We're not producers. We don't know everything you do." Jacobs offered Liberman a job, albeit a vague one as there was as yet no show for him to work on. Even so, Liberman agreed to work for expenses—about $250 a week—until they found a show.

"When do you want me to start?" he asked Jacobs.

Jacobs laughed. "Well, you're working for nothing, so start tomorrow."

Within a few months Liberman had a lead. In 1973, Liza Minnelli was at the height of her popularity, having just won the Oscar for *Cabaret*. She'd also scored a triumph with *Liza with a Z*, a television special taped at the Lyceum Theatre, in 1972. In October 1973, Liberman went to see Stevie Phillips, Minnelli's agent at ICM. Phillips told him Liza had a few weeks open in January 1974 and wanted to do a Broadway concert. As it happened, one of the Shubert's prime houses, the Winter Garden, was free. But Minnelli's terms were tough. She wanted 90 percent of the profits. Still, Jacobs leapt at the chance. He told Liberman, "Our aim here is to get a show on. We don't care if we make money. Just break even. We want to say, 'The Shubert Organization Presents Liza Minnelli at the Winter Garden.'"

Jacobs gave Liberman near autonomy. But there wasn't much time. It was October, and the concert was scheduled to open the first week of January. Another of Minnelli's demands was that there had to be a full-page ad announcing the concert in the *New York Times*. Liberman and Phil Smith went to Blaine Thompson, a Broadway ad agency, and met with illustrator Joe Eula to come up with the poster art. Eula took out a sketch pad and a red marker and scribbled an elongated *L* followed by *i z a* in smaller letters. On top of the *L* he drew a tiny face with cropped black hair, black eyes, and black eyelashes. "It was perfect," Liberman recalled. "That meeting took five minutes." Liberman showed the poster to Jacobs.

"It doesn't say Minnelli!" he snapped.

"Bernie, she just won the Oscar for *Cabaret*," Liberman argued. "It's like 'Sammy,' it's like 'Frank.'"

"It has to say 'Minnelli'!" Jacobs said.

They compromised. Above the big red "Liza" Liberman wrote, "Liza Minnelli records for Columbia Records."

"OK," said Jacobs.

The ad ran in the *New York Times* one week before the box office was to open. It offered, as all ads did back in those days, to sell tickets through the mail. As phone sales did not exist yet, there were only two ways to buy tickets—via mail order or at the box office. The mail orders came in that week, but only at a trickle. Schoenfeld and Jacobs began to panic. They were producing Liza Minnelli—and she wasn't selling. Liberman begged them to calm down. People would come to the box office, he said, where they could be sure of their seat locations. Secretly, though, he was worried. The following Monday, the day the box office opened, Liberman decided to bike to the office from his apartment on the Upper West Side. The box office opened at 10:00 a.m. and Liberman thought he'd go by the theater at 9:30 to see if there was a line. As he came down Broadway, he saw a line of people that snaked down Broadway from the Winter Garden box office to Forty-Ninth Street, then over to Seventh Avenue, then up to Fiftieth Street and back to the theater. Minnelli fans circled the Winter Garden. "Boy, was I a happy camper," he said. By four o'clock that afternoon, the concert was sold out.*

Liza opened at the Winter Garden on January 6, 1974. The opening night credits read: "Produced by the Shubert Organization (Gerald Schoenfeld, Chairman; Bernard B. Jacobs, President)." It was the first time the name Shubert had appeared above a title since John Shubert put his name above the play *Julia, Jake and Uncle Joe* in 1961 (it ran one performance). The United States government said nothing.

The name of the third member of the Shubert triumvirate—Irving Goldman—did not appear above the title. But he was at opening night with his pal Abe Beame, the city's new mayor. Secretary of State Henry Kissinger was a guest that night as well, and the theater was crawling with Secret Service. Goldman worried Kissinger would overshadow the mayor. Phil Smith was standing at the back of the theater when a porter came up to him and said, "Mr. Goldman is outside and he wants to see you." Smith found Goldman in his car with the mayor.

"Phil, I've got to bring the mayor in, but I want him entering with fanfare. I want you to get him a big round of applause. Can you do it?"

"I can do it, Irving, but you have to follow my instructions," Smith said. "Stay in the car with the mayor until I come and get you."

---

*   Not everything went according to plan, however. Later that day, Minnelli's agent called and screamed, "Stop selling tickets! They spelled Liza's name wrong!" Liberman still has his opening night tickets, uncut. They read: "Liza Minelli."

The crowd was getting restless, everybody was looking for Henry Kissinger. Smith decided to take advantage of the excitement. He lined up a bunch of Shubert employees and told them to start applauding when he came in with Goldman and the mayor. "I figured that would start the whole place applauding because they'd think Henry Kissinger had arrived. Goldman was short, his wife was short, and Beame was short, so nobody would be able to see them. We walk down the aisle, the place is cheering, Beame is waist high, everybody's standing up looking for Henry Kissinger!"

Goldman was thrilled. "That was fantastic, Phil! Now I want you to arrange to have the mayor photographed with Liza after the show." Smith did as instructed, bringing Kissinger, Beame, and others backstage to meet the star. The next day photographs of Minnelli, the secretary of state, and the mayor of New York appeared in all the newspapers. "My God, Irving had an orgasm that day," recalled Smith. "I think he would have given me the company if he could have."

Aside from looking after the mayor on opening nights, Goldman didn't do much around the Shubert offices. "He had a nothing job," said Smith. "Bernie and Jerry ran the company. Irving was along for the ride." He was also along for something else—ice. Goldman called Smith into his office one day. He had a list of ticket brokers he wanted to have access to Shubert seats. Smith said the company already had a list of approved brokers. "I can't make changes to the list, Irving," Smith said. "We have to watch this thing very carefully." Goldman was blunt. "Phil, these overpayments I hear about to ticket brokers. I want a piece of it." Smith replied, "Irving, if I find anybody here taking such payments, I will fire them. We are not going to be a part of that."

"Irving was just a bad guy," Smith recalled. "He was rotten to the core." But Schoenfeld and Jacobs had made their deal with the devil, and "they had to tolerate him," said Smith.

Soon, though, the devil overreached. In March of 1974 Mayor Beame rewarded Goldman by appointing him commissioner of cultural affairs for New York City. Broadway producer Alexander H. Cohen supplied a bus to shuttle theater people from Shubert Alley to the swearing-in ceremony at City Hall. Goldman took up his new post to the applause of Harold Prince, Carol Channing, Arlene Francis, Joseph Papp, and Vincent Sardi Jr.

Harvey Lichtenstein, the head of the Brooklyn Academy of Music, was on hand as well. He told the *New York Times*, "I don't know Mr. Goldman. I don't know anything about him."

Discussing Goldman's appointment nearly forty years later, Jerry Leichtling, the onetime Shubert office boy, laughed and said, "Irving Goldman as cultural affairs commissioner is like having Dolly Parton as defense secretary."

CHAPTER TEN

Horsing Around

The Shuberts needed shows. As luck would have it, one was taking shape some three thousand miles away in the English country-side. In the spring of 1972, James Mossman, a popular BBC reporter, invited his friend, the playwright Peter Shaffer, to spend the week-end with him at his cottage in Norfolk. Driving through the fog, they passed a stable. Mossman told Shaffer he'd heard an "extraordinary story" a few years earlier at a dinner party. A local magistrate told the gathering, "A most awful thing has landed on my plate. A local boy has blinded seventy horses."

"Seventy horses? How is that possible?" Shaffer wondered. He knew Mossman was an embellisher, so he pressed his friend. "Well, maybe not seventy," said Mossman. "Maybe she said twelve or something like that. But that boy did blind a bunch of horses one night."

"The story was repellent to me," Shaffer recalled. "Repellent as an idea, as a theme. And then it took hold of me in a way that I really wanted to account for this, somehow, in my head. It was the enormity of this horror that gripped me. I was thinking about it all the time, and the only way I could lay it to rest was to write about it."

Shaffer tracked down the magistrate. The case had been passed on to another judge, she said, and she'd heard nothing more about it. Shaf-fer tried to locate the boy, but got nowhere. He looked at Norfolk court records, but could find no such case. He checked with the local papers to see if they'd covered the story. They had not. He did find a woman who worked in the psychiatric wing of a local hospital. "She admitted she had heard of the boy," Shaffer said. "I said, 'You've more than heard of it. You know something.' But she refused to say anything. And that's all I ever found out. A boy blinded horses and . . . vanished. There was obviously something enormous behind this action, but, in a way, not knowing what it was, was delightful. It meant I could do anything."

Shaffer was gaining stature as one of England's leading playwrights. He'd had a few hits in London and on Broadway, including *The Private Ear* and *The Public Eye*, a pair of one acts about love and infidelity; *The Royal Hunt of the Sun*, a spectacular epic about the Spanish conquest of the Incas, breathtakingly staged by John Dexter; and *Black Comedy*, a farce that takes place in the dark.

Born in Liverpool on May 15, 1926, Shaffer and his twin brother, Anthony (who would go on to write *Sleuth*), were conscripted during World War II to work in the coal mines. Both had bad eyesight, which meant they could not go down into the mines. They were assigned the grueling task of pulling coal bins along a railway. To keep boredom at bay, Peter Shaffer memorized huge patches of Shakespeare and re-cited them, in his head, while at work. "It kept me from going mad," he said. "I'd do *Hamlet* one day, and *King Lear* the next." He learned to write plays, he believed, by absorbing the structure of Shakespearean monologues and scenes.

At Cambridge after the war, he wrote mystery novels, none of which were published. He moved to New York in 1950 and worked as clerk in the Doubleday bookstore at Grand Central, and then behind the lending counter of the New York Public Library. He wrote plays in his spare time. He returned to London a few years later and started writing radio plays for the BBC. Shaffer's breakthrough stage play was *Five Finger Exercise* in 1958, directed by John Gielgud.*

In 1972, gripped by the story of a boy who blinded horses, Shaffer turned for help to a friend who was a child psychologist. He gave Shaf-fer a list of reasons why a child might maim animals, but also admitted

---

* Rehearsals for *Five Finger Exercise* were chaotic, with the actors stumbling all over the stage. Gielgud, aghast, said, "What are you all doing banging into each other?" Juliet Mills, one of the performers, replied, "We are doing, or rather trying to do, John, what you have given us to do!" Gielgud said, "What on earth for? Everyone knows I can't direct!"

that the reason might remain a mystery. That's when Shaffer began to see the play as a psychological mystery.

He told his favorite director, John Dexter, about his new play. Shaffer trusted Dexter's theatrical instincts from the day they met to discuss his earlier play *The Royal Hunt of the Sun*. It contained a scene that depicted Pizarro and his men climbing the Andes. "I hope climbing the Andes and all that won't be too difficult to stage," Shaffer said. Dexter replied, "I hope it is!"

I've found my director, Shaffer thought at the time.

"John was a marvelous, very clever, but a very difficult man," Shaffer said. "He would always call me dear, but those 'dears' could be like daggers."

Shaffer's first draft focused on the boy and his "act of sadism." There was a psychiatrist, but he had yet to come into focus. Dexter read the draft and told Shaffer to concentrate on the psychiatrist. "Dig into yourself to find the analyst. He'll unlock the door for you," Dexter said. It was a breakthrough. Shaffer's psychological mystery now had its detective—Martin Dysart, the child psychiatrist.

By this point, Shaffer had decided the boy would blind six horses—"which is quite enough, thank you." And he had a title, *Equus*. Dexter began experimenting with ideas of how the horses should be portrayed on stage. He wanted the horses to be played by actors, but he didn't want the actors in horse costumes trotting around making neighing sounds—"none of that rubbish," he said. He had the actors study horses. "He wanted them to see the way the horses held their heads, he wanted them to turn themselves into horses without any visual aids," Shaffer said. "It was John at his most experimental. He was creating an amazing equine image using only the actors' bodies."

Everything had to be stylized. Instead of neighing, the actors learned to make a sound like the crack of bell around a horse's neck. John Napier, a young designer, fashioned skeletons of horses' heads from cane, leather, and wire wrapped in silver foil. The actors wore the skeletal horse heads on top of their heads. They stood on skeletal hooves as well. The rest of their costumes were black shirts and black pants.

To play the psychiatrist, Dexter and Shaffer cast Alec McCowen,

who'd received raves for his performance in *The Misanthrope* opposite
Diana Rigg. Casting the role of the boy was difficult, however. He had
to be beautiful, remote, haunted, and frightening. One night Shaffer
was watching a show on the BBC that featured a handsome boy named
Peter Firth. He had the qualities Shaffer sought. Shaffer called Dexter. Without even exchanging pleasantries, Dexter said, "I assume you
are ringing about Mr. Firth. I have seen him, too. That is the boy you
wrote about, dear," and then hung up.

Equus went into rehearsal at London's National Theatre during the
hot summer of 1973. Shaffer had written a scene he knew would be
controversial. The boy, Alan, has a sexual encounter with a local girl
in a stable. They take off their clothes, but just as he is about to have
sex with her, he hears hooves smashing wood. As he later tells Dysart,
he could no longer see the girl. He could only see his beloved horse,
Nugget. "I wanted the foam of his neck. His sweaty hide. Not flesh!
Hide! Horse-hide." The girl flees, and Alan, naked, takes a pick and
blinds the horses.

Dexter put off staging the blinding scene until late in rehearsals.
One day at a run-through, he told Shaffer he had come up with some
ideas. One thing he didn't want, however, was nudity. "It's gilding the
lily," he said. "It's as if we're being deliberately scandalous. I'm sorry,
but I don't like it."

Shaffer was furious. A naked boy blinding horses in a frenzy was
primitive, terrifying, and erotic. Sexuality was an important dynamic
in the play. Dexter let Shaffer stew. Finally, at the end of the day, Dexter said he was going to stage the scene. Shaffer and a friend, the stage
designer Jocelyn Herbert, took their seats. Shaffer noticed Dexter whispering something to Peter Firth. He's telling him not to strip, Shaffer
thought, fuming. The scene started. The girl fled the stables, and Firth
began stalking the horses. And then he ripped off his clothes, grabbed
the pick, and stabbed the eyes out of six horses. Herbert screamed and
grabbed Shaffer's wrist. "This was the first time we had seen the nude
scene, and it was astounding," said Shaffer. "The tension went up and
up and up. It was alarming and amazing and right."

Shaffer realized what Dexter had done. He wanted to gauge the impact of the nudity, but if Shaffer, his audience, knew it was coming, he wouldn't be shocked.

"You are a monster," Shaffer said.

"Who else was I going to find to try it out on, dear?" Dexter replied.

A "dear" like a dagger, Shaffer recalled decades later. "Marvelous."

Equus opened July 26, 1973, to an audience packed with critics. "I thought some people might get up and boo. Or call me obscene," Shaffer said. Dexter, in a letter to Stephen Sondheim before the opening, wrote, "*Equus* is going very very slowly but is, I think, interesting and stands a good chance of working as Peter intended it to. Success with the public is another matter. Anyway, as you have often said, who cares?" [1]

Clive Hirschhorn, then reviewing for the *Sunday Express*, left the National Theatre after the opening performance with two friends. As they walked across Waterloo Bridge to go to a restaurant in Covent Garden no one uttered a word. They ordered drinks. Only then could they begin to discuss the play. The next morning the critics called *Equus* a modern masterpiece. Dexter noted in his diaries that not since Laurence Olivier appeared in *Othello* had a play caused such a frenzy at the National Theatre box office.

Broadway wasn't paying much attention to new shows at the National Theatre in the summer of 1973. The Shuberts may have been vaguely aware of *Equus*, but nobody from the company flew to London to attend the opening night and grab it for a Shubert house. It wasn't until September that *Equus* began to cause a stir in Shubert Alley. And that was because Walter Kerr, the most respected critic of his era, went to London and saw it.

"The closest I have seen a contemporary play come—it is powerfully close—to reanimating the spirit of mystery that makes the stage a place of breathless discovery rather than a classroom for rational demonstration is Peter Shaffer's remarkable *Equus*," Kerr wrote in his influential Sunday *New York Times* column. "Mr. Shaffer is the author of *The Royal Hunt of the Sun*, and he may have been trying for just such iconography—a portrait of the drives that lead men to crucify themselves—there. Here, I think, he has found it." He added, "At once we are lured, with infinite skill, into a psychiatric detective story, the tensions of which account for half the evening's force." Forty years later, talking about *Equus* in his Riverside Drive penthouse, Peter Shaffer pulled out a copy of Kerr's review. He had underlined the words "a psychiatric detective story."

Kerr's review, as well as the London raves, set off a scramble for the Broadway rights to the play. The flamboyant Alex Cohen, one of the most prolific producers around, was an early suitor. Cohen kept an apartment in London and was friendly with the major producers, directors, and writers. But a rival producer, who hadn't had a hit in a long time, was looking to make a comeback. *Equus*, he thought, was the ticket. Kermit Bloomgarden had been a force on Broadway in the forties and fifties, having produced *The Little Foxes*, *Death of a Salesman*, and *The Music Man*. But by 1970 his luck had run out. And his health was poor. His right leg was amputated in 1971 due to hardening of the arteries. He had a steel prosthetic, which his office boy, a teenage Scott Rudin, picked up every morning to have oiled at a shop in Harlem. (Shaffer remembers, "His leg creaked!") To outmaneuver Cohen, Bloomgarden called his friend Lillian Hellman, whose plays he had produced. She was friendly with Shaffer, and she told him, "Kermit needs this." Shaffer gave him the Broadway rights. Bloomgarden, no longer as flush as he once was, teamed up with a rich lady—Doris Cole Abrahams, whose husband owned Aquascutum, one of England's best known makers of luxury outerwear. As they began laying plans for a Broadway production, Bernie Jacobs, having read Kerr's review, requested a script. He and his wife read it one weekend at the kitchen table in their house in Roslyn. They weren't sure what it was about, but they couldn't stop talking about it.

A New York producer who had seen it in London advised Jacobs not to take it.

"It's a homosexual play," he said. "It'll never work here. Too gay."

"Bullshit," Jacobs said. "I've read it. It's terrific. We want it."

The Shuberts got *Equus*. It opened October 24, 1974, at the Plymouth Theatre on Forty-Fifth Street. Peter Firth came to New York, but Alec McCowen, who originated the role of the psychiatrist, did not. He was living with his companion, who had become ill and he would not leave him. So Dexter and Shaffer had to find another actor to play Dysart. Anthony Hopkins was a formidable young talent at the National The-atre, a protégé of Laurence Olivier. But he'd had a drinking problem and was nearly fired from a production of *Macbeth* in 1972. A year later he entered AA. He was better, and Dexter had even considered him for the role of Dysart in London. But a lunch meeting had gone awry. "Shifty, spineless, Welsh cunt," Dexter wrote in his diary. "Has AA helped him? I don't think so, so once a cunt *always* a Welshman. . . . At least I didn't offer him *Equus* as I had planned." But by 1974, Dexter had changed his opinion. He offered Hopkins the part in New York. Shortly before the opening of *Equus* at the Plymouth, he wrote, "Tony Hopkins is on the way to being superb in *Equus*. He is calm, disciplined, and every word is crystal clear."[2]

Hopkins was unknown in New York in 1974, but the reviews that October morning launched his career in America. Clive Barnes, the chief drama critic of the *New York Times*, wrote, "Anthony Hopkins, articulate and troubled, is superb. . . . It is a virtuoso performance gauged to a fraction."

"Anthony was a nobody at that point," said Shaffer. "*Equus* made Anthony a star."

Equus was a sensation. The day the reviews came out, the Plym-outh box office took in $134,000, thought, at the time, to be the single largest one-day take for a play in Broadway history. For the first year, weekly grosses hit $50,000, unheard of for a nonmusical. The run, though, was not always smooth. Dexter could be brutal to the actors, recalled Dennis Erdman, who understudied Alan. Marian Seldes, play-ing Alan's mother, had a tendency to wave her arms around while she was saying her lines. One day, Dexter stopped her in the middle of a scene and said, "Keep your hands to your side, Ms. Seldes. You're an actress, not Helen Keller's older, aging sister."

When Hopkins left the play, Anthony Perkins replaced him. But Dexter had little patience with him. Perkins was in the habit of looking down while he delivered Dysart's speeches. "Mr. Perkins, your cock isn't that long so stop looking on the floor for it," Dexter snapped.

A larger problem (so to speak) was that Perkins turned out to be a mediocre draw at the box office. To keep the show running, the producers needed a bigger star. They found one—Richard Burton. When he was announced, lines of ticket buyers formed outside the Plymouth box office. And then Actors' Equity kicked up a fuss. The play had opened with a foreigner (Hopkins), and Equity insisted that from then on, the role had to be played by an American. The union threatened to veto Burton. Bloomgarden turned to his friend Bernie Jacobs, who negotiated Equity contracts. Could he reason with Equity?

Equity is an unruly union. Key decisions are made by its council, which consists of seventy-five actors (many, it's often said, who are unemployed). When a producer goes to Equity to make an appeal, he appears before the seventy-five actors and must field all their questions and suffer through their soapbox speeches. As one producer says, "They're actors. They love the sound of their voice." Jacobs privately called Equity "an entire galaxy of lunatics."

But on the day he appeared before the council in support of Richard Burton, Jacobs, accompanied by Phil Smith, treated the actors with deference. He argued that Burton as an international star would extend the life of *Equus*, providing work for the American actors who were in the cast. A journeyman actor at the back of the room raised a hand. "Mr. Jacobs," he said, "why are you hiring an English actor when many of us in this room could play this part?" Jacobs replied, "Well, sir, I'm sure many of you could play this part very well. In fact, I'm sure some of you could play it even better. But that is not what the public wants. The public wants to see Richard Burton play this part." Jacobs carried the day, and Equity approved Burton.

But there was more trouble. Burton had not been on stage in eight years. His recent movies—*The Voyage, Klansman, Massacre in Rome*—were box office disappointments, and he was in the midst of breaking up with Elizabeth Taylor for the second time. He'd cut back on his drinking, allowing himself an "occasional glass of very special Burgundy," as he told the *New York Times*. But he was weary and wondered if he "could command the attention of the audience as I once did." Still, he told the paper, "It was quite essential that I should go back to the stage now. . . . I thought, if I don't take the plunge now, I probably would never go back."

But he was not on his game. Dexter thought he'd become lazy. Burton admitted to Shaffer he was "terrified." He kept saying, "I'm such a fake." Shaffer thought he was "full of self-loathing." Burton assured Dexter, whom he did not like, that his performance would come together once he got in front of an audience. Dexter decided to test him. Burton's first official performance was on a Monday. The theater world would be watching. Dexter told him he needed a trial run. So at the Saturday matinee before Burton's scheduled debut, Perkins stepped aside so he could play the role. The press was not tipped off. "I've never been so bloody scared in my life," Burton later told the *Times*. "I was trembling."

Over the loudspeaker the stage manager announced, "At this performance the role of Martin Dysart, usually played by Anthony Perkins"—the audience groaned—"will be played by Richard Burton." The audience roared.

But it was not a performance for the ages. Burton raced through his first big speech "as if it were Noel Coward," he later said. He was shaky on his lines and unsure of where he was supposed to be on stage during his scenes. After the performance, Dexter marched backstage and said to him, "Well, dear, you've had your chance in front of an audience. What are you going to do now?" Shaffer went back to see him as well. When he knocked on the dressing room door, Burton opened it and said, "You will never see that performance again." And then he shut the door.

That weekend, Dexter, Shaffer, and Burton's agent, Robert Lantz, moved into Burton's hotel suite, rearranged the furniture so that it resembled the set, and drilled him on the play. Burton had memorized the speeches, which he called "arias," but "not the other bits." By "the other bits," Shaffer wanted to know, "do you mean my play?"

Fueled by endless cups of coffee, they ran the play again and again (Shaffer played the boy) until Burton knew his lines. Comfortable in the role, he made his debut on February 26, 1976, to mixed reviews. Clive Barnes wrote, "This is unabashedly a star performance. He is not one's idea of a man who would be a moderately failed psychiatrist . . . yet somehow his larger-than-life approach works." Martin Gottfried, in the *New York Post*, was not impressed. He called the performance "self-centered," "mannered," and "superficial." Gottfried concluded, "Inactivity has caused his formidable talents to go to flab." But Walter Kerr, in the Sunday *Times*, delivered a money review: "The actor's performance in *Equus* seems to me to be the best work of his life."

Despite the mixed notices, audiences flocked to the play. Weekly grosses had been slipping under Perkins. They now soared above $50,000. Jacobs, knowing Burton would be a draw, pressed the producers to raise ticket prices. Jacobs thought ticket prices, which had not risen much in several years, were artificially low. Orchestra seats for a musical at the time were about fifteen dollars; for a straight play, nine fifty. Jacobs pushed for a fifteen-dollar ticket for Burton, the highest ever for a play. The public snapped them up. When Burton left, and Perkins returned to the role, the producers wanted to lower the price for fear he wouldn't sell at fifteen dollars a head. But Jacobs held the line. The top price to *Equus* was now fifteen dollars. And it wasn't coming down. "If the public wants the show, they'll pay for it," he said. "And now they're used to a fifteen-dollar ticket." From that point on, ticket prices began to rise on Broadway. But Jacobs was right; the public would pay just about any price to see a hit show. (They'd been paying huge markups to scalpers for years.) Anything less than a hit probably wouldn't be around long, even with lower prices, Jacobs thought. And the higher the ticket, the more money there would be for everybody, especially theater owners.

Equus ran three years on Broadway and sent out two national touring companies. Produced all over the world, it set box office records everywhere it opened. Running two years at the Plymouth Theatre, it provided the Shuberts much-needed cash. Many years later, at an event honoring Vanessa Redgrave, Gerald Schoenfeld introduced a group of young reporters to Peter Shaffer. "I want you to meet," he said to them, "the man who saved Shubert."

CHAPTER ELEVEN

The Paintman Cometh

In the spring of 1974, as the Shubert Organization and the producers of *Equus* began planning the Broadway production, State Attorney General Louis Lefkowitz attacked Schoenfeld and Jacobs. Prompted by Larry Shubert's complaint, the attorney general's office had spent a year investigating the Shubert Foundation and its board. On March 28, Lefkowitz filed suit in Surrogate Court against Schoenfeld and Jacobs, charging them with "conflicts of interest" and "self-dealing," as well as siphoning off hundreds of thousands of dollars from the Shubert Foundation in legal fees that were "grossly excessive, unjustified and unreasonable." The foundation's money, Lefkowitz charged, should have gone to charities rather than the lawyers' pockets. He accused them of taking nearly $550,000 in legal fees from various Shubert entities in the years after J. J. Shubert's death—but without submitting proper bills. He noted that, in addition to those fees, both men received salaries of $173,000. He objected to their photocopying bill—$17,534 over ten years—and the $15,092 they spent renovating their offices above the Shubert Theatre. He also noted they didn't pay rent for those offices. "Such use of rent-free space constitutes self-dealing and a conflict of interest in that [Schoenfeld and Jacobs] were at all . . . times . . . attorneys for and executors of [J. J. Shubert's] estate."

In all, Lefkowitz lodged sixty-six objections to the way Schoenfeld and Jacobs handled Shubert business. He attacked Schoenfeld for putting his mother-in-law, Mabel Miller, on the payroll from 1965 to

1972 (she received $31,083). Her compensation was "unwarranted and unjustified," the attorney general wrote. He also criticized the lawyers for representing theater producers who worked with the Shubert Organization—an obvious "conflict of interest," the attorney general noted.

Ironically, given the fact that his complaint set off the attorney general's investigation, Lawrence Shubert Lawrence Jr. came in for some stinging criticism as well. Lefkowitz excoriated him for taking $1 million in salaries from 1965 to 1972 and for using foundation money for a chauffeur-driven Cadillac limousine, trips to London, flowers for "Shubert women," and regular meals at Sardi's (nothing was said about his bar bill, which must have been considerably larger than Schoenfeld and Jacobs's photocopying bill). The attorney general noted Larry Shubert was once reimbursed $252.38 for a hotel bill, though the purpose of this business expense was never declared. And he complained that Stuttering M-M-Murray Helwitz remained on the Shubert payroll despite his conviction in 1965 for taking $70,000 in ice. Helwitz, Lefkowitz said, had earned $132,000 at Shubert since he'd gotten out of jail.

Irving Goldman's name did not appear in the suit. But Lefkowitz objected to a bill for $1,030,583 paid to the Campbell Paint Company in Flushing for painting Shubert theaters. As *New York Post* reporter Joseph Berger pointed out, the Campbell Paint Company obtained its paint from a company called Gothic Color, which was owned by . . . Irving Goldman.

The paintman cometh.

In the weeks ahead, Berger, a tough and tenacious investigative reporter, scrutinized Goldman. Berger found out the Campbell Paint Company was hired to paint at least three Shubert theaters in cities other than New York, even though it would have been cheaper to hire local painters. Berger also discovered that Goldman's paint company had been listed in *Playbills* in the 1960s, but according to a Shubert employee, the listing was changed to the Campbell Paint Company because the name "Gothic" would have made Goldman's self-dealing "too obvious." George Campbell Jr., the owner of the company, refused to comment. But Berger noted Campbell had pled guilty in 1967 in a conspiracy-bribery case involving "rigged bids" on $42 million worth of painting contracts from the city Housing Authority. Berger also reported that Goldman family members received commissions from Campbell totaling thousands of dollars.

But the most explosive charge against Goldman and the Shuberts was made by Robert Brustein, the head of the Yale School of Drama. Brustein told the *New York Times* that Schoenfeld approached him in 1972 with an offer to supply paint to the school at a lower price through Goldman's company. Yale bought Goldman's paint, but only for a short period of time. The Shubert's annual grant to Yale of $30,000 was slashed to $10,000 because Goldman complained the school wasn't buying his paint anymore, Brustein said. Schoenfeld denied he had anything to do with Goldman's paint dealings. Goldman didn't speak to the reporter. But a woman who answered the phone in his Shubert Alley office barked, "He's not here and doesn't want to talk to you," and then slammed down the receiver.

For reporters, a "no comment" often means a "license to kill." The *Times* began its own investigation of Irving Goldman. Reporter Ralph Blumenthal wrote that, in addition to Yale, several other university drama departments saw their Shubert Foundation grants canceled or slashed when they didn't buy enough paint from Goldman. Catholic University received $2,500 annually from the foundation. But at a grant meeting in 1971, Goldman said that Father Gilbert Hartke, head of the drama department, "never bought a quart of paint from me—he doesn't get a dime." The grant was canceled. Officials at three other schools—the University of Indiana, the University of Texas at Austin, and the University of Kansas—told the *Times* that, upon receiving grants from the Shubert Foundation, Goldman told them of his connection to the Gothic paint company. "He identified himself first as the president of Gothic Color, then brought up the Shubert money," one university official told the *Times*. After receiving their grants, all three university drama departments began buying paint from Gothic. Goldman, another official said, was pleased with the arrangement. As for the situation at Yale, a professor from the university ran into Goldman at a theater party in New York. Goldman brought up Yale's application for a grant and said, "If they can't buy paint from us, why should I bother with them?" [1]

The *Times* also reported that Nicholas Scoppetta, New York's commissioner of investigation, warned Abe Beame against making Goldman cultural affairs commissioner because of rumors of Goldman's unsavory business connections. Scoppetta was concerned about Goldman's connection to a company called New York Sportservice, Inc., a sports concession conglomerate run out of Buffalo, New York, by Louis Jacobs. Goldman represented the company's interests in New York City during the 1960s. In 1972, a congressional investigation into Mafia involvement in professional sports turned up a thicket of underworld connections to Louis Jacobs and his empire, including secret ownership of the Frontier Casino in Las Vegas. Jacobs's partners in the casino included two high-ranking members of a Detroit Mafia family. Jacobs died in 1968, but after the congressional investigation, *Sports Illustrated* put him on its cover, posthumously, under the headline THE GODFATHER OF SPORTS.

Scoppetta, the *Times* reported, presented his concerns about Goldman to Beame. But the mayor dismissed them. Goldman, he said, was his close friend and a loyal supporter. So long as he'd done nothing illegal, he would be the city's cultural affairs commissioner.

With the *Times* now on the trail, the *Post*'s Berger stepped up his investigations. In a series of articles, he rehashed Goldman's friendship with Surrogate Court Judge DiFalco and the alleged fixing of John Shubert's estate back in 1963. Berger also explored Goldman's involvement with the Jola Candy Company, which supplied candy to subway vending machines. Jola, which was named after Goldman's daughters, Joy and Laurie, also collected 17 percent of the gross receipts from photo booths throughout the subway system. Berger reported that Goldman did not reveal his business connections to the Transit Authority when city officials vetted him for the job of cultural affairs commissioner. "Failure to answer such questions could be grounds for dismissal," Berger wrote. The reporter also uncovered more ties to the mobbed-up Sportservice, Inc. Goldman's candy company was a subsidiary of a company called Interborough News Company, Inc., which owned vending machines throughout the subway system. And Interborough, Berger reported, was controlled by Sportservice, whose business associates included such pillars of the community as Gerardo Catena, head of the New Jersey Mafia; Raymond Patriarca, head of

the New England Mafia; Moe Dalitz, a Cleveland mobster; and Jimmy
Plumeri, a New York loan shark and a capo of the Lucchese crime
family, murdered in 1971.

Berger's articles on Goldman's murky business dealings appeared
in the *Post* almost daily. The reporter discovered that trucks with the
name Gothic Color emblazoned on their sides made stops at subway stations to pick up "canvas bags bulging with coins." The coins
were then taken to Interborough's offices, located at the Fourteenth
Street and Eighth Avenue subway station in a "closed-off passageway."
Pressed to explain why his paint trucks were collecting bags of coins
for Interborough, Goldman said he was doing it "as a favor, an accom-
modation."[2] Goldman railed against Berger in private. Every time one
of the reporter's stories appeared in the paper, Goldman yelled, "I'll
fuck him! I'll fuck him where he breathes!"

Berger also investigated Goldman's pet charities, which received
tens of thousands of dollars in grants from the Shubert Foundation.
The City of Hope hospital in Los Angeles, for instance, received
nearly $110,000 in 1972 from the foundation. Goldman was national
vice president of City of Hope and hosted lavish fund-raising dinners in New York attended by city and state officials, including Mayor
Beame and Goldman's old crony, Judge Samuel DiFalco. A source told
Berger, "The Shubert Foundation had no favorites to any marked degree. Irving Goldman came in with the favorites. The dam was broken."[3]

Meanwhile, Schoenfeld and Jacobs, new to the spotlight, were rattled by Lefkowitz's charges. They hired their old friend James Vaughan,
the lawyer who advised them for years, to defend them in the press.
The two men, Vaughan told reporters, "were the most qualified theatrical men in town." Their "excessive legal fees," he said, were justified
by the work they did for J. J. Shubert's estate and the Shubert Foundation. "Lawyers have a claim for compensation," Vaughan said. "The
question is whether they were reasonably compensated. I believe they
were."[4] As for the rent-free office space, Vaughan said J. J. Shubert had
given them the offices above the Shubert Theatre years ago. As Phil
Smith would say decades later, J. J. gave them free offices "precisely
because he never paid them very much." As for the various fees and

bills they submitted over the years, Vaughan noted, pointedly, that the IRS had scrutinized Shubert operations over the years (including that $17,534 photocopying bill) and had not raised a red flag. "They are in a goldfish bowl as far as the IRS is concerned," Vaughan told the *New York Post*.

Mabel Miller, Schoenfeld's mother-in-law, was indeed on the payroll—but she worked, Vaughan said.

"I got her the job!" Phil Smith said. "She processed mail orders at the Majestic Theatre. Jerry called me up and asked if I could find a job for his mother-in-law—she needed something to do. We had the job at the Majestic, so I gave it to her. She wasn't making much money—maybe ninety dollars a week. Not a huge sum. And she was very good."

Vaughan glossed over the awkward fact that convicted iceman Murray Helwitz still had a job, saying that the Shuberts "don't regard a man who has committed a crime and has been punished for it as an outcast." [5]

Lefkowitz returned fire. He demanded that all six board members of the Shubert Foundation—Schoenfeld, Jacobs, Goldman, Eckie Shubert, Irving Wall, and Lawrence Shubert Lawrence Jr. (on the board in name only now)—step down until the charges of misconduct were investigated. In the meantime, he would appoint a seven-member board to oversee Shubert business. If they did not resign, Lefkowitz threatened legal action to remove them.

Franklin Weissberg was a young lawyer whose show business clients included director Hal Prince. He was also well connected in Republican political circles, having worked as Mayor Lindsay's consultant on the performing arts. Schoenfeld and Jacobs invited him to their offices. "We are in a terrible pissing match with Louis Lefkowitz," Jacobs told him. "We all need lawyers and we thought it would be a good idea to have a Republican in the mix." Lefkowitz, a Republican, was friendly with Weissberg.

"I liked Louis, he was a very good politician," Weissberg said. "He was an indefatigable campaigner and the first attorney general who styled himself the people's lawyer. But he had an unsavory past. He was a liquor lawyer, and he remained a liquor lawyer at heart."

Schoenfeld and Jacobs also knew of the attorney general's "unsavory past." They'd been told that, as head of the Alcohol Beverage Control Board, Lefkowitz was notorious for demanding bribes to grant liquor licenses. If a bar or restaurant owner needed a license, he would meet Lefkowitz at his office. Lefkowitz would open the bottom drawer of his desk and point at it. The applicant was expected to drop an envelope of cash into the drawer. No words were exchanged.

Schoenfeld and Jacobs mapped out their strategy against the attorney general over dinners at Wally's & Joseph's steakhouse on Forty-Ninth Street. They learned there, through a lawyer tapped into Lefkowitz's office, why the attorney general was going after them. A classic machine politician, Lefkowitz loved to dispense patronage. Seats on the board of the Shubert Foundation were plum patronage, with such perks as tickets to Broadway shows, opening night invitations, and control of a large pot of grant money. Lefkowitz, Schoenfeld and Jacobs were told, wanted to stack the board with his friends and supporters. "This is what Louis wants," their source told them, "and what Louis wants, Louis gets." The tip emboldened them.

They toughed it out in public, but the attacks took a toll in private.

"Jerry was falling apart," Weissberg recalled. "The investigation was horrible. Louis went after them with guns blazing."

Phil Smith said, "It was a tough time, no question about it. But the good part was that, for whatever reason, the days or weeks that Bernie got weak and upset and started to bury his neck in his chest, Jerry would get strong. Then there would be a period where Jerry got very weak, and wanted to back down, and Bernie would get strong. It was like a switch. When one went out, the other went on."

Jacobs's only daughter, Sally, having heard her friends at school talking about the mud being flung at her father in the papers, asked him, "Daddy, are you a crook?" Not long after, Jacobs traveled to London to see some plays. He checked into a room at the Berkeley Hotel with a balcony overlooking Hyde Park. Phil Smith was in the room next door. At dinner one night, Jacobs confessed, "Phil, this is terrible. My children think I'm a criminal. You know, I looked out from the terrace and I thought about jumping."

Smith replied, "Bernie, that is the act of a crazy man. You are not crazy."

"No," Jacobs said, "but I gave it a thought."

"Well, thank heavens your sanity has returned to you," Smith said.

Back in New York, Schoenfeld and Jacobs informed Lefkowitz they had no intention of stepping down from the board of the Shubert Foundation. "You propose that seven new directors be appointed by your office as the sole disinterested party," Milton Gould, another lawyer who was defending them, wrote, "I respectfully suggest that your office is not the 'sole disinterested party.'"[6]

A different lawyer represented each board member. Weissberg had been given the choice of representing either Rocky Wall or Irving Goldman. "I made a couple of phone calls about Irving Goldman," Weissberg said. "And I said, 'No way.' So I represented Rocky. And he became a close friend."

Rocky Wall, who had been bayoneted in the neck on the battlefields of Italy, "was not a man to be trifled with," Weissberg said. "He was not afraid of anyone."

Lefkowitz's point man for the Shubert battle was a ferocious, Javert-like prosecutor named Maurice H. Nadjari. He had thin, tight lips and coal-black eyes that blazed with contempt for his targets. A man was guilty until proven innocent, he believed. Nadjari was sworn in as special prosecutor in 1972. Four years later, he had spent $14 million of taxpayer money to bring indictments against eleven judges. Not one was convicted. He obtained the indictments through "inaccurate testimony" and "illegal wiretaps," reported *Village Voice* columnist Jack Newfield. "He ruined careers with baseless charges," Newfield wrote, adding, "He sees the world in black and white, without doubts, without ambiguities. He is obsessive and without a sense of proportion."

In an infamous speech to a group of lawyers, Nadjari compared the thrill of hearing a jury foreman say "guilty" to having sex. One prominent criminal attorney told Newfield, "In my opinion, Nadjari is mentally disturbed."[7]

During the Shubert battle, Nadjari summoned Rocky Wall and Frank Weissberg to his office.

"You guys are all in a lot of trouble," he told Wall. "Unless we get this resolved, we're going to bring you all down."

Wall looked him in the eye and said, "You can do anything you want to me, but you're not going to get me off that board because I've done nothing wrong, and I am not afraid of you. And if I'm the last person left on that board, I'll reconstitute it and you can go fuck yourself."

With the battle against the attorney general in full tilt, the Broadway community rallied around Schoenfeld and Jacobs. Eugene Wolsk, a low-key producer and general manager, called Phil Smith. He had an idea. What if, he asked, we bring together a group of prominent Broadway people, go down to Lefkowitz's office, and make our case for Bernie and Jerry? "I think that would help," Smith said.

Wolsk pulled together an impressive slate, including producers David Merrick, Hal Prince, Elizabeth I. McCann, and Robert Whitehead; union leaders Solly Pernick (stagehands), Max Arons (musicians), and Lloyd Richards (directors and choreographers); and the theatrical lawyer John Wharton.

Alex Cohen was at his house in the south of France when Wolsk called. Not one to miss an opportunity to make a splash in the press, Cohen told the *Times*, "I had a distress call when I was in France"—and then took credit for organizing the flotilla of theater people.[8] Cohen always claimed that he hired a fleet of limousines to ferry everyone to the attorney general's office from Shubert Alley, and that he spoke for the group, convincing Lefkowitz to lay off.

"I saved them," he once told a reporter.

In fact, the group traveled downtown in a bus. And the person who spoke for the group was John Wharton, founder of Paul, Weiss, Rifkind, Wharton & Garrison. On the bus before the meeting, Wharton told the group, "When we go in there, nobody speaks but me." It must have been difficult for such a colorful cast of characters to hold their tongues, but, according to Liz McCann, they did.

Lefkowitz received the delegation in his baronial office. After brief introductions, Wharton spoke. "Gerald Schoenfeld and Bernard Jacobs deserve to be praised, not hunted," he said. "They are trying to do a good job. They are trying to take this business and save it. They are trying, Louis, to pull it out of the garbage. They shouldn't be punished for that. They should be supported, and as you can see from all of us here today, they have the full support of the theater community."

"John was wonderful," Liz McCann recalled years later. "He knew how to talk to Lefkowitz. I'm not sure Louis would have listened to a bunch of Broadway producers, but he could not ignore John Wharton."

Lefkowitz refused to comment publicly on the meeting, but the producers, now off Wharton's leash, talked to reporters.

"This is the first time in my whole nineteen-year career that I've seen all of these people in one room with such a display of unanimity," David Merrick pronounced. "I went on behalf of Mr. Schoenfeld and Mr. Jacobs. Their conduct has always been absolutely impeccable and honest."

"This is the best management of the Shuberts and we have no complaint with the board or with the people in the organization with whom we do business," Alex Cohen said.[9]

Max Arons, head of the musicians union, declared, "In comparison with years ago, this is the best management of all. There is no question of dipsy-doodle as twenty-five years ago, when musicians felt they had to give back something of what they made to theater managements. Mr. Schoenfeld and Mr. Jacobs negotiate contracts with us. Everything is put on the table, there are no deals. It's healthy, a million percent improvement."

Nobody, though, said anything in support of Irving Goldman. The *Times* reported: "Broadway's major concern was with the retention of Mr. Jacobs and Mr. Schoenfeld, with whom Broadway theater people work on a day-to-day basis. Most said they had had little contact with Mr. Goldman."[10]

"Irving Goldman? The paint man?" Liz McCann said years later. "Who would speak up for him? Certainly not John Wharton."

The meeting had an impact. Lefkowitz cooled his investigatory zeal. "After that meeting, the sting sort of went out of the whole thing," Smith said.

Lefkowitz never attempted to remove the board. Schoenfeld and Jacobs outmaneuvered him by expanding the board themselves. They appointed three new members—John Kluge, founder of Metromedia and destined to become, in the 1980s, the richest man in America;

Helen Hollerith, a member of the Pew family, which owned Sun Oil Company; and Lee Seidler, a professor of economics and accounting at New York University.

"That was a very smart move," said Foley Vaughan, whose father represented Schoenfeld and Jacobs. "These were three people with impeccable credentials. Why would they agree to accept an appointment like that if they were going into a snake's nest? And, now, if Louis wanted to remove the board, he would have to remove three people about which there was no controversy. He would have looked stupid."

Kluge, Hollerith, and Seidler would remain on the Shubert board until their deaths.

Lefkowitz's battle with Schoenfeld and Jacobs ground on for another three years, but slowly and with little publicity. In the end, on April 13, 1977, there was a settlement. Schoenfeld, Jacobs, and other lawyers and executors of J. J. Shubert's estate, including Morgan Guaranty, agreed to reduce outstanding claims of $7 million in fees and commissions—claims that reached as far back as J. J.'s death in 1963—to $5 million. The $2 million difference was funneled into the Shubert Foundation, then doled out in grants to theatrical causes. Lefkowitz dropped all charges against the lawyers and the executors. He called the decision "fair." [11] Others said it was just a way of saving face.

Schoenfeld and Jacobs had battled with one of the most powerful men in New York State—and won. They were now "the Shuberts."

Irving Goldman remained a target, a nice, fat, juicy one. Lefkowitz unleashed Nadjari on him. Nadjari indicted him on charges of defrauding the Transit Authority by inflating invoices from his candy company. Nadjari also indicted him on a kickback scheme involving $1 million worth of contracts to the Campbell Paint Company. Goldman, Nadjari claimed, received a 50 percent kickback. Nadjari then indicted Goldman on a bribery scheme, accusing him of giving $4,350 to a witness to flee to Mexico to avoid a subpoena. (The witness, Anne Levinson, ran off to Mexico City but was brought back to New York by federal agents.) Goldman tried to hang on to his perch at the Shubert Foundation, but by now he had become an embarrassment to the company.

The board forced Goldman out on March 19, 1975. He also stepped down as cultural affairs commissioner. He exited the stage with a ringing protestation of innocence: "The charges against me are false. And I will fight them. And I am sure that I will be exonerated." [12] As usual, Nadjari overreached. Some of the indictments were overturned. At one point, a judge declared a mistrial. Irving Goldman was never found guilty of any crimes. By 1980, his health began to fail. Nadjari, his pursuer, had been fired by Lefkowitz in 1976 after a series of controversial prosecutions. Lefkowitz himself left office in 1979. His successor, Robert Abrams, had little interest in hounding an ailing old man. Irving Goldman died, at seventy-three, in 1983. The *New York Times* didn't even run an obituary.

"Irving escaped by dying," Phil Smith said.*

---

* One afternoon in 1995, I got a crash course in the history of the Shubert empire from Gerald Schoenfeld. Sitting behind his grand desk in his elegant office above the Shubert Theatre, he described what it was like to work for J. J. Shubert; he talked about the coup against Larry Shubert; and he recalled, with a pained expression, his bruising battle with Louis Lefkowitz. But when I brought up Irving Goldman, Schoenfeld looked at me and said, only half-jokingly I thought, "Michael, that is not a name we mention in these hallowed precincts."

CHAPTER TWELVE

The Jockey

Though engulfed in scandal at the close of 1974, Schoenfeld and Jacobs still had a job to do—find shows to fill empty theaters. The Plymouth had *Equus*, but several Shubert theaters were dark. And then there was a phone call for Bernie Jacobs. It was Michael Bennett, a thirty-four-year-old talented, charismatic, and ambitious choreographer. Jacobs had gotten to know him while Bennett was choreographing *Coco*, a musical by André Previn and Alan Jay Lerner about Coco Chanel, starring Katharine Hepburn. It wasn't a good show but it ran from 1969 to 1970 at the Mark Hellinger Theatre on the strength of Hepburn's name. Though Bennett was billed as the choreographer, everybody knew he had taken over the direction from Michael Benthall, who could not handle the star. Bennett could. He ran into Jacobs at Wally's & Joseph's one night and told him, "I've finally found a way of working with Kate Hepburn. If I want her to go stage left, I tell her to go stage right!"

On the phone that day, Bennett told Jacobs he was working on a new musical called *A Chorus Line*. He wanted to know if he and his collaborators—composer Marvin Hamlisch and lyricist Edward Kleban—could come up to the office and play some songs from the show for him. Of course, Jacobs said. He always had time for a talented person with a new show.

In the cab to Shubert Alley, Bennett told Hamlisch, "Just play a couple of the funny songs. Don't do anything too esoteric." The funniest song they had was called "Dance 10; Looks 3," about a dancer who surgically enhances her body to kick-start her career. Bennett, Hamlisch, and Kleban squeezed into the tiny elevator at the side of the Shubert Theatre that took them up to the executive offices. In the reception room was a grand piano that "looked like it hadn't been played in twenty-five years," Hamlisch said. "It was covered in dust." [1]

Hamlisch lifted the lid on the keyboard and placed his fingers on the cracked yellowed keys. He hit the first note of "Tits and Ass," and one of the legs on the piano gave way. The piano fell on its side with a crash. Jacobs, Bennett, Hamlisch, and Smith scrambled to lift it back in place.

My God, this is how we get money for a Broadway show? Hamlisch thought. But he played the song, and this time the piano didn't fall on its side. Jacobs wanted to hear more. "Marvin played through the whole score for us that afternoon," Phil Smith said—"I Hope I Get It," "I Can Do That," "At the Ballet," "What I Did for Love," "One."

Afterward, Bennett met privately with Jacobs and explained the show to him. It was based on hours of interviews he'd done with dancers in Broadway shows. He'd been working on it for nearly a year down at the Public Theater, where Joe Papp had given him space and money. But the day before Papp had said to him, "I'm going to have to close you down after next week because we're out of money." Bennett looked at Jacobs and said, "You can have the show, Bernie."

Jacobs thought for a moment and said, "No. We could never do that to Joe. We could never do that."

Bennett was crushed. "But Joe isn't going to do any more for me. It's going to die right here."

"No, no," Jacobs replied. "We'll talk to Joe and we'll see what we can work out. We'll take care of things."

Bennett floated out of the office. Between the Public Theater and the Shubert Organization, his show would go on.

Jacobs and Smith weren't sure what the show was. They liked the songs, but the idea of a musical about Broadway dancers, based on what sounded like group therapy sessions, was vague, at best. But Jacobs was learning to bet on the jockeys, and Michael Bennett was one hell of a jockey.

•   •   •

He was born Michael "Mickey" Bennett DiFiglia on April 8, 1943, in
Buffalo, New York. His mother, Helen, was a secretary for Sears, his father, Salvatore, a machinist at a Chevrolet plant. Salvatore was also an
inveterate gambler who was usually in hock to low-level members of
the Magaddino crime family, known as "The Arm," that controlled upstate New York. The Bennett household was an unhappy one, strapped
for cash due to Salvatore's gambling debts. Helen was bitter and depressed by the shabbiness of her life. At the age of two, Bennett found
his escape. He began "to dance around the living room," as a line from
A Chorus Line goes, to the music on the radio.

By the time he was ten, Bennett was so good he began earning
money dancing freestyle at bar mitzvahs, weddings, even on street
corners. When he wasn't dancing, he was choreographing, using his
brother Frank's marbles as dancers and creating patterns for imagi-
nary dance routines. He devoured *Dance* magazine, especially articles
about Jerome Robbins, who became his idol. Robbins's *West Side Story*,
which opened on Broadway in 1957 and which Bennett saw on tour
in Buffalo, was his favorite show. There is a home movie of him doing
the "Dance at the Gym" number from the show in the driveway of the
family's tiny one-story house at 181 Florida Street. A snippet of it can
be seen in the excellent documentary *Every Little Step*, about the 2006
revival of *A Chorus Line*. Bennett, eight years old, performs the number
flawlessly and with such intensity it's clear that every part of his lean
body bends toward Broadway.

Though Salvatore derided his son's sissy pirouetting, he liked the
extra income it brought in. He began pocketing most of it, saying it
would help with household expenses. He lost it at the track and the
card tables. The searing event of Bennett's childhood—one that would
haunt him throughout his life and, when he began to use cocaine heavily, cause him extreme paranoia—took place one day in the kitchen of
the house on Florida Street. Salvatore was heavily in debt to a local
mobster. But he had a plan: He would sell his son's talent to the Mafia.
He invited two local mobsters to the house and ordered Bennett to
dance for them. "The kid whirled, spun, kicked, slid, turned, a midget
dancer," Kevin Kelly writes in *One Singular Sensation*, his gossipy biography of Bennett. Salvatore offered a deal. His kid was going to make
some serious money as a dancer one day, and he offered a percentage

of Bennett's future income to the mob. The mob passed. It dealt in gambling, prostitution, racketeering, and extortion, not in sissy boys who knew every step to Agnes de Mille's dream ballet from *Oklahoma!*

In 1960, at Melody Fair, an amphitheater in North Tonawanda, New York, that presented musicals starring veterans like Van Johnson, Ruby Keeler, and John Raitt, Bennett met Jack Lenny, a onetime performer who had become a manager. Lenny saw Bennett, then sixteen, perform. They met after the show. Lenny said Bennett should consider trying his luck in New York. Early in his junior year of high school, Bennett received a telegram from Lenny informing him that Jerome Robbins was auditioning dancers for a European company of *West Side Story.*

"I went to my locker and I took everything out of it and I left," Bennett recalled. "And I got on a bus to New York and I said, 'I am not coming back. I am getting this job, and I am not coming back.'"[2]

He got the job, playing Baby John, and went off to Europe. Bob Avian was also in the show. He and Bennett became good friends. Bennett began to think of Avian as his older brother, the first member of a surrogate family he would assemble around himself. Bennett could not function without a family, and since his real one was a source of pain and unhappiness, he had to create a new one. The family would expand as he became more and more successful, and there would be bitter fallings out. But Avian would always be there.

After the *West Side Story* tour, Bennett returned to New York and began making the rounds as a Broadway "gypsy," the name for chorus kids who float from show to show. His talent was obvious, and he never lacked for work, appearing in the choruses of *Subways Are for Sleeping, Here's Love,* and *Bajour.*

Along the way Bennett was picking up dancers he would use in shows he would choreograph one day—Baayork Lee, Leland Palmer, Sandy Roveta. After *Bajour* (a musical, ironically, about real gypsies) flopped, Bennett took a job dancing on the TV show *Hullabaloo,* where he met Donna McKechnie, who would become his muse, lover, and, briefly, wife.

"If you ever figure out where I fit into the family," she once said, "let me know. I never did."

McKechnie, perhaps the greatest Broadway dancer of her generation, remembers bouncing around the set of *Hullabaloo* and asking Bennett what he wanted to do for the rest of his life. "I'm going to be a choreographer," he said, while doing the jerk.[3]

He got his chance in 1966 with *A Joyful Noise*, a Broadway musical about hillbillies based on the novel *The Insolent Breed* by Borden Deal.

"I was having lunch with Ed Padula, who wrote the book for the musical, and he said they needed a choreographer," Norman Twain, the producer of *Bajour*, said. "I suggested Michael. Ed wanted to know if he was ready. 'I think so,' I said. 'You'd better try him. Somebody's going to.'"

While casting *A Joyful Noise*, Bennett met another person who would become an important part of his family. Tommy Tune, from Wichita Falls, Texas, arrived in New York in 1965 to become a Broadway dancer. At six feet, six inches, he towered above every Broadway gypsy in town. After a stint in the short-lived musical *Baker Street*, Tune went to an audition for a show that was going to open Caesars Palace in Las Vegas. The audition was held at the Variety Arts, a seven-story building next to the Lunt-Fontanne Theatre on Forty-Sixth Street that was a beehive of rehearsal studios. Bob Fosse had a key to the building and could come and go as he pleased. He could often be found in the middle of the night on the top floor, working out dance routines. The Variety Arts was at the heart of the Broadway theater world in the 1960s. When it burned down in the 1970s "we lost our center," said Tune. Presiding over this buzzing showbiz honeycomb was the switchboard operator, who also functioned as an unofficial casting director.

Tune recalled, "You'd walk in and she'd say, 'You! You're a tall dark swarthy type, Peter Gennaro is looking for tall dark swarthy types for his new show, *Bajour*. Get over there now!' The minute you walked in the door, she knew where to send you."

On this particular day, Tune was in the elevator with a small, wiry man wearing a baseball cap. Michael Bennett looked up at him and said, flirtatiously, "Well, who are you?"

"I said, 'My name's Tommy Tune. Do you think I should change it?' I always asked everybody that. The minute I got to New York I asked everybody that question. 'Cause I knew it was catchy, but I also knew it was unbelievably unbelievable. And he said, 'Not if you want to go around being Tommy Tune.' And you know, I never asked the question again."

Tune told Bennett he was auditioning for the show at Caesars Palace. "Well, stop on three when you're done," Bennett said as the elevator door opened on the third floor and he got out.

Bennett dispatched his assistant on *A Joyful Noise*, Leland Palmer, to peek through the door at Tune's audition. Tune figured out he'd been spied on when he stopped on three to see Bennett.

Palmer asked him, "Well, did you get it?"

"Yes, and I'm going to take it," he said. "It's good money."

"Oh, come on," Palmer said. "You're gonna want to do this?" She stood up and executed the combination Tune had just done for the Vegas people.

"She mocked it," he said. "She made me realize how lousy it was."

"Why don't you want to do this?" Palmer said, and turning to Bennett added, "Let's show him."

"And they did a combination that I could do for you right now," Tune recalled. "I had never seen anything like it. Michael had taken 'street' and 'western,' because *Joyful Noise* was set in Tennessee, and put them together. It was brilliant."

"Come with us," Bennett said.

Tune turned down the job at Caesars Palace.

A Joyful Noise opened on December 15, 1966, at the Mark Hellinger Theatre, and closed nine days later. The critics hated it but praised Bennett's choreography, and he became Broadway's leading Mr. Fix It, the man you called when your show was in trouble. Bennett worked faster than just about anybody. He could take a lackluster number and turn it into a crowd-pleaser. He "doctored," as the saying on Broadway goes, *By Jupiter*, *Your Own Thing*, and *How Now, Dow Jones*.

At night he would stay up till the wee hours in his small West Seventy-Ninth Street apartment, thinking about what he wanted most: total control. Total control not just over a show but over Broadway itself.

"He saw himself in an office building, the highest floor of an office building in New York, looking down on all of Broadway," Tune said. "And if you wanted a choreographer, you had to come to him. And he would say, 'This is the right person for that show. You can have him. But only for this show.' You had to come to him before you could do anything. That was his fantasy."

Although Bennett projected confidence in public, in private he battled periods of depression, self-doubt, and paranoia, a state he called "Black Friday." When Black Friday came around, he could barely function. Hired to doctor the musical *How Now, Dow Jones*, Bennett stopped showing up to rehearsals one week. Charles Blackwell, the stage manager, took aside Tune, who was playing a waiter, and told him to find Bennett. "We need him here at ten a.m. tomorrow," Blackwell said.

At 8:30 the next morning Tune, who lived near Bennett, went to Bennett's apartment and found him in bed with the covers over his head. "I can't do it," he said. "I can't face them anymore." Tune put a wet cloth on his face, hauled him out of bed, turned on the shower, and pushed him in. "I don't want to go," Bennett protested. In the cab on the way to rehearsal, Bennett curled up into a ball and said, "I can't face them, I can't face them." As the cab pulled up to the Variety Arts rehearsal studios, Tune said, "Come on, Michael. This is going to be a great day."

Outside the door of the rehearsal studio, Bennett closed his eyes, took a deep breath, and then entered the room. "OK, let's go!" he shouted at the dancers, and proceeded to fix the opening number.

"*Boom*! Like that he was another person," Tune recalled. "He was incredibly complex. He was as sure as he was in the rehearsal room as he was unsure outside it. And that's where the drugs came in. He needed them to bolster himself."

Bennett experimented with just about every drug available in the 1960s, often washed down with vodka. But he was remarkably resilient, never showing the effects of drugs and alcohol in the rehearsal studio. "I remember him talking about cancer," Tune said, "and he said, 'We'll never get it. Not us. That'll be somebody else. But not us.' And of course you believed him. I believed everything he told me."

The show that cemented Bennett's reputation as a leading Broadway choreographer was *Promises, Promises*, a big hit in 1968. He received his third Tony Award nomination. It was also the first show on which he worked with Donna McKechnie, whom he called "my favorite instrument."[4] Bennett put McKechnie at the center of a show-stopping number called "Turkey Lurkey Time." Two years later, he used her in *Company*, where she danced the "Tick Tock" number. "Bennett created passionately expressive movement . . . only McKechnie could do full justice to it," Ken Mandelbaum writes in his book *A Chorus Line and the Musicals of Michael Bennett*.

Hal Prince directed *Company*, Stephen Sondheim's urbane and cynical musical about a single man and his married friends. Prince realized that Bennett was more than just his choreographer. Sometimes, Prince would step aside and say to Bennett, "Take it for a minute and move them somewhere."[5] What Prince noticed was that Bennett never relied on steps. Characters inspired him, the movement flowing from who they were and the situations they found themselves in.

"What I did in *Company* was choreograph the characters," Bennett would later say. "I think a lot more of the show was choreographed than most people realize."[6]

Larry Cohen, a young stringer for the *Hollywood Reporter*, saw *Company* five times and became friendly with Prince at the recording session for the cast album. He asked Prince if he could watch the development of his next show from rehearsals to opening night. "Hal gave me complete access," he said. "I thought I would write a book about it." (He never did.)

The next show was Stephen Sondheim's landmark *Follies*, about a reunion of middle-aged ex-*Follies* girls in a dilapidated theater. The show contained one breathtaking Michael Bennett number after another, from the opening sequence in which ghosts of showgirls intermingled with the living ex-*Follies* dancers, to the thrilling "Who's That Woman?"—which show buffs always refer to as the "Mirror Number." As the middle-aged women re-created an old number downstage, young versions of themselves, wearing costumes dangling with mirrors, performed a mirror image of the number upstage. The past and the present came together at the climax. "It was both an all-out showstopper, a reflection of the show's theme of self-confrontation, and another scary reminder of the ravagement of time," writes Ken Mandelbaum.

Watching the creation of the show from the sidelines, Cohen "was in awe of Michael. When the show went out of town to Boston, they couldn't come up with an opening number. Michael tried dozens of opening numbers, and I don't mean little changes. I mean completely different numbers every time until he finally found the one that worked. Michael had no fear of throwing it all up in the air and starting all over again. The discipline and the drive were incredible."

What also became clear to Cohen was a rift developing between Prince and Bennett over the show's tone. Prince wanted to keep the show dark, haunting, and sad. Bennett thought it too bleak. In a snit one day he summed up his feelings about the characters in *Follies*: "I don't give a shit about two middle-age couples who lost it in a rumble seat!" Bennett wanted to bring in his friend Neil Simon, whom he knew from *Promises, Promises*, to add some jokes to James Goldman's script. The characters were either brittle and cynical, or sad and pathetic, and the audience didn't care about them. A few well-placed Simon jokes might help the audience warm to them.

But Prince refused to change a word. He was the director. He had total control. Bennett found sections of the show unendurable. During those scenes, he would flee to the alley behind the Colonial Theatre with Avian and Cohen, light up a cigarette, and talk about how he would solve problems that Prince couldn't—or wouldn't—acknowledge. Watching him in the alley, Cohen thought, There is no way he is going to be in this position again. He's ready to be a director. He wants total control.

Wanting to be a director and finding the right show to direct do not always coincide. Bennett cast about for a musical, but settled on a play, *Twigs*, by George Furth (who had written the book to *Company*). It was about three sisters and the men in their lives. Bennett cast Sada Thompson, who played all three sisters. The play had a decent run, and Thompson won the Tony for Best Actress. Bennett was now ready to direct a musical, and many producers offered him shows. One that came up was *Seesaw*, an adaptation of William Gibson's charming two-hander, *Two for the Seesaw*. The show had a score by Cy Coleman and Dorothy Fields and a book by Michael Stewart (*Hello, Dolly!*). Bennett, Avian, and Cohen, who was now working informally for Bennett as an in-house dramaturge, read it. "It was total crap," said Cohen. "We passed."

Still in demand as a show doctor, Bennett was turning down most assignments. Tune had an embroidered pillow made for him that said, "Thou Shalt Not Doctor."

And then Tune and Cohen both got calls summoning them to Detroit to work on the Broadway-bound *Seesaw*.

Cohen, then in Los Angeles, got his call at three in the morning.

"I need you to get on a plane to Detroit," Bennett said. "We have taken over *Seesaw*. Put down everything else and get here. You'll see the show and we'll have dinner and talk about it."

"But, Michael, we turned this down," Cohen protested.

"I know, I know. Just get here."

Tune got the call the day he returned from London, where he'd been filming *The Boyfriend*. He'd given up his apartment in New York, so he asked Bennett if he could stay in his until he found another. (Bennett had moved from the Upper West Side and was now living at 145 West Fifty-Fifth Street, 13A; the previous tenant had been Tennessee Williams.) "I got there, there was a note that said, 'The key is under the doormat. Call me.' I went in and the phone was ringing. It was him. He said, 'Oh good, you're there. I'm in Detroit. I'm directing a show. It's called *Seesaw*. I need you to choreograph a couple of numbers. I'll pay you $500 a number. Don't unpack. Go to the airport and come to Detroit. We'll reimburse you. Just go to the airport.'"

Why did Bennett take over a show he thought was "total crap"? He had a soft spot for the producer, Joe Kipness. Kippy was a colorful and beloved character around Broadway. He owned popular restaurants and was a friend of the "bent-nose gang," as one of his friends said, referring to the Mafia. There's a story about him being backstage at one of his shows in a theater that was still under construction. Work was going slowly, so Kippy confronted one of the theater's owners. "Get this place finished, or the garbage workers won't pick up at your buildings!" he screamed.

Another time, he was screaming at someone over a pay phone until he cut himself off by ripping the phone out of the wall.

When Kippy was having a feud with David Merrick, somebody

broke into Merrick's office above the St. James and trashed it. Around Broadway, people secretly applauded Kippy for hiring some of the bent-nose gang to put the fear of God into Merrick.

Despite his mobster reputation, theater people found Kippy hopelessly sentimental. His other nickname was "Cryin' Joe," because whenever his shows were in trouble and he needed someone to help him out, tears would come to his eyes. *Seesaw* was in serious trouble in Detroit. Cryin' Joe called Bennett for help and didn't stop sobbing until Bennett said yes.

Another reason Bennett took the job was money. He was broke. He never earned much from his shows because they didn't run that long. And he never saved. "Money meant very little to him," said John Breglio, who would become his lawyer. "If a producer wouldn't pay for something he needed in a show, he'd pay for it. He gave money away to dancers who needed it."

His accountant, Marvin Schulman, kept him afloat. Years later, Tommy Tune discovered how. Tune was making money from appearances in the movies at the time. Schulman was his accountant, too. Whenever Bennett needed money, Schulman dipped into Tune's account and transferred some cash to Bennett's.[7]

But the main reason why Bennett took over *Seesaw* was because Kippy agreed to his terms: total control.

Within a week of taking over *Seesaw*, Bennett fired twenty-six people.[8] Edwin Sherrin, the original director, quit. When Bennett demanded script changes, the writer, Michael Stewart, threw a fit and went back to New York. Performers Bennett had worked with for years were let go if they didn't fit his new concept of the show.

"He was doing what he had to do, which was to take a show that was going to flop and turn it into a show that was going to run," said Cohen. "Everything he did was in service of the show."

The most brutal firing was of the leading lady, Lainie Kazan. The character she was playing was a dancer, but Kazan was forty pounds overweight. She'd promised to slim down, but never did. Bennett wanted to replace her with the beautiful (and thin) Michele Lee.

When someone has to be let go from a Broadway show, the producer delivers the news. But Cryin' Joe couldn't face Large Lainie. Bennett had to wield the ax.

The scene was "an *All About Eve* on steroids moment," recalled Cohen.

Kazan begged to stay. This was her shot at Broadway stardom.

"You're too fat," Bennett told her.

"I'll cut off my tits if you let me stay!" she screamed.

He cut off her head.

"Because of what happened on *Seesaw*, Michael had a reputation of being ruthless," Cohen said. "He steeled himself to deal with Lainie, but it killed him inside. He was not a brutal person. It was all about the show."

Bennett liked the score and persuaded Coleman and Fields to write four new songs, including what would prove to be the show's most popular, "It's Not Where You Start." An aspiring and openly gay choreographer performed the song. Bennett cast Tune as the choreographer and gave him complete freedom to choreograph the number. Because Tune had not unpacked his bags in New York, he arrived in Detroit without his tap shoes. But he had a pair of clogs. Bennett liked the idea of a clog dance.

"But I'll break my neck," Tune protested.

"No you won't!" Bennett replied.

Tune performed the number in his clogs holding a bunch of balloons.

The "Balloon Number," as it came to be called, stopped the show and eventually won Tune the first of his ten Tony Awards.

Bennett worked fast. The company performed the old (bad) *Seesaw* at night, while Bennett created a new show during the day. "He did two years' worth of work in eight weeks," Cohen recalled. "He set a certain amount that he was going to accomplish each day and if you couldn't keep up, you were out."

The original play, *Two for the Seesaw*, was about the romance between a button-downed lawyer from Nebraska and an eccentric struggling dancer from the Bronx. Enlarged to fill a big stage, the musical had lost the charm of its simple story. Bennett and Cohen went through Stewart's script and tossed out every line that wasn't in the original play. Bennett asked his friend Neil Simon to contribute some jokes. As for the staging, Bennett took a cumbersome and clunky show and turned it into a slick contemporary musical comedy.

"It was the beginning of what he would eventually achieve in *Dreamgirls*," said Cohen. "He knew people were attuned to the movement of the movies, so he created the stage equivalent of wipes and dissolves. The old vocabulary of a show was to stop after each number for applause. Screw the applause, Michael thought. Keep going. You'll get even more applause two numbers later because the audience will need the release."

The overhaul of *Seesaw* in Detroit was costing Cryin' Joe Kipness a lot of money. He came to Bennett one day and said he couldn't afford to go on anymore. Bennett paid for the final week of the run in Detroit himself.

Back in New York the Broadway grapevine hummed with the news that Michael Bennett was saving *Seesaw*. The show was an advertisement for Michael Bennett, Broadway's best director. Bennett wanted the theater world to know that he could restage a major musical in record time. Jerome Robbins, Gower Champion, and Bob Fosse did the same in their day. And now it was Bennett's turn.

When it came time to do the billing in New York no one would take credit for the script. Stewart wasn't interested and Neil Simon didn't think a few jokes entitled him to be sole author. Bennett asked lyricist Dorothy Fields. "I can't be the author," he told her. "I didn't even graduate from high school." Fields demurred. "Absolutely not," she said. "I'll be laughed out of the business."

Bennett suggested Cohen. But Cohen had a better idea. "In a weird way, you're the author of the show," he said. "You may not have written five lines, but you directed the storyline."

Seesaw opened on Broadway at the Uris Theatre (now the Gershwin) on March 18, 1973. The opening night *Playbill* read, "Written, directed, and choreographed by Michael Bennett."

It would not be the last time.

The boys from Syracuse, New York, who began it all: J. J., Sam, and Lee Shubert. Sam (*center*) went to work as a teenager at the Grand Opera House in downtown Syracuse. Within a few months, he was running the box office. Within a few years, he owned several theaters in upstate New York. Lee (*right*), the eldest, opened a haberdashery store, but was bored. He soon joined his younger brother Sam in the theater business. J. J. (*left*), the youngest, joined the business as well. Sam and Lee were cool and deliberate in business. J. J. was a hothead and a tyrant.

Sam S. Shubert on a ship's deck striking a characteristically contemplative pose. But his dreamy, gentle look masked an enormous ambition that propelled him to New York City and into a ferocious battle with Abe Erlanger, whose Syndicate controlled the theater business.

A rare candid photograph of Sam looking prosperous and satisfied with the empire he was building. The people with him were probably actors in a touring Shubert show. Actors liked Sam because he paid them well and treated them fairly. Major stars of the day such as Minnie Maddern Fiske and Joseph Jefferson supported him in his fight with the ruthless Syndicate.

J. J. Shubert inspecting the chorus girls in a traveling Shubert show. He bedded many of them, and didn't hesitate to chew them out or hit them if they displeased him. One chorus girl he slapped sued him, complaining of a swollen eye and a bleeding lip. He accused her of sticking him with her hatpin.

Lee Shubert greeting a soldier at the Stage Door Canteen during World War II. He loved the sun, and could often be found in Central Park in the summer tanning himself in the open tonneau of his Isotta Fraschini. "His upturned eyebrows and the deep wrinkles at the corners of his eyes make him look something like a good-natured Indian," A. J. Liebling wrote in a *New Yorker* profile.

LEFT: J. J. greeting his biggest box-office star—Al Jolson. J. J. cast Jolson in one of the Shubert *Passing Show*s at the Winter Garden Theatre. Jolson brought down the house singing "Paris Is a Paradise for Coons" in blackface. He left the Shubert stable in 1926 to make movie history, singing "My Mammy" in *The Jazz Singer*.

CENTER: Lee looking very much like a cigar-store Indian with his wife, Marcella, a former show girl, and producer John Golden. Lee was not a model of fidelity. After his daily shave in a barber chair in his office, some girl or other from one of his shows would swing by for a little afternoon delight. They were called the "Five O'Clock Girls" because that was the appointed time. Lee had at least one bastard son, whom he installed in the box office of the Plymouth Theatre.

RIGHT: A grumpy-looking J. J. with his stylish second wife, Muriel, who had been a chorus girl at the Winter Garden Theatre. They met in 1921 but didn't marry until 1951. Muriel was on the Shubert payroll. Every week she received a check for $546.38, which she cashed at a Shubert box office. Pablo, her chauffeur, would then drive her to the Empire Bank, where she'd put the money in a safety deposit box. "Nobody knew what Muriel did with all her cash," said a Shubert employee. "Maybe she was planning on making a fast getaway."

LEFT: An aging J. J. with David Merrick, one of Broadway's most prolific producers of the 1960s. Born David Margulois in St. Louis, he came to New York in 1939 and changed his name to Merrick, inspired by the eighteenth-century English actor David Garrick. He promoted the first play he produced, *Clutterbuck*, by calling bars and restaurants during the cocktail hour to page a "Mr. Clutterbuck." It was the beginning of many legendary—and increasingly diabolical—David Merrick stunts.

10

CENTER: J. J. confers with his only son and heir, John Shubert, whose mother was J. J.'s first wife, Catherine Mary. J. J. groomed John to take over the business, but could be as nasty to him as he was to his other employees. "My son has no more authority here than the porters in my theaters," he said. John Shubert predeceased his father. He had a massive heart attack on a train to St. Petersburg, Florida, where he kept a second wife and two secret children.

11

RIGHT: James M. Nederlander (*center*) learning the business from his father, David Tobias (D. T.) Nederlander (*left*), and the head box-office treasurer of D. T.'s theaters in Detroit. D. T. gave his son plenty of advice, including "Stay away from the backstage area or they'll want you to paint their dressing rooms." Jimmy Nederlander would eventually bring the family business to New York, challenging the Shuberts' hold on Broadway.

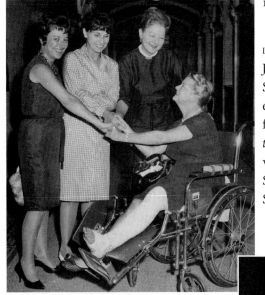

LEFT: A wheelchair-bound Eckie Shubert, John Shubert's legal widow, celebrates a Surrogate Court ruling that kept the Shubert empire intact after a scandal tarnished the family name. Congratulating her are (*left to right*) Betty Jacobs and Pat Schoenfeld, whose husbands, Bernard Jacobs and Gerald Schoenfeld, were J. J. Shubert's lawyers; and Shannon Dean, one of Eckie's close friends.

13

RIGHT: Irving Goldman (*far left*) "had the charm of a guy who sells you used Chevrolet upholstery," said producer Albert Poland. Goldman is celebrating his rise to the top of the Shubert Organization with (*left to right*) Bernard Jacobs, Eckie Shubert, and Gerald Schoenfeld. Schoenfeld and Jacobs needed the corrupt Goldman's support to take over the company. "We didn't know how high the price would be," Jacobs would say.

14

Anthony Hopkins as psychiatrist Martin Dysart and Peter Firth as the boy who blinds horses in the Broadway production of Peter Shaffer's *Equus*. John Dexter, who directed the play, initially had doubts about Hopkins. "Shifty, spineless Welsh cunt," he called the actor in his diary. But shortly before the play opened at the Plymouth Theatre, he wrote: "Tony Hopkins is on the way to being superb in *Equus*. He is calm, disciplined, and every word is crystal clear."

Composer Marvin Hamlisch (*left*) with lyricist Ed Kleban at the original cast recording of *A Chorus Line*. At the time, Hamlisch, an Oscar-winning film composer, was the only person working on the show who had any money. Kleban was scratching by teaching musical theater workshops and writing for a children's theater. In an updated yearbook being put together for his high school reunion, he contemplated writing, "Occupation: Failure."

Dorothy Loudon at Sardi's with her longtime agent and friend, Lionel Larner. Mike Nichols suggested Loudon for the part of the evil Miss Hannigan, who runs the orphanage in *Annie*. Her performance was perfect "because she hated kids," said writer Tom Meehan. At an early reading of the show, Loudon told Andrea McArdle, who was playing Annie, "If you make one move on any of my laugh lines, you will not live to see the curtain call."

The creators of *Annie* (*left to right*): composer Charles Strouse, lyricist and director Martin Charnin, and bookwriter Thomas Meehan in front of the Watergate Hotel in Washington, D.C., where the musical played its out-of-town tryout. After opening to enthusiastic reviews at the Kennedy Center, producer Mike Nichols took the team to dinner and said, "You're going to be here six weeks. You've gotten good reviews and you're going to be a hit here. But if you do nothing and bring the show in as it is, you are going to have one of the biggest flops in history. So get to work."

Tommy Tune (*left*) getting advice from his friend and mentor Michael Bennett at a rehearsal for the 1980 Tony Awards. Bennett gave Tune his first shot at choreographing in the 1973 musical *Seesaw*. But when Tune's first show as a director, *Nine*, went up against Bennett's *Dreamgirls* for the Tony Award in 1982, Bennett turned on his protégé. He called Tune up one night and threatened him in a voice that sounded like a mobster's.

Bernard B. Jacobs (*center*), president of the Shubert Organization, looks adoringly at Michael Bennett, the director of Broadway's two biggest hits, *A Chorus Line* and *Dreamgirls*. The father-son relationship between these two powerful men affected everyone on Broadway. "If anyone said anything against Michael, they'd be in trouble with Bernie," said set designer Robin Wagner.

19

David Merrick on the set of *42nd Street* with one of the show's stars, Lee Roy Reams. *42nd Street* was Merrick's Broadway comeback. He had gone to Los Angeles to make movies but discovered that the studios controlled Hollywood. Only on Broadway could he run the show.

One of the last photographs of Gower Champion (*left*), the director of *42nd Street*. His arm is around Lee Roy Reams. Champion was suffering from a rare blood disorder during the tryout in Washington, D.C. He died the morning the show opened in New York, on August 25, 1980. Merrick announced Champion's death at the curtain call, putting *42nd Street* on the front pages of newspapers around the world.

22

Jack Benny, James M. Nederlander, and Elizabeth I. McCann celebrating a contract Benny signed to play some of Nederlander's theaters in 1971. McCann was one of the few producers who could shuttle between the Nederlanders and the Shuberts. "You were either a Shubert man or a Nederlander man," said producer Emanuel Azenberg. McCann managed to be both.

23

The final curtain call for the Tony Award–winning *The Life and Adventures of Nicholas Nickleby* at the Plymouth Theatre on January 3, 1982. Director Trevor Nunn and leading man Roger Rees are in the front row, far left. The Shuberts and the Nederlanders coproduced *Nicholas Nickleby*, though they remained suspicious of each other throughout the run. Every aspect of the show was negotiated "like the Treaty of Ghent," said press agent Josh Ellis.

CHAPTER THIRTEEN

The One

Clive Barnes understood what Bennett had achieved with *Seesaw*. Though he noted in his *Times* review that the show had "quite obviously been built rather than inspired," Barnes praised its "efficient slickness" and fresh look. "The American musical theater has for long neglected projection techniques," he wrote. "*Seesaw*, which has its scenic design by Robin Wagner [who would come to be one of Bennett's closest friends and collaborators], makes a determined effort to catch up, and with its projection of skyscrapers and cityscapes it really does look very good."

Bennett, along with Wagner, was beginning to change not only the way musicals moved but how they looked.

Despite the strong reviews, Kippy and his coproducers were, once again, out of money. They'd already spent $1 million on *Seesaw*, and there was nothing left to advertise the good reviews. *Seesaw* was about to join the six other musicals that season that had closed after fewer than twelve performances. But Bennett could not let his calling card die. He rallied the cast and crew. Tune led the actors in performing numbers from the show outside the theater, while stagehands distributed *Seesaw* flyers to passersby. Bennett, meanwhile, sought to raise money to keep the show going. He turned to one of the people he respected most in the business, the lawyer John Wharton. During their meeting Wharton introduced Bennett to his smart young associate, John Breglio, just out of Harvard Law School. Bennett and Breglio liked each other. They met for lunch, and Bennett, who was four years older, cast his spell over Breglio. "I was taken with him right away," Breglio said.

Breglio had begun to learn the movie business at Paul, Weiss, Rifkind, Wharton & Garrison. "The theater was dead," he said. But after he got to know Bennett, he cast his lot with the theater. He became Bennett's lawyer and a crucial member of his surrogate family. If Bob Avian was Bennett's older brother, John Breglio was his younger brother.

"They were two Italian boys in a world of old Jews," producer Elizabeth I. McCann said with her usual bluntness.

The campaign to save *Seesaw*, aided in no small part by *New York Post* columnist Earl Wilson, who loved the show and wrote about it almost every day, succeeded, to a point. The show didn't close overnight. It ran till the end of the year, but it didn't make a dime. Bennett was nominated for a Tony for his direction, and won for his choreography. More importantly, his work on the show vaulted him to the top of the list of musical directors. He was "the One."

Joseph Papp, the energetic, ferocious, and mercurial head of the Public Theater, disdained Broadway. Public Theater productions occasionally moved uptown—*Two Gentlemen of Verona*, *Sticks and Bones*, *Much Ado About Nothing*—but Broadway was mainstream, safe, commercial, all of which Papp despised. He often said, "Broadway is shit." The comment got back to Richard Rodgers and Oscar Hammerstein, who had donated the money from a pair of house seats at every performance of *The Sound of Music* to Papp's New York Shakespeare Festival. Broadway's pashas were not amused, and Papp had to apologize to keep that *Sound of Music* money flowing.

Bernard Gersten, Papp's second-in-command, did not hate Broadway and kept on top of its shows and gossip. He'd seen *Seesaw* and heard what Michael Bennett had done with the show out of town. He thought Bennett would be a good choice to come downtown and overhaul a musical that was in trouble at the Public—*More Than You Deserve*, which had a score by Jim Steinman and featured a performer named Meat Loaf. Papp had never heard of Bennett. He checked out *Seesaw* and liked the staging. A few days later, he told Gersten he thought Bennett should direct a revival of Kurt Weill's 1938 musical, *Knickerbocker Holiday*. Gersten sent the script and the score to Bennett. But Bennett wasn't interested. A revival of a musical from the thirties was not going to be his ticket to the top. He had another idea, however, and wondered if he might come down to the Public and pitch it.

Bennett arrived at Papp's office at the Public Theater carrying a bulky Sony reel-to-reel tape recorder and several reels of tape. He had nearly twenty-four hours of interviews with Broadway dancers—the gypsies. He thought there might be a show somewhere in those hours and hours of tape. He played some of them for Papp. After listening to the recordings for forty-five minutes, Papp said, "OK, let's do it."

"That's all there was to it," Gersten said. "Joe liked Michael, so we gave him space and some money to go to work."

For many years those tapes languished in a vault in the law offices of Paul, Weiss, Rifkind, Wharton & Garrison. In 2004, John Breglio, Bennett's executor, decided to revive *A Chorus Line* on Broadway. He also wanted to make a documentary about Bennett and the show. "I wanted to use the tapes," he said. "But nobody had listened to them in thirty years. I went to the vault and thought, Oh, my God. I'm going to open them up and they're going to be ashes. It would be my own scene out of *The Artist!*"

The tapes did not crumble in his hands. Breglio transferred them to MP3s before listening to them. And when he did, the first person he heard was Michael Bennett. "I really want to talk about us. Now I don't know whether anything will come of us, or whether there is anything interesting. I think we're all pretty interesting, all of you are pretty interesting, and I think maybe there is a show in there somewhere, which would be called *A Chorus Line*."

A Chorus Line.

Bennett didn't know what the show would be, but he had the title from the start. It was the original title of *Twigs*, the play Bennett had directed before *Seesaw*. He called the writer George Furth and asked if he could use the old title. Furth said yes.

The first taping session took place at midnight, January 18, 1974, at the Nickolaus Exercise Center on East Twenty-Third Street. It was late at night because most of the dancers Bennett corralled were working on Broadway and couldn't meet until after their shows. Bennett provided food and wine—"very cheap red wine," said Donna McKechnie. Among the dancers who took part in what amounted to a group therapy session for dancers were Nicholas Dante, Priscilla Lopez, Michon Peacock, Wayne Cilento, and Kelly Bishop. Most, but not all, were longtime friends of Bennett.

"We wanted the biggest cross section possible so that we could try to find what the common experience was," said choreographer Tony Stevens. "And Michael wanted some enemies in the room, so there were rivals there, people who had histories that were not so great." [1]

With Bennett asking most of the questions, and fueled by cups of cheap red wine, the dancers told their stories. Many, like Bennett, had grown up in unhappy households. Some talked about alcoholic parents. Others spoke about philandering fathers and broken marriages. Many of the men talked about their sexuality, and the consequences of having to hide it from friends and family. Nicholas Dante recalled his experiences as a teenager working at night as a drag queen in a tawdry club. His story would inspire what would become the show's climax, Paul's monologue about meeting his parents, unexpectedly, at the stage door of a drag club where he worked. One dancer talked about her weak singing voice and how it hurt her at auditions ("Sing"). Another spoke about her father's string of infidelities and how she found solace in ballet class ("At the Ballet"). A third recounted her humiliation at the hands of an acting teacher in high school ("Nothing"). The session lasted twelve hours, and was so fruitful that Bennett decided to hold another one on February 18. By all accounts, the second session was not as successful as the first. It was, as Ken Mandelbaum notes in *A Chorus Line and the Musicals of Michael Bennett*, unfocused and repetitious. Most of the material for the show would come from the first session.

When Bennett told Breglio about the tapes and his plan to make a show from them, the lawyer blanched. "Wait a minute. You can't have all these people sitting around telling you their life stories for a show. You're going to have twenty authors—and twenty lawsuits. You've got to get them to sign a release."

In the end, the dancers who took part in the tapings waived their right to their life stories for a dollar each—and the stipulation that if their stories were used, their names would be changed. When the show became a hit, Bennett had Breglio draw up a contract that gave a share of his royalties to the dancers who had participated in the tape sessions and in the workshops at the Public Theater. At the height of its popularity, *A Chorus Line* was earning close to $10,000 a year for each dancer. That, of course, was nothing compared to the millions it earned Bennett and the other creators. And many of the original dancers would later complain that they had sold their lives for a pittance. But nobody had any idea that two twelve-hour tape sessions would became the basis for the biggest hit in Broadway history.

"They trusted Michael not to screw them," said Breglio. "And every single one of them signed the release."

Working with Dante, who was an aspiring writer, and his friend the playwright James Kirkwood, Bennett fashioned a rough script from the tapes. To write the music, he turned to another friend, Marvin Hamlisch, who had been the dance arranger for *Henry, Sweet Henry*, one of the first shows Bennett choreographed. In the intervening years, Hamlisch had won Oscars for *The Way We Were* and *The Sting*. He was one of the most sought-after composers in Hollywood, and stood to earn millions scoring movies. But Hamlisch loved Broadway musicals. He had dreamed since childhood of writing one. His agent was not happy. Papp was paying everybody who worked on *A Chorus Line* a hundred dollars a week. But Hamlisch didn't care. *He* would have paid for the chance to write a musical with Michael Bennett. For his lyricist, Bennett turned to Ed Kleban, a songwriter whose work was starting to get noticed around New York. Bennett put Hamlisch and Kleban together. They "kicked the tires," Hamlisch recalled, on a possible relationship, sat down at the piano and went to work. Kleban poured over transcripts of the tape sessions, looking for song hooks and titles. "Most of it was intensely boring, the same nonsense over and over again," he said.[2] But every now and then, he'd find something that inspired a song. For instance, one of the dancers recalled going to his sister's dance class. "I can do that!" the dancer remembered thinking.

And there was a song.

Kleban's drafts of lyrics for *A Chorus Line* show the importance of rewriting a song until it conveys, in the most direct way possible, a thought, an emotion, a story. Here, for instance, is an early draft of a song called "Love":

> *Talk about the past*
> *Talk about tomorrow*
> *But I can't regret*
> *What I did for love*
> *Talk about the joy*
> *Talk about the sorrow*
> *Where do I belong?*
> *The day after tomorrow*
> *Funny, but it's hard to say*
> *And I can't regret*
> *What I did for love*
> *What I did for love*

Several drafts later, most of the lines have been jettisoned and Kleban has found the hook that would give the song its driving idea and its title:

> *Can't regret*
> *What I did for love*

Kleban recorded the state of his pre–*A Chorus Line* finances on his lyric manuscripts. He was picking up a few hundred dollars here and there teaching musical theater and writing a show for a children's theater. For his work on *A Chorus Line* he received $1,000 from the Public Theater. He attended his high school reunion just after *A Chorus Line* opened on Broadway. Had the reunion taken place six months prior, he said he would have written in the updated yearbook, "Occupation: Failure."

And indeed, with the exception of Hamlisch, nearly everybody working on *A Chorus Line* was broke. But that didn't deter them from committing nearly a year to the show. As usual, Bennett never tired of restaging numbers until he got what he wanted. "The Music and the Mirror," Cassie's celebrated dance in front of five rehearsal mirrors, was originally staged with four boys dancing behind her. But it wasn't right. Cassie (Donna McKechnie), who had almost been a star, had fallen on hard times. She was alone, desperate for a job. And she was dancing for one person, the director of the show and her ex-lover Zach (clearly, Bennett's stand-in). Out went the four boys. Now it was Cassie, alone, dancing as she's never danced before, with Zach watching and deciding her fate.[3]

While there were some exciting dances, nobody was quite sure if *A Chorus Line* worked as an evening of musical theater. Tommy Tune was living with one of the original cast members, Michel Stuart, at the time. "Michel would come home and tell me, 'We ran the whole show today, and Joe Papp fell asleep. It was three hours long.' I said, 'Don't worry. Michael will trim it. He knows what he's doing.'"

Hamlisch said the collaboration on *A Chorus Line* was the most exciting and enjoyable of his career in show business. There was little bickering. Everyone trusted Bennett's judgment. The one big fight was over the show's anthem, "What I Did for Love." Papp, who only occasionally dropped by rehearsals (he believed in leaving artists alone to do their work, interceding only if he thought they were screwing up), loathed it.

"Joe wanted to cut it," recalled Gersten. "He thought it was 'just a Broadway number.' It was pandering to the Broadway audience."

But Hamlisch, whose music was all over the radio, wanted a hit song from the show. And Bennett, always attuned to what an audience wanted, knew the show needed its tearjerker.

"Fine," said Papp, and walked out of the rehearsal room.

A far more serious stumbling block was money. Bennett conceived the song "One" as his finale, with the chorus kids dancing, anonymously, behind the big star—the "singular sensation" (who, of course, the audience would never see). *A Chorus Line* was not an expensive show. It took place on a bare stage. The costumes were dancers' tights and sweats. But "One" needed the full Broadway treatment: gold lamé tuxedos and top hats and a sparkling curtain, called a drop. The cost of each costume was $1,000. The drop wasn't cheap, either. "One" would cost $25,000. Papp didn't have it. He'd already sunk $100,000—most of which was on credit—into the show. Jack Lenny, Bennett's agent, offered to give Papp the $25,000 in exchange for 50 percent of the show. Papp said no. "The idea that we would give Jack 50 percent of the show for just $25,000 seemed absurd," Gersten recalled.

And so Papp told Bennett that was it. *A Chorus Line* was over. That's when Bennett and Hamlisch hightailed it up to the Shubert offices and broke the old piano. Papp must have gotten wind that Bennett was up to something because he turned to someone who had always given him money in the past: LuEsther Mertz, heir to the Publisher's Clearing House fortune. She believed in Papp and the mission of the Public Theater, and had always been a soft touch when the theater was in trouble. Nobody remembers the exact deal today, but between the Shubert and LuEsther Mertz, Papp got the $25,000, and *A Chorus Line* played its first preview on April 16, 1975.

A few minutes before the show started, Bennett and Tune stood in the alley next to the Public Theater smoking. Tune was disappointed he could not be part of *A Chorus Line*, but after *Seesaw* and his Tony Award, he was no longer a gypsy. Bennett looked up at his good friend and, crying, said, "I promise you, if this works I will take you with me on the next one." He paused and added, "But I don't think it will. They're not going to understand what it is that we do. I'm going to have to bring it down, and I don't want to do that. I want it to be real. I don't want it to be fake."

"What are you talking about, Michael?" Tune replied. "This show is going to be wonderful."

They went inside, stood at the back of the house, and heard Zach say at the start of the show, "Again . . . step, kick, kick, leap, kick, touch . . . Again!"

Anybody who was at the Newman Theater at the Public that night—and most were friends of Bennett—will never forget the experience of seeing *A Chorus Line* for the first time. At the end of the opening number—"I Hope I Get It"—the audience of 299 stood and cheered and cried. In theater circles that night, phones rang off the hook with the news that the Public Theater had a massive hit.

"I don't think there was a ticket left the next day," said Gersten. "People, celebrities, started coming down and sitting on the steps to watch the show." At any given performance, you could see Liza Minnelli, Diana Ross, Mikhail Baryshnikov, Shirley MacLaine, David Geffen, or Cher crowded on the stairs of the Newman.

"Fire laws were ignored," said Breglio. "You hear today about people trying to get tickets to *Book of Mormon*. It was twenty times that. People would do anything to get in. And Joe wasn't charging them $20,000 a seat—he wasn't doing anything like that."

(Papp did raise ticket prices, but by only a few dollars. And most of the money went to up the actors' salaries from $100 a week to $200.)

News of Bennett's triumph reached the Shubert offices. A few days later, a Shubert limo brought Betty and Bernie Jacobs, Phil Smith, and producer Manny Azenberg down to the Public. Alex Cohen—who had become a trusted friend and advisor to the Shubert ever since he defended them against Louis Lefkowitz—and his wife, the writer Hildy Parks, met them at the theater. After the show, the group headed to Pearl's, a popular Chinese restaurant in Times Square, to discuss its prospects. Cohen delivered a long lecture about what was wrong with the show, concluding that it was fixable but that only he and Hildy knew how to do it. There were also concerns about whether an uptown audience would accept the candid accounts of homosexuality in the show. "The consensus was, It's really good, but it won't work uptown," said Azenberg.*

"The audience was hysterical that night, but the show had flaws," Jacobs recalled years later. "Michael called me the next day, and I told him I loved it, and then I gave him my notes, which was the most ridiculous thing in the world, in retrospect, assuming I could see anything wrong with the show Michael could not. But we went through this charade, with Michael pretending to listen to me."

Bennett himself wasn't sure Broadway was the place for *A Chorus Line*. He thought it needed to remain in an intimate house, that it would lose its emotional wallop in a fifteen-hundred-seat Broadway theater.

---

* Phil Smith has a different recollection: "There was never any doubt it would come to Broadway. Bernie and I had a conversation that night about where we would put it. We really needed something. And there it was."

But a week later, he asked Jacobs and his wife, Betty, to come back and see the show. It was tighter, sharper, swifter, more dramatic and compelling. "Michael had accomplished a miracle in one week," Jacobs said. "It was as good as anything I've seen on stage."

Jacobs met Bennett in the greenroom after the show and told him he could have a Shubert house. He even offered him one of his largest, the Winter Garden. But Bennett was wary. He knew Hal Prince and Stephen Sondheim had a new show called *Pacific Overtures* that was headed to the Winter Garden in January 1976.

"You'll kick me out in six months," he said. "You've got a Hal Prince show."

Jacobs replied, "Michael, if this show is what I think it is neither Hal Prince nor fifty sticks of dynamite will blast you out of the Winter Garden."

"You like my show!" Bennett exclaimed. He threw his arms around Jacobs and "before I knew it for the first and only time in my life a male tongue was down my throat," Jacobs said. "After that, I learned to always keep my lips tightly sealed whenever I was dealing with Michael Bennett."

("Bernie loved to tell that story," Smith recalled years later. "As soon as he told it to me the first time, I knew we had the show.")

The kiss was the start of an intense relationship that would come to affect many people who worked on Broadway. Michael Bennett had assembled his surrogate family, but he was missing a key figure: a father. And there was Bernie Jacobs, old enough to be Bennett's real father, a powerful man who controlled the real estate of Broadway. (As an added bonus, Michael would also come to adore Betty Jacobs.) Bennett would have the shows; Jacobs the theaters. As Manny Azenberg observed, "I think, in essence, Michael was a hustler. And he thought he was going to hustle Bernie. He wanted a theater. He wanted things. And on the way to hustling Bernie, he fell in love with Bernie. And Bernie and Betty fell in love with him. And so what started out to be opportunistic, wound up being real."

Whatever doubts there were about the viability of *A Chorus Line* on Broadway vanished the day the reviews appeared. "The conservative word for *A Chorus Line* might be tremendous, or perhaps terrific,"

Clive Barnes wrote in the *Times*. Bennett, Martin Gottfried declared in the *New York Post*, "is now a major creative force and *A Chorus Line* is purely and simply magnificent, capturing the very soul of our musical theater." And *New York* magazine's John Simon, a tough critic, especially when it came to musicals, wrote: "*A Chorus Line* is something new and historic . . . the first musical-verité . . . You can find faults in *A Chorus Line*, even incontrovertible and not inconsiderable ones. But, in the last analysis, they don't matter."

With the critics on board, the *Chorus Line* train was headed to Broadway. The Public Theater would be the sole producer. Bennett wanted 15 percent of the profits plus 5 percent of the weekly box office gross. "We didn't say no," Gersten recalled. Not long after *A Chorus Line* moved uptown, that deal would make Bennett the richest director in the history of Broadway.

A few hurdles remained, however. For one, the Public did not have the money to produce the show on Broadway. The estimated cost for the move was $550,000. Once again, the Shuberts and LuEsther Mertz came to the rescue. The Shuberts picked up the load-in cost of the show. The "load-in" is the moving of the show into the theater. Stagehand-heavy, it is often the most expensive part of producing a show. Back then it would have cost $15,000 a day. If it took two weeks, the cost would be $150,000. The Shuberts also paid many of the show's initial bills, including advertising. And they agreed to cover the weekly overhead until the show got rolling. "We believed the show would be a hit, and we'd collect whatever we laid out over time," said Smith.

Mertz, meanwhile, gave Papp a grant of $250,000 for the move.

The Shuberts also helped reduce the cost of running the show through their close relationship with Broadway's unions. Smith called Robert McDonald, the head of the stagehands union, and asked him to go down to the Public, take a look at *A Chorus Line,* and let him know if he could see any problems with moving it to Broadway.

"You have one problem, Phil," McDonald told Smith the next morning. "The mirror scene. You have all these people moving mirrors, and they're actors. On Broadway, they're going to have to be stagehands. That's the contract."

Smith reported back to Jacobs, who called McDonald and exploded. "We cannot pay four or five stagehands for one scene in the show—absolutely not!"

McDonald replied, "Well, I have a suggestion. Fly 'em in. Fly the mirrors in. One man is all you need."

"You think that will work?" Jacobs asked.

"It will."

And that's the way it was done, saving the Shuberts and the Public Theater, over time, hundreds of thousands of dollars.

Another issue was which Shubert theater best suited the show. Bennett and Papp did not believe the show would hold up in a large house. They ruled out the Winter Garden. Jacobs offered them the Shubert. That was too big as well. Then Bennett spoke to his friend Mike Nichols, who told him the best house on Broadway was the Ethel Barrymore, which had 1,058 seats. "Mike's right," Bennett told Jacobs and Smith. "I'm going to put it in the Barrymore." Jacobs and Smith were shocked. The Shubert had four hundred seats more than the Barrymore, which meant thousands of dollars more each week, hundreds of thousands more each year, millions more in the end.

Smith spoke up. "Michael, you're giving up a fortune going to the Barrymore. You, Michael Bennett, are going to give up a fortune, and you shouldn't do that. And don't you want your show in a theater where it's going to be seen by fourteen hundred people a night?"

("We thought the show would run five years," Smith said years later. "And that was a fortune. But, my God, it ran fifteen years. And that was an even bigger fortune.")

Smith's argument carried the day, and though Bennett eyed a few other theaters, he eventually settled on the Shubert, the theater named after Sam S. Shubert, the founder of an empire that, having struggled for a decade, was poised to rise again with the success of *A Chorus Line*.

In the spring of 1975, *A Chorus Line* was the hottest show in town. Within three months—July 25, to be exact—it opened on Broadway to even better reviews. The advance built to well over a million dollars (enormous in 1975) and the press coverage was endless. *A Chorus Line* appeared on the covers of *Newsweek,* the *New York Times Magazine,* and

Saturday Review. Broadway, mired in the doldrums since the late sixties, was stirring again as a result of this one show.

"It was good for us all," said McDonald. "It lifted all the boats."

A small boat: There was a restaurant called Ma Bell's across the alley from the Shubert. It was struggling. Smith had an idea. The Shubert Theatre had a second balcony, and second balconies, because they're so high up from the stage, are always hard to sell, even for a hit. Smith offered to sell the restaurant fifty tickets a night, which the restaurant could use as a package deal. Eat at Ma Bell's and see *A Chorus Line.* Ma Bell's wasn't struggling for long, and Smith was filling his second balcony.

Another beneficiary of the success of *A Chorus Line* was *Playbill,* the theater magazine that had been handed out in Broadway theaters since 1884. By the early seventies, it was losing money, a victim of Broadway's prolonged downturn. Metromedia, the company run by Shubert board member John Kluge, owned it, and Kluge wanted to sell it. Arthur Birsh, Kluge's second-in-command, wanted to go out on his own and offered to buy it. Kluge sold the magazine to Birsh, with payments to be made in the future. "It was losing money," said Birsh. "If it ever made money, I'd pay him. He didn't think it would." Birsh took control of *Playbill* in 1974. "We had three ads," he said. His wife, Joan Alleman, the editor of *Playbill* at the time, was shocked. "Arthur had been doing very well under Kluge," she said. "And now he owned a magazine that was losing money!" But a year later came *A Chorus Line.* Birsh, who was close to Schoenfeld and Jacobs, had access to house seats. Potential advertisers began clamoring to see the show, and Birsh had the tickets. The advertisers looked around the Shubert and saw fifteen hundred well-heeled consumers, all reading their *Playbill*s. The ads came rolling in.

Papp and his Public Theater were, of course, enormous beneficiaries of *A Chorus Line.* The show would, over the course of its run in New York and around the world, earn $40 million for the Public, making it, as Helen Epstein writes in her book *Joe Papp: An American Life,* "the most affluent institutional theater in America." Papp poured the money back into the Public, giving a home to actors, writers, and directors who continue to influence the theater today—Meryl Streep,

Kevin Kline, Kevin Spacey, Larry Kramer, Tony Kushner, Ntozake Shange, George C. Wolfe, and JoAnne Akalaitis. Papp himself was affected by the success of *A Chorus Line*. The man who once called Broadway "shit" started dressing like a Broadway producer, with a long coat draped over his shoulders and a cigar in his mouth. He even appeared in ads for *A Chorus Line* on the sides of telephone booths. "Nothing's more New York than a Broadway curtain call," the ads read, picturing Papp wearing a tuxedo and a flowing white silk scarf. "Joe took to being a Broadway producer like catnip," said Bernard Gersten.

Michael Bennett was now the most sought-after director in the world. He could create an empire of his own. He had, friends said, ideas for dozens and dozens of shows dancing in his head. And he was only thirty-two.

A Chorus Line reversed the fortunes of the Shubert Organization. Though the company was not the producer, the rental income from the Shubert in New York, as well as Shubert theaters around the country the show would play on tour, would add up to tens of millions of dollars. The Shuberts could now refurbish decaying theaters and produce other Broadway shows. Schoenfeld and Jacobs ruled an empire that was growing rich.

And, of course, Broadway itself reaped rewards from *A Chorus Line*. In 1974, attendance was 6.6 million. The next year, when *A Chorus Line* opened, it shot up to 7.2 million. In 1976, it hit 8.8 million. The "Fabulous Invalid," as Broadway was called whenever it looked to be in trouble, was getting out of her wheelchair.

Decades later, Phil Smith summed up the impact of *A Chorus Line* this way: "Before *A Chorus Line* there was no money. After *A Chorus Line* there was nothing but money."

CHAPTER FOURTEEN

The Interloper

In 1963, Manny Azenberg got a job in David Merrick's office. His first assignment was as the company manager for the national tour of *I Can Get It for You Wholesale*, which had a decent run in New York, with Barbra Streisand making her Broadway debut in the role of the secretary, Miss Marmelstein.

The first stop on the tour was Detroit. It was known in the business as "Nederlander country." David T. Nederlander, or "D. T." for short, controlled the city's major theaters—the Fisher, the Riviera, and the Shubert-Lafayette.

Azenberg, just a few years out of the army, went to D. T.'s offices in the Fisher Theatre to introduce himself. As he walked into the office he saw a little man, shriveled up in a chair "ripping the kishkas" out of a tall man standing in front of him. The tall man was crying, while the little man, in a high-pitched nasal whine, yelled, "And you're going to lose your job for this, you son of a bitch!"

A younger man in the room pleaded, in that same high-pitched nasal whine, "Dad, please don't do this. He didn't know."

D. T. was having none of it. "Get him out of here!" he screamed, his voice rising so high dogs were fleeing Detroit.

Still crying, the man who'd been fired left the office. In the hallway he was stopped by a different young man who said, in the now-familiar high-pitched voice, "Don't worry. You're rehired."

The man was being fired—and rehired—at the same moment.

Azenberg thought, These people are crazy. Maybe the army was better.

That was Azenberg's introduction to the Nederlander family—D. T., the father who fired the man; Jimmy, the son who begged his father not to fire him; and Joey, the son who rehired him.

Azenberg later learned that the man who'd been fired and rehired was the new house electrician at the Fisher Theatre. He'd read the meter and given the electric company the correct number of kilowatts used that month. That was his offense. It was customary, in Nederlander country, to save money by shaving off at least a hundred kilowatts.

(The man got his job back—and worked for the Nederlanders for the rest of his life.)

Azenberg arrived at the Shubert-Lafayette—where *I Can Get It for You Wholesale* was to play its first performance that night—to find D. T. standing in the lobby yelling at the show's star, Lillian Roth. Her offense? There was a snowstorm that night, and it was easier for her to get into the theater through the lobby than through the alley at the side of the building. It was an hour before the show, and although there was no one else in the lobby, D. T. was throwing her out. "Actors go in the stage door!" he shouted.

Azenberg steered clear of D. T. "I was afraid of him," he said. But he got to know Jimmy and Joey. And he soon saw another side of the Nederlanders. If you were in trouble, they took care of you. If anybody in the business, a manager, a press agent, an actor, arrived in Detroit down on his luck, Jimmy or Joey would go to the box office and get some cash. "You're in trouble, here, take this," they'd say.

Azenberg got to know the Nederlanders at an opportune time, for in just two years—1965—Jimmy Nederlander would leave Detroit and try his luck in New York. In time, he would build his own empire on Broadway and become the Shuberts' first rival since Lee and J. J. vanquished Abe Erlanger and the Syndicate in the 1920s.

James M. Nederlander—"Jimmy"—was born in Detroit on March 31, 1922, to D. T. and Sarah Nederlander. He was their third child, after Harry and a daughter, Frances. There would be three others—Robert,

Joseph, and Fred. When Jimmy was born, his father had been in the theater business for ten years. D. T. started out as a jeweler and pawn-broker, but in 1912 he was offered a ninety-nine-year lease on the De-troit Opera House. He took it. Why? "Well, he was like me," Jimmy said. "You gotta take a chance in life. You oughta do somethin'. If you don't take a chance, you'll never get anywhere. If you see an opportu-nity, grab it."

The only trouble: D. T. knew nothing about operating a theater. So he went into business with two people who did—Lee and J. J. Shu-bert, who at the time were expanding their empire in their battle with Erlanger.

The Detroit Opera House became the Shubert Detroit Opera House.

And Jimmy grew up there. When he was five, he saw comedian Joe Cook in *Rain or Shine*. He saw touring companies of the *Ziegfeld Follies*, *George White's Scandals*, *Earl Carroll's Vanities*. He laughed at Ed Wynn in *The Perfect Fool*. Al Jolson loved his mother's roast chicken. He often went on stage at the Opera House eating a leg of it while singing.

D. T. made such a success of the Opera House that in 1928 United Artists offered him $850,000 for the lease. He turned it down and expanded his holdings, taking over some smaller theaters and other pieces of real estate throughout the city. Jimmy and his siblings grew up in a large house in a fashionable section of downtown Detroit. They spent weekends at an elegant country house on Pine Lake. And then the stock market crashed, and the Great Depression ruined his father's business. The Shuberts declared bankruptcy, and stuck D. T. for $800,000 in back rent and various other bills. The Opera House was empty, and in an act of desperation, D. T. paid the leaseholder $100,000 to get out of the lease, a lease that five years before had been worth $850,000 to United Artists. The Opera House where Joe Cook, Ed Wynn, and Al Jolson had played to standing-room only crowds be-came a discount men's clothing store called Sam's Cut Rate.

Though D. T. was in trouble, he did not, like the Shuberts, declare bankruptcy. Jimmy and his siblings were pulled from their fancy pri-vate schools and sent to public schools in poor neighborhoods. "It was a shock," Jimmy said. "We were comfortable, then we weren't. But what are you gonna do? When things go bad, you adapt. We adapted." Jimmy went to work as a caddy at the Pine Lake Country Club, where his father had once been a member. He got a dollar a round, and gave it to his parents. He also worked at a General Motors plant fitting valves. Somehow, with his older brother also working and his father holding on to what real estate he could, the family weathered the Great Depression. "I learned one thing," Jimmy said. "Don't be poor."

When the Depression lifted, D. T. went back into the theater business, once again with Lee and J. J. Shubert, even though they'd stuck him for $800,000. In 1940, D. T. and the Shuberts took over the Orpheum Theatre and renamed it the Shubert-Lafayette. By this time, Jimmy had decided he wanted to be a lawyer. He enrolled in a local prelaw program but soon ran out of money. He needed a job. So he asked his father if he could work for him. His father handed him a broom, and told him to start sweeping the lobby of the Shubert-Lafayette. He also worked as an usher, a press agent, and a box office treasurer. Around election time, he delivered envelopes full of cash to all the judges in Detroit. "Son," D. T. said, "I'd rather know the judge than the law."

Jimmy learned a few other things from his father as well:

"If you make a deal, stick to it. Lawsuits are for lawyers."

"There are two things that will kill you in life—ego and greed."

"Stay away from the backstage area or they'll want you to paint their dressing rooms."

"When they come to the box office, tell 'em you only have good seats on Tuesday and Wednesday and Thursday. Fridays and Saturdays take care of themselves."

And, when it comes to looking for the next big hit, "Nobody can pick 'em."

In 1942, Jimmy went into the war as an aviation cadet. He wanted to be a flier, but he had no depth perception. The first time he tried to land a plane, he missed the field by six hundred feet. He went to gunnery school, but he could never hit the target. The army didn't know what to do with him. Then he heard about *Winged Victory*.

Written and directed by Moss Hart, *Winged Victory* was a play with music commissioned by the United States Army as a fund-raiser for the

Army Emergency Relief Fund. With a cast of three hundred, including servicemen and actors, it was a smash on Broadway in 1943 and then toured the country for more than a year. Jimmy worked in the box office. He was also cast in the movie, directed by George Cukor. But he lasted only a day on the set. "They shot the first scene thirty times, and I thought, Get me outta here. I'm not an actor. I don't want to do the same damn thing thirty times."

After *Winged Victory*, Jimmy was sent to Guam. "Tropical thing," he said. "One minute it rains, the next minute the sun's out." There wasn't much to do, so, because of his show business background, he decided to produce plays to entertain the troops. He returned to Detroit when the war ended and struck out on his own, leasing a theater in Toledo from the Shuberts. It was a small house (a thousand seats), so he could only book plays. Musicals went to the bigger houses. He went broke. He then moved to Minneapolis to run a theater, but discovered the city was too far afield from the traditional Broadway touring route—Boston, Philadelphia, Pittsburgh, Cleveland, Detroit, and Chicago.

He learned how to deal with temperamental stars, however. "The best thing is to get along with 'em, keep 'em happy," he said.

Beatrice Lillie was touring in a play called *Inside U.S.A.* She was doing a split week in St. Paul and Minneapolis. The show had a strong advance sale in Minneapolis, but died in St. Paul. She didn't make a penny. Furious and humiliated, she wanted to close the show.

"Jesus, don't do that," Nederlander told her producer. "Play Minneapolis, and then close it when you get to Boston. I'll get her the money she thought she should have made in St. Paul."

He didn't have it himself, so he went to three restaurants he frequented and borrowed $2,500 from the owners. He put the money in an empty ticket box and went to Lillie's dressing room. "Here's your money from St. Paul," he told her.

She took the money and threw it up in the air.

"It went all over her dressing room," he recalled. "But she went on in Minneapolis."

Jimmy returned to Detroit and becme the booker for his father's theaters. "We need shows," D. T. told him. "Go to New York and get some." Jimmy started making frequent trips to New York. He cajoled, wheedled, and begged for shows from agents, managers, and producers.

In 1957, the U.S. government ordered J. J. Shubert to break up his empire. He had to unload theaters in New York and around the country. And he had to dissolve partnerships either by selling theaters or buying out partners such as D. T. Nederlander in Detroit. J. J.'s lawyers offered D. T. a fraction of what his share of the Shubert-Lafayette was worth. Jimmy believed J. J. was "trying to force my father out." Furious, D. T. told the Shubert lawyers, "Tell Mr. Shubert I am not ready to get out of show business!"[1] After months of wrangling, D. T. bought out the Shuberts. He told Jimmy to go to New York and settle up the terms with J. J.

In his office in the Sardi Building, J. J., ever the petty tyrant, snarled at Jimmy. "You've got my scenery from *The Student Prince* in the basement of your theater."

"I don't think so, but you could be right," Jimmy replied. "What do you want me to do about that?"

"I'm going to hold back $2,500 until I get my scenery."

J. J.'s son, John, overheard the conversation. He was fond of Jimmy, so he made a call to the Shubert warehouse in Fort Lee, New Jersey, and was told that the sets for *The Student Prince* were there. He took Jimmy aside and said, "Let's not upset my father. Let it go, and in six months I'll send you a check. He signs all the checks. I'll put one in the pile and he won't notice."

Sure enough a check for $2,500 signed by J. J. arrived in Detroit six months later.

"John was a lovely guy," said Jimmy. "J. J. was mean."

Over the next few years, during his frequent trips to New York to get shows, an idea began taking shape in Jimmy's head. John Shubert died in 1962; J. J. the following year. And Jimmy knew that Larry Shubert, the titular head of the company, was a boozer.

"There was really nobody to compete against the Shuberts, so I decided I would. I had the training from my father. I was the logical successor to the Shuberts. My father had been their partner. I wanted to be their competitor."

The consent decree barring the Shuberts from buying theaters in New York gave Jimmy his opening. One day in 1965, walking through Times Square with his friend the producer Joseph Harris, he passed the Palace Theatre on Broadway and Forty-Seventh Street. "You know, RKO wants to sell the Palace. Why don't you buy it?" Harris said.

"Okay," said Jimmy. "Where's the guy?" Harris took Jimmy to the office of RKO president Harry Mandel. Mandel told him he wanted $1.4 million—$400,000 down—for the fifty-two-year lease on the theater (the land was owned by two old ladies from the Upper East Side). "Okay, you got a deal," Jimmy told him.

Jimmy didn't have any money at the time, so he went back to Detroit and raised the $400,000 from his father and his father's friends in the automobile business. His father thought he was "crazy" to set up shop in New York. "The unions will kill you," he told his son. Jimmy replied, "Listen, New York's the name of the game. And if it's good enough for the Shuberts, it's good enough from me."

Jimmy opened the first Nederlander office in New York above the Palace Theatre in August 1965. A rickety elevator took him up to the seventh floor. Julius, who'd been working at the theater for nearly twenty years, operated the elevator. He always had his Bible with him, and he prayed for everybody who rode in his elevator. "Julius came with the theater," said Jimmy, who would employ the elevator operator until his retirement in the 1990s.

Once the mecca of vaudeville, the Palace by the mid-sixties was ramshackle. Judy Garland, Danny Kaye, and Harry Belafonte enjoyed successful engagements there in the 1950s, but for the most part it was a second-rate movie house. Jimmy refurbished it and reopened it as a legitimate Broadway theater. His first tenant was Bob Fosse's *Sweet Charity*, starring Fosse's wife, Gwen Verdon. It ran over a year. "Should have run even longer," Jimmy said, "but Gwen and Bobby were fighting, and you never knew when she was gonna show up."

Jimmy started buying other theaters. He picked up Henry Miller's Theatre (now the Stephen Sondheim) from the widow of producer Gilbert Miller, whose father built it. He paid $500,000. "Mrs. Miller went right out and bought a diamond bracelet with the money!" he remembered.

He took a half interest in the Brooks Atkinson Theatre for another
$500,000. He also bought theaters in other cities, including San Fran-
cisco, San Diego, and Los Angeles. He'd go on to buy the Billy Rose on
West Forty-First Street (which he renamed the Nederlander, after his
father), the Lunt-Fontanne on Forty-Sixth, the Alvin on Fifty-Second
Street (now the Neil Simon), and the 46th Street (now the Richard
Rodgers), which he bought from two men in prison for fraud.

The *New York Times*, profiling Jimmy in 1967, asked him why he
was buying theaters at a time when "some believe the legitimate theater is dying." Jimmy replied, "Because we're making money." [2] He
told another reporter, "Ever since I've been in the theater business,
I've heard one thing, that the theater is dying. Thirty years later it's
still operating. If you have something that the public is interested in,
they will come." [3]

But finding something the public was interested in, in the early seventies, was not easy. Jimmy needed shows. Like Schoenfeld and Jacobs,
he was forced to become a producer.

"If you're gonna be a theater owner, you gotta be a producer
whether ya like it or not," he said. "The only way you can make money
with theaters is to keep 'em booked, so I had to give money to all these
guys who were trying to do shows."

He had plenty of flops and a few hits, his biggest being *Applause*
with Lauren Bacall at the Palace, which ran a little over a year. Bacall
could be a handful. When the run ended she asked if she could have
her dressing room furniture for her house in the Hamptons. "Take it,"
said Jimmy.

From their offices above the Shubert Theatre, Jerry Schoenfeld and
Bernie Jacobs watched Jimmy Nederlander assemble his empire. They
did not, at first, see him as a rival. He was buying theaters that, in their
view, were not top-tier houses. And though he refurbished the Palace,
he didn't have the money to spend on his other theaters, which were
in disrepair. "Jimmy was the biggest buyer of Scotch Mystic Tape in
town," an old producer joked. "Every time there was a hole in one of
his carpets, he'd cover it up with Mystic Tape. There was Mystic Tape
all over his theaters!"

"If you booked the Brooks Atkinson, chances were, in certain parts of the building, you could get hit on the head with plaster," joked Harvey Sabinson, a Broadway press agent at the time.

The Shuberts, meanwhile, controlled the two most desirable blocks in the Times Square area—Forty-Fourth and Forty-Fifth Streets between Broadway and Eighth Avenue. Their theaters lined both streets. And they had *A Chorus Line*, which dwarfed any show that played in a Nederlander house.

But in 1977, Jimmy Nederlander stumbled on his own blockbuster, one that would make him so much money the Shuberts finally had to acknowledge they had a competitor on the block.

And it was all because of a little red-headed girl and her dog.

In December 1971, Martin Charnin, an actor turned lyricist and director, was shopping at Brentano's bookstore on Fifth Avenue. He was looking for a gag Christmas gift for a friend and picked up a collection of Harold Gray's *Little Orphan Annie* comic strips. As he was wrapping the book, he thought there might be a show in the beloved comic strip. He called his friend Thomas Meehan, a writer for the *New Yorker*, and asked him if he'd like to take a stab at a musical. Charnin wouldn't tell Meehan what his idea was over the phone—"He was always a little bit paranoid; he thought Rodgers and Hammerstein had bugged his phone," Meehan said—so they arranged to meet in person. Meehan was thrilled. "I'd never been involved in the theater, though I loved to go. But I was forty, and I thought that ship had sailed."

When Charnin told Meehan his idea was a *Little Orphan Annie* musical, Meehan said, "I don't think so."

"I was thinking *West Side Story* or *My Fair Lady*," Meehan recalled years later. "Not a comic strip. Besides, when I hear *Little Orphan Annie* I cringe. I was a *Dick Tracy* fan."

"That's too bad," Charnin said, adding, "Charlie Strouse is writing the music." Strouse was the successful composer of *Bye Bye Birdie* and *Applause*, with two Tony Awards on his shelf. Meehan changed his mind. "Who was I to tell Charles Strouse to go take a hike?"

Meehan went off to the library at the *New York Daily News*, which had the complete run (beginning in 1924) of *Little Orphan Annie* on microfilm. He spent hours looking at the strip—and grew more and more disheartened. "There wasn't much there," he said. "There was a rich man, a girl and a dog—and that was it." A few days later, however, he found a way in. "I suddenly saw orphans in darkness. I love Dickens and I began to think maybe we could make this Dickensian. Nixon was president, and it was a dark time. I thought it might be interesting to write something set in the Depression that starts off dark but then becomes hopeful with a president—FDR—who radiates optimism and a New Deal. I want to be clear: We were not thinking of it as a family show. We wanted to write something about the American experience."

As it happened, Strouse and Charnin captured the Dickensian spirit Meehan was aiming for in the first song they wrote, "It's the Hard-Knock Life." And they captured the musical's fundamental optimism in their second song, "Tomorrow."

"We decided we wanted to write an old-fashioned musical," Meehan said. "At the time, Hal Prince and Steve Sondheim were doing the so-called concept musical—*Company, Follies.* But *Little Orphan Annie* was not going to lend itself to that form. We wanted to write the kind of musical we loved as kids—tuneful, funny, straight ahead with the story."

Meehan fleshed out the comic strip, adding new characters, the most important of which was the villain, Miss Hannigan. She was inspired by a minor character in the comic strip—Miss Asthma, who ran the orphanage. "Hannigan was my grandmother's maiden name," said Meehan.

By 1976, with a first draft in hand, they began holding backers' auditions. Nobody gave them a dime. At one audition at Strouse's apartment, Meehan saw a woman pass a note to her husband. Meehan later found the note on the floor. It read: "I'll kill you for having brought me to this thing!"

"That was our first review," said Meehan.

The Shuberts passed on the show. Schoenfeld told Meehan, "A little girl and a dog are not commercial." Michael Price, who ran the Goodspeed Opera House in East Haddam, Connecticut, also passed. Discouraged, Meehan took all his *Little Orphan Annie* research, put it in a box, and stuck it in his attic. He was broke and went back to writing freelance magazine stories to make ends meet. Charnin was out of money, too, and the rights to the comic strip, which were held by the *Chicago Tribune*, were about to expire. He needed $25,000 to retain them, so he begged twenty-five friends to give him $1,000 each.

And then he got a call from Michael Price. "I just got back from London," Price told him, "and while I was walking through Hyde Park, I couldn't get that damn song of yours ['Tomorrow'] out of my head. So we might as well try the show."

Charnin, who would direct the musical, wanted to cast adults as the orphans. He and Meehan took Bernadette Peters to the Russian Tea Room for lunch and offered her the role of Annie. "What can I say? She was short and she could sing and she had red hair," Meehan said. "We were going to do the *Peter Pan* thing, and have a guy in a dog suit as Sandy. Thank God we came to our senses and figured out the thing had to be real, with real kids and a real dog. We needed a ragamuffin bunch of girls. We forbid them from washing their hair for two weeks before we opened at Goodspeed."

Meehan was pleased with the character of Miss Hannigan, but the woman playing the part—Maggie Task—wasn't landing the jokes. Lines such as "Why anybody would want to be an orphan, I'll never know" were met with silence. After the first preview, Meehan was standing in the lobby with his notebook. A man came up to him and asked if he was with the show. "Yes," Meehan said. "It stinks," the man replied. The local reviewers were split—half loved it, half thought it was the worst show they'd ever seen. Walter Kerr, from the *New York Times*, came up that summer to see it, and dismissed it as "a right-wing" musical. "He completely misinterpreted the politics because he knew that Harold Gray had been a right-winger," Meehan recalled. "There were a couple of guys in New York who had an option on the show but, not surprisingly after the Kerr review, we couldn't get them on the phone."

Annie looked like it would open—and close—in East Haddam. But during the final week of the run, the producer Lewis Allen, who was friendly with Charles Strouse, brought Mike Nichols to the show. After the performance, Nichols told the creators, "You guys are sitting on a million dollars."

A few days later, Sam Cohn, Nichols's agent, called with the magic words, "Mike wants to produce your show." Nichols met with Charnin, Strouse, and Meehan and told them, "I'm going to be the kind of producer I always wanted as a director: After the first day of rehearsal, I'm going to go away and let you do your work. You won't see me again until the first preview out of town." He did have one suggestion, however. He had a friend, a cabaret performer named Dorothy Loudon, who he thought would be perfect for the role of Miss Hannigan.

Tough, sharp-tongued, and bitter about a career that had stalled out—"people thought I was retired or dead," she once said—Loudon auditioned with "Hard Hearted Hannah" and got the job. She landed all the jokes, and ad-libbed a few of her own. When Rooster, Hannigan's brother, introduced his girlfriend, "Lily St. Regis, named after the hotel," Loudon quipped, "Which floor?" Meehan added the line to his script. Loudon's performance was helped immensely by the fact that "she hated kids," said Meehan. At the first reading of the show in New York, Loudon went up to Andrea McArdle, who was playing Annie, and said, "Listen to me, kid. If you make one move on any of my laugh lines, you will not live to see the curtain call."

Although Nichols would be billed as the lead producer of *Annie*, he was smart enough to live by Mel Brooks's rule from *The Producers*: "Never put your own money in the show." And so he left it to his agent, Sam Cohn, and his lawyer, Robert Montgomery, of Paul, Weiss, Rifkind, Wharton & Garrison, to raise the $750,000 to bring *Annie* to Broadway.

Montgomery called Jimmy Nederlander.

"We've got a show that looks very good, and we need some money," he said.

"How much do you need?" Jimmy asked.

"Three hundred thousand dollars."

"Three hundred thousand dollars! Jeez, that's a lot of money. What's the show?"

"*Annie*, based on the comic strip."

"I don't know."

"Mike Nichols is producing it."

"Mike Nichols! He's a talented guy," Jimmy said. "Let me think about it."

Jimmy called his friend Roger Stevens, a producer who ran the Kennedy Center, and told him about the offer. They decided to do it together, each putting up $150,000. They had 40 percent of *Annie*.

The musical opened out of town in Washington to enthusiastic reviews. Nichols took the creators to dinner and said, "You're going to be here six weeks. You've gotten good reviews and you're going to be a hit here. But if you do nothing and bring the show in as it is, you are going to have one of the biggest flops in history. So get to work."

"He scared us to death," said Meehan. The next day, in Nichols's suite at the Watergate Hotel, the creative team went through the show beat by beat, eliminating every scene, every lyric, every snatch of dialogue that slowed down the narrative.

Annie opened in New York on April 21, 1977—two years after *A Chorus Line*—at the Alvin Theatre on Fifty-Second Street. It rode into town on the wave of goodwill sweeping the country after the election of folksy, plainspoken Jimmy Carter. As Jack Kroll wrote in *Newsweek*, Little Orphan Annie is "the mascot of the new age of hope, optimism, and simplicity that's coming in with President Carter." John Simon, in *New York* magazine, understood exactly what Meehan was trying to do. He called the show "*Oliver* in drag."

For Jimmy Carter and the country, that wave of "hope, optimism, and simplicity" would be short-lived. Carter lost the 1980 election to Ronald Reagan in the midst of a recession. *Annie*, however, would endure, racking up 2,377 performances. It would also, despite its creators' intention to write a musical comedy for grown-ups, become one of Broadway's first family shows. During the early weeks of the run, the audience comprised the usual Broadway crowd—adults from the Upper East and West Sides. "No kids," Meehan said. "And then, about six weeks into the run, the same people started coming back with their kids."

Annie, which opened with hardly any money in the bank, took off. Meehan remembered going to Saks Fifth Avenue to buy a tie a few weeks after the opening. "Tomorrow" was playing in the background. Goddamn it, he thought, this really is a hit. Where are the expensive ties?

For Jimmy Nederlander, *Annie* was the best bet he'd made up to that point. His $150,000 investment returned a profit of $1 million from

Broadway alone. And that was just the beginning. There would be rent for years at the Alvin Theatre, money from three national tours, and a share of the $9.5 million movie sale.

While Tom Meehan went shopping for expensive ties, Jimmy Nederlander went shopping for more theaters. And soon Broadway was divided. By 1980, "You were either a Shubert man or you were a Nederlander man," said Manny Azenberg.

"The Great Duel," as the *New York Times* would call it, was underway.

CHAPTER FIFTEEN

I Love New York,
Especially in the Evening

In 1975, the year *A Chorus Line* opened and Broadway began to regain some of its luster, New York City nearly went bust. "Out of the blue, the richest city in the world suddenly became one of the poorest," Roger Starr wrote in *The Rise and Fall of New York City*. Or, as Ernest Hemingway put it in *The Sun Also Rises*, "How do you go bankrupt? Two ways. Gradually, then suddenly."

The storm clouds that had been gathering over the city for more than a decade—soaring municipal wages and pensions; the perverse economics of rent control; ever-expanding welfare programs and middle-class subsidies; short-term, sleight-of-hand borrowing to papering over ballooning deficits; and a crippling tax burden that chased businesses away—burst. The crisis began in February when the Urban Development Corporation, a state agency created to develop moderate-income housing, ran out of money. Its failure signaled to the markets that New York State itself was in trouble, which in turn highlighted New York City's financial plight. Later that month, lawyers for a group of powerful banks about to buy more city bonds demanded to examine the municipal books. They discovered a short-term deficit of $3.4 billion. "They professed shock at the irregularities and shortfalls they discovered, even though the banks they represented had overlooked such accounting practices in happier days," George J.

Lankevich wrote in *New York City: A Short History*. But now the music had stopped. When their report was made public, the city was frozen out of the credit markets. Bonds that had already been issued lost two-thirds of their face value. Standard & Poor's "acted with indecent speed and suspended [the city's] comically high A credit rating for the city," Lankevich wrote.

For the rest of the year the city lurched from crisis to crisis, requiring bailouts totaling hundreds of millions of dollars from the state. Abe Beame, elected in 1973 because he "knows the buck," lost credibility. He'd papered over budget shortfalls in the past, declaring the city solvent and warnings of impending fiscal doom overblown. Now, with the crisis in full tilt, nobody believed anything he said. Hugh Carey, the newly elected governor, spoke up for the city and seized power from the mayor. But there wasn't enough money in Albany to cover the city's financial obligations. Carey pressed Beame to wield the ax. Daily life became a struggle as transit fares went up, city payrolls were cut, and city services, such as garbage collection, reduced. Fearing pay cuts and loss of jobs, sanitation workers staged a wildcat strike, leaving fifty-eight thousand tons of garbage on the streets. Firefighters struck back with a "sick-in." Police officers distributed pamphlets in Times Square warning people to stay off the streets after 6:00 p.m. "At such times it seemed as if the city was only one step from anarchy or madness," Lankevich wrote in *New York City*.

The storm unleashed its full ferocity on October 17. The city needed $477 million to cover its obligations but had just $34 million on hand. Beame announced, "I have been advised by the comptroller that the City of New York has insufficient cash on hand to meet debt obligations due today. This constitutes the default we have struggled to avoid." Carey, along with such key city leaders as Richard Ravitch and former mayor Robert Wagner, convinced the New York City teacher's union to invest $150 million from its pension fund in city securities to stave off bankruptcy. But such emergency measures could not go on forever. Carey turned to the federal government for help. He cabled President Gerald Ford begging that he recognize New York "as part of the country."[1]

A few days later, at a National Press Club luncheon, Ford gave his answer. He would veto any attempt by Congress to bail out New York City. He then took the city to task for its inept hospital system, its swelling welfare rolls, its crumbling educational system, and its high wages and pension funds for city workers. The next day the *New York Daily News* summed up Ford's response to New York's fiscal crisis with the headline: FORD TO CITY: DROP DEAD.

For Broadway, the fiscal crisis meant the complete collapse of its neighborhood, Times Square. If the city seemed on the verge of "anarchy or madness,"[2] the situation was, as is everything about New York, amplified in Times Square. The streets were strewn with garbage. Prostitutes and drug dealers did their business with little interference from the police. Crime escalated. Schoenfeld and Jacobs were fighting to save the Shubert Organization and now, just as they had *A Chorus Line* up and running, their customers were being told by the police to get off the streets by 6:00 p.m. From the start of their reign, Schoenfeld and Jacobs made cleaning up Times Square a priority. As Schoenfeld often said, "Corporations can leave the city. But the theater industry can't move."* When they divvied up responsibilities, government relations fell to Schoenfeld. He was gregarious where Jacobs was dour and taciturn. "Jerry could talk you to death," said Harvey Sabinson, a press agent and Shubert confidant. "Bernie would scowl you to death. People thought Jerry was a windbag, but he was a feisty advocate for the theater industry."

A veteran Broadway producer said, "Honestly, I don't think Bernie cared much about Times Square. He'd step over a homeless person to get to a show. But for Jerry, cleaning up Times Square became a crusade."

Not long before Schoenfeld became chairman of the Shubert Organization, he met with Donald Manes, a powerful member of the New York City Council, and pressed the case for a sustained effort to reduce the smut and crime in Times Square. Manes told him, "Jerry, forget it.

---

* Ten years later, when the city aggressively offered tax breaks to retain corporations, Schoenfeld would rant to city officials: "Morgan Stanley can threaten to leave the city and get millions and millions of dollars in tax breaks. The Yankees can threaten to leave the city and get millions and millions of dollars in tax breaks. We get nothing because we can't threaten to leave the city!"

Your business is going down the tubes." Manes, who became Queens borough president in 1971, opposed any effort to rehabilitate Times Square. He feared the sex industry would decamp to Queens.[3]

"Jerry never forgot that—he repeated that story over and over," said Sabinson. "He was furious. And he developed issues. Panhandlers in Times Square drove him crazy. He harassed city officials to do their jobs. He became very close to the top police officers in Midtown South and Midtown North, which cover the theater district. He was a one-man band when nobody thought you could do anything about Times Square."

In the early seventies the Shubert Organization was not so powerful that it could sway city officials on its own. So Schoenfeld had the idea of presenting the theater industry as a united front. The vehicle he chose was the League of New York Theatres and Producers (today's Broadway League), a sleepy gentlemen's club for old producers where they could hang out and play cards. "Jerry perceived that the League could become a political arm of the theater business," said Sabinson.

Sabinson retired as a Broadway press agent in 1975 and retreated to his house in the Berkshires to write a book. Schoenfeld brought him back into the business with an offer to run the League. "My mandate was to establish a relationship with the government. The League never had anything to do with the government, but Jerry wanted it to become a lobbying organization." The Shuberts expanded the League's budget, and Sabinson hired economists and statisticians. Schoenfeld wanted studies of Broadway's economic impact on New York City, so he could make the case that the theater business was essential to the city's financial health. He could then argue that the city should pay attention to Broadway's needs, chiefly making the neighborhood safe for its customers.

Schoenfeld, who was close to Beame, pressed the mayor to form a group of Times Square businessmen, residents, and religious leaders to address the deterioration of the neighborhood. Since the Shuberts had supported Beame's election in 1973, the mayor could not ignore Schoenfeld. And so on January 16, 1976, Beame announced the creation of the Mayor's Midtown Citizens Committee, which would "provide policy guidance and assist in monitoring and evaluating the performance of city agencies in the cleanup of the Midtown area," the *New York Times* reported. Schoenfeld became the chairman, and the Shubert Organization agreed to cover many of the committee's expenses.[4] Other members included Vincent Sardi, owner of the eponymous restaurant; the Rev. Robert Rappleyea of Holy Cross Church; Barry McCarthy, an executive with the *New York Times*; and Seymour Durst, a real estate mogul who owned swaths of Times Square. Part of their job was to raise private funds to repair potholes, remove graffiti, install litter baskets, and pay for garbage pickup. It was a measure of how desperate the city's finances were in 1976 that private money had to be found to install litter baskets in Times Square. Producer Alex Cohen, never one to miss an opportunity to place a good quote in the paper, told the *Times*, "We're going to buy a thousand brooms to have artists and technicians help with the street cleaning. We're going to keep our own cages clean!"[5]

The city received a grant of $432,000 from the federal government to create the Midtown Enforcement Project. Its mandate was to investigate porno houses, dirty bookstores, and massage parlors with the goal of shutting them down if illegal activity was uncovered. The Midtown Enforcement Project would work with the Midtown Citizens Committee to clean up Times Square.

Schoenfeld took up his chairmanship with gusto. "I think Beame thought he'd form that committee to keep Jerry quiet," said Phil Smith. "You know, make him chairman of something, and he'll be happy. But Jerry turned it into a bully pulpit. He had a megaphone, and he was relentless."

Schoenfeld found an ally in Sidney J. Baumgarten, whom Beame appointed to run the Midtown Enforcement Project. Baumgarten "brought a ferocity to smut-busting not seen since the heyday of Fiorella La Guardia."[6] A graduate of Brown University and New York University Law School, Baumgarten was a tough, no-nonsense ex-army officer. "I became Eliot Ness," he said, "because the only person I had to report to was the Mayor."

Reporters were skeptical of yet another effort to clean up Times Square. After all, Mayor Lindsay had created a law enforcement task force in the early seventies to go after the pimps, prostitutes, and drug dealers, with negligible results. As Baumgarten noted, "We identified, in 1976, four hundred and fifty illicit establishments from Fifty-Ninth Street to the Battery. And that included prostitution, pornography, and drug dens. And many of them were multiple uses. Lindsay's efforts didn't have any real bite."

The *New York Times* cast doubt on Beame's new committees. "The Mayor was reminded that crackdowns on urban vice date to Sodom and Gomorrah, at least, and he was asked why the public should place greater faith in this one. . . . The attempt to stop prostitution is perennially controversial, touching on the rights of streetwalkers, their patrons and the public."

Keenly aware that civil libertarians were scrutinizing his every move, Baumgarten, with the help of two other lawyers, including a Fordham law professor, outfoxed them by crafting the Nuisance Abatement Law. It stipulated that if a sex shop had racked up at least two convictions for prostitution or five for drugs and gambling or had more than three zoning violations, Baumgarten could go to a judge and get an ex parte order to shut the place down—"ex parte" meaning the judge could issue the order without notifying the owners of the sex shop. Due process was guaranteed, however, as the law stipulated the defendants had a right to a public hearing within seventy-two hours of the ruling. The City Council passed the law in 1977. "It was challenged several times, but was always upheld and is still in use today," said Baumgarten.

Baumgarten used other, less public, strategies as well, some fiendishly clever. Most of the establishments he targeted were involved in some sort of illegal activity—drugs, gambling, prostitution. Once he had a conviction in hand, he would go to the bank that held the mortgage and point out that every mortgage forbids the running of an illegal operation in a building. "Foreclose!" he'd say. "Here's the evidence!"

"We put a lot of pressure on the banks," he said.

Most of the sex shops were run by people for whom criminal activity was a way of life. Many eliminated Con Edison charges by tapping into electrical services from adjoining buildings. Baumgarten flooded the sex shops with Con Ed inspectors. If they found wires had been jumped, they shut off the electricity. The next day the owners would put out candles—and Baumgarten would have the fire department investigate them for having open flames without an open flame permit. The fire department would order the store shut.

Dirty bookstores were more difficult to close, since they were protected by the First Amendment. So Baumgarten sent undercover men in to browse around and make a note of the volume of sales. An undercover man would buy a bunch of books, and then Baumgarten's office would check sales tax records to see if the stores were reporting sales tax. Since much of the sex industry was run by the Mafia as a way of avoiding taxes, the bookstores fell into Baumgarten's trap. He hit them with tax violations.

Baumgarten's tactics were controversial, and he was opposed, at times, by the police department itself. "One of the major problems we saw right away was that there was an enormous amount of corruption in connection with the vice business," he said. "We had an informant who estimated that at least $10 million a year was going into NYPD pockets, some of it going to fairly high echelons of the police department."

Police officers assigned to a block might go into three massage parlors and make arrests, but leave another three free to do business. "I'd call up the men and say, 'How come you don't ever go into that place?' And a big tough cop would say, 'Well, they have a big dog and I'm afraid of dogs.' The excuses were bizarre."

To steer clear of pervasive corruption, Beame allowed Baumgarten to handpick his own force—police officers as well as building, fire, health, and consumer affairs inspectors. His second-in-command was a retired three-star police chief named Fred Kowsky. "He had the greatest reputation in the police department," said Baumgarten. "This guy would arrest his own grandmother if she committed a crime. I told him, 'Fred, we've got to pick the right people for this job because if there's any hint of corruption, we've had it.'"

The NYPD wasn't the only law enforcement agency unhappy about this special force beholden only to Baumgarten and Kowsky. The district attorney's office had doubts about using law enforcement to rid

Times Square of the sex industry. Prosecuting sex offenders created a revolving door, Manhattan DA Robert M. Morgenthau told the Midtown Citizens Committee. Pimps and prostitutes would be arrested, fined (about a hundred dollars), and let go. Even those who did jail time were out on the streets in little more than a week. The whole business, Morgenthau said, was a waste of time.[7]

Civil libertarians and disgruntled city agencies fired away at Baumgarten. But he had cover—the Midtown Citizens Committee. "We could not have done what we did without the backing of Jerry Schoenfeld and the Shuberts and the committee," Baumgarten said. "Having that group of prominent citizens behind us gave us political power. If we didn't have their backing, we would have been considered a bunch of renegades going off and doing our own thing. But we had Jerry and others, including Alex Cohen, the producer, supporting us. They could not be ignored."

Which is not to say all criticism was muted. One misstep involved the Shuberts and Cohen. The police department had a rule that an undercover officer could not disrobe to obtain a solicitation from a prostitute. The rule had been in place for years, going back to a time when the police force was largely Irish and the Catholic Church thought it immoral for a policeman to remove his clothes in a whorehouse. The hookers got wise to the rule and "the minute a guy walked in, they'd say, 'Take off your clothes,'" said Baumgarten. "If they refused, they knew the guy was a cop."

Then Baumgarten remembered an incident that had occurred at the Commodore Hotel on Forty-Second Street (the site of the Hyatt next to Grand Central Terminal today). The Archdiocese of New York held all of its functions at the hotel. But there was a whorehouse on the mezzanine, and when Cardinal Cooke found out about it, he told the hotel to get rid of the place or the church would take its business elsewhere. The hotel hired a law firm to start an eviction proceeding. The law firm flooded the whorehouse with private investigators, who later gave affidavits to the court about sex acts. The hotel was granted an eviction order.

Private investigators were not, of course, subject to the police union's no-disrobing policy. Baumgarten wondered if his task force could employ private investigators. But he worried that the private investigators could lose their licenses by engaging in illegal sexual encounters. Baumgarten sought guidance from the secretary of state of New York, who licenses private detectives. The secretary was Baumgarten's old friend from their Queens neighborhood—Mario Cuomo. "I sent Mario a formal letter asking for an opinion whether using private investigators to engage in sexual acts in order to close up offending premises would endanger their licenses," Baumgarten said. "And I got back a formal reply saying it was perfectly okay."

Then the question arose of how to pay for the private investigators. It was not, after all, an approved line in the task force's budget. Baumgarten turned to his two ardent supporters—Jerry Schoenfeld and Alex Cohen. They went out and raised private funds, much of it from the Shubert Organization and the League of New York Theatres and Producers, to pay for the private detectives. "We used them for six months, and really knocked the hell out of a lot of places where the cops couldn't do anything," said Baumgarten.

But the program remained controversial. Robert Morgenthau said the practice would "repel and disgust" a grand jury.[8] Beame ordered Baumgarten to discontinue it "immediately." Baumgarten himself came under heavy criticism for what detractors called "Nadjari-like tactics," a reference to Maurice Nadjari, the zealous special prosecutor.

Another controversy—embarrassing to Schoenfeld and his Midtown Citizens Committee—erupted when Baumgarten discovered that Seymour Durst, one of the most prominent members of the committee, owned the notorious Luxor Baths, Times Square's largest whorehouse.

Durst said he'd take care of the situation, which he did by selling the building to Betty Vicedomini, the madam running the whorehouse. Baumgarten and Schoenfeld were furious. "We threw him off the committee," Baumgarten said. "The mayor made the announcement that he was resigning." Durst laughed it off, telling the *Times*, "I hear I've just lost another job." Schoenfeld, who considered Durst a good friend, never spoke to him again.

Despite relentless press criticism (*Screw* magazine publisher Al Goldstein thought Baumgarten was a First Amendment–trampling

"ogre"), the controversial use of private detectives, and the embarrassing Vicedomini-Durst affair, Baumgarten's task force was effective. More than two hundred sex stores and massage parlors shut
down, never to reopen. But when Ed Koch was elected mayor in
1977 he unceremoniously dumped Baumgarten. "Just before he was
sworn in, somebody walked into my office and said, 'Give me the
keys to your car and clear out.' Swear to God. He took my city car.
I had to ask my wife to come in from Long Island and pick me up."
Koch dispensed with the sharp-elbowed Baumgarten, but he kept the
Midtown Enforcement Project. He replaced Baumgarten with another lawyer, Carl Weisbrod, who was far more sensitive to ruffled
feathers.

"Syd probably did a lot of things right, and a lot of things wrong,"
said Weisbrod. "But it was, to his credit, the start of a sustained effort
to address Times Square's problems. We continued a lot of the inno-
vative civil enforcement techniques that Syd introduced, although in a
much more collaborative way with the district attorney and the police
department. I would have to have been Attila the Hun to be hated
more than Syd was."

Weisbrod took a more expansive view of his new job. The focus
should not be solely on the sex industry, he thought. You could drive
the smut out, but law enforcement crackdowns could only get you so
far. Businesses, legitimate businesses, had to be lured to Times Square
for the neighborhood to thrive. And that meant redevelopment.
Schoenfeld was coming to the same conclusion. On a trip to Washington, D.C., he met with officials at the U.S. Department of Commerce.
They told him, "You have to create a climate for redevelopment in the
theater district and Times Square."

In December 1977, at Schoenfeld's urging, the League released its
first serious study about Broadway and its economic influence on the
city. It was titled *The Broadway Theatre: A Key to the Redevelopment of
Times Square*, and it began: "Wherever one travels the transcendent
image that emerges of New York City is Times Square. This gateway
to America, whose music and comedy attract millions yearly, is now
playing a tragedy whose sets are vacant hotels and buildings, whose
players are prostitutes and pimps, and whose theme is sex, crime and

violence. The unfavorable notices warn of retardation in the excep-
tional growth rate Broadway has experienced over the last four years
(100 percent), and the phenomenal increase in tourism it has generated."

The League pointed out that Broadway was the "single greatest"
tourist attraction in New York, generating $217 million annually for
the city. The theater business boosted revenues for restaurants, hotels,
taxis, parking lots, airfares, bus rentals, and tours. But, the report concluded, Broadway's attraction was being undermined by the sex, crime,
and violence engulfing Times Square. Redevelopment—improving
"the physical and ambient qualities of . . . Times Square in order to
foster public confidence"—was the solution.

Soon, a project would come along that both the city and the Shuberts could embrace, a new hotel, in the heart of Times Square, designed by an architect who believed in airy but insular urban spaces
that kept tourists safe from the filth on the streets.

The effort to rehabilitate Times Square was underway by the late
1970s, though it would take another fifteen years before tourists would
consider the Crossroads of the World as safe and fun as a theme park in
Orlando. The perception of Broadway, however, changed sooner. The
turning point was a 1978 television commercial featuring actors from
Broadway shows, a catchy jingle, and a slogan that became famous all
over the world.

Success has many fathers, and the I Love New York campaign is no
different. It seems that every New Yorker who had anything to do with
government, marketing, public relations, or Broadway in the late 1970s
was the genius behind it.

Publicist Bobby Zarem, the "superflack" of the seventies, was walking home in January 1976 after a late-night dinner at Elaine's when
he "realized you could roll a quarter down Second Avenue and there
wasn't a car or a person to stop it." The city Zarem fell in love with as
a boy in Savannah, Georgia—the city of the Stork Club and the Co-
pacabana, Walter Winchell and Broadway—"was dead and dropping
into the East River."

Zarem wanted to do something. He claims he came up with the

I Love New York slogan that night. On Monday morning he wrote a proposal for a campaign to save New York. It was inspired by the one thing New York had that no other city had—Broadway. The first three people he wrote to for help were producers Alex Cohen, David Merrick, and Hal Prince. "Alex and David never wrote back," he said. "Hal Prince did, but he said he was in Boston with *Pacific Overtures*, and couldn't get involved with anything else right now." Eventually, Zarem got his proposal to Charles Moss, creative director of the advertising agency Wells Rich Greene. The agency took charge of the campaign and got Albany on board.

That's one version of how it all began. Here's another. Accepting her award as a New York City Living Landmark in 2013, Mary Wells Lawrence, a founder of Wells Rich Greene, recalled having lunch with Governor Hugh Carey after Ford, in *Daily News* parlance, told the city to drop dead. Carey was upset. "I love New York so much," he said. "If I get your agency a lot of money can you make everybody love New York?"

Wherever the truth lies, everybody credits Charles Moss and William Doyle, deputy commissioner of the Department of Commerce, for putting the campaign together. Moss called Steve Karmen, who'd written many jingles for Wells Rich Greene clients, including Budweiser and Nationwide ("is on your side"). Moss told him, "We're doing a campaign for the state. The line is 'I Love New York.' We need a song. Call me tomorrow." Karmen, born and raised in Brooklyn, sat down at his piano and began his jingle with a dramatic and catchy major ninth chord. He finished it that afternoon and sang it over the phone to Moss the next day. Moss gave him the green light to go into the studio with an orchestra and singers and make a full-blown recording. His budget, Moss told him, was unlimited. Karmen knew he'd come up with a winner when his handpicked singers said the tune was fun to sing. "These guys sang everything," he said. "A Budweiser commercial in the morning, a Miller commercial in the afternoon. If they liked something, you knew it was good."

For the logo, Doyle and Moss turned to graphic designer Milton Glaser, who designed *New York* magazine, and had cofounded it with Clay Felker. Glaser came up with two black lozenges side by side. The first contained the words "I love," the second, "New York." But as the printing presses rolled out the logo, Glaser, doodling in the back of a cab, came up with a better image: I ❤ New York. Stop the presses, he told Doyle. It put the campaign over budget, but Doyle agreed the new logo was better.

The state's initial budget for the I Love New York campaign was $4.3 million. The logo would appear on posters and T-shirts, and the song would be heard in bars, hotels, taxicabs, and airports in the city. But the centerpiece would be a television commercial.

The first commercial opened with a fisherman saying, "I live in New Hampshire, but I love New York." There was also a woman from West Virginia. She loved New York, too. And a man from "Cape Cad." There was footage of the Hudson River Valley, the Adirondack Mountains, Niagra Falls. The spot promoted New York State as a place to vacation in the summer. There wasn't a single shot of a Broadway show or New York City. And then somebody—again, everybody takes credit—had the idea of spotlighting the theater. The second commercial Wells Rich Greene produced focused exclusively on Broadway.

Shooting took place during the week of January 25, 1978, at Stage 2 West at 460 West Fifty-Fourth Street. A blizzard was pounding the city, but the show must go on, so the League of New York Theatres and Producers arranged for a fleet of cars to ferry the Broadway actors to the taping. Michael Bennett was on hand to direct the snippet from *A Chorus Line* (dancers in the "One" formation), the first show to appear in the spot. Joining the cast of *A Chorus Line* were actors from *Annie*, *The Wiz*, and *Grease*. Yul Brynner was there, too, surrounded by the boys and girls in the revival of *The King and I*. Frank Langella, Broadway's newest star as the title character in *Dracula*, worried about appearing in a commercial dressed as a vampire. He didn't want to be typecast as a villain.

The *New York Times* covered the taping. "The theater is simply the carrot because it is the most unique and most desirable thing about New York," a Wells Rich Greene executive told the paper.[9]

The actors were instructed to sing "I Love New York." They were not allowed to say the name of their show or sing a song from it. The point was to advertise Broadway, not individual shows. But Yul Brynner managed to sneak in one "et cetera," and Sandy got to bark during the *Annie* segment.

The final shot was to be of Frank Langella, as Dracula, engulfed in fog. His line was, "I love New York. Especially at night." But Langella didn't like the word "night." Dracula, he said, would never say "night." Dracula would say, "evening." True enough, but this was a one-minute commercial, timed to a fraction of a second. "Night" was one syllable. "Evening" was two. It added a shade too much time. Langella did several indifferent takes saying the word "night." To keep him happy, the director let him do one take his way. Langella looked straight into the camera and purred, "I love New York. Especially in the eeee-ven-ing." Then he turned his back to the camera, swirled his cape, and walked off into the fog.

Joshua Ellis, the press agent for *Dracula*, watched the take. "It was glorious," he said. "The smoke and the cape, that one take was superior to everything else. They asked him to do it the same way again but using the word 'night.' He kept doing crappy versions so they'd have no choice but to use the one he liked. It required internal surgery to fit it in, but the effect was immediate and thrilling."

The Broadway version of the I Love New York commercial was unveiled February 14, 1978, at a luncheon at Tavern on the Green. Zarem, who did the press for the launch, rounded up fifty New York celebrities and placed them at tables representing the state in which they were born. (Diana Ross sat at the Michigan table amid dignitaries from that state.) There was plenty of behind-the-scenes jockeying for a position on the dais. Governor Hugh Carey, who hosted the luncheon, refused to invite the city's newly elected mayor, Ed Koch. Koch had defeated Mario Cuomo, Carey's handpicked candidate. Zarem feared the press would zero in on the mayor's absence from an event celebrating one of his city's greatest assets, Broadway. "I had to beg the governor to let me invite the mayor," Zarem recalled. "Finally, at eleven o'clock, one hour before the lunch, they gave me the go-ahead."

At 12:30 the curtains were drawn at Tavern on the Green and the lights turned down. A screen at one end of the banquet room flickered. The first shot was of a conductor in a Broadway pit leading the orchestra as it played the "I Love New York" theme song. The conductor pointed to the viewer and then, as the dancers from *A Chorus Line* appeared, the narrator said, "There's only one Broadway. It's in New York." The crowd cheered. By the time Langella swirled away in the fog with his "Especially in the eeee-ven-ing," they stood and applauded. The next day, newspapers around the country carried a photograph of Yul Brynner, Koch, Carey, Diana Ross, and Frank Langella holding the sheet music to "I Love New York" and singing the song.

The commercial ran in markets throughout the Northeast for a little over a month. Within two and a half weeks of its first airing, gross weekly theater revenues jumped 30 percent, the *New York Times* reported. Restaurants in the Theater District reported a revenue increase of 15 percent. Thirteen thousand travel agents requested Broadway package tour brochures after seeing the commercial. In July, Deputy Commissioner Doyle announced that the spot was so successful it was going national. He estimated that the $4.3 million the commerce department invested in the I Love New York campaign had generated $14.3 million tax dollars for the state, and another $8 million for New York City and other local governments. "It's a profit-making operation," he said. "For every dollar we're spending we're getting three or four back. Every other state but New York seemed to know that until now." [10]

The I Love New York campaign spread across the country, and then the world. A couple of years after the launch, Steve Karmen, who donated the royalties from the song to New York State, took his children to Egypt. He was astounded to see I ❤ Cairo T-shirts all over the place.

By the close of the 1970s, Broadway was in better shape than ever. In 1979 attendance hit 9.4 million. Not since 1968 had that many people taken in a Broadway show. The Shubert coffers were swelling, and Schoenfeld and Jacobs were on the prowl for more shows. Michael Bennett was planning his next musical, which everybody was sure would be a hit. Jimmy Nederlander was flying off to London looking for shows. While there he made a deal with the Royal Shakespeare Company for first dibs on productions. The RSC was putting together an eight-and-a-half-hour adaptation of *Nicholas Nickleby*, to be directed by an up-and-comer named Trevor Nunn. It hardly seemed commercial, but Jimmy was game. As his father told him, "Nobody can pick 'em."

Back in New York, over lunch at the Palm Court in the Plaza Hotel, a Broadway impresario who'd been out of the game for several years was plotting his comeback. His ticket would be a musical about Broadway itself.

CHAPTER SIXTEEN

The Coiled Cobra

Schoenfeld and Jacobs's dealings with David Merrick stretched back to their days as lawyers for J. J. Shubert. It usually fell to them to negotiate terms for Merrick's latest show. They found him by turns exasperating, duplicitous, nasty, hilarious, and ridiculous. Schoenfeld once observed that Merrick's power came from the fact that "he didn't give a damn what people thought about him. Most people care about the impression they make on others. David did not."

Jacobs, who spent more time with Merrick than Schoenfeld did, had a different take on the impresario. While admitting that "negotiating with David gave me a stomachache," he added, "I think the person David enjoyed fighting with was me. Somehow I represented a challenge. But I learned that, despite his penchant for fighting and being disagreeable and nasty, David was susceptible to flattery like no other person I ever met in my life. You could pour it on with David as if you were taking a quarter pound of butter and putting it on a piece of bread. I would say, 'David? Why are you getting so excited? Without you there'd be no American theater. You're the most important producer of our time.' And he'd say, 'You're right,' and all of sudden he becomes meek."

David Merrick was indeed "the most important producer" of his time. His hits included *Gypsy, Irma la Douce, A Taste of Honey, Oliver!, Hello, Dolly!, Play It Again, Sam,* and *Promises, Promises.* At his height in the mid-1960s, *Time* magazine estimated he employed 20 percent of the workforce on Broadway. His face—cold black eyes, a black moustache nearly hiding a permanent sneer—appeared on the cover of *Time* in March 1966. Merrick hated the picture and, with typical verbal flair, threatened to sue for "defamation of caricature." Howard Kissel, Merrick's biographer, said the image was "an uncannily accurate portrait of a brooding, wary, deeply disturbed man."[1]

He was born David Margulois in St. Louis on November 27, 1911, the youngest of five children of a failed salesman, Samuel, and a mentally unstable mother, Celia. They were divorced when he was seven. Years later he'd say they were both alcoholics and that his childhood "was like living on the set of *Who's Afraid of Virginia Woolf?*". He bounced from relative to relative, never experiencing the warmth of a stable, loving home. Later in life, the only relative he ever spoke of was his older sister Sadie, who looked after him as best she could. Once established, he brought her to New York and took care of her for the rest of her life.

His unhappy childhood made him secretive and misanthropic. "I have the soul of an alley cat," he liked to say. As an associate of his once said, "His whole career is a colossal plot to prove he doesn't need anybody."[2]

He was smart enough to win a scholarship to Washington University in St. Louis and then went on to earn a law degree from St. Louis University. He spent his free time hanging around theaters in St. Louis and was friendly with Tennessee Williams when both were at Washington University. When he became famous, he often claimed that he placed second in a playwriting competition. Williams entered as well—and didn't place at all. There's no record of such a competition and, as Howard Kissel notes, Williams never mentioned it in interviews. But it gave Merrick a good quip: "It only proved that the judges knew nothing about playwriting."

Merrick acted in plays in school, but he never thought about pursuing a career as an actor. There wasn't any money in it, and money was what he sought. Money and power. He wanted to be a producer, making the decisions and collecting the box office receipts. Penniless, he needed a stepping-stone to get out of St. Louis. That turned out to be a young woman named Leonore Beck, who'd recently inherited $116,000 from her mother. David married her, and with her money at his disposal, took her to New York in 1939. He changed his name to Merrick, a combination of Margulois and David Garrick, the eighteenth-century English actor and manager. He invested $5,000 of Leonore's money in a play by James Thurber called *The Male Animal*. It was a success, earning him $18,000. It also gave him valuable behind-the-scenes experience working alongside the show's producer and director, Herman Shumlin. He was quick to pick up on all the scams and secret deals associated with the theater, in particular kickbacks and ice.

Merrick hung around Shumlin for a couple of years before going off on his own to produce a comedy called *Clutterbuck*. It's all but forgotten today but it does have the distinction of being the first production Merrick publicized with a gimmick. Every night during cocktail hour, he called bars and restaurants to page a "Mr. Clutterbuck." Success came in 1954 with his first musical, *Fanny*, which had a score by Harold Rome. The show got good reviews, but the box office faltered a few months after opening night. Stickers began appearing above urinals in men's rooms all over the city that read: "Have you seen Fanny?" There was a sexy belly dancer in the show named Nejla Ates. Merrick had a nude, life-size sculpture made of her and, in the dead of night, installed it in the Poet's Corner in Central Park. He called the police, who came to take it away in the morning, surrounded by photographers and reporters. Merrick's *Fanny* antics did the trick. The show returned its investment in seventeen weeks and ran another two years.

Shows and stunts started piling up. When John Osborne's *Look Back in Anger* struggled at the box office, Merrick hired a woman to sit in the audience, leap on the stage, and slap the leading man, who was being cruel to his wife in the play. The incident and the play were discussed in the papers for three weeks until Merrick, chuckling, admitted he paid the woman $250 to enact her little scene. Merrick took great pleasure in baiting critics. When Stanley Kauffmann, drama critic for the *New York Times*, announced he would start attending previews rather than opening nights so that he'd have time to write more thoughtful notices, Merrick sent him tickets to the final preview of his latest play, *Philadelphia, Here I Come!*. Enclosed was a note: "At your peril."

When Kauffmann showed up at the theater that night, Merrick announced the performance was canceled because a "white rat" had
been found in the generator (Kauffmann had white hair). The *New
York Times* carried the story on its front page the next day.

In London, Merrick learned about a trashy sex novel, *The Philan-
derer*, that Kauffmann had written years earlier to pay the bills. It was
out of print, so Merrick searched bookstores all over New York and,
according to *Vanity Fair*, mailed eighty-nine copies to critics and editors at major American newspapers. The books arrived with a card
that read: "Compliments of David Merrrickk," a joke inspired by the
spelling of Kauffmann's name.

Kauffmann lasted less than a year as chief critic of the *Times*. An
awkward, shy man, he was uncomfortable being a public target, which
inevitably comes with such an influential job. His replacement, Clive
Barnes, approached the position with good humor. After his appointment was announced, Merrick sent him a note: "The honeymoon is
over." Barnes responded, "Why David, I didn't know we were married.
And furthermore, I had no idea you were that kind of boy!"

Merrick's most celebrated stunt involved his 1961 musical *Subways
Are for Sleeping*. The show received mostly negative reviews out of
town, so Merrick and his press agent, Harvey Sabinson, scoured the
New York phone book for people who had the same names as the
seven major newspaper critics of the day. He invited them to a preview
and gave them a steak dinner at Sardi's afterward. Then he created an
ad featuring endorsements of the show by his "critics," "Walter Kerr,"
"Howard Taubman," and "Richard Watts." (This stunt had been in the
works for years, but Merrick couldn't pull it off until Brooks Atkinson
left his post at the *Times*; he was the only Brooks Atkinson in the New
York City phone book.) The *Times* spiked the ad. *The Herald Tribune*
missed it, and ran it in an early edition of the paper. The publicity from
the stunt was enormous, and despite poor reviews *Subways* managed
to last a few months.*

---

* In 2013, producer Scott Rudin, who studied Merrick's career in detail, pulled off his version of the
stunt. This time the *Times* didn't catch it. Furious about theater reporter Patrick Healy's piece on the
closing of his show *The Testament of Mary*, Rudin slipped the following note into an ad for the play: "Let's
give a big cuddly shout-out to Pat Healy—infant provocateur and amateur journalist at the *New York*

As he conquered Broadway, Merrick divorced Leonore (she found out he'd given a mink coat to a dancer in *Gypsy*) and bedded hundreds of girls. He married six times, one wife, Etan, twice. "Women either leave the door open or they find me dead on the bottom of the cage," he once said. Asked by a female writer in the early sixties for his thoughts on feminism, he replied, "A woman's place is in the oven."[*]

If, as Schoenfeld thought, a key to Merrick's success was his indifference to what people thought of him, another was his ruthlessness. He fired people with abandon. *Hello, Dolly!* had its out-of-town tryout in Detroit. During the intermission of the first rocky performance, a furious Merrick was firing everyone in sight. Michael Stewart, who wrote the book, hid behind a door that opened onto the lobby. Just before the second act began, an usher kicked the doorstop, and as the door began to close, Merrick spotted Stewart. "And you can be fired, too!" he yelled.

He reveled in sowing seeds of anxiety among his creative teams. Merrick hired Peter Stone to write the book to *Sugar*, a musical version of *Some Like It Hot*. During the tryout in Washington, Stone went to take his customary seat on the aisle only to find Neil Simon sitting in it. That's how he learned he'd been fired.

Merrick ruled his empire from an office above the St. James Theatre. It was all red—red walls, red carpet, red lamp shades. "Really, the devil's color," said Richard Seff, an agent who represented several actors who appeared in Merrick productions. "He always looked at you like a coiled cobra," Seff recalled. "That was the image I had of him. You never knew when he was going to strike." One afternoon Seff went to the office to negotiate a contract for his client Anna Maria Alberghetti, who was director Gower Champion's choice to play the lead in the 1961 musical *Carnival!*. Merrick offered Seff a cup of coffee and got right to the point.

"How much does she want?"

"Well, David, you know pretty much what stars of her caliber get

---

Times. Keep it up, Pat—one day perhaps you'll learn something about how Broadway works and maybe even understand it." Broadway insiders loved it. Executives at the newspaper of record were mortified.

[*] Despite the diabolical bravado, he remained friendly with his first wife Leonore and paid her alimony, without contest, until the end of her life.

on Broadway these days," Seff said. "I'd say $2,500 a week plus a percentage over the break even."

The coiled cobra stared at the agent. "Are you out of your mind," he hissed. "She's a nobody. Her last movie [*Cinderfella*] was a stinker. Hollywood's dumped her. She doesn't have any talent."

"Well, what do you want for her then?" Seff asked.

Merrick thought a moment and said, "Gower seems to like her. She's not wrong for the part. It's a good break for her. I'll give her scale plus ten percent."

Seff laughed. "Oh come on, David."

And then the cobra struck. Merrick walked round his desk and snatched the coffee cup out of Seff's hand. "Get out of my office," he hissed.

"I had to go home and wait for him to call," Seff said. "Eventually he did, because Gower wanted her, and we got her asking price."

Because he was paying her so much money, Merrick despised the twenty-four-year-old Alberghetti. During rehearsals she fell ill and was temporarily replaced by her understudy, Anita Gillette, who worked for Equity minimum. Merrick told the press Gillette was better than Alberghetti. When Alberghetti returned to the show, he sent her a dozen dead roses.

By the end of the 1970s, the coiled cobra who baited critics, hissed at agents, taunted leading ladies, and produced hit after hit in the sixties was a has-been. His last major show of the seventies was songwriter Jerry Herman's *Mack & Mabel*. It was a miserable experience for everyone. During the tryout in San Diego, Merrick confronted the book writer, Michael Stewart, in a crowded elevator and shouted, "You're a hack." The two men who'd had success with *Hello, Dolly!* and *Carnival!* stopped speaking to each other. But Stewart had a mole in Merrick's office, a young assistant named Mark Bramble, who turned red every time Merrick spoke to him. This habit tickled Merrick, and from time to time he'd pop out of his office, point at Bramble, and say, "Blush!"

Stewart feared he was about to be fired, so he asked Bramble, his spy, to keep him abreast of what Merrick was plotting. Not much, it turned out. Merrick was involved in producing a movie at the time—

The Great Gatsby, starring Mia Farrow and Robert Redford—and wasn't focused on *Mack & Mabel*. The musical, which starred Bernadette Peters as Mabel Norman and Robert Preston as Max Sennett, ran just sixty-six performances in the fall of 1974. Merrick's next show, Stephen Schwartz's *The Baker's Wife*, closed out of town.

Merrick, it seemed, had lost his touch. He abandoned Broadway for Hollywood. He had the rights to *Semi-Tough*, a novel about professional football. He thought it would make a good musical but changed his mind and decided to turn it into a movie. With Burt Reynolds as the star, it was a minor hit. His third movie, *Rough Cut*, was a flop despite the presence of Reynolds and David Niven (who had to sue Merrick to get nearly $100,000 in salary payments that were not forthcoming). Hollywood was not for Merrick. On Broadway, in his heyday, he ruled unchallenged. But he was no match for the studios, which were owned by corporations for whom the phrase "David Merrick presents" meant nothing.

On a trip to Los Angeles, Bernie Jacobs and Phil Smith ran into Merrick at the Beverly Hills Hotel, where he was living. "I never leave the grounds," he told them.

"We knew then that he had gone completely wacko," Smith recalled. "He never leaves the grounds? What is he, a fucking prisoner? But he was around the hotel night and day. It was pathetic. He thought he was going out there to be a producer. But there was nothing for him to do. We were told by some people that they gave him a chair with his name on it and told him to sit right there while they went about doing their job making the movie. It drove him fucking nuts."

Merrick returned to New York, but there was something different about him. He had, of course, always been diabolical, manipulative, and mercurial. But he could outfox a forest of foxes. And he was always in control. Even when he yelled, which was rare since he preferred a chilly monotone, it was done with calculated effect. Now he seemed "off the wall," said Bob McDonald, the head of the stagehands union. "We heard he was on something."

Rumors spread through Shubert Alley that the legendary producer had become a cocaine addict. "Bobby McDonald was the first to spot it," said Smith. "He said to me one day, 'You know what the change is? He's sniffing coke.' I couldn't believe it. David never smoked, he never drank—he wouldn't even stand in the sun! But Bobby was right. I was friendly with Etan [Merrick's third and fifth wife] and she once said to me, 'Phil, you could have bought a beautiful house in the country for the amount of coke I ran down his toilet.'"

Though his behavior was more erratic than ever, there were flashes of the old, calculating Merrick. One of the things he had always been good at was soaking up gossip. While in California he heard that his ex-office assistant, Bramble, and his ex-friend, Michael Stewart, had acquired the rights to an old novel by Bradford Ropes called *42nd Street*, which, in 1933, had been made into a far more famous musical movie by Busby Berkeley.

Bramble and Stewart hit on the idea of a stage musical of *42nd Street* while they were writing another show, *The Grand Tour*, with Jerry Herman. They would work on the script in the afternoon at Stewart's apartment near Carnegie Hall. When things weren't going well—"and on *The Grand Tour* that was frequently the case," said Bramble—they'd knock off work and take in an old movie at the Carnegie Hall Cinema. "It didn't matter what was playing as long as it wasn't *The Grand Tour*," said Bramble. One afternoon the movie was *42nd Street*. They both agreed it would make a good stage musical. They called Jerry Herman and asked him to write the score. "No way," said Herman. "I don't want to be compared to Al Dubin and Harry Warren,"who'd written the score to the movie, which featured such standards as "You're Getting to Be a Habit With Me," "Shuffle Off to Buffalo," and the title song.

"You really should use their songs," Herman said.

They took his advice and filled out the score with other songs from the Dubin and Warren catalogue, including "Lullaby of Broadway," "We're in the Money," and "About a Quarter to Nine." Gower Champion came on board as director, but he wanted to put the show together in Los Angeles with Cy Feuer and Ernie Martin as producers. Stewart and Bramble hated the idea of working in Los Angeles. "I don't believe theater happens there," said Bramble. And then Bramble got a call from Merrick.

"Tell me about *42nd Street*," Merrick said. "I understand you have the rights to the novel."

"Yes, we do."

"Would you consider me as your producer?" Merrick asked.

"Of course, I would!"

Merrick chuckled. "Well, you're going to have a problem with your collaborator. He doesn't speak to me anymore."

"You're probably right," Bramble replied.

"If you can get him to come to lunch tomorrow at the Plaza Hotel, I will fly in tonight," Merrick said. "Shall we say one o'clock?"

Bramble called Stewart. "Absolutely not," Stewart said. "I have no interest in talking to David ever again." Bramble persisted. "Look," he said, "we have to be realistic about this. Your biggest hits, and Gower's biggest hits, have been in collaboration with David Merrick. Whether you like him or not, the fact is he made you both wealthy men and he took very good care of the productions. We've got to talk to him and hear what he has to say."

Stewart agreed, but he entered the Plaza Hotel the next day ready for battle. Neither man extended a hand, exchanging only the most perfunctory of hellos.

As they sat down for lunch, Stewart said, "It's a big show, David. We want scenery, we want many costumes, and we want sixteen girls."

Merrick looked at him and said, "I don't see it that way. I don't see it that way at all. I won't do it with fewer than twenty-four girls, and frankly I would prefer thirty-six."

"And he never lost the idea of doing a great big Broadway musical for his comeback in the theater," Bramble later recalled.

Bramble and Stewart agreed to work with Merrick, but Champion, who wasn't speaking to Merrick after the debacle of *Mack & Mabel*, quit as soon as he found out Merrick was on board. Merrick offered the show to Michael Bennett, Bob Fosse, and Hal Prince. All turned him down. It was a bad idea, they said. The Broadway musical had changed. With *Company*, *Follies*, and *A Chorus Line*, musicals were darker, more adult, more dramatic. A musical comedy with a lot of tap dancing and a bunch of songs from the 1930s was old hat. The show must go on as its theme? How hokey.

Merrick couldn't raise any money. His investor pool had dried up, and even Warner Bros., which had made the movie, passed. Bramble and Stewart did a backers' audition at the studio for five executives, including a lady who ran the theater department. When they were done, the woman said, "I really don't know you, but I must tell you, don't do this. It's a terrible idea." All Merrick could scrape together for a production budgeted at nearly $3 million was $150,000, put up by three Canadian businessmen.

To raise the rest of the money, Merrick offered the negative of *Rough Cut*, which had not yet been released, to Chemical Bank as collateral for a loan of $2.5 million. Because Burt Reynolds was at the height of his stardom, the bank agreed. "We stopped looking for investors," said Bramble. Now they had to get Gower Champion back on the show. Champion had directed three flops in a row—*Mack & Mabel*, *Rockabye Hamlet*, and *A Broadway Musical*. Merrick heard he was hard up. So he offered him a generous deal to direct and choreograph *42nd Street*. Champion accepted. The two men who had such success with *Carnival!*, *Hello, Dolly!*, and *I Do! I Do!* were back in business.

They clashed immediately.

Champion wanted to design the show in black and white, evoking the spare, hard edge of the Depression-era movie. Robin Wagner designed a set model that, said Bramble, was a "gray spectrum." He and Stewart took one look at the model and ran to a phone booth to call Merrick, who was in Los Angeles. "The set is fucking awful," Bramble told him. "You really need to get here now before a terrible mistake is made." Merrick was in New York the next morning and within a day the "gray spectrum" set was red—David Merrick red.

Champion asked the creators to give him two weeks alone with the cast. When Bramble and Stewart returned to rehearsals they were shocked by Champion's appearance. This tall, elegant, handsome man had withered almost overnight. He was thin, gaunt, gray. He was wearing a heavy coat. "I have a cold," he told them. It was June.

In July, the company headed to the Kennedy Center in Washington for the out-of-town tryout. Merrick moved into the Watergate Hotel, which became his command center. "He was having a blast," said Bramble. Which meant, of course, torturing his creative team. Bramble and Stewart were lovers at this point, and Merrick delighted in turning them against each other. He'd call Bramble up in the middle of the night and snicker, "Your partner is ruining the show." *Click*. Then he'd call Stewart. "That book your boyfriend wrote? He just ran the screenplay through his typewriter." *Click*. Then he'd call them both, "Gower Champion has never read an entire script in his life." *Click*.

Merrick wasn't wrong. The show was a mess in Washington. Songs were in the wrong place, and Champion was so busy with the choreography he didn't have time to direct the actors. But every now and then a happy accident would occur. At one rehearsal there was a problem with the scenery at the top of the show. The stage manager stopped the curtain just as it was going up, revealing a row of legs in tap shoes. Everybody said, "Wow! Look at that!" Champion kept the curtain at three-quarters of the way down and ordered the chorus to start tapping. One of the most thrilling openings in the musical theater was born.

But the show wasn't ready. Previews had to be canceled, the budget was soaring past $3 million, and advance ticket sales were negligible. Merrick said, "I don't care what's not finished. We're playing a performance tomorrow night." Somehow he rounded up about three hundred and fifty people to attend the first preview at the Opera House in the Kennedy Center—a theater that seats 2,350 people.

"It was like a graveyard," Bramble recalled. "The overture started and when it went into 'Shuffle Off to Buffalo' the audience started to laugh. And we thought, Oh, shit. They're laughing at us." As one chestnut after another was played, the audience tittered. When the orchestra went into "Lullaby of Broadway," the audience started whispering. Bramble and Stewart were devastated. We're fucked, they thought.

What they didn't realize was that the audience wasn't laughing at them. The audience was laughing with them, enjoying songs they hadn't heard in years. What they were whispering to each other was, "Do you remember that one?"

The show ran three hours. It was all over the place. But the three hundred and fifty people in the theater loved it. "And that's when David really started bearing down on everybody," Bramble said. "He smelled it. He smelled a hit." Merrick demanded new sets and costumes. He wanted everything bigger and brighter. Champion tried to resist—he still wanted to retain some of the edge of the Depression—but he was

now too weak to fight Merrick. He was also preoccupied with his leading lady, twenty-two-year-old Wanda Richert. The sixty-one-year-old
married director had fallen in love with her, and they'd begun an affair.
Merrick knew about it, of course. He'd also heard that shortly before
the affair began, Richert had had a one-night hookup with Champion's
son Gregg after a cast party. Merrick's suite was next to Champion's at
the Watergate, and he'd put a glass to the wall so he could eavesdrop.
"You should hear what goes on in there," he told Bernie Jacobs and Phil
Smith. "And this man is supposed to be sick." He also told them about
Richert's hookup with Gregg Champion. He paused and, twinkling
maliciously, sang, "She's got the son in the morning and the father at
night."

42nd Street opened in Washington to lukewarm reviews, including
a pan from the Washington Post. But Merrick charged ahead. "I know
where we are," he told the creative team. "We're not finished. I don't
care about the reviews. I believe in the show. And you can have anything you want to fix it. Anything you want. All it takes is time and
money and we have both."

Merrick took advantage of the reviews. He invited his three Canadian investors to Washington to see the show. He took Bramble aside
and ordered him to join them for dinner at the Watergate after the
performance.

"What do you want me for at that meeting?" Bramble asked.

"Because I want you to look miserable. I want you to look like you
are dying."

At dinner, Merrick appeared gloomy. "Gentlemen, I don't know
what to say about this. I've never been in this situation in my entire
career. I am mortified at the mess that's on the stage."

He kicked Bramble under the table. As instructed, Bramble began
to moan.

"I think," Merrick continued, "I'm probably going to close the show
here. I think that's the only thing to do."

He kicked Bramble again.

"No, don't close. Please David," Bramble pleaded.

The Canadian investors looked ashen.

"I might have to, that's all," Merrick said. "But you gentlemen be-

lieved in me when no one else did. You believed in what we were doing. And I will never forget it. I think you should let me give you your
money back with a one hundred percent profit."

He took out three checks totalling $300,000 and handed them to
the Canadians. They brightened and thanked him profusely. Merrick
put them in a cab. And then he danced a little jig outside the hotel and
said, "It's all mine now."

It was time to start playing games with the New York press. Merrick
again took advantage of the poor reviews, this time to dampen ex-
pectations for the show on Broadway. He played theater reporters
and gossip columnists "like a fiddle," Bramble said. He took ads in
newspapers, but then pulled them. He announced previews, and then
canceled them. The show wasn't ready, he said. It had to go back into
rehearsal. Champion, meanwhile, was growing paler and thinner by
the day. He staged one last number—"You're Getting to Be a Habit
With Me"—and then vanished. Only Merrick and a few of Champion's
close friends, including set designer Robin Wagner, knew where he
was—Sloan-Kettering, dying of a mysterious blood disease.

For most of the period when there should have been previews in
New York that summer of 1980, the cast played to an empty theater.
Merrick wouldn't let anyone in. He was, however, forced to admit dele-
gates from the Democratic National Committee, which was having its
convention at Madison Square Garden. He'd donated a performance
to the DNC months earlier and had to live up to his commitment. The
performance was a disaster. The audience was "half loaded," Bramble
recalled. "They had no interest in being there. They talked throughout the show." The next day Merrick canceled more previews and the
cast continued to run the show every night to an empty theater. One
day the actors brought stuffed animals and placed them in the front
row. They had an audience. Merrick loved it. "We'll start previews," he
said. "We'll let the audience in." The critics, including a novice named
Frank Rich who had recently joined the staff of the *New York Times*,
were planning to attend the final preview. Merrick canceled it at the
last minute, forcing them to attend the August 25 opening and file
overnight reviews.

At six that morning, Merrick phoned Bramble.

"I don't think Gower is going to live through the day," he said. "I'm calling everybody to the theater at 1:00 p.m., and I want you to go and make sure that everybody just keeps busy because I don't want them to find out how bad the situation is. I'm going to Sloan-Kettering and as soon as I know anything, I'll come to the theater."

In the Winter Garden that afternoon the cast did warm-ups and drilled lines. Jerry Orbach, who was playing impresario Julian Marsh, kept spirits up with jokes and songs. At four o'clock, Bramble spotted Merrick backstage. "Come here," Merrick said. They hid behind stacks of scenery.

"He's dead," Merrick said, and fell on top of Bramble.

"I never saw him like that," Bramble recalled. "He was devastated."

"No one can know this before we play the show tonight," Merrick said. "If the public finds out that Gower Champion is dead, we'll never be able to open." He paused. "I don't know how to tell the public."

Over the years there's been speculation that Champion died several days before opening night and that Merrick kept him "on ice" as he cooked up his greatest publicity stunt. But Bramble and others who worked on *42nd Street* say that is a myth. Champion died that morning, officially of a rare blood disorder called Waldenstrom's disease.*

To Bramble, Merrick at first seemed too distraught to plot any kind of public announcement. But his impresario instincts kicked in and he told his press agent, a young man from Queens named Fred Nathan, to invite camera crews from the local television stations to cover the curtain call. Nathan also called all the critics and told them to remain in their seats after the bows.

The opening night audience filed into the Winter Garden not knowing what to expect from a show that had produced some bizarre rumors. Frank Rich, admitting years later he was a "wreck" since this was the biggest opening he'd yet covered, took his fifth-row seat on the aisle and composed himself by recalling the excitement he

---

* Wagner, who was at the hospital when Champion died, believes Merrick was up to something, however. "His room was right next to Gower's at the Watergate, and I think he may have tapped the phone. I'm sure he knew how sick Gower was. He was getting blood transfusions almost every day in Washington. I think David was waiting for him to die before he would open the show."

felt as a teenager watching Barbra Streisand at the Winter Garden in *Funny Girl*.[3]

Bernie and Betty Jacobs settled into their aisle seats, not far from Rich. Somebody walked over to Jacobs, tapped him on the shoulder, and whispered into his ear. He got up and as he passed Phil Smith a few rows behind him, leaned down and said, "Merrick wants to see me."

A few minutes later he was back at Smith's side. "Gower Champion is dead," he whispered, "and David doesn't want anybody to know."

The overture began, the curtain went up—only a quarter of the way—and the audience roared with delight as a line of legs tap-danced to the title song. But then the dramatic scenes began, and the show deflated. "My heart sank," Rich would later write. "*42nd Street* was no match for *Hello, Dolly!, Oliver!, Carnival!*, or any other Merrick musical with an exclamation point in its title from my youth."[4]

Still, there was good buzz at intermission, except in Jacobs's row. Word began spreading among the Broadway elite that Champion was dead. John Breglio and his wife, Nan Knighton, heard the news. They took their seats for the second act, stunned.

The audience roared its approval throughout the second half of the show. Jerry Orbach brought down the house when he told Wanda Richert (playing the ingenue Peggy Sawyer), "Think of musical comedy—the most glorious words in the English language!"

There were eleven curtain calls that night. Frank Rich stayed for one and then dashed out of the theater. A friend accosted him on the street. "I have to talk to you," the friend said.

Rich brushed him aside. "I'm on deadline!"

"Gower Champion is dead," his friend said, and then disappeared into the theater.

Inside the Winter Garden the crowd roared. David Merrick, the greatest producer of his time, perhaps the greatest producer of all time, had returned to Broadway triumphant. He walked out on stage and the roar became deafening. Merrick had never before made an appearance at the end of a show. But he did not look pleased. His arms were folded, he was hunched over, and one hand covered his mouth. "This is tragic," he said. The audience laughed. "No, no. You don't understand. Gower Champion died this morning."

People screamed and collapsed into their seats. Merrick walked over to Richert and put his arms around her. Jerry Orbach yelled to the stagehands, "Bring it in! Bring it in!"

And the curtain came down.

Merrick's dramatic announcement of Champion's death made the front pages of every newspaper in New York, and many more around the world. It also made *42nd Street* the most famous show on Broadway. There were lines around the Winter Garden for three days, breaking box office records every day. Frank Rich's lukewarm review did not dent the show. A few months later, on a cold day in November, Merrick summoned Bramble to the theater right before a performance. Pointing to the limousines lined up and down the block, he said, "That's a hit. Now let's go eat." In the car up to Elaine's restaurant Merrick told Bramble, "Gower Champion staged his exit perfectly. And nobody could have promoted it better than me."

Merrick had made Champion more famous in death than he had ever been in life.

But soon after opening night, Merrick's behavior became odd even for him. He fired Nathan, his young press agent who had corralled the media on opening night. He also fired longtime associates, including Helen Nickerson, who had been his loyal secretary since 1963. "Pack your bags. You're fired," he told her.[5] He demanded a meeting with Bernie Jacobs and insisted that the price of house seats be raised to a hundred dollars—at a time when the top ticket price was thirty. Jacobs balked. The press would play up the price hike, he said. The public would think every ticket was a hundred dollars. That perception could kill the show.*

Merrick countered with another plan. He didn't think the Winter Garden was big enough to contain his hit. He wanted to increase the seating capacity from fifteen hundred to seventeen hundred by alternating the size of the seats. One seat would be eighteen inches. The

---

* Merrick eventually raised the price of house seats to fifty dollars. House seat orders dried up, and Merrick took a beating in the press. Albert Poland felt "that was a turning point and a part of the regular theater-going audience was lost."

one next to it would be fourteen inches. Husbands would sit in the bigger seats, wives in the smaller ones. "What are we going to do when somebody comes to the box office to buy a ticket?" Phil Smith asked. "Take out a ruler and measure their ass to make sure they can fit in the seat?"

Merrick didn't laugh.

He came up with another idea. "I'm going to open a second company of the show on Broadway," he told Phil Smith one day. Smith, who saw that Merrick was dead serious, replied, "Well, David, that's a great idea, but you might have a problem with the press. They'll rereview the show and they're liable to say it's not as good as they thought it was. Don't forget that Gower died that night. Maybe his death influenced their reviews."

"You're right," Merrick said, and never spoke of a second company again. But he wanted out of the Winter Garden, partly because he hated the box office treasurer, Bill Friendly. "Bill Friendly is not friendly," he'd say. He thought Friendly was stealing from him. Once he showed up at the box office pretending to be a ticket buyer. He pulled his coat up over his head and disguised his voice. "I want two tickets for tonight," he mumbled. Bill Friendly replied, "How are you, Mr. Merrick?"

Merrick stormed out of the lobby.

Jacobs finally gave in to Merrick's demand for another theater. The Majestic, which was larger than the Winter Garden, became available. Merrick could move *42nd Street* there. The show was scheduled to close at the Winter Garden on Friday, move to the Majestic over the weekend, and reopen on Monday. On Friday, Merrick turned up at the Majestic to inspect the theater. He exploded. The curtain was brown. He wanted a red curtain—David Merrick red. "This will not do," he said. He announced to the stagehands working in the theater, "I'm canceling the show. Go home." That afternoon Jacobs received a letter from Merrick's lawyer. "This is to advise you that *42nd Street* is closing tonight," it read. But then the lawyer called. "Bernie, David's gone too far out on the limb this time, and he doesn't know how to get back in," he said. "Can you help? Can you get the stagehands back to the theater?" Jacobs used his influence with the union, while Phil Smith went from one Shubert theater to another in search of a red curtain.

He found one at the Belasco that fit the stage of the Majestic. "It was crazy, but you know he was right," Smith said. "A red curtain was the right color for his show."

But Smith and Jacobs became increasingly concerned about Merrick's judgment and behavior. One day during the Jewish holidays when Schoenfeld and Jacobs were off, Smith got a call from Merrick. "I need to talk to you about something very important," he said. "Where are you?" Smith was in his office in the Sardi Building. "I don't walk down that side of the street anymore," Merrick said. He'd been boycotting the south side of West Forty-Fourth Street ever since his landlord, Jujamcyn Theaters, refused to renew his lease on his office above the St. James. "Can you open Bernie and Jerry's offices and we can talk there?" Smith thought to himself, Why am I going to open their offices for this lunatic? He persuaded Merrick to meet him in the Sardi Building. "He looked like he hadn't been asleep," Smith recalled. "His hair was askew. His wig wasn't on straight. He looked pathetic."

"You know what my problem is, Phil?" he said. "I've got to find someone to maintain the show. Otherwise the show is going to fall apart."

Ironically, Smith and Jacobs had been discussing that same subject at a dinner several days before with Michael Bennett. How do you maintain a show when the director is dead? Bennett said the best person to do it would be Marge Champion, Gower's ex-wife. The two had danced together for years. She knew every step he ever choreographed. Smith suggested her to Merrick.

"I couldn't do that," Merrick said.

"Why not?"

"Gower wouldn't like it."

"Don't tell him!"

"But if he calls, Phil, I'll have to tell him," Merrick said.

Champion had been dead for six months. Smith thought, I'd better call an end to this meeting. This man is nuts.

Not long after, Smith and Jacobs got further confirmation of the rumors they'd been hearing about Merrick. The treasurer of the Majestic called them. "Jesus, Merrick's off to the races," he said. "I just went down to the men's room and he's on the stairs sniffing coke off the steps!"

In 1983, Merrick went down to Rio de Janeiro, a city he knew well. He went down with one of his few friends in life, a doctor from New York. When they returned, the doctor died, suddenly, of a heart attack. Not long after that, Merrick suffered a stroke. He later admitted to Bramble that it was a cocaine stroke. He and the doctor had picked up some "bad stuff" in Rio. Merrick lost his most potent weapon—his dagger-like tongue. He could no longer express his quick, vicious wit. One of his ex-wives, Etan, took over his care. She took him to the south of France to recuperate. Bramble went to visit him at a villa overlooking the sea, but the staff told him Merrick was too sick to see anybody. Bramble demanded to be taken to his room. He found Merrick wrapped up in a heavy blanket even though it was the middle of August. He was moaning. But as soon as they were alone in the room, Merrick threw off the blanket. He was wearing a three-piece suit. "Can I please come back to New York with you?" he struggled to say.

And he did. He had no place to live, since his various houses were being renovated or were tied up in litigation with yet another ex-wife, Karen Prunczik, who played Anytime Annie in *42nd Street*. They were married ten months. Merrick moved in with Bramble at his 321 West Fifty-Fifth Street apartment. They went around town collecting cash Merrick had stashed in safe deposit boxes. Merrick was hiding money from his ex-wives and the IRS. At one point, he stashed $250,000 in an antique Victrola in Bramble's cupboard.

With Bramble's help, he kicked his cocaine addiction. They flushed bags of cocaine down the toilet.

Merrick saw almost no one while he lived with Bramble. But almost every day at lunchtime, Bernie Jacobs came to the apartment. The two warriors gossiped about box office grosses, rival producers, or the reviews for the latest show. And they talked about the old days, when the phrase "David Merrick presents . . ." caused a stir on Broadway.

CHAPTER SEVENTEEN

The Bernie and Jerry Show

With *42nd Street* selling out at the Winter Garden and *A Chorus Line* still selling out at the Shubert, hundreds of thousands of dollars a week were now flowing into the Shubert Organization. And *42nd Street* and *A Chorus Line* weren't the only hits in the Shubert stable. In 1978, Richard Maltby Jr., a lyricist and director, began auditions for a revue of Fats Waller songs in the cabaret space of the Manhattan Theatre Club (MTC), an Off-Broadway theater. He asked the performers to audition with a 1930s-style song. Since the performers were black, most came in with songs from the heyday of the Cotton Club. But not Nell Carter. The ample singer auditioned with Noel Coward's "If Love Were All." She knocked Maltby out with her heartbreaking rendition and got the job. Filling out the cast were Ken Page, André De Shields, Armelia McQueen, and Irene Cara (who would be replaced by Charlayne Woodard). Called *Ain't Misbehavin'*, the revue opened to raves in February at MTC. In April, it transferred to Broadway's Longacre Theatre. Its producers were Emanuel Azenberg, Dasha Epstein, and the Shubert Organization.

"Bernie and Jerry took me to practically every theater in New York," Maltby recalled. "In those days you had your pick of straight play theaters. They were empty. I picked the Longacre because it had a low stage and I wanted the connection with the audience. They couldn't believe I wanted the Longacre. Nobody wanted it."

Ain't Misbehavin' ran four years and became an ambassador for

Broadway. Because it was a small show and could tour easily, the I Love New York campaign sent a company to South America to encourage tourism to New York City.

The Belasco, another straight playhouse that was difficult to book, had a popular black musical called *Your Arms Are Too Short to Box With God*. The Imperial was home to *They're Playing Our Song*, Marvin Hamlisch's next show after *A Chorus Line* and a solid hit. At the Music Box, Ira Levin's *Deathtrap* was thrilling packed houses. Other popular shows in Shubert houses included *Evita*, *Morning's at Seven*, and *The Elephant Man*.

And at the Broadhurst, Bob Fosse's *Dancin'* had, by 1980, been running two years. Fosse's previous show, *Chicago*, opened in the same season as *A Chorus Line*. It was swamped by Michael Bennett's triumph. Fosse, according to biographer Martin Gottfried, resented the accolades lavished on Bennett. *Dancin'* was his response to *A Chorus Line*. But it was not a happy production, and he did not like his producers, the Shuberts. The feeling was mutual. Schoenfeld and Jacobs thought Fosse, who once said "I lift up a rock and choreograph what's underneath," pushed the sleaze factor beyond the limits of mainstream taste in two numbers, "Welcome to the City" and "The Dream Barre." The first depicted a tourist under assault from prostitutes, peep shows, and massage parlors. The second featured dancer Ann Reinking acting out a sexual fantasy with her dance master. Jacobs referred to "The Dream Barre" as "the cunnilingus number." When Schoenfeld expressed his concerns to Fosse right before the first preview in Boston, the director shoved him and snarled, "That's a goddamn lousy thing to say!" Schoenfeld thought Fosse was going to hit him. He didn't, but if he had, Schoenfeld "would have punched him right there."[1]

Their position at the top of the Shubert empire secure, Schoenfeld and Jacobs began to assert control over the theater industry. Long involved in union negotiations, they now dominated the bargaining tables. Schoenfeld handled musicians, ushers, managers, and press agents. Jacobs dealt with the actors and the stagehands, whose union was one of the most powerful in the city. With so many shows making so much money in their theaters, a strike was the last thing Schoenfeld and Jacobs wanted. But independent producers grumbled they were

giving away the store for the sake of peace. Production costs were
going up—and ticket prices along with them. Schoenfeld and Jacobs
countered that theater employees had a right to a decent wage and
good benefits and that a strike would be a disaster for the industry. They
remembered the actors' strike of 1960, when Broadway shut down for
thirteen days. Several shows could not reopen after the strike. A three-
week musicians' strike in 1975 also killed shows. Schoenfeld and Jacobs
thought the theater business was too fragile to risk losing productions
over labor disputes. As for ticket prices, Jacobs believed they'd been low
for too long. If a show was popular, the audience would pay a higher
price to see it. When Schoenfeld and Jacobs took over the Shubert Organization in 1972, the top ticket price was fifteen dollars. By 1980, it
was forty dollars. Every time Jacobs wanted to raise prices to *A Chorus
Line*, Joe Papp resisted—"but just a little," said Bernard Gersten, Papp's
right-hand man.

Schoenfeld and Jacobs were friendly with their labor adversaries. Jacobs and Bob McDonald, the head of the stagehands union, got along
especially well. Every now and then Jacobs would call him up and say,
"I hear you have an election coming up. Meet me in the alley [Shubert
Alley] and we'll yell at each other. It'll look good for you in front of
your men."

Which is not to say all negotiations were pleasant. In the seventies
and eighties, Irish Americans ran the ushers union. The head of the
union was a short, fat, feisty Irish lady. She once came to a negotiation
armed with a list of demands, including a day off whenever there was
a death in the family. "I've never heard of such a thing," Schoenfeld responded. The Irish lady jumped up and yelled, "God forbid—he won't
let us bury our dead!" Schoenfeld went white. Elizabeth McCann, the
producer, recalled, "The moment she would say, 'Holy Mother of God,
Jesus, Mary and Joseph!' Jerry thought he was being condemned to
hell. He got out of there so fast. I said to him, 'Jerry, you know a wake
lasts three nights. And they drink a lot. So they won't be in the next
day, either.'"

Schoenfeld and Jacobs took active roles in other Broadway institu-
tions, including the Actors Fund and the Theater Development Fund,
whose TKTS Booth in Duffy Square (the half-price ticket booth) they
helped create in 1973. (Duffy Square, the northern part of Times

Square, had been a magnet for vagrants, drug users, dealers, and prostitutes. The TKTS Booth was developed, in part, to clean up the area.) They also changed the way tickets were sold on Broadway. For years, box offices refused to accept credit cards or personal checks (ice melts much faster when it's in cash). The Shuberts accepted both, and they instituted, for the first time, phone orders. Their company, Telecharge, turned into a gold mine as each transaction came with a handling fee. It was only fifty cents, but fifty cents on thousands of tickets to *A Chorus Line*, *42nd Street*, *Ain't Misbehavin'*, and *Evita* added up.

Under J. J. Shubert and then under Lawrence, Schoenfeld and Jacobs toiled in obscurity. Until 1972, when they took over the company, their names rarely appeared in the papers. But by the end of the seventies, they were public figures.

"It is unlikely that any two people dominate their part of the entertainment business as thoroughly as do Gerald Schoenfeld and Bernard B. Jacobs," John Cory wrote in a profile that ran on the front page of the Arts & Leisure section of the *New York Times* on April 1, 1979. They "tower over the world of commercial theater. Collectively, they are known as the Shuberts, and individually, on every part of Broadway, as Bernie and Jerry. Either way they are flourishing, and while they do not necessarily take all the credit for the fact that Broadway flourishes with them, they do not entirely eschew it, either. Their hearts and Broadway's, they suggest, beat as one."

With critic Clive Barnes, they didn't "eschew" credit at all. Barnes, profiling them in the *New York Post*, asked, "This increase in the quality of the product—why has that come about?"[2]

"Us," said Schoenfeld.

"You mean the theatrical community?" Barnes asked.

"No, Gerald means us, Gerald and myself," Jacobs said. "This sounds immodest, and it really is not meant to. But the two of us have swung around the Broadway product. We simply have gotten better things on Broadway than we have ever had before. . . . Everyone with any sense knew ten years ago that the old image of Broadway was totally dead."*

---

* Barnes was one of the few critics friendly with Schoenfeld and Jacobs. He got to know them when he arrived at the *Times* in 1966. He enjoyed the occasional lunch with them at Sardi's. "They were smart

Despite the carping about Schoenfeld and Jacobs's control over union negotiations, Broadway producers thought the Shubert Organization was in good hands. They were, as Hal Prince called them, "good guys." They changed the theater rental agreement in their favor, but they were quick to lower or waive the rent if a show was struggling. They were loath to exercise the stop clause, which allowed them to evict a money-losing show, because they believed that a producer with a struggling show one season might come up with a smash next season.

Theater people also liked them because they were fun. The charge made by some producers who later came to resent their power that they were just lawyers was preposterous to anyone who knew them well. They were, in their own way, Broadway characters. Jacobs had a dry, cutting wit. The day after *'night, Mother*, Marsha Norman's play about a lonely woman who kills herself, opened on Broadway, Albert Poland was in Jacobs's office. "How was *'night, Mother*?" Poland asked. "It was fine," Jacobs replied, "but the depth of the suicide audience remains to be seen."

Schoenfeld could be pompous, a trait that became more pronounced as he accumulated more power. But he could poke fun at himself. Not long after Schoenfeld and Jacobs took over the Shubert Organization, Poland, who was working both as a producer and an actor, appeared in a play Off Broadway at La Mama called *Elegy to a Down Queen*. He played a parrot. He was on his perch as the audience filed into the theater on East Fourth Street. He spotted Jerry and Pat Schoenfeld. Jerry came up to him and said, "How are you, Albert?" Poland responded, in character. "Hello, Jerry!" he squawked. "How are you? Squawk, squawk." The next day Schoenfeld called him. "Albert, when we are in private, you may call me Jerry," he said. "But when we are in public, you must call me Mr. Schoenfeld." There was a pause. "Especially, Albert, when you are a parrot."

---

men," he said. Barnes was both the theater and dance critic at the *Times* when, in 1977, Rupert Murdoch tried to lure him to the *New York Post*, which he had just bought. Murdoch offered Barnes $100,000 a year—an enormous amount of money for a journalist back then. Barnes was flattered, but turned him down. Few people left the *Times*, the most powerful paper in the world, in those days. A few months later, Abe Rosenthal, the paper's managing editor, took the theater beat away from Barnes. The critic called Murdoch and told him he was available. "I know," said Murdoch. "I'll take you. But you're not worth $100,000 anymore."

But when they gave an order, they expected it to be followed. *Ain't Misbehavin'* was nominated for the Tony Award for Best Musical in 1978. Dasha Epstein, the Shuberts' coproducer, was excited. "Bernie, if we get the Tony, I'm going up on stage with you," she said. Jacobs glared at her. "No you're not. Gerald and I are going up," he said. "But Bernie, I was there from the beginning," Epstein protested. "If we win, I'm going up."

"You'll do what I say," Jacobs snapped.

Ain't Misbehavin' won the Tony, and Epstein, looking splendid in a Zandra Rhodes dress, walked up on stage. She looked down and saw Jacobs, in the second row, scowling at her. "He did not move," she said. "Jerry came up on stage, but Bernie did not." The next day Schoenfeld received several calls from people wanting to know who the pretty woman in the great dress was standing next to him at the Tonys. Epstein said to Jacobs, "You see what you missed? I would have been next to you!" Jacobs didn't say a word. "He refused to speak to me for two weeks," Epstein recalled.

But he remained fond of Epstein and always looked out for her. When Epstein's husband Henry, a multimillionaire real estate mogul, died, Jacobs and his wife, Betty, took her with them on a vacation to Fisher Island, Florida. Epstein walked by their room one evening and saw the two of them on the bed, watching TV and holding hands. "Here was this man who was so powerful just lying on the bed, holding hands with his wife. Like a little boy and girl. And he said, 'Dasha, come on. Come sit here and watch television with us.' He knew. He knew I was lonely because I missed Henry so much."

Jacobs stepped in to help Epstein settle her husband's vast estate. When she found herself at war with one of the trustees of the estate, Jacobs told her, "You don't just need a fancy lawyer—you need a fighter." He found one for her, but when he thought the lawyer was overcharging her, he said, "You're not paying that," and fired him.

Schoenfeld was a grudge holder, especially against anyone who, he believed, had betrayed him or "Shubert," as he called the company. "You are dead to me" was one of his favorite phrases. But like Jacobs, he could also be kind and wise. Albert Poland was once at Frankie & Johnnie's, a steakhouse on West Forty-Fifth Street frequented by the

Shuberts. He'd just returned from a painful Christmas visit to his family in Michigan. After an ugly fight with his father on Christmas Eve, Poland cut the visit short. He was drinking heavily at the time and on this particular evening parked himself at the bar with a grappa. Schoenfeld and Smith came into the restaurant. Oh, God, I don't want them to see me like this, he thought. "Albert, come and join us," Schoenfeld said. "What's the matter with you? You look unhappy, Albert." Poland told them about the fight with his father. Schoenfeld listened and said, "When my father died, we were estranged and I will regret it to my dying day. You can't let that happen. Go back there, even if it's for a day, or a few hours. Have a car and driver waiting at the curb so if you have to leave you can do so immediately. But you must do it." A few weeks later Poland was back in Michigan, having it out with his father. It was painful, but they reconciled. As soon as Poland got back to New York, "I rushed to see Jerry. To tell him I was in his debt. His words made all the difference."

If by 1980 Schoenfeld and Jacobs towered, as the *Times* put it, over Broadway, there was one element they could not control—the press, particularly the *Times* itself, which towered over Broadway in its own way. *Times* critics and reporters had near make-or-break power over shows. Press agents begged and wheedled to get their shows on the front page of the Arts & Leisure section the Sunday before opening night. If they didn't, their producers would often fire them. As powerful as the paper was in 1980, it was about to become even more powerful with the arrival of Frank Rich.

Born and raised in Washington, D.C., Rich attended Harvard and came to the attention of Stephen Sondheim and Hal Prince when he wrote a rave review in the *Harvard Crimson* of *Follies* during its Boston tryout. Rich arrived in New York in the seventies and became a movie critic for the *New York Post*, when it leaned left under publisher Dorothy Schiff. Rich was out of a job when Rupert Murdoch took over the paper in 1977. "Frank came over to my apartment in tears," said Martin Gottfried, who was pushed out of the paper to make way for Clive Barnes. "He didn't know what he was going to do." Rich landed at *Time* as a movie critic but was then lured away to the *New*

York Times by the powerful managing editor, Arthur Gelb, who, early in his career at the paper, had been a theater reporter and critic. Rich was second-string drama critic to Walter Kerr. His early reviews were not of much note, but his nimble work on the opening night of *42nd Street* (Kerr was sick and could not cover it) caught executive editor Abe Rosenthal's attention. When Kerr decided he only wanted to write on Sunday, Rosenthal made Rich, then just thirty-one, chief drama critic.

One of his first assignments was to review Peter Shaffer's new play *Amadeus*, about the rivalry between Mozart and Salieri. The Shuberts were producing it at the Broadhurst. Having seen how Merrick had manipulated the critics into covering *42nd Street* on opening night rather than a preview performance, they decided they wanted the critics at their opening as well. The theater would be packed with cheerleaders for the show, ginning up the excitement, which would spill over into the reviews, they thought. Schoenfeld called Gelb and badgered him about returning to the old days, when critics dashed up the aisles on opening night and knocked out copy in the heat of the moment. But Rich wanted more than just forty-five minutes to make sense of *Amadeus*. He could handle *42nd Street*. It was an old-fashioned musical, and he'd been a musical theater buff since childhood. But *Amadeus* was serious stuff. It was about classical music and kapellmeisters and the Viennese court of the eighteenth century, not exactly territory that a young critic who could act out every scene from *Mame* knew well. Gelb told Schoenfeld, "I promise you that Frank Rich will be at *Amadeus* on opening night." What he didn't say was that Rich was going to buy a ticket, in the mezzanine, to the final preview.

Rich attended, unnoticed by anyone involved in the production, including Schoenfeld, who was greeting people in the lobby. Rich filed his review and then, as Gelb had promised, attended opening night. Schoenfeld and Jacobs were pleased with themselves. At the party after the show, Schoenfeld told friends that there would be no review in the *Times* until the next morning. "Frank Rich was at the opening," he said. "We have stopped the reviewing of previews. We told the *New York Times* what to do and from now on they will be coming to opening nights. No more previews."

Jon Wilner, the ad executive on the show, went back to his office after the performance and picked up the early edition of the *New York Times*. And there it was—Frank Rich's review of *Amadeus*, in the early edition. Wilner ran over to the party with the paper. When Schoenfeld and Jacobs saw it, they exploded.

"How dare he do this?" Jacobs yelled.

Wilner interrupted. "It's an out-and-out rave," he said. "This is the best review you've ever had for a straight play, ever!"

"That cocksucker!" Schoenfeld screamed.

"I never saw them that angry again," Wilner said. "It was just mind-boggling. They had a huge hit and all they cared about was their power. They were so hungry for this power, but the *New York Times* had said to them, 'We're more powerful than you are.'"

The one man to whom the review meant the most, Peter Shaffer, noticed the commotion. He saw Jacobs clutching the *Times*. "What is the review like?" he asked.

"Oh, it's fine, but that's not what we're talking about!" Jacobs snapped.

"Well, that's what I'm talking about!" Shaffer said.

Years later, Shaffer, laughing at the memory, added, "Yes, Frank Rich liked your play very much. Now let's talk about real things. The *New York Times* is defying the Shubert Organization. Oh, the conceit of it!"

Someone else the Shuberts couldn't dominate was their rival, Jimmy Nederlander. They battled Nederlander in the spring of 1980 over control of the National Theatre in Washington, D.C. The Shuberts made a bid to manage the not-for-profit theater, but Nederlander took them to court, arguing that their control of the theater would "unduly restrain competition."[3] Nederlander invoked the consent decree from 1956, which enjoined the Shuberts from acquiring more theaters. Schoenfeld and Jacobs were furious that Nederlander would drudge up a twenty-four-year-old document. They retaliated by canceling Nederlander's house seats to Shubert theaters. "I don't want any courtesies from him, and I don't care to extend any to him," Schoenfeld told the *Times*.

A court dismissed Nederlander's case, and the Shuberts eventually got control of the National Theatre. But that only inflamed the feud.

Nederlander struck back in his own mischievous way. He hired Irving Goldman, Schoenfeld and Jacobs's ex-partner, as a business consultant.*

Both companies also got into a bidding war for the Broadway rights to Ronald Harwood's hit London play *The Dresser*. The Shuberts usually refrained from bidding wars, but they were so angry with Nederlander, they wanted to snatch the play away from him. Nederlander outbid them, paying $75,000 in advance plus 50 percent of the net profits. Producers watched from the sidelines, aghast. They could not afford such a price for a play, and they feared they'd be muscled out of the market by future bidding wars between the two theatrical empires.[4]

Schoenfeld and Jacobs positioned themselves as stewards of the American theater, pointing out that they produced shows with artistic merit. Nederlander, Jacobs sniffed, "worries about theaters—whether he can fill them up or not."

Nederlander's main gripe about the Shuberts was their foundation, which had grown in size and influence with the success of the Shubert theaters. He argued that Schoenfeld and Jacobs could afford to gamble on shows because the money wasn't theirs. It belonged to the foundation. He had to put his own money into shows. He also claimed the foundation's grants to non-profit theaters gave the Shuberts an advantage. He pointed out that many productions from the Public Theater and L.A.'s Mark Taper Forum, both beneficiaries of Shubert grants, played Shubert theaters. "It's like competing against Ford Motors and the Ford Foundation all in one," he sniped. "If somebody gives you $100,000 a year—sure, you'll be more likely to do business with them."

Nederlander's charge, at least according to the judge who ruled the Shuberts could take over the National Theatre, was unfair. Shubert grants were "unconditional," the judge said.[5] But Nederlander was onto something unusual about the foundation. Had he explored it more fully, he might have been able to block his rivals' path. J. J. Shubert left his theaters, which were owned and operated by the Shubert

---

* Many years later, asked why he would hire someone with such a black reputation, Nederlander said, "Well, he had experience in the theater." When it was pointed out that Goldman had been accused of using his position as head of the Shubert Foundation to secure paint contracts for his company, Nederlander laughed and said, "What's wrong with that?"

Organization, a for-profit company, to the non-profit Shubert Foundation. In 1969, Congress passed the Tax Reform Act, which took aim at
philanthropies that owned profit-making businesses. Supporters of the
law believed the profit-making businesses shielded incomes by funnel-
ing them into the philanthropies. As a result of the Tax Reform Act,
more than a hundred charities had to divest themselves of for-profit
companies.[6] The Shubert Foundation would have to sell off the Shubert theaters. Schoenfeld and Jacobs were in no position in 1969 to buy
the theaters themselves, and new owners might not have kept them in
their jobs. But the foundation was never forced to sell the theaters. No
one at the Shubert Organization fretted about the 1969 ruling. "We
were putting our finger in the dike everywhere we turned. We were so
inundated with problems of surviving," Schoenfeld said.[7]

In the 1970s, Nederlander could have pressed the government to
invoke the Tax Reform Act against the Shubert Foundation. He never
did. And by 1980 it was too late. In 1977, the Shubert board petitioned
the IRS for a private letter ruling, which would allow the foundation
to hold on to the theaters. The board argued that the legitimate theater would be destroyed if the theaters were sold. New owners, the
board said, would turn the theaters into porn houses or parking lots,
or would sell them off, piecemeal, to the highest bidders. The theaters
were vulnerable because they only returned a marginal profit. The
board said the foundation's main purpose was to perpetuate theater in
America, which it could do best by maintaining control of the Shubert
theaters.

In October 1979, the IRS gave the board everything it wanted. The
IRS agreed that the legitimate theater would be in peril if the theaters were sold. Owning theaters, the IRS said, is not a good business,
"characterized by long periods of losses and relatively short periods of
profits."[8] It would appear that nobody from the IRS had seen *A Chorus
Line* or *Ain't Misbehavin'* or *Annie* or *Evita* or *They're Playing Our Song*.

The ruling received little attention at the time, but it was highly
unusual. To this day, the Shubert Foundation is thought to be the only
charity that controls what has now became a multibillion-dollar for-
profit company, the Shubert Organization. A 1994 *New York Times*
article exploring the ruling carried expressions of disbelief from tax
experts. "It is a case without parallel," said Pamela Mann, who ran

the charity division for the New York State attorney general. "Nutty," said William Lehrfeld, a lawyer specializing in foundation law. "That's absolutely the silliest thing I've ever heard."

Whatever the experts thought about the ruling fifteen years later made no difference to Schoenfeld and Jacobs. They were presiding over a vigorous, powerful, and wealthy empire. And they pointed out that the success of the theaters meant more money for the foundation, which in 1993 doled out grants totalling $5.4 million, a far cry from the $400,000 the foundation gave out in 1970.

Aside from Nederlander, who told the *Times*, "There's no question about it—they have an unfair advantage," nobody in the theater in 1994 seemed bothered by the unusual arrangement between the Shubert Foundation and the Shubert Organization. Rocco Landesman, then the head of Jujamcyn Theaters, Broadway's third landowner, said, "I haven't bumped up against any conflict. There's a real separation of church and state."[9]

The Shubert-Nederlander feud had reached such a fever pitch by 1980 that producers had to start taking sides. A few could straddle the divide. Elizabeth I. McCann, for instance, worked both sides of the street. But for the most part, in a male-dominated business, you were either a "Shubert man" or a "Nederlander man." At the 1980 Tony Awards, Alex Cohen, the producer of the Tony telecast, tried to bridge the divide in flamboyant fashion. Just before the start of the show, he walked Nederlander across the aisle of the Mark Hellinger Theatre and, in front of the entire Broadway community, made him shake hands with Schoenfeld and Jacobs. The audience applauded, but the three men barely smiled. Privately, they yelled at Cohen for putting them in an awkward situation.

It would take more than a handshake to end the feud. It would take a business arrangement, which in the theater meant a show. As it turned out, one was coming together in England, though the inspiration came from the Soviet Union. In 1978, Trevor Nunn, the thirty-eight-year-old director of the Royal Shakespeare Company, visited the Gorki Theater in Leningrad. The head of the theater told him that for the next six months, the company would be preparing a stage adaptation of *The Pickwick Papers*.

"It emerged that such large-scale adaptations of Dickens are commonplace in Soviet theater," Nunn told *Time* magazine.[10] The RSC was strapped for cash. It could only afford to do one new play instead of the usual five. Nunn decided the production would have to be big enough to employ all thirty-nine members of the acting company. He decided on an eight-and-a-half-hour stage version of *Nicholas Nickleby*, adapted by David Edgar. The company developed much of the production through improvisation. The actors studied daily life in Victorian England, each memorizing a chapter from the book and then performing it for the rest of the company. "We had a crazy theory," Nunn said, "that if thirty-eight of the cast died, the one survivor could come in and tell the story all by himself."

The first part of the play was in good shape, but the second half didn't gel. Nunn began to have doubts about the production. He and his codirector, John Caird, disappeared to a hotel in the English countryside to sort out the situation. Caird persuaded Nunn not to abandon the show, shouting at him over food and wine in the hotel's Michelin-starred restaurant. "We must have resembled nothing so much as two gays who'd gone away for the weekend to sort out their relationship," Nunn told *Time*. Sort it out they did, and *The Life and Adventures of Nicholas Nickleby*, with a brilliant young Roger Rees in the lead, opened at the Aldwych Theatre in the West End in June 1980.

Jimmy Nederlander had brought a number of RSC productions to New York in the 1970s, and had a first-look deal with the company. He loved the show, though the prospect of doing an eight-and-a-half-hour play on Broadway was daunting. The budget was $4.4 million. And he didn't have a theater. All of his were booked. But Elizabeth McCann and her producing partner Nelle Nugent had an idea. The two women were on good terms with both the Shuberts and Nederlander. McCann had worked for Nederlander in the 1970s, and she and Nugent had coproduced a number of shows with the Shuberts, including *Amadeus*. The only way to bring *Nicholas Nickleby* to Broadway would be as a joint venture between the Shuberts and Nederlander, they argued. Jimmy Nederlander had the rights to the show; the Shuberts had the perfect theater—the Plymouth on Forty-Fifth Street. McCann negotiated the deal, shuttling between Nederlander's rundown office above the Palace and the Shuberts' elegant offices above the Shubert Theatre. The crux of the deal was this: The three producers—McCann and Nugent, Nederlander, the Shuberts—would each have one vote. Decisions would be made by majority. Once the vote had been cast there would be no squabbling about the outcome. When it came time to pick a press agent, McCann and Nugent and Nederlander cast their vote for Joshua Ellis; the Shuberts voted for their longtime flack, Merle Debuskey.

"It was two-to-one, so I got the job," said Ellis. His big coup was landing *Nicholas Nickleby* on the cover of *Time* magazine on October 5, 1981. To accompany the article, the editors wanted a group picture of the producers. "The photograph had to be negotiated like the Treaty of Ghent," Ellis recalled. "We couldn't take the picture in the Plymouth, since the set was being built. So Jimmy offered the Nederlander Theatre. But Bernie and Jerry wanted it to be in one of their theaters, so they offered the Shubert. And then there was the question of left to right because the person on the left is the first one named in the caption. Everybody was vying to be on the left."

In the end, Jimmy Nederlander was on the left, but a cherubic-looking Schoenfeld was in the center, standing a bit higher than everybody else.

That fall, the talk on Broadway was the ticket price to the show—one hundred dollars, the highest in Broadway history. But when the rave reviews came out—"The RSC has fashioned an epic of feeling and intelligence, a vertiginous celebration of life upon the splendid stage" (*Time*)—the show was a sellout. *Time* also ran a story about Broadway's resurgence, "And Another Boffo Season." Attendance for the 1980–81 theater season was 11 million, up 15 percent from the previous year, the magazine reported. Box office receipts hit $196.9 million, quadruple those of the 1969–70 season. "As theater folk welcome *Nicholas Nickleby* to help launch the new season, they . . . can pat their pocketbooks with pride," *Time* noted.

Nothing brings people together like success, and the success of *Nicholas Nickleby* took some of the sting out of the Shubert-Nederlander feud. When the show won the Tony for Best Play in 1982, Schoenfeld and Jacobs shook hands with Nederlander without any prompting from Alex Cohen.

But every now and then the rivalry flared up. In 1986, producer

Manny Azenberg was preparing to put Neil Simon's new play, *Broad-way Bound*, into Nederlander's 46th Street Theatre. David Mitchell, who was designing the sets, went over to inspect the theater. It had not been cleaned in a while, and when he leaned up against a wall his white shirt turned black. He also saw rats. Mitchell wrote to Azenberg and Simon, "People should not be allowed in this theater. It is an embarrassment." Azenberg gave the letter to Nederlander and his second-in-command at the time, Arthur Rubin. "Read this," he said. Rubin read it aloud and then said, "The Shuberts are redoing the Imperial next door. That's where the rats are coming from. They're not Nederlander rats. They're Shubert rats."

CHAPTER EIGHTEEN

The Jockey and the Godfather

The success of *A Chorus Line* cemented a father-and-son relationship between Bernie Jacobs and Michael Bennett. Jacobs watched the show from the back of the Shubert Theatre almost every night, marveling at Bennett's stagecraft. Over long dinners at Wally's and Joseph's, Bennett taught Jacobs how to examine a show, from its book to its choreography to its music, right down to its scene changes. Jacobs, in turn, taught Bennett all about the business. "Michael was not a businessman," said John Breglio. "He'd never be able to understand the complications of a royalty pool, but he wanted to know. He wanted to know all about the business. And Bernie was the ultimate businessman. It got to the point where Michael was completely dependent on Bernie. Before he made a decision, he'd say, 'I have to talk to Bernie about it. I'm going to go see Bernie and see what he thinks.'"

They were an odd couple—Jacobs, in his sixties, dour, gruff, sober; Bennett, in his early thirties, wiry, energetic, a smoker, drinker, and drug-taker. But those who saw them together noticed the chemistry. "They loved each other," said Robin Wagner. "Bernie thought Michael was as good a son as you could get. And Bernie was the perfect father—wealthy, strong, powerful, and protective. If anybody said anything against Michael, they'd be in trouble with Bernie."

Bennett was a frequent guest at Bernie and Betty Jacobs's weekend house on Shelter Island. Designed by Norman Jaffe, the house had a long hallway that opened onto the kitchen. Bennett used it as dance ramp. Seated in matching white leather chairs, Bernie and Betty would watch with delight as Bennett demonstrated a new dance on the ramp. He taught the older couple how to do the Hustle. He gave Jacobs his first joint. "I remember Michael dancing on the ramp, and Bernie lying on the floor, smoking pot and laughing," said critic Martin Gottfried, another frequent guest on Shelter Island.

As the money from *A Chorus Line* rained down on him—$90,000 a week, according to *Variety*—Bennett began to play the part of the Broadway impresario. He couldn't drive, but he bought a white Rolls-Royce and hired a full-time chauffeur. He moved into a penthouse on Central Park South. He took to wearing a long white fur coat at Broadway openings. And he married his star, Donna McKechnie. Jacobs encouraged the marriage. "Bernie's attitude toward homosexuality was, You just haven't met the right girl yet," said his friend Albert Poland. (Jacobs admitted the marriage was his idea. "I made some comment, which in retrospect was kind of stupid," he told Kevin Kelly, author of *One Singular Sensation*. "I said, 'Why don't you straighten out and marry Donna?'")[1]

Bennett's drug and alcohol use accelerated as well, and with it his paranoia. He showed up in London to direct *A Chorus Line* with "an entourage of people who spoke of him in hushed tones as if the Almighty was about to descend," said Robert Fox, a young producer at the time. Fox was working with Michael White, an established West End producer who was presenting *A Chorus Line*. Fox was drawn to Bennett—"he was unbelievably charismatic"—and it was his job to look after the director in London. "He didn't want to have dinner with Harold Pinter or Tom Stoppard," said Fox. "He wasn't remotely interested in any of that. He wanted to hang out at the hotel and drink and chat and watch TV. That's how I got to know him. I'd go over to the Berkeley Hotel and have dinner with him almost every night."

Soon after he arrived in London, Bennett caused a public scandal. White had hired Elizabeth Seal, England's leading musical theater star, to play Cassie. Ten minutes into a rehearsal, Bennett turned to Fox and said, "I'm going to fire her. She can't do it. I'm telling you it won't make any difference if I sit here for another eighty minutes and watch the rest of the show. She's gotta go."

Fox was taken aback. "We have to be very careful," he said. "Her husband is a photographer for the *Sunday Times*. She's very connected with the press, and it will cause a huge scandal."

"I don't give a fuck," Bennett said. "She can't do it."

After the run-through, he met Seal in the stage manager's office. "Look, darling, it's not going to work."

"What do you mean?" replied a flustered Seal.

"You can't do it, and I can't make you do it. So here's what we're gonna do. We're gonna tell them that you broke your foot, OK?"

But Seal and her husband were having none of it. As Fox had feared, they gave the story to the papers, which pit the arrogant Broadway director against one of the West End's beloved performers. Bennett wanted to put McKechnie in the show, but British Equity, led by Vanessa Redgrave, kicked up a fuss. The union would not permit an American actor to replace a British actor. Photographers began chasing Bennett all over London. "And he was being driven around in Michael White's Bentley by a chauffeur who was buying coke for him in ounces, not grams," said Fox.

Bennett left town. *A Chorus Line* opened at the Drury Lane to mixed reviews. It managed to run three years but was never the phenomenon it was in New York.

Bennett's next port of call was Hollywood. Universal bought the film rights to *A Chorus Line* and wanted him to direct it. They paid him $6.5 million upfront, and agreed to give him 20 percent of the distributor's gross after the first $20 million. "There had never been a deal like that in the history of Hollywood," said Breglio. In addition, Universal agreed to produce three more movies of his choosing and provided him with fancy offices on the lot. He lasted six months. He tried to develop a movie for Bette Midler called *Road Show*, which was about his experience in Detroit fixing *Seesaw*. Universal didn't like that idea and it became tangled up in studio bureaucracy. Bennett was discovering what David Merrick had learned about Hollywood: The studios had all the power.

He called Breglio.

"I'm out of there," he said. "I hate it here. I hate all these people. I never want to look at Hollywood again. I'm leaving, and I'm leaving a note on the door and it's going to say, 'Gone Fishin'.'"

And that's what he did. He and Bob Avian made a big sign that said GONE FISHIN' and stuck it on the door of their fancy studio offices. They left without telling anyone. Universal "went berserk," said Breglio. "They'd paid $6.5 million for *A Chorus Line* and they assumed Michael was going to direct it. But you can't force someone to do something they don't want to do. He said, 'Tell them I don't want their money.' And he was gone."

When Bennett abandoned Hollywood, Universal approached every major director—Mike Nichols, Sidney Lumet, Sydney Pollack—to direct *A Chorus Line*. Bennett met with them all. Over lunch or dinner he would dazzle them with his concept for the movie. After the meeting, the directors would call Universal and turn down the offer. Bennett, they said, was the only person who could direct the movie. His ideas were far better than anything they could come up with. "Remember," said Breglio, "his motivation was to never have the movie done. In those days, everyone was convinced that when a movie came out, the show would close. We had a six-year hold back on the movie because we assumed *A Chorus Line* would be closed by then. No one thought it would run fifteen years. So Michael didn't want a movie. He would drop enough of his ideas, which were brilliant, to scare everybody away."

Richard Attenborough, who had just won the Oscar for *Gandhi*, didn't scare so easily. Bennett had dinner with him and when they were through, he called Breglio. "He didn't say he was going to do it, but I know he is."

"How do you know?" Breglio asked.

"Because we just had a lovely dinner and he never asked me one question about the show or what I would do. He just told me everything about what he was going to do."

Attenborough directed the movie version of *A Chorus Line*, which was released in 1985. It was one of the biggest flops in the history of Hollywood musicals.

Bennett returned to New York ready to work on his next Broadway show. He shed the trappings of the Broadway impresario. Gone was the fur coat. He was now wearing his old uniform—jeans, a T-shirt, and a baseball cap. Gone was the Rolls-Royce, replaced by a van with a state-of-the-art sound system so he could listen to tapes of new scores while he was being driven around the city. To Bennett's friend Robert Fox, the van represented "the beginning of quite severe psychosis and paranoia" fueled by increasingly heavy cocaine use. "The van was kind of a paranoid fantasy—that you could be on the move and nobody would be able to get you," said Fox.

Another trapping Bennett shed was McKechnie. The marriage lasted only a few months, though the friendship endured. Bernie Jacobs helped draw up the divorce agreement and, through his contacts in the real estate business, set McKechnie up in her own apartment at 710 Park Avenue.

Now that he was back in New York, Bennett needed a base of operations. And he didn't mean an office. He wanted a building, with rehearsal studios, music studios, a theater, a gym, and space for his designers. He wanted his own self-contained theatrical empire, the one he dreamed about years ago over dinner in a greasy spoon with Tommy Tune. And he found it—890 Broadway, an eight-story warehouse on Broadway and Nineteenth Street. Jacobs and Breglio put together the deal, and Bennett got the building for $700,000.

"The first thing he did was put in dressing rooms and lockers for the dancers," Wagner said. "Most of the rehearsal spaces back then were filthy. He wanted a place where people weren't embarrassed to work." He put in a restaurant and hired a chef who had the unfortunate habit of getting drunk while cooking. "The first course was always terrific, but the second course was terrible, burnt, because he was smashed," said Wagner. Bennett also leased out space, at low rents, to the American Ballet Theater, the costume designer Theoni V. Aldredge, Barbara Matera, who made the costumes, a milliner named Wally who made the hats for Broadway shows, and Woody, who made shoes for dancers. Bennett gave Wagner half a floor to use as his design studios. As a gift to his good friend, he did not charge him rent.

Bennett also put Betty Jacobs to work as a script reader. "I hadn't worked since Bernie and I got married," she said. "Michael used to say to me, 'When people ask you, 'what do you do?' what do you say?' I said, 'I don't do anything.' And Michael said, 'Well, tell them you work for Michael Bennett.' It was very nice. It really was." Bennett was inundated with scripts for musicals, and Jacobs read them all. "But I decided then that you really can't read musical scripts," she said. "I mean, if I had read *A Chorus Line*, I don't think I would have done it. So much of it is the director's vision."

Bennett also drew up plans for a theater in the basement where he could workshop his shows. It would be called the Bernard B. Jacobs Theater.

One night after the renovations to the fourth-floor dance studio at 890 Broadway were completed, Bennett invited Breglio and his wife, Nan Knighton, to ride down in his van to see the building. It was a beautiful winter night, a fresh blanket of snow covering the city. They went up to the fourth-floor dance studio. Moonlight poured in through the windows. The floor-to-ceiling-length mirrors were covered with paper. Bennett turned on the lights and tore down the paper. Then he began dancing in front of the mirrors. "Look at this!" he exclaimed. "Is it really mine? Isn't it wonderful?"

Bennett had a raft of ideas for his next show. He wanted to do a musical version of *Love Me or Leave Me*, the 1955 movie about singer Ruth Etting and her stormy affair with gangster Martin Snyder. He was also drawing up plans for an extravagant stage adaptation of *Easter Parade*. And he wanted to do a new adaptation of *Peter Pan*. In the end, though, he went back to what he knew best—dancers. *A Chorus Line* provided work for Bennett's friends and contemporaries. But there was a whole group of older dancers who, Bennett knew, might never work again on Broadway. He wanted to employ them, and so he acquired the rights to *Queen of the Stardust Ballroom*, a 1975 television drama about a lonely widow who falls in love with a married postal worker she meets at a dance hall. It was a poignant, kitchen-sink story written by Jerome Kass. Bennett would turn it into a Broadway musical by expanding the dance hall numbers, making them fantasy sequences.

The Shuberts wanted to produce it. Anything Bennett wanted to do would be a smash, Jacobs believed. He also believed that the Shuberts, and only the Shuberts, should be his producer. But Bennett decided to finance the entire show himself. He was cynical about show business, and he knew that whatever he did after *A Chorus Line* was going to be a target. He told Breglio, "Nobody can be as successful as I am. My next show is going to be a flop because they will go after me no matter what it is. They will bring me down." And so *Ballroom* was born of cynicism—and Bennett didn't want anyone to risk a dime on a cynical venture. He wrote the check for the $1 million production cost. He also asked Breglio to join him as coproducer. The thirty-two-year-old lawyer was thrilled. He'd always wanted to be a producer, and this was his chance. He was going to leave his law firm and work full-time for Michael Bennett, the most powerful theater director in the world. Joining them would be Bob Avian and Susan MacNair, Bennett's indispensable secretary. They decided to call their company Quadrille Productions. And they swore one another to secrecy. No one was to know about the partnership until they announced it. Bennett knew Jacobs would not be happy. "Bernie was paranoid someone else would come into Michael's life," said Wagner. Bennett wanted to prepare Jacobs for the news. But Jacobs had the Broadway grapevine at his disposal. He soon heard what Bennett and Breglio were doing.

The phone rang early one Saturday morning in Breglio's apartment.

"I know the deal you guys are doing," Jacobs said. "You know how close I am to Michael. I don't want this to get in the way of my relationship with Michael."

"There's no reason for it to get in the way," Breglio replied. "All I can do is make things even better for Michael. We'll produce more shows. Fill your theaters up even more."

"Yeah," Jacobs said, "but just keep in mind—if I want to, I can crush you."

To play the lonely widow in *Ballroom*, Bennett hired Dorothy Loudon, now a Broadway star after winning the Tony as Miss Hannigan in *Annie*. Vincent Gardenia was cast as the married postal worker. Kass adapted his teleplay, and Billy Goldenberg wrote the music. The lyrics were by Alan and Marilyn Bergman.

Marilyn Bergman took on the role of mother hen, bringing chicken soup to rehearsals and fussing over Bennett as if he were her son. But when Bennett began demanding changes to her lyrics, she turned on him. She started calling Bennett "that little faggot."

"And that was probably the nicest thing she called him," said Breglio. "By the end of the process they hated each other. I think they would have killed each other if it was legal."

Bennett was battling on other fronts as well. In putting together *A Chorus Line*, he had created the workshop process. In the past, shows rehearsed three or four weeks, played an out-of-town tryout, and then opened on Broadway. It was a brisk production schedule. But in a workshop, a show comes together over an extended rehearsal period, with cast and creatives experimenting and improvising. There was no timetable, no deadline. The show was ready to go when Bennett said it was. For such a process to work financially, nobody could expect to be paid much money. But after the success of *A Chorus Line*, Actors' Equity was determined that its members be compensated fairly for their time and effort. The union feared the workshop process would become a way of exploiting actors. Bennett resisted Equity's involvement, but Breglio—and Jacobs—knew it could not be avoided. An Equity representative told Breglio that "unless we formalize the workshop process, make sure our actors get paid a decent salary, and get a piece of the show's future, we're not going to let them work on *Ballroom*." Jacobs arranged a meeting in his office with Breglio and the representative from Equity. They started negotiating at seven in the evening and by morning had hammered out a workshop contract that remains in place to this day. Actors are paid for their services, but at a lower rate than they are when formal rehearsals begin. Should the show become a hit, the union and the workshop actors get a share of the profits.

"This was not a business proposition," said Breglio. "It was an artistic imperative." Bennett wanted more time to create shows. But he couldn't do it without the cooperation from the union. The final agreement "was good," Breglio said.*

Though Jacobs helped Breglio negotiate with Equity, he still re-

---

* It quickly became perverted, however. Instead of a place for creative people to develop a show, the workshop became a backers' audition. "There are all these people watching to see whether they are going to put money in the show," Breglio said. "Michael never intended that."

sented the young lawyer's presence at 890 Broadway. "The tension was palpable all the time," said Breglio. "He wasn't happy I was there. He was on the phone with Michael every day, telling him he didn't need me. His message to Michael was: 'I can do everything and anything for you. I have the Shuberts. I have the theaters. I have the knowledge. I have the experience. What do you need him for?'"

Psychologically, Bennett was not in good shape. He was cynical about *Ballroom*, but he felt the pressure to deliver another hit. He eased the tension with pot, Quaaludes, and cocaine. His drug dealer visited his office every day. "He had a briefcase with every drug under the sun in it," Wagner said. "Michael would lay out lines of coke every day at lunch." The cocaine heightened his paranoia. The mob, he said, was coming to collect on his father's old debts. But there was someone who could protect him, Bernie Jacobs, the most powerful man on Broadway, "the Godfather," as some began to call him. In the end, Jacobs had his way. Breglio lasted just five months at 890 Broadway. Bennett walked into Breglio's office one day and said, "It's not going to work. *They* won't let us do this."

"It was traumatic for both of us," Breglio recalled. "For me it was traumatic because I'd been in the arts my whole life. I became a lawyer by accident. But now I was going to do what I wanted to do all my life—produce. And do it for Michael Bennett. It was traumatic for Michael because all his life he dreamed of having his own theater empire. And here was somebody very powerful telling him you can't have it. Do your dancing and your directing and your creative stuff. But don't build your empire. We, the Shuberts, will give you all your business support. You will depend on us."

That night Bennett phoned Breglio and asked him to come over to his penthouse at 40 Central Park South for dinner. Breglio declined, but Bennett insisted. "I want to play something for you," he said. As soon as Breglio arrived at the apartment, he could tell Bennett was drunk. He'd been listening to Billy Joel's new album, *The Stranger*, over and over again, especially the song "Vienna." He wanted Breglio to hear it, to pay attention to the lyrics—"Slow down, you crazy child/ . . . When will you realize. . . . Vienna waits for you?"

Downing another vodka, Bennett said, "This is about us. We're kids. 'Slow down, you crazy child.' Vienna waits for us. We'll do it some day. We're young. They're old. They're all gonna die. They're all going to die. And then we'll do what we want to do."

With Breglio gone, Bennett needed a new executive producer to run the day-to-day operations on *Ballroom*. As it so happened, Bernard Gersten, second-in-command at the Public Theater, was about to break from Joe Papp. Gersten had thrown a surprise birthday party for Papp at the Delacorte Theater in Central Park. Papp arrived thinking he was going to watch a rehearsal. Instead, the place was packed with actors, directors, writers, and politicians. The lights went up, and everybody sang "Happy Birthday." There were fireworks and sketches and songs about Papp and the Public. The food store Zabar's provided picnic baskets. Gersten had orchestrated the whole event. And Papp resented it. "I began to think, 'Wait a second—I wonder how much this cost? And how come I didn't know about it at all?' I mean, after all, I'm running an organization. I slowly began to realize that the thing had been done under my nose, without me knowing it, and money—some $40,000, which was substantial at the time—had been spent without my approval." [2]

The break came after the party. It was over *Ballroom*. Gersten thought the Public Theater, raking in money from *A Chorus Line*, should produce *Ballroom*. But Papp wasn't interested. He didn't do shows that weren't developed at his theater. Besides, he said, Bennett was now part of the Broadway establishment. He was no longer a struggling artist who needed a place to work.

Bennett and Gersten had grown close because of Gersten's work on *A Chorus Line*. Gersten offered to coproduce *Ballroom* on Broadway. He went to Papp and asked him for a favor. Could he continue to work at the Public but also work for Bennett on *Ballroom* in his spare time?

"If you do, you'll have to quit the Public," said Papp.

"I'm not going to quit," Gersten replied.

"Then I'll have to fire you."

"Then fire me," said Gersten.

"OK, you're fired."

The next day Gersten went to work at 890 on *Ballroom*—and incurred the wrath of Bernie Jacobs. Every decision Gersten made—advertising, marketing, budgets, ticket pricing—Jacobs questioned. Bennett and Bergman already were fighting, and now the two Bernies were as well. Making matters worse was the fact that, at the box office, *Ballroom* was a bust.

The Sunday *New York Times* carried a full page ad announcing: "From the director of *A Chorus Line*—Michael Bennett's new show, *Ballroom*." "And nobody bought tickets," said Gersten.

The Shuberts were so sure the show would be a hit, they carved out an extra box office between the Shubert and Booth theaters in Shubert Alley to handle the demand (The space had once been the star dressing room at the Booth.) "We all got crazed," said Phil Smith. "We thought *Ballroom* would be the biggest thing since 7 Up. We had four box office people in there waiting for the crowds. Well, the crowds never showed up." (The Shuberts soon closed the extra box office. It eventually became One Shubert Alley, a shop that today sells Broadway mugs, T-shirts, posters, key chains, etc.)

Jacobs was furious. If the show wasn't selling, it wasn't Bennett's fault. He was the greatest director in the world. It was Gersten's fault. He didn't know what he was doing. Only the Shuberts knew how to produce a Michael Bennett show, he insisted.

Breglio went to see *Ballroom* in Stamford, Connecticut, during its out-of-town tryout. He found a dejected Bennett in his makeshift office in a trailer behind the theater. "I don't know how I'm going to get out of this," Bennett said. "This is a mess. It's never going to work. Everybody's fighting with everybody else. It's just a catastrophe. I just got to ride it out."

Ballroom opened December 14, 1978, at the Majestic on Forty-Fourth Street. Bennett masked his doubts about its prospects behind a lavish opening night party at Windows on the World, the five-star restaurant on top of the north tower of the World Trade Center. He ferried Loudon, his star, downtown in a chauffeur-driven Rolls-Royce. He escorted her to a private room where champagne and caviar were on ice. "When you're ready," he told her, "I will escort you into the main room." Loudon's date was her agent, Lionel Larner. As they stood looking out over the Hudson River, drinking Cristal, Larner said, "Now that you're a star, Dorothy, all this is yours—New Jersey!"

The reviews that night cast a pall over the party. While the critics praised Bennett's staging, most found the story of the lonely widow dreary and undramatic. The death blow was dealt, of course, by the *New York Times*. "With someone of the caliber of Michael Bennett in charge, the natural assumption is that he and his authors are keeping their powder dry," wrote Richard Eder. "The assumption holds for a while. But around the halfway mark the suspicion begins to grow that the powder is never going to be lit at all. And finally it becomes evident that it is not powder, but dust."

A few days after the review appeared, Bennett got a call from one of his father's mobster associates in Buffalo. The mobster asked if there was anything Bennett would like to have done to Richard Eder. "It's a little late in the day for that," Bennett replied.[3]

As *Ballroom* staggered at the box office, Bennett fled New York. He went on a month-long trip to China sponsored by Columbia University. His traveling companions included Robin Wagner, the arts philanthropist Martin Siegel, producer Bill Oakes, Bernie and Betty Jacobs, and Phil Smith and his wife, Phyllis. The trip lifted Bennett's spirits. Flying from Belgrade to Mongolia, Bennett played soccer in the aisle of the plane with a Chinese soccer team and traded bits of his clothing for theirs. On their first morning in Beijing, Bennett and Wagner awoke at 5:00 a.m. to "an incredible ringing sound," said Wagner. They went out on the terrace of the Beijing hotel and saw thousands of Chinese on bikes ringing their bells on their way to work. Jacobs, in the room next door, was already up. He was on the phone trying to get through to New York to find out what the grosses were for *Ballroom*.

Before the group's first ceremonial dinner near the Forbidden City, Bennett went to a friendship store and bought a Chinese army uniform. He made his entrance at the dinner wearing the uniform, to the cheers of Chinese diplomats. He met with a dance troupe and taught the kids how to do the Hustle from *Saturday Night Fever*. As the Americans prepared to depart Beijing, the dancers showed up at the train station to say good-bye to Bennett. He asked them if there was anything else he could do for them. Their leader took him aside and said, "Please don't dance in Shanghai."

Jacobs continued to monitor the grosses back in New York. *Ball-room* was falling apart. Toward the end of the trip, Smith was in a hotel lobby when he heard Bennett being paged. Bennett was sitting with Jacobs in a tour bus outside the hotel. Smith went to get him so he could take the call. Bernie Gersten was calling from New York. *Ballroom*, he told Bennett, would have to close.

Back in New York a week later, Robin Wagner was walking down Forty-Fourth Street to see *Ballroom* one last time. He ran into some of the dancers. They were furious with Bennett. They felt he'd abandoned them by touring China while they were dying at the Majestic. One said, "That fucker went to China, closed the show, and couldn't face us." Wagner thought, They don't know he did the show for them. They don't know it's his money. Nice.

Though he thought *Ballroom* would fail, it still took Bennett nearly two years to recover from his first big flop. He eased the pain with drugs and vodka, which fueled his paranoia. He started calling the Shuberts "the Mafia," and Jacobs "my Mafia godfather." He told Wagner the Shuberts had planted a bug in his teeth while he was at the dentist so they could listen to everything he said. But he still relied on Jacobs's counsel, calling him in the middle of the night, often high on drugs and drink. "He called me last night at three, and his tongue was thick," Jacobs would tell Albert Poland. Jacobs did not know what to do about Bennett's addiction. Booze, drugs, and anonymous sex were not part of his world. "Bernie used to say, 'I don't go to parties where they have white powder,'" said Poland.

The only thing that might get Bennett back on track was a new show. As it happened, one was right under his nose at 890 Broadway.

Tom Eyen, a writer and director, and Henry Krieger, a composer, collaborated on a successful Off-Broadway musical called *The Dirtiest Musical in Town* in 1975. Their star, Nell Carter, stopped the show every night with a song called "Can You See?" When the show closed on New Year's Eve 1976, Eyen and Krieger had lunch at a coffee shop on LaGuardia Place in Greenwich Village and talked about writing a show for Carter. It would be about three black singers from Chicago, The Dreamettes, who go to Harlem to compete at Amateur Night at the Apollo. Eyen wanted to call it *One Night Only*. He scribbled a lyric on

a napkin while Krieger sketched out a melody. They went to Joe Papp
with the idea, and he gave them a six-week workshop. They continued
working on the show, tailoring it to Nell Carter. But in 1980 she landed
a pilot called *Gimme a Break*. Papp wanted to wait for her to come back.
Eyen and Krieger "didn't want to wait for anybody," Krieger said. They
took their show to 890 Broadway and with Sheryl Lee Ralph singing,
auditioned ten songs for Bennett and Bob Avian. They liked what they
heard and gave them rehearsal space. Eyen was directing. If the show
was any good, Bennett and Avian would produce it.

To replace Carter, Eyen and Krieger cast Jennifer Holliday, who impressed them in *Your Arms Are Too Short to Box With God*. When she
came in for her audition she had big red circles on her cheeks and
reminded Krieger of *Pagliacci*. Her energy was "weird but she sang
great," he recalled. She would play Effie, the overweight lead singer of
the Dreamettes.

Eyen staged two workshops for Bennett. After the second, Bennett
told Eyen and Krieger, "I'm going to make you rich. I want to direct
your show."

Eyen was hurt, but "he accepted it," said Krieger.

With Bennett at the helm, the energy and pacing of the show, now
called *Dreamgirls*, accelerated. Eyen played ping-pong with the actors,
taking their ideas, refining them, trying to make them work. That was
not Bennett's way. The show was unfolding in his head, and he was
dictating it to the cast. He wanted it to move cinematically, swiftly,
barely pausing for the audience to catch its breath. And, with its tale of
show business success and excess, friendship and betrayal, he wanted
the audience to feel its brutality. Rehearsals could be hair-raising. In a
key scene, Effie walks into her dressing room and comes face-to-face
with her replacement, Michelle Morris. "Who is she?" Effie demands.
Sheryl Lee Ralph, as Deena, was not responding to the dramatic situation the way Bennett wanted. She wasn't responding to anything.
She just stood there, statuesque. Bennett exploded. "Get the fuck out
of rehearsals! Get out of the room! You have no fucking feelings! Get
out of my life!" Ralph burst into tears. Bennett went over to her, put
his arm around her, and said, "That's what I want, honey. And I want
it every night."

A turning point came one afternoon at 890 Broadway when Bennett prodded Eyen and Krieger to come up with a strong first-act ending. Eyen dashed off a lyric, and Krieger went to a piano in a small studio to set it to music. Krieger diddled around for an hour, but couldn't come up with anything. He thought the lyric "And I am telling you I'm not goin'" was awkward. "I was discouraged because usually everything comes to me really quickly. There was a knock at the door, and it was Ray Stark, the producer. He was filming the movie *Annie*. He said he was sorry to bother me, but he needed to use the phone in the room. He made his phone call, thanked me, and I went back to work. At which point the song wrote itself."

Krieger returned to the rehearsal room to play the song for Eyen, Bennett, and Avian. He taught Holliday the song while she was performing it, the two of them singing back and forth. It brought down the house, with Bennett leading the applause.

Bennett was still calling Bernie Jacobs at three most mornings, but now he was explaining his ideas for *Dreamgirls*. Jacobs was also hearing good reports from his wife, Betty, who attended many of the rehearsals. After the failure of *Ballroom*, Jacobs had convinced Bennett that he needed the Shuberts as his producers. *Dreamgirls* would be a Shubert show. But it was expensive—$3.5 million—and the Shuberts wanted to share the risk with other investors. First, though, they had to see what Bennett had put together. A presentation was arranged on the stage of the Shubert Theatre, where *A Chorus Line* was still selling out. Jacobs, Schoenfeld, and a few key Shubert executives were on hand. An hour before the presentation, Eyen and Krieger were downstairs in the theater at a piano by the men's room finishing the title song.

Auditioning for Schoenfeld and Jacobs was nerve-racking. Jacobs sat stone-faced. Schoenfeld might smile if he liked something, but he, too, showed little emotion. Around Broadway the two were known as "Mount Rushmore." Eyen went through the show, with Krieger's musical assistant playing the piano. Bennett demonstrated some of his choreography. "Quite frankly, no one knew what to make of it," said Breglio. "You had a lot of big numbers, but there was no production. So it was hard to assess." But that didn't matter. Bennett was back in the Shubert fold. When it was over, Jacobs said, "We're doing it, Michael, and this is going to be fabulous."

Bennett leapt into Jacobs's lap and threw his arms around him.

•   •   •

The Shuberts financed *Dreamgirls* with David Geffen, who'd met Jacobs through their mutual friend Marlo Thomas. Geffen had also be-
friended Bennett around the time *A Chorus Line* opened on Broadway.
The two had talked about doing a show together one day. *Dreamgirls*
headed to the Shubert Theatre in Boston in late October 1981. There
was tension in the theater the moment rehearsals began. Eyen, resent-
ful he'd been muscled aside as director, clashed with Bennett over the
script. Bennett was issuing his usual demands for better scenes and
songs, but Eyen resisted. "I'm the writer, not him!" Eyen would explode. Though only three years older than Bennett, Eyen referred to
the Tony-winning director as "this kid running around."

"Tom was a wild, hot-headed Arab-American. He gave Michael the
hives, literally," said Krieger. When they blew up at each other, Avian
would take Bennett aside and calm him down, and Krieger would do
the same with Eyen. "They were both explosive types," said Krieger.
"When they were happy, it was like the sun coming out. When they
were depressed and angry, it was, book me a ticket someplace else."
At one point, Bennett wanted to cut the song "One Night Only" because he thought it was too Jewish (it was in a minor key). He wanted
something more contemporary, so Eyen and Krieger wrote a disco
song called "Going to Be My Time." The first time the cast performed
it, "there was an insurrection from everybody in the theater," said
Krieger. "Everybody turned on Michael for cutting 'One Night Only.'
He finally put it back."

The original poster for the show read: "Michael Bennett's *Dreamgirls*." Eyen saw it and went berserk. "He thought it suggested Michael
had written it," said Breglio, "so we changed it to Michael Bennett's
production of *Dreamgirls*—which was a huge concession, considering
Michael's stature in the theater."

There was also tension between Bennett and Holliday. At one point
during the workshop, he fired her because she wasn't acting the role
to his satisfaction. But he couldn't find anyone who sang "And I Am
Telling You I'm Not Going" as powerfully as she did, so he took her
to see *Lena Horne: "The Lady and Her Music,"* then the hottest show in
town, bought her dinner, and rehired her. And then she fell in love with

him. He led her on. She was under his spell and he could manipulate the performance he wanted out of her. He gave her $100,000 to buy a condominium in New York. Some in the company believed they were sleeping together, but Krieger knew better: "Think about it. She was five thousand pounds and a girl and black."

Bennett was under tremendous pressure—from the Shuberts, the company of *Dreamgirls*, and himself—to deliver another hit after the failure of *Ballroom*. He had a recurring nightmare, which he talked about in a *New York* magazine profile. *Dreamgirls*, in "the shimmer of its half-light, became a black-cast *Ballroom*, a $3 million flop." [4]

Bennett invited his friend Larry Cohen, who had moved to Los Angeles, to see the show in Boston. Afterward, he asked Cohen, "Am I the best?"

"Yes," Cohen replied. "You are the best."

Bennett relaxed. "Okay, what did you think of the show?" he said.

Cohen thought it was dazzling, but found a "cosmic flaw" in the second act. After being replaced by Deena at the end of Act I, Effie was gone for good. "Bring the fat girl back," Cohen said. "The audience wants her. No matter how good the second act is, you keep thinking, When am I going to see the fat girl again?"

Cohen's advice echoed something Elia Kazan said to Tennessee Williams during rehearsals of *Cat on a Hot Tin Roof* in 1955. In the original draft of the play, Big Daddy was not in the third act. Kazan urged Williams to bring him back. Big Daddy was such a force, the audience needed to see him one last time. Williams wrote a scene between Big Daddy and Brick for the third act that is one of the most potent in the play.

Over the objections of Eyen, who did not want to pander to the audience, Bennett brought Effie back in Act II of *Dreamgirls*.

Despite the tension among the creative team and the show's second-act problems, *Dreamgirls* began to feel like a hit. Marvin Krauss, the general manager, offered to buy out Krieger's share, including his royalties, for $250,000. Krauss had seen Krieger play poker with the company and thought he wasn't much of a gambler. But Krieger had been working on this show every day for more than two years. He was not about to sell off his baby to a shark like Krauss.

Dreamgirls opened to positive reviews in Boston, including a near rave from Kevin Kelly in the *Globe*. Bennett, he wrote, accomplished a "staging concept with the rapidity, if not the fluidity, of the movies. . . . The theater's sparse and limited vocabulary suddenly finds itself in the wide open library of the cinema."

Kelly and Bennett were good friends, and many believed they had been lovers in the 1970s. Kelly's review meant a great deal to Bennett, and the critic met privately with him to give more advice on how to improve the show for New York. Kelly's review circulated in New York. Broadway was humming with the news that Michael Bennett had another winner. Ticket sales began to take off. But Bennett was still nervous. A few days before the New York opening, he told the *Times*, "This show is not about dancers. This show is about singers. . . . It is not *A Chorus Line II*. It's not a black version of *A Chorus Line*."

Dreamgirls opened December 20, 1981, at the Imperial Theatre, to a first-night audience that stood and cheered after "And I Am Telling You I'm Not Going" and stood and cheered again at the end of the show, though many felt Act II was a letdown after Holliday's show-stopping solo. At the opening-night party, Bennett worried about the reviews. He knocked back vodka to calm his nerves. At 9:45 the *Times* hit the streets. Someone handed Bennett a copy of Frank Rich's review. "When Broadway history is being made, you can feel it," Rich wrote. "What you feel is a seismic emotional jolt that sends the audience, as one, right out of its wits. While such moments are uncommonly rare these days, I'm here to report that one popped up at the Imperial last night. Broadway history was made at the end of the first act of Michael Bennett's beautiful and heartbreaking new musical, *Dreamgirls*." Rich then described, in detail, Holliday's performance of "And I Am Telling You I'm Not Going." Buried in the review were complaints of "a few lapses of clarity" and "overpat" resolutions in Act II. But Rich concluded: "Mr. Bennett has long been [Jerome] Robbins's Broadway heir apparent, as he had demonstrated in two previous *Gypsy*-like backstage musicals, *Follies* and *A Chorus Line*. But last night the torch was passed, firmly, unquestionably, once and for all."

Not all the overnight notices were raves. Douglas Watt, in the *Daily News*, spoke for many when he wrote that *Dreamgirls* "is all style and no substance." Walter Kerr, writing in the Sunday *Times*, would call it "very efficient. It is also, I regret to say, all very remote."

Bennett phoned Jacobs and Breglio the next morning at 10:00 a.m. He'd been up all night, drinking and going through the reviews. Despite the rave in the *Times*, he was "terrified that the show was not going to do well," said Breglio.

Jacobs spoke to him, paternally. "Michael, we've got some good reviews. And we've got Frank. We've got the *Times*." Jacobs began to discuss the ad and marketing campaigns, but Bennett interrupted him.

"Cut the crap!" he screamed into the receiver. "Do I have a hit or not? Do I have a hit? I want to know. Do I have a hit?"

"Michael, you have a hit," Jacobs said. "You have a big hit. Believe me, you have a hit."

Bennett took a deep breath.

"I'm glad. I'm happy for that. I'm thrilled we have a hit."

And then he hung up.

CHAPTER NINETEEN

Civil War

In December 1978, Herb Sturz, a deputy mayor, received a phone call from his boss, Ed Koch. The mayor had on his schedule a meeting with Gerald Schoenfeld, chairman of the Shubert Organization. He wanted Sturz to sit in.

Sturz, an able and diplomatic civil servant, had never met Schoenfeld. His first impression of the Shubert chief was of a man whose head was about to explode. Schoenfeld was "up in arms," Sturz said, over Father Bruce Ritter's plan to expand his shelter for runaways and homeless kids in Times Square. The Under 21 shelter, which was part of Ritter's Covenant House network of safe places in the city for homeless teenagers, was located on Forty-Fourth Street near Eighth Avenue, Shubert's backyard. Ritter was trying to evict some merchants so he could expand his facility to keep pace with the growing number of runaways flooding New York City at the time. Schoenfeld had supported Ritter's Under 21 shelter as part of the effort to make Times Square safer. But when he saw that it had become a crash pad for druggies who loitered in front of it day and night, he changed his mind. He wanted Ritter and the riffraff out of the neighborhood.[1]

At the meeting with Koch and Sturz, Schoenfeld angrily expounded that "the shelter, with all those drug addicts, is going to destroy our business. It will scare away our audiences." Ritter had little time for Schoenfeld's objections. Indeed, he seemed to delight in sticking it to the fancy Broadway types. He said he wanted to open a soup kitchen at the shelter for the homeless. "My heart rejoiced," he wrote in a newspaper column, "at the thought of a couple hundred Times Square derelicts lined up in the lobby of the St. James Theatre." [2]

Sturz thought Schoenfeld was overstating the case—"I think some of his anger was for show"—but he acknowledged the point. Ritter was running what he thought was a rehabilitation center, but not every drug addict cleans up overnight. In fact, there had been complaints from other merchants in the area about the number of teenagers loitering—and doing drugs—in front of the shelter. Carl Weisbrod, director of the mayor's Midtown Enforcement Project, also had concerns about the expansion of the shelter. "These kids clearly need [its] services," he told the *New York Times*. "But the city has been trying to attract legitimate commercial uses to Times Square." [3]

Sturz and Weisbrod found another location for the shelter—Tenth Avenue and Fortieth Street, far away from the Shubert's stomping ground—and persuaded Ritter to take it. Schoenfeld liked the solution. He became close to Sturz and Weisbrod, often meeting them for breakfast at the Pierre Hotel, or lunch at Orso, Joe Allen's upscale Italian restaurant on West Forty-Sixth Street. Over these meals, Schoenfeld, Sturz, and Weisbrod discussed plans to continue the rehabilitation of Times Square. The Midtown Citizens Committee, of which Schoenfeld was still chairman, and the Midtown Enforcement Project, had achieved some success. The number of massage parlors had been reduced and the police force in the neighborhood had tripled in size. The half-price ticket booth had driven the vagrants, drug dealers, and addicts out of Duffy Square.

But Times Square in 1980 was not Disneyland. It was still seedy, rough, and dangerous. It was also the last patch of Midtown that had yet to undergo a building boom. In the 1960s and seventies, office towers sprang up along Sixth and Park Avenues. But aside from a couple of office towers, including One Astor Plaza (which housed the Minskoff Theatre), there was little new construction in Times Square. On many blocks the tallest buildings were the old Broadway theaters, which loomed over tenement buildings that housed family-owned businesses such as bars, restaurants, modestly priced hotels, dance studios, acting schools, ticket brokers, souvenir shops, and musical instrument repair stores.

Plans to redevelop and modernize Times Square—and Forty-

Second Street in particular—had been put forward since the 1960s. The Broadway Association, a group of Times Square businessmen, drew up a plan in 1962 to rid Forty-Second Street between Broadway and Eighth Avenue of the flourishing penny arcades and grinder movie houses. The association wanted to turn ten run-down movie houses into fancy supper clubs and cabarets. Victorian-style sidewalk arcades would run the length of the block on both sides of the street. Escalators would take pedestrians up to latticework footbridges spanning the block. In the center of the street would be "seasonally appropriate potted plants." [4]

Nothing came of the project, however, and Times Square continued its slide into sleaze. In the 1960s and 1970s, two maverick developers, Irving Maidman and Fred Papert, acquired a number of buildings along Forty-Second Street between Ninth and Tenth Avenues, a block that was even more seedy and dangerous than the one between Broadway and Eighth. They tried to create a neighborhood of experimental, Off-Broadway theaters, along with restaurants, bars, and rehearsal spaces. But when the fiscal crisis hit in the mid-seventies "a chill descended on this small-scale investment activity." [5]

But Papert was not down for long. As the financial crisis eased in the late seventies, Papert put forth an ambitious plan to salvage the three-block area from Forty-First to Forty-Third Streets between Seventh and Eighth Avenues—a neighborhood he called "a garbage dump." [6] Papert envisioned a playland for New York, complete with theaters, theme park rides, museums, and family restaurants. Called the City at 42nd Street, the plan attracted the backing of the Ford Foundation, which supplied $500,000 to get it rolling. The head of the board of directors of the City at 42nd Street was John Gutfreund, managing partner of Salomon Brothers. The goal was to take over the area, condemn many of the old buildings and seedy businesses, and restore or build theaters that would contain live musical shows, exhibitions, and multiscreen surround-sound movies. There would also be a giant ferris wheel from which riders could view all of Times Square. The plan could not be implemented, however, without the support of the city, which could exercise eminent domain to rid Forty-Second Street of its sleazy establishments. The project also came with a steep price tag—estimated to be $600 million. It needed tax abatements and help from the city to secure $40 million from the federal government to purchase parcels of land and begin the restoration of the old theaters.[7]

The Ford Foundation presented the plan to Mayor Koch at a luncheon at its elegant Kevin Roche–designed headquarters on East Forty-Third Street.

"I remember it very well because it was not a very good lunch," Koch recalled. "It was very dry tuna fish. They showed me their plan and a model. And the model had a ferris wheel. And I looked at it and said to myself, 'This is ridiculous. This is Disneyland. That's not what New York wants or should have. This is orange juice, and what we need is seltzer.'"

Koch used the seltzer line in an interview with the *New York Times*. "New York cannot and should not compete with Disneyland—that's for Florida," he told Paul Goldberger, the paper's architectural critic.

Gutfreund and the other members of the City at 42nd Street were furious.

"You're not going to stop us," Gutfreund told Koch.

"I'm not here to stop you," Koch replied. "If you want to use your money, build it! But you're not using city money."

Gutfreund, Papert, the Ford Foundation, and the other powerful supporters of the project probably could have raised the money even without tax abatements and federal grants. But they did not have the city's power of eminent domain. Without it, the City at 42nd Street was dead.

Critics of Koch's decision said he killed the project because it was not his idea, and since his ego was gigantic—"How'm I doin'?" he always asked voters as he strode through the city—he couldn't allow other people to take credit for the cleanup of Times Square. But Koch's famous "seltzer" response was a snappy way of putting something he believed: New York City could never be a planned Utopia. It was a hodgepodge of its history, of its immigrants, of its crooks, artists, dreamers, winners, and losers.

Liberal on most social issues, Koch had swung to the right on economics in the wake of the fiscal crisis. The city, he knew, could not

survive without businesses, without corporate headquarters, without
Wall Street. His administration, in its early days, was business friendly,
offering tax breaks and other incentives to retain or entice companies
to come to New York. He also sensed that Times Square was ready
for redevelopment. Why not try to attract businesses to the area? He
asked Herb Sturz, chairman of the city planning commission, to come
up with an alternative plan to clean up Forty-Second Street. Sturz's
plan called for the restoration of nine theaters, most of which had
become porno houses, and the construction of a four-tower office
complex, to be controlled by Park Tower Realty, which paid $25 mil-
lion to buy the site. Park Tower hired architects Philip Johnson and
John Burgee to design the complex. But as soon as they revealed their
plans, powerful critics such as Goldberger at the *Times* and Brendan
Gill at the *New Yorker* denounced them, saying the buildings were ugly
and soulless. Others complained that the skyscrapers would block out
the sunlight and turn Times Square into a tunnel. At the same time,
politicians representing the west side of Midtown sued the city to stop
the plan.

"I never forgave them for that," Koch said. "I asked them, 'Why are
you bringing these lawsuits against us?' And they said, 'Well, if you're
successful and this place becomes gentrified, it will raise the rents for
our constituents over in Chelsea and Hell's Kitchen.' Because the area
would get better and more valuable, they wanted to stop us. I never
forgave them."

In the end, it would take the city ten years to battle the lawsuits.
The salvaging of Forty-Second Street, in the 1980s, stalled out. And so
Koch turned his attention to another project a few blocks up Broad-
way, one that would become the linchpin for the redevelopment of
Times Square. It would also pit theater people who had been friends
for years against one another.

In the 1970s, John Portman, an Atlanta-based architect, was considered
a savior of the inner cities. As businesses and residents fled to the suburbs, Portman was designing and building luxury hotels in some of
the most blighted urban areas in the country—the Peachtree Plaza in
Atlanta, the Westin Bonaventure in Los Angeles, and the Detroit Marriott at the Renaissance Center in Detroit. Sleek and contemporary,

the outstanding features of these hotels were their soaring atriums and glass elevators. They were open and airy, filled with restaurants and shops. You could stay at a Portman-designed hotel and never have to leave the complex. And that was precisely the point. They sheltered their guests from the dangers of the inner city.

In 1973, Mayor John Lindsay announced that New York would get its own Portman Hotel, to be located on the west side of Broadway between Forty-Fifth and Forty-Sixth Streets. Lindsay believed the hotel, which would cost $150 million, would help spur the revival of Times Square. But the financial crisis of 1975 scuttled the plan, and the Portman Hotel appeared to be another failed attempt to save a neighborhood sliding into chaos and decay. When Koch's plans to redevelop Forty-Second Street stalled, he decided to revive the Portman Hotel idea. But the cost of the project was now $241 million. To entice Portman back to Broadway, the city offered him a host of tax abatements, tax deferrals, and zoning incentives. The city also pledged to secure federal grants of up to $21.5 million. Portman was pleased. Times Square, he said, "is the most famous area in the country and we had the chance to do something of substance, to be a catalyst for saving the area. You always try something out on the road first, New Haven and places like that, before bringing it to Broadway. Thank God this isn't a play. Critics can kill a play. But not a hotel."[8]

Portman's hotel would soar forty-seven stories and contain 2,020 rooms. It would also have a fifteen-hundred-seat theater, ideal for lavish, tourist-friendly musicals. Critics complained that it looked like a bunker—"something out of *The Guns of Navarone*," one wrote.[9] Its lobby was on the eighth floor, high above the seedy streets of Times Square. But, mindful of his critics, Portman's plan also included a pedestrian plaza outside the hotel. The League of New York Theatres and Producers endorsed the hotel. So, too, did the Shubert Organization. The hotel, designed in part to attract conventions, would be located in the heart of Shubert territory. The company had six theaters on Forty-Fifth Street alone. The hotel would funnel hundreds of people a night into Shubert shows. Schoenfeld became a vocal proponent of the hotel, though he and other producers had reservations about the pedestrian plaza. He feared it would become a gathering place for junkies and hookers. Alex Cohen referred to it as "Needle Park."

To build this modern new hotel, several buildings from another era would have to be demolished, including the Piccadilly Hotel (whose bar had been a Shubert watering hole for years) and three theaters—the Bijou, the Helen Hayes, and the Morosco. Portman's plan had always called for the destruction of the theaters. But Broadway was in such bad shape in 1973, nobody paid much attention to three old theaters that, more often than not, stood empty. After the successful campaign to save Grand Central Terminal from the wrecking ball in 1978, however, urban preservation, not demolition, took hold.

The Helen Hayes Theatre was an architectural gem. Opened in 1911 as the Folies-Bergère at 210 West Forty-Sixth Street it had a glazed terra-cotta facade of turquoise blue, old ivory, and gold. The lobby was white marble. The Beaux-Arts auditorium, with seating for just under a thousand, mixed soft colors of rose, pearl gray, and gold.[10] Tenants included George Jessel in *The Jazz Singer*, Bela Lugosi in *Dracula*, and Imogene Coca and Henry Fonda, making their Broadway debuts, in *New Faces of 1934*. In 1955 it was renamed the Helen Hayes to mark the First Lady of the American Theater's fiftieth anniversary on the stage. A year later, it was home to *Long Day's Journey Into Night*, for which Eugene O'Neill won a posthumous Pulitzer Prize.

Architecturally, the Morosco was not in the same league. It was a straight-forward brick building with a rather cumbersome iron and glass canopy. But over the years, the 954-seat theater, built by the Shubert brothers in 1917, housed some of the most important plays in theater history, beginning with O'Neill's first full-length play, *Beyond the Horizon*, in 1920. Arthur Miller's *Death of a Salesman* premiered there in 1949, followed six years later by Tennessee Williams's *Cat on a Hot Tin Roof*. Richard Burton and Helen Hayes appeared in *Time Remembered*, Henry Fonda starred in *Silent Night, Lonely Night*, and Melvyn Douglas played a presidential candidate in Gore Vidal's brilliant political drama *The Best Man*. In 1973, Jason Robards and Colleen Dewhurst appeared in a heartbreaking revival of O'Neill's *A Moon for the Misbegotten*. The Morosco was prized for its acoustics, said by actors to be the best on Broadway.

The Morosco was located at 217 West Forty-Fifth Street. Right next door, at 209, was the 603-seat Bijou, the smallest theater built by the Shuberts. It was never a desirable theater.

The playwright John Guare and his wife Adele Chatfield-Taylor, who served on the New York City Landmarks Commission, were appalled that three historic Broadway theaters were to be sacrificed for the Portman Hotel. They contacted their friend Roberta Brandes Gratz, a journalist who covered urban planning. "Oh, Bertie, you've got to write about this," they said. "No one is paying any attention."

Gratz's article—"Save the Helen Hayes"—appeared in the November 19, 1979, issue of *New York* magazine. "Do we really have to destroy three good theaters and give away millions of dollars to get this hotel built?" she asked. She quoted Stephen Sondheim, then the president of the Dramatists Guild, who said the theaters were "intimate houses," well suited to nonmusical plays. "They have an atmosphere you seldom get in the new theaters. It's less tangible—a sense of continuity and tradition. Like the patina of an old painting."

But Koch officials made it clear to Gratz that they were not interested in the plight of old theaters. "Implicit in the beginning was our willingness to accept demolition of the Helen Hayes," said Kenneth Halpern, director of the Mayor's Office of Midtown Planning and Development. "We were looking to do whatever was necessary to get the hotel built."

Gratz's article galvanized the theater community against the destruction of the theaters. "You have to understand," she recalled, "the *New York Times* was not covering this story. From the *Times*'s point of view, the hotel was going to lead to the rebirth of Times Square." The Municipal Art Society, which had led the fight for historical preservation, didn't raise any objections to the destruction of the theaters, either. One of its most influential members was Fred Papert, an early champion of cleaning up Times Square.

Gratz went to Papert and said, "Fred, how can this be happening? We can't lose these theaters."

"Roberta, leave it alone," he responded. "It will be fine."

But she didn't. After her article came out Lenore Loveman and Sandy Lundwall formed the Save the Theatres campaign. Colleen Dewhurst, the president of Equity, became a fierce advocate for the theaters. Some of the biggest names on Broadway—Jason Robards, Tony Randall, José Ferrer, Celeste Holm, Tony Roberts, Christopher Reeve, Arthur Miller, Edward Albee, Lauren Bacall, James Earl Jones—joined her.

Bernard Hughes, who'd starred in *Da* at the Morosco, wrote an impassioned editorial in the *New York Times*. Forty-Fifth Street, he wrote, "was the quintessential Broadway street," a collection of theaters that housed musicals, comedies, and straight drama "thriving in proximity." To those who believed the hotel would help wipe away the sleaze on the streets, he protested: "After playing 549 performances of *Da* at the Morosco, I have a right to take that last crazily expedient statement personally. For the business of those streets is my business. They do not contain a single porno shop or massage parlor." [11]

The campaign to save the theaters got a spectacular boost when Joe Papp joined the fray. He was, Gratz said, a bit late to the game, but he played it with the showman's flair for publicity.

He started by requesting a meeting with the mayor.

"We're on opposite sides of this issue," he told Koch, "but I need something from you. I have a flatbed truck, but I need a permit so that we can park it in front of the theaters and use it to make our case to passersby. We will not use it to denounce you. We're going to talk about saving the theaters."

"Sure," Koch said, and issued the permit.

As soon as Papp climbed on top of his flatbed truck, he shouted into his bullhorn, "Shame on Ed Koch!"

"You know, on reflection and the passage of time, you forgive everybody," Koch said many years later. "I forgave him because he was an extraordinary asset for the city of New York, and he was a genius."

The battle to save the theaters wore on for two years. Papp and Actors' Equity mobilized their supporters, with actors standing on the flatbed truck talking about the importance of the theaters and acting out scenes from the great plays once performed on their stages. The papers and local news shows covered the protests almost every day. Papp and other famous theater people were carted off to jail for acts of civil disobedience. They were, of course, immediately released. Shirley Herz, a press agent, said everybody got on well with the police, who thought the actors were great fun to have in the paddy wagons, especially when they led everybody in songs from old musicals. Phil Smith, walking by the protesters one morning, saw Papp being arrested. Smith then caught a train to Washington, D.C., for an event at the National Theatre. At the dinner later that night, he was surprised to see Papp at his table.

"I thought you were arrested today, Joe?" he asked.

"Oh, I have a deal with the police," Papp said. "They arrest me first—and release me first."

Behind the scenes, aided by money from the J. M. Kaplan Fund (which was set up by the former owner of Welch's Grape Juice and run by his daughter, Joan Davidson), the Save the Theatres campaign brought a number of lawsuits, many concerning the environment, against the city to stop the destruction of the theaters. Every time the bulldozers closed in on the theaters, there were more lawsuits and injunctions. The group also commissioned architect Lee Harris Pomeroy to come up with a plan to incorporate the theaters into the design of the hotel. Portman and the city rejected that proposal as too costly.[12]

As they watched the battle unfold, the Shuberts and the League of New York Theatres and Producers seethed. No one was more furious than Schoenfeld, who'd made it his mission to clean up Times Square. He argued that the three theaters were obsolete because they were not big enough to house musicals, which were what the public wanted. His opponents countered that the Shuberts didn't care if the theaters were torn down because they hadn't owned them in years. Lester Osterman, a producer, owned the Hayes and the Morosco. His booker was Leonard Soloway. "The truth is, the Hayes was hard to book because it had a second balcony," said Soloway. "The Morosco, though, was a very good house for straight plays." As for the Bijou, the joke around Broadway was that if you wanted to deep-six a show, you'd stick it there.

The Shuberts' adversaries also said they didn't care about three historic playhouses because they were angling to manage the new musical house in Portman's hotel. And, in fact, Schoenfeld asked Michael Bennett, set designer Robin Wagner, and lighting designer Jules Fisher to come up with their dream theater, which he presented to Portman.

But the Shuberts had competition. Jimmy Nederlander was making a bid to run the theater.

Schoenfeld worked the press as aggressively as Papp did. He met with the editorial boards of the major papers, most of which supported the hotel. Paul Goldberger, the architectural critic for the *Times*, handed Schoenfeld a victory when he wrote, "We may well be faced with the choice between the Portman design or no hotel at all. And as important as the Helen Hayes and the Morosco are, they are not, in the view of this critic, enough by themselves to justify the scrapping of the entire project."

Schoenfeld convinced Helen Hayes, whose very own theater was in peril, to come out in support of the hotel. But when she did, her actor friends pressured her to change her mind. In the end, she waffled, saying "I'm torn between sentiment and good sense. That's all I can say—you've come up with someone with no position." [13]

Schoenfeld attended every city hearing on the Portman Hotel and the fate of the theaters. His disdain for his opponents was palpable.

"He couldn't bear to look at any of us," Gratz recalled. "He was annoyed by any opposition. The arrogance of power was well exhibited in Jerry Schoenfeld."

During the battle, Alex Cohen, who initially supported the hotel, switched sides, pressured, his friends said, by his wife, Hildy Parks. He joined Papp on the flatbed truck and denounced the Shuberts for trying to wipe away theater history. Schoenfeld and Jacobs were furious. They'd been friends with Cohen for years. His office was above theirs in the Shubert Theatre. They'd even given him parking privileges in Shubert Alley. They cut him dead.

Schoenfeld didn't shy away from public confrontations with his opponents. Outside the Plymouth Theatre one night before a performance of *Nicholas Nickleby*, playwright David Mamet accosted him: "You call yourself a producer, but you don't know how to create anything. All you know how to do is destroy!" "And you don't know how to write plays!" Schoenfeld snarled, referring, perhaps, to *The Water Engine / Mr. Happiness*, which had flopped earlier at the Plymouth. [14]

Resentment toward the Shuberts had been building in the theater community even before they began advocating for the demolition of the theaters. Schoenfeld and Jacobs had amassed power over union negotiations, the TKTS Booth, ticketing, real estate, Michael Bennett. The Shuberts were richer than ever from *A Chorus Line* and had just produced another hit, *Dreamgirls*, which looked poised to sweep the Tony Awards in 1982. Schoenfeld and Jacobs were not shy about exercising their power. As Jacobs told Breglio, "We don't need producers anymore. We have everything right here—money, theaters, talent. All we need are good general managers."

Some of the resentment stemmed from jealousy. In the theater, as David Merrick once said (perhaps by way of Gore Vidal), "It's not enough that I should succeed—others should fail."

Bob Fosse, in particular, envied the success of *Dreamgirls*.

"How is that flop show of yours?" Fosse asked Jacobs at a party shortly after *Dreamgirls* opened.

"Bobby, which flop show? I have so many of them," Jacobs replied, laughing.

"You know that piece of garbage Michael Bennett did."

"Piece of garbage that Michael Bennett did? Did you read Frank Rich's review?"

"I never read Frank Rich," Fosse said.

"Well, if you read Frank Rich you would know that the torch had passed from Jerome Robbins to Michael Bennett—and you didn't get a chance to touch it on the way!"

But the battle against the Shuberts to save the Bijou, the Morosco, and the Hayes was serious. The actors on the barricades believed in their cause. Hundreds of years of theater history were in danger of being destroyed. The Shubert Organization was on the wrong side of the fight. Schoenfeld and Jacobs were putting real estate above history and art. It was easy to paint them, as Joe Papp did, as "greedy landlords." Or, as Breglio put it, "they were starting to be seen as the Evil Empire."

As the fight reached its climax in the spring of 1982, many on Broadway looked to strike back at the Evil Empire.

CHAPTER TWENTY

And the Winner Is . . .

Just about the only person in the theater world not preoccupied with the fate of the Helen Hayes and the Morosco was Tommy Tune. He had a show to put on.

The show, a musical version of Fellini's 8½—about a famous Italian film director on the verge of a nervous breakdown—came to Tune's attention in the form of a cassette tape pushed through his mail slot. He was living at 145 West Fifty-Fifth Street, 13A (Bennett's old apartment), when the cassette dropped from the slot. A handwritten note accompanied the tape: "I'm your upstairs neighbor, and I'm working on my musical version of 8½. I call it *Nine*."

Tune knew the movie. He chuckled to himself, "And we'll love him even more because he's grown by half an inch!" The note was signed by Mario Fratti, who was writing the script. The score was by Maury Yeston, a professor of music at Yale. He had been working on the show since 1973. The tape was of a workshop in 1979 at the Eugene O'Neill Theater Center in Waterford, Connecticut. Tune threw the cassette into his weekend bag and headed out to Fire Island. The next morning he went for a walk on the beach. He put on his Walkman headphones and listened to the tape. The first thing he heard was a sweeping, gorgeous overture played on the piano. It was called "Overture delle Donne." Tune envisioned a bath house in an elegant European spa. He'd been looking for a show to direct. He had found it.

"I had to do it," he recalled. "I had to do it."

To produce the show, Tune turned to his boyfriend, Michel Stuart, one of the original cast members of *A Chorus Line*. Other members of the team included Thommie Walsh, who would assist with the choreography, and writer Arthur Kopit, brought in by Tune to rework Fratti's script. Kopit was represented by ICM, headed by the powerful agent Sam Cohn.

Cohn liked the score, too, and convinced Paramount Pictures to put up $150,000 for a workshop.

In addition to his producing responsibilities, Stuart would design the costumes. Walsh thought Stuart needed an assistant. He suggested a friend, William Ivey Long, a young designer who had recently graduated from the Yale School of Drama. But Long turned down the job "with tears in my eyes," as he recalled, "because I didn't want to be anybody's assistant." He went on to design the costumes for James Lapine's play *Twelve Dreams* at the Public Theater. The day before the first preview, Walsh called him and said he was bringing Tommy Tune to see the show the next day. The set was all white, and Long had designed several glamorous costumes, including a black velvet gown in which Carole Shelley made her entrance. Tune only stayed for the first act. Long never found out what he thought of his work.

But a few weeks later, in early December, he received a phone call.

"Can you measure all the girls today, and also do a shoe tracing?" the caller wanted to know.

"Excuse me, who is this?" Long asked. "What show is this?"

"This is for *Nine* the musical," said the caller, who identified himself as the stage manager. "We're rehearsing on top of the New Amsterdam Theatre."

"Would you look at the call sheet and tell me what my job is?" Long said.

"You're the costume designer."

Stuart, Long later learned, was overwhelmed raising money for the show. He never had time to do the costumes. Tune decided Long should do them, though nobody bothered to tell him. *Nine* was being thrown together, with minor details such as offers, contracts, schedules—even rights—being overlooked.

Long took his tape measure to the New Amsterdam Theatre on Forty-Second Street to begin designing costumes that, it seemed, "had been an afterthought."

•   •   •

The New Amsterdam Theatre, an art nouveau palace built by the vicious Abe Erlanger in 1903, had a storied past. Its most famous productions had been Florenz Ziegfeld's *Follies*, which played the New Amsterdam from 1913 until 1927. Will Rogers, Fanny Brice, W. C. Fields, Ed Wynn, and Eddie Cantor graced its stage. With its orchestra, two balconies, and twelve spacious boxes, the theater could seat 1,750. Elaborate vines and flowers, molded from emerald-green porcelain, covered the auditorium. The art nouveau elegance extended throughout the building. In one lounge was an enormous, elaborately carved Irish marble fireplace. A ceiling dome supported by twelve marble columns capped the smoking room.

Atop the New Amsterdam was a six-hundred-eighty-seat theater initially called the Aerial Gardens and later, the Frolic. It was here that Ziegfeld produced his *Midnight Frolics* starting in 1915, the last in 1929. After the *Follies* concluded in the ground-floor auditorium, the well connected retreated upstairs for dinner, dancing, and more risqué entertainment. On any given night the audience might include Diamond Jim Brady, William Randolph Hearst, various Astors and Vanderbilts. With dancing, eating, drinking, and a show, the Frolic became New York's first nightclub, according to theater historian Ethan Mordden.[1] But since most of the profit came from the bar, the Frolic was done in by Prohibition. The Aerial Gardens became a playhouse, but it struggled to compete with larger theaters during the Depression. It eventually became a radio studio, then a television studio, and, finally, rehearsal space for Broadway shows.

By 1980, both the Aerial Gardens and the New Amsterdam were in disrepair. The main auditorium had been a movie house for many years, its twelve art nouveau boxes ripped from the walls to improve sightlines. Gone, too, were most of the emerald-green porcelain vines and flowers. Murals in the lobby depicting scenes from Shakespeare, Wagner, and *Faust* had been painted over long ago.

The Aerial Gardens—now called the New Amsterdam Roof—also had been stripped of its decor. The blue velvet seats were still there, though they were rotting and smelled of mold. The windows had been painted black. But the paint was peeling and shafts of light shot into the decrepit theater. There were holes in the walls and a gaping hole in the ceiling. The wind howled through the theater, and snow fluttered onto the stage.

"It was a very Miss Havisham kind of place," said Long. The first thing he saw when he arrived were several women sitting on the stage—a tall, angular Karen Akers; a buxom, fiery redheaded Anita Morris; a raven-haired beauty named Shelly Burch; and a rail-thin, temperamental former Folies-Bergère performer named Liliane Montevecchi. The only man in the cast was Raul Julia, whom Long knew from his performances at the Public Theater in *Two Gentlemen of Verona* and *The Threepenny Opera*.

Initial drafts of *Nine* had several male characters (as there are in the movie), but Tune hit on a daring idea. The show was about Guido Contini and all the women in his life—his mother, his wife, his lovers, his producer, the whore who seduced him as a boy. There would be four boys playing young Guido and his friends, but Raul Julia would be the only adult male in the cast. He would be surrounded by twenty-one women. *Nine*, Yeston would later say, "became an essay about the power of women by answering the question, 'What are women to men?'" [2]

Because it was freezing in the New Amsterdam Roof, the women wore winter coats. Long noticed they each had their own box on stage made out of wood. Tune explained, "I love putting things in the way, so I have to choreograph around them. An empty stage scares me." The boxes, Tune said, represented each woman's world on which Guido would alight—like a bee gathering pollen. Long was baffled, even more so when he watched some of the rehearsal. Yeston, a bundle of energy, was there, writing songs to order. Melodies, beautiful, elegant melodies, poured out of him. If you needed one song, he'd give you three. You could take your pick. But the script was all over the place, and there was barely a second act.

And Long was put off by Tune and his team.

"I thought they were preposterous and pretentious," he said. "They held hands and talked about Karma, and Michel Stuart carried around a bag of crystals that, he said, had magic powers. Somebody would blow up a balloon before rehearsals, and they'd pass it around because it contained the 'soul' of the show. Really? Tommy had his head in the clouds, but of course he is taller than everybody else. I definitely had no idea what was going on."

That night, after rehearsal, Tune convened a meeting of the designers at his apartment on West Fifty-Fifth Street. Lawrence Miller, the set designer, presented sketches of ideas for scenery, and Tune explained the visual concept of the show. It was to be set in a spa in Venice. The set would be all white tiles, and all the women would be dressed in black. "Who here has been to Venice?" Tune asked. Long was the only one who raised his hand. "I had done the grand tour, as all young southern—gay!—gentlemen did back then. They said, 'Tell us about Venice!' They had all these books about Venice, but no one had ever been there. So I started talking about the water and the shimmering light and the silence because there are no cars. What did I really know about Venice? Nothing! I was free associating."

While Tune and the company rehearsed in the freezing cold of the New Amsterdam Roof garden, Long spent weeks researching Italian fashion designers. Postrehearsal production meetings were usually held at Charlie's, a pub on West Forty-Fifth Street. The creators were putting *Nine* together over beer and hamburgers. Long would often explain his ideas for costumes, but several weeks into rehearsals, he still hadn't drawn anything. Then one night his assistant said, "We're not leaving here until you draw every single black dress you've been talking about." The napkins at Charlie's were long and thin, perfect for sketching costumes for the tall women Tune had cast in *Nine*. By three in the morning, Long had sketched over thirty black dresses on the napkins.

On February 7, 1982, Tune staged a workshop for the show's backers, including Barry Diller, who was running Paramount. Diller arrived with his friend Warren Beatty. A few days later, Diller told Sam Cohn that Paramount was dropping out of the project. He didn't think Raul Julia was a big enough star to carry the show. And there was one more thing. "Warren Beatty told him he thought the show was awful," Tune recalled.*

Rehearsals were suspended while Michel Stuart and Cohn scram-

---

* Beatty may have disliked the show, but the gorgeous Shelly Burch caught his eye. He sent word round to the New Amsterdam that he'd like to take her to dinner.

bled to find new backers. An aspiring young producer named Francine LeFrak, whose father was the real estate developer Samuel J. LeFrak, had attended the presentation and loved the show. One of the things that impressed her most was a steamy dance performed by Anita Morris, playing one of Guido's lovers. Her number was titled "A Call from the Vatican," and it was the first—and thus far only—phone-sex number in a Broadway musical. Morris had choreographed it with her husband, Grover Dale, on a trunk in their living room. LeFrak thought it was a showstopper. She offered to help raise money. "Maury came over to my office and played the score, and I filled the room with potential investors," LeFrak said. "Maury is the biggest schmaltz operator in the world, and when he played 'Be Italian' and 'Unusual Way,' I just collected checks."

Stuart, whose family was in the garment business (his real name was Kleinman), tapped the rag trade business for backers. Cohn turned to the Shuberts, arranging for Jacobs and Smith to see a presentation of *Nine*.

"It was an interesting show, and you could tell that Tommy Tune had a lot of talent," Smith said. "But at that point, with *Dreamgirls* such a big hit, there was no room in Bernie's life for anyone but Michael."

The Shuberts passed.

But Jimmy Nederlander, who had recently bought the New Amsterdam with the intention of restoring it, jumped in. He also offered the producers a theater, the 46th Street, which was right next door to the Imperial, where *Dreamgirls* was playing to sold-out houses.

Nine was back on. But there was no money for an out-of-town tryout. The show, which was capitalized at $2.5 million, would open cold on Broadway. The opening night for *Nine* was set, appropriately enough, for May 9, which also happened to be the cut-off date for Tony Award eligibility. That was press agent Judy Jacksina's idea. She knew *Nine* had to make a splash in a field dominated by *Dreamgirls*. She told Cohn, "Sam, listen, this is an esoteric piece. We got people on boxes singing 'La-la-la-la-la!' We have to create some excitement." Opening on the ninth was gimmicky, but it meant that the reviews would be out on the morning of the tenth, and the Tony nominations would be announced that afternoon. If, as Jacksina suspected, the show received many nominations, "we would take over the newsstands."

Jacksina had other stunts up her sleeve. Her greatest weapons were the show's twenty-one striking women. Why not cover the front of the theater with life-size photos of them in their black costumes? "I wanted to seductively represent what was going on inside the theater," she said. "I didn't want cute little tap dancing photos. I wanted sex."

There was one hitch, however—the costumes had yet to be made. All that existed were Long's sketches on his napkins. "I had to make twenty-seven costumes in two weeks," Long recalled. "I've never worked under such pressure in my entire career. We were killing ourselves."

Long brought his twenty-seven dresses to the photo shoot, which lasted twenty-three hours. Two days later, at 7:30 a.m., workmen started covering the front of the 46th Street Theatre with life-size photos of the gorgeous women dressed in black—everyone except Anita Morris, whose costume had been rejected because Tune didn't like it. She was represented by a giant head shot. At 11:00 a.m., Jacksina received a phone call from a friend. Traffic was tied up on Forty-Sixth Street. Drivers were stopping to look at the photos. And there were five camera crews from local TV stations shooting the front of the theater.

Nine had yet to play a performance and already it was news.

"You know what those photographs were?" Long said. "They were a 'Fuck you!' to *Dreamgirls*."

A few nights later, Tune, exhausted from a marathon rehearsal at the New Amsterdam, was about to climb into bed when the phone rang.

"Darling!" Michael Bennett said. "You have to go out of town with your show. That's what we do!"

"I know. But, Michael, we don't have any money. We can't afford to go out of town," Tune replied.

"But, darling, you must go out of town," Bennett insisted. "You will go out of town, and I will help you, and you'll come in in the fall."

"It's not possible, Michael," Tune said. "We have no money. We have to open now."

"You will go out of town, do you hear me?" Bennett hissed. *"You will go out of town."*

Bennett's tone frightened Tune. It was, he remembered years later, "black, it was the devil, it was Mafia-like. He had become the thing he feared."

"I can't talk to you Michael," Tune said. "I'm sorry. I have to go."

He hung up the phone and stood in the kitchen shaking. His friend who had once told him, "Never fear, never fear," had frightened him.

In March, the cast and crew of *Nine* left the New Amsterdam and decamped to the 46th Street for further rehearsals. Every night around 9:30 they heard people cheering next door at the Imperial. That was the time Jennifer Holliday brought down the house with "And I Am Telling You I'm Not Going."

"You could hear the screams through the brick wall," Long said.

On the other side of the 46th Street Theatre another drama was reaching its climax. The wrecking ball was closing in on the Helen Hayes. On their lunch break the women from *Nine* would run to the Hayes or the Morosco (around the corner on Forty-Fifth Street) and join the protesters. They would return to rehearsals in tears. "I'm going to lie down in front of the bulldozers," Karen Akers declared.

Tune had little patience for the histrionics. "I'd say, 'Girls, come on. Pull yourselves together. We have work to do!' I felt like I was unloyal to Broadway, but I had a show to put on."

The little Bijou Theatre fell to the bulldozers in January. By March, all that stood between the Morosco and the Hayes and the bulldozer was the Supreme Court, which had agreed to hear one last legal challenge to their demolition. Local and state lawsuits had been resolved in Portman's favor. A campaign to have the Morosco and the Hayes designated national landmarks failed. Portman's hotel got a significant boost when the J. W. Marriott Corporation agreed to manage it. As soon as Marriott signed on, the Reagan administration approved $22 million from the Urban Development Action Grant (UDAG) program for the project, despite administration officials openly advocating ending UDAG. Opponents of the hotel pointed out that J. Willard Marriott, founder of the corporation, had been chairman of Reagan's finance committee during the 1980 presidential campaign.[3]

For Joe Papp, the fight to save the theaters had become a full-time job. He commandeered office space from the Broadway advertising agency Serino, Coyne & Nappi. The company was located on the fourth floor of One Astor Plaza, and its conference room looked down on the Morosco. "I'm moving in," he told Nancy Coyne, and made free use of her faxes and phones to wage his battle. He was frequently photographed gazing down at the doomed theater.

On March 22, while vacationing in Puerto Rico, Ed Koch took a phone call from an aide who told him the Supreme Court had lifted the stay against the destruction of the theaters that morning.

"If we're going to do it, we should do it now," the aide advised.

"Go ahead," Koch replied, and headed to the pool.

When Papp got word the Supreme Court had lifted the stay, he burst into the conference room at Serino, Coyne & Nappi trailed by a phalanx of reporters, photographers, and cameramen. He leapt up onto the radiator so that the Morosco and the bulldozer were in his frame, and as the cameras clicked and whirred he shouted, "Arrest me, arrest me! They're going to have to arrest me to get me out of the way!"

The press conference over, he rushed down to the Morosco where a crowd of more than a thousand had gathered. The celebrity protesters included Richard Gere, Christopher Reeve, Susan Sarandon, Estelle Parsons, and Raul Julia and the cast of *Nine*. Several actors were reading scenes from O'Neill's *Strange Interlude*. Papp jumped up on the flatbed truck with his bullhorn. "These theaters are going to come down," he told the crowd. "The Supreme Court has lifted the stay."

There were screams and tears and angry shouts of "Shame on Koch! Shame on Koch!" And then the crowd, led by Papp, scrambled over the barricades to block the demolition crew from doing its job. All the demonstrators were arrested, peacefully, and carted off to a nearby precinct where they were charged with criminal trespass and then released.[4] Most returned to the Morosco, but this time they stayed behind the barricades. Shortly after 2:00 p.m., as a giant wrecking claw from DeFilippis Crane Service began closing in on the Morosco, the crowd began to sing "Give My Regards to Broadway" and "America the Beautiful." And then the claw took a chunk out of the theater's facade. The mezzanine, with its chandeliers and rows of horsehair-stuffed seats, was exposed. Another swipe from the claw, and the last two letters of the name "Morosco" on the theater's marquee came loose and dangled above the sidewalk.

"We were in tears," Roberta Gratz recalled. "Everybody there was in tears. We were in disbelief that they could really destroy something so important."

By the end of the day, the Morosco and the Helen Hayes were piles of rubble. Technically, the facade of the Hayes was supposed to be preserved. But in the melee of protest and destruction it was, said Gratz, "dispersed."

Every now and then a chunk of it winds up on eBay.

As the crane tore into the Hayes, Tommy Tune was racing to finish *Nine* next door. Previews were to begin April 22, and the second act was still a mess. There were "twelve different endings," Jacksina said, as well as a long homage to rococo opéra bouffe in the middle of the second act called "The Grand Canal."

"Oh God, it was longer than *Aida!*" Jacksina said.

There were other hurdles as well. During an advertising meeting one of the producers announced he had to go to Rome.

"Why are you going to Rome?" Jacksina asked.

"I have to go talk to Mr. Fellini. We don't have the rights."

"What? What? What?" Jacksina exploded. "We're about to start previews in two weeks and you don't have the rights from Mr. Fellini? *What?"*

"Would you stop saying, 'What!' the producer responded, and then headed to the airport.*

Long, meanwhile, still hadn't cracked Anita Morris's costume. She and her husband "sent word," Long said, that she would be wearing black pants and a black turtleneck in the show. It would be a dramatic look—flaming red hair atop a black body. Against the white tiles, the black costume would accentuate Morris's double-jointed extensions in "A Call from the Vatican."

But Long wasn't ready to admit defeat. He asked Tune to lunch and

---

* He returned a few days later with "a half-assed document," said John Breglio, who, representing Jimmy Nederlander, first noticed the oversight. "It wasn't great, but at least they could get the show on."

begged for one last chance. "If this doesn't work, tell her I will go to Bonwit Teller and buy her the most expensive silk turtleneck and pants in the store," he said.

"OK," said Tune. "You can have a second chance. But that's it. She's very delicate, and she's very nervous about her costume."

Long dashed to the costume shop at 890 Broadway and began designing. "I saw lace, stretch lace from head to toe," he said. "I was going to take her idea of a long black costume, but make it nude—a nude body suit covered in lace."

A few days later Morris showed up for the fitting.

"Thank you for coming, Anita," Long said. "I'm sorry that I have failed you. I missed who you are. I was successful with the other ladies, but their characters are one note. You're more complicated."

"I have the mumps," Morris whispered. "I feel terrible. I don't think I can stay here."

"Please give me one more chance," Long implored. "I see lace. I see a stretch version of what you and Grover want, but nude."

"Can you get me some tea?" Morris asked.

She stripped down to her bra and thong, and Long began wrapping her in lace. But the lace didn't stretch, which would make it impossible for Morris to pull off her double-jointed dance numbers. Long noticed some fabric in the trash can that had been used for some capes in the show. It had patterns on it and was stretchable. He grabbed a roll of it from the trash can. "Shut your eyes," he told her. Then he held it out in front of her. She opened her eyes and "her mumps were gone," Long recalled, laughing. Off came the bra and thong, and for the next two and a half hours Long and his assistants pinned the fabric to her naked body.

They had her costume—a neck-to-ankle stretchable bodysuit covered in black patterns. Morris would wear nothing underneath.

"Oh, let's not tell Tommy!" she said. "Let's surprise him."

On April 19—three days before the first public performance of *Nine*—Long staged a costume parade for Tune at the theater. There was Karen Akers in her chic, understated black jacket and skirt. There was Liliane Montevecchi in a black mink hat and black Folies-Bergères boa.

There was Shelly Burch in her low-cut blouse, revealing her ample bosom. And there was Anita Morris in her see-through body suit. Tune turned to Long, and "shot daggers at me," Long recalled. "And then he began a slow, cold clap."

The entire cast and crew burst into applause. But not Tune. He continued to glower at Long, clapping his hands slowly, deliberately.

"I learned an important lesson that day," said Long. "Never, ever surprise your director."

And now the race was on to haul *Nine* to the May 9 finish line. The set was still being built and painted in the theater; the "Grand Canal" number was still running longer than *Aida*; and Long was still finishing the costumes, including another thirty that were all white for the finale. Tune wanted doves released over the audience during the final scene. The first time the doves were released in rehearsal, they relieved themselves on actress Taina Elg's white hat.

"Dove doo is gray when it first drops," Long said. "But when you try to wash it, it turns lime green. And so Taina's hat was now lime green. She didn't get a new white hat until after we opened because they didn't have any money."

The painting of the set was completed an hour or so before the first preview. The ladies in the show were told not to sit on their boxes that night, or they'd have white paint on their behinds. Some of them were drying their boxes with their hair dryers.

The first preview was rocky. There was no intermission, and some baffled audience members walked out in the middle of the show. Those that remained could hear the roar that went up next door at the Imperial when Jennifer Holliday sang "And I Am Telling You I'm Not Going."

Tune and Jacksina lingered outside the theater after the first performance so they could hear what people were saying.

"What was that?" one woman asked her friend.

The other woman replied, "I think it was a heroin trip. I think the Italian director is having a heroin trip."

"How do you know?" the first woman asked.

"Well, I've been reading up on heroin trips and that's what they're supposed to be like."

At the next performance, as people once again began walking out of the theater midway through the show, Jacksina turned to Tune and said, "If you don't put an intermission in this show, I am going to die. Do you hear me? *I am going to die.*"

An intermission went in the next day. And then Tune began to cut, mercilessly. Out went most of "The Grand Canal," and with it many of Long's costumes. The ending still wasn't working. One night writer Arthur Kopit said, "Let's cut the white finale. Nobody understands it. It looks like they're all getting married." Long had had enough. He'd already lost most of his costumes from "Grand Canal" and he didn't want to lose anymore. He didn't want his first Broadway show to be nothing but black costumes. "Fuck you, Arthur!" he screamed. "It's about rebirth, it's about hope!" Tune, who never lost his temper amid the chaos, listened impassively. Then he said, "The finale stays."

Despite its problems, *Nine* was generating strong word of mouth in theater circles during previews. People were struck by Tune's swirling, cinematic staging and Yeston's gorgeous melodies. And they were raving about Anita Morris, though they didn't know her name. They were calling her "the redhead in the cat suit."[5]

The critics saw *Nine* on May 8, the day before opening night. The show had been "frozen"—theater lingo for no more changes—that afternoon. Another coat of paint had just been applied to the set, something Clive Barnes picked up on in his review in the *New York Post*: "*Nine*, which panting slightly and still faintly smelling of fresh paint, skidded in under the Tony nomination deadline last night."

After Frank Rich saw the show, Francine LeFrak gave him a cassette of the score. They'd been friends since his days as a writer for *Time* magazine, and LeFrak had been telling him for months how much she loved *Nine*. "This was my baby—I was so passionate about it," she said. That Rich wanted to hear the score again was, she thought, an encouraging sign.

The night *Nine* opened, Michael Bennett threw a party at his Central Park South penthouse for a few close friends, including John Breglio and Nan Knighton, who had seen the show.

"There were touches of genius in it," Breglio recalled. "It wasn't all great, but I remember thinking, this is the dark horse."

At 11:20 Bennett turned on the local news to see what the television critics had to say about his protégé's musical. "*Nine* is an extraordinary show," said Dennis Cunningham on CBS. "A show to treasure. Tommy Tune has done masterful work. A startling act of imagination, independence, and daring, *Nine*—"

Smash!

The television screen shattered. Bennett had hurled a tumbler of vodka at Dennis Cunningham. The room fell silent. Then Bennett went into his kitchen and returned with two bottles of Cristal. He poured out champagne for everyone and said, "I want to toast my friend Tommy Tune tonight on his success. Here's to Tommy. And here's to *Nine*."

At the opening night party, the cast and crew of *Nine* nervously awaited the reviews. The Associated Press was out, and it was excellent. They'd heard through the grapevine that Barnes, in the *Post*, was also a rave. But it was the *Times*—it was Frank Rich—that counted. Jacksina came into the party with an early edition of the *Times* and handed it to LeFrak.

"There are two unquestionable reasons to cheer *Nine*, the extravagantly uneven musical that opened at the 46th Street Theatre last night," Rich wrote. "Their names are Tommy Tune and Maury Yeston." He praised Tune as "a man who could create rainbows in a desert," and said Yeston had written some of the season's "most novel and beautiful songs."

LeFrak's heart sank, however, when she read on. "For all the brilliantly styled moments in *Nine*, there are others where stylization curdles into vulgarity of kitsch and camp." Rich complained that, at its center, the show was hollow, that the creators never made the audience care about Guido or the women "who gnaw at his soul."

And then came the punch. "For all his musical inspiration, Mr. Yeston can write pedestrian lyrics," Rich wrote. He cited, as an example, a line from the song "My Husband Makes Movies"—"No need to carry out this masquerade"—which he called a "standard-issue" sentiment about unhappiness in love.

LeFrak was stunned. She'd given Rich a tape of the score, and he used it to bash Yeston's lyrics.

"It was the worst decision I ever made as a producer," she said. "I should never have given him that tape. I couldn't believe I could be that stupid. I was heartbroken. I felt I let everyone down. I never spoke to Frank again. I've forgiven him, but I've never spoken to him since."

The next morning it appeared that *Nine*, which opened with paltry advance ticket sales, might sag under the weight of mixed reviews. The critics who didn't care for it echoed Rich's charge that it was glitz over substance. But concerns about the reviews were dispelled that afternoon by the Tony nominations. *Nine* received twelve, just one shy of the thirteen for *Dreamgirls*. The two shows were going head-to-head in several categories, including Best Score, Book, Direction, Choreography and, most crucially, Best Musical.

In the *Nine* production offices there were screams of delight. The decision was made to treat the show as if it were a massive hit. Ignore the mixed reviews, the poor advance ticket sales. Concentrate on the Tony nominations. "We decided that whatever *Dreamgirls* did, we would do it bigger," Jacksina said. "If they took out a half-page ad, we'd take out a full-page ad. We were fighting for our show, and we were going to blindside them."

Up in the serene, elegant offices of the Shubert Organization, there was consternation. Schoenfeld and Jacobs had indeed been blindsided by *Nine*. The reports they'd heard during previews were mixed, and it was inconceivable that a show that "came out of nowhere," as Breglio put it, would threaten *Dreamgirls*, which the *Times* had anointed the best show of the season. But *Dreamgirls* was a "soft hit." The Shuberts looked at the numbers and saw that it was no *Chorus Line*. A Tony for Best Musical would extend its life in New York and on the road.

And now it had competition.

Nine had powerful champions, including *Daily News* gossip columnist Liz Smith, who rallied the town for her fellow Texan, Tommy Tune. Earl Wilson, the grand old nightlife columnist at the *Post*, was also a fan. He touted the show in his columns. But *Dreamgirls* had the *Times*, which showered the show with puff pieces. *Nine* took another critical hit from Walter Kerr in the Sunday *Times*, who dismissed it as "a gimmick, top to closing."

A few days after the Tony nominations came out, the nominees gathered in the Eugenia Room upstairs at Sardi's for brunch with the press. Jacksina arrived before her nominees—Karen Akers, Raul Julia, Liliane Montevecchi, and Anita Morris—and noticed that *Dreamgirls* had taken over the room. "They were all standing in front of the Tony Award medallion having their picture taken and being interviewed and being fabulous," she said. "It looked like there were seven hundred of them. OK, they got there before me, and they've obviously planted their flag on the moon. They were not going to let *Nine* get near this hootenanny."

Jacksina knew she had to make a splash. She went downstairs to the main dining room and asked Vincent Sardi if she could use the back entrance to the Eugenia Room's kitchen. Sure, he said. Then she waited for her nominees to arrive. She escorted them all upstairs to have their pictures taken—all except Anita Morris, who wore a low-cut green dress and not much underneath. "Wait down here," she said. "I'll be right back." When she returned, she took Morris up the back staircase and into the kitchen.

"OK, do what I say," she said. "There's a table right outside the kitchen door. I want you to jump up on that table and do your Marilyn Monroe thing."

Morris did as instructed. She burst through the doors, jumped up on the table, shook out her flaming red hair and said, "Hi everybody!"

"Well, that stopped the room," Jacksina recalled. "That low-cut dress, all that white, white skin and all that red hair. Oh my God, she was like a Vegas girl come to life. The photographers turned away from all those seven hundred *Dreamgirls* people and then they ran over to the table and were fighting each other to get the best shot. And for the next hour, it was all about Anita Morris and *Nine*."

Jon Wilner, an ad executive who worked on *Nine*, said the war between the shows "affected everyone in and around the industry. I am not making a joke here, but if the Shuberts went to this deli, then the *Nine* people wouldn't go to that deli. That's how bad it was. And it was quite serious. You couldn't kid about it, you couldn't laugh about it. You could not walk into the Shubert office and say anything remotely nice about *Nine*, and you couldn't walk into the *Nine* office and say anything remotely nice about *Dreamgirls*. You had to watch your step."

Behind the scenes, the battle was being fought by the generals— Bernie Jacobs, for *Dreamgirls*, and Sam Cohn, for *Nine*. They'd known each other for years, and their relationship was, as a reporter for the *Times* once characterized it, "mutual suspicion mingled with mutual respect." [6]

The battle turned ugly. Rumors spread that the Shuberts had offered Cohn $1 million to delay the opening of *Nine* until the fall. Another rumor had it that the Shuberts lobbied Con Edison to withhold the extra power allotment that the 46th Street Theatre needed to operate the sets for *Nine*. Jacobs was convinced Cohn was fanning the rumors to make the Shuberts look like bullies. Cohn denied the charge. He did, however, remind everyone that Schoenfeld and Jacobs wanted the Hayes and the Morosco torn down so the much-loathed Marriott Marquis Hotel could go up.

Jacobs, meanwhile, bad-mouthed *Nine*. He called most of the six hundred-plus Tony voters to make sure they were in the *Dreamgirls* camp. "He lobbied hard," one voter recalled years later. "He made it clear that, if you wanted to do business with the Shuberts, you'd better vote for *Dreamgirls*."

LeFrak's office was in the same building as Cohn's, and she often delivered strategy memos about the *Nine* Tony campaign to him. "We didn't do anything without Sam's blessing," she said. "We were all novices. We wanted his approval."

"The producers of *Nine* knew as much about producing a Broadway show as I know how to do plumbing," said Wilner. "And most of the time, they were high as kites. They could only have advertising meetings when there was a nine—it had to be on the ninth, the nineteenth, or the twenty-ninth of the month. And before the meetings, they'd close the conference door and meditate for fifteen minutes. Sam Cohn's name wasn't on anything, but he was calling the shots."

Cohn would read the memos—and then, as was his habit, eat them.*

He also fielded angry phone calls from Jacobs. "When *Nine* closes, I am going to throw the biggest party Broadway has ever seen!" Jacobs bellowed. LeFrak remembered one call during which Cohn turned white. "I believe Bernie was threatening him," she said. "He was saying, 'I will never hire any of your clients again.' I've never seen Sam so shaken. He was eating tissue paper, and he set it on fire with a match. Bernie was yelling into the phone, and smoke was coming out of Sam's mouth."

The producers of *Nine* didn't, at first, think they could topple *Dreamgirls*. The Shuberts had a solid bloc of votes that consisted of Shubert employees and other Shubert loyalists. In addition, "there was the sense that we had crossed the Shuberts, and we would pay for it," LeFrak recalled.

And then one day she ran into a woman who, she knew, was firmly in the Shubert bloc. The woman, whom to this day she will not name, said to her, "They think I'm voting for *Dreamgirls*. But I love *Nine*, and I'm voting for it. Don't tell them."

"That was the first sign there was a chink in the armor," Le-Frak said. "Other than that, going up against the Shuberts was miserable."

There were others on Broadway who began to sense that *Dreamgirls* was not impregnable. The producer Albert Poland was one. Driving along Fifty-Seventh Street one afternoon with Poland, Jacobs began talking about the upcoming awards.

"When *Dreamgirls* wins the Tony—"

Poland interrupted him.

"I wouldn't be so sure of that, Bernie," he said. "There is a big Shubert backlash."

Jacobs slammed on the brakes. "What do you mean?" he barked.

"There is a lot of anger about your position on the theaters. And Sam is fanning the flames."

---

* Cohn's paper-eating habit was legendary around Broadway. Once, after breakfast with Bernie Jacobs and Phil Smith, he reached for the check. "Where is it?" he said. "You ate it, Sam," Smith replied.

• • •

The thirty-sixth annual Tony Awards took place on June 6, 1982, at the Imperial Theatre, home to *Dreamgirls*. The atmosphere was tense. Alex Cohen, the wily producer of the telecast, ratcheted up the tension by sitting the *Dreamgirls* camp on the right side of the theater (facing the stage) and the *Nine* camp on the left side.

In other words, one side of the theater belonged to the Jets, the other to the Sharks.

The Shuberts, who owned the Imperial and could sit wherever they wanted, had a foot in both camps. Schoenfeld was the interloper on the *Nine* side of the theater, while Jacobs remained in *Dreamgirls* territory.

The design awards were presented before the live broadcast on CBS. When Tharon Musser won Best Lighting Design for *Dreamgirls*, the right side of the house screamed and applauded. Next up was Best Costume Design, which went to William Ivey Long. As he was getting up, someone sitting behind him kicked his seat in anger. It was John Napier, who'd been nominated for his costumes for *Nicholas Nickleby*.

But Napier's turn was next. He picked up the Tony for Best Scenic Design for *Nicholas Nickleby*.

Then, a moment later, the *Nine* camp shouted and cheered Maury Yeston, who won for score.

The final award before the start of the live broadcast went to Tom Eyen, for his book to *Dreamgirls*.

The score was *Dreamgirls*, two; *Nine*, two.

The Tony Award broadcast began with a shot of Times Square and the theme from the I Love New York Campaign. Had the audience in the Imperial Theatre that night not been so focused on the battle between *Dreamgirls* and *Nine*, perhaps they would have recognized that their once-dying industry, and their once-dying city, were making a comeback.

Broadway and I Love New York, on national television.

But they didn't care.

"All we thought about was who's going to win," said Judy Jacksina.

Tony Randall was the host, and he came out wearing an oversize turtleneck and a tan corduroy jacket. "I am a critic, and we don't dress," he said to the black-tie audience. After that came a low-key number from a nominated show that had no chance—Andrew Lloyd Webber and Tim Rice's *Joseph and the Amazing Technicolor Dreamcoat*—and then Tony Awards to featured actors, Amanda Plummer (*Agnes of God*) and Zakes Mokae (*Master Harold and the Boys*).

Milton Berle walked out on stage. He was once in a musical satire called *Saluta!* he said. "And as George Kaufman said, 'Satire is what closes on Saturday night.'"

There was a loud thud from the wings of the theater.

"What the hell?" a startled Berle said, looking to his right. Then he turned back to the audience and said, "Don't tell me they're tearing this one down, too!"

The crowd roared and applauded . . . and applauded . . . and applauded.

Berle calmed them down and said, "The nominees for Best Direction of a Musical are: Michael Bennett, *Dreamgirls*."

There was a quick cut to Bennett, his shiny black eyes wide open, his hands clasped.

Berle continued: "Martin Charnin, *The First*, Tony Tanner, *Joseph and the Amazing Technicolor Dreamcoat*, and Tommy Tune, *Nine*."

Another cut to Tune, smiling and eager.

"And the winner is . . ."

Someone in the audience shouted, "*Dreamgirls!*"

Berle said, "*Dreamgirls*. Big mouth! And the winner is . . ."

He looked up and said, "*Nine!* Tommy Tune, Tommy Tune!"

The left side of the house erupted in screams and cheers. The right side, the *Dreamgirls* side, sat on its hands. Alex Cohen, calling the shots from the control room, cut to Schoenfeld, who was clapping but not smiling.

Tune tap-danced across the stage and said, "Well, this is just great! Thank you. I have to do a gesture because words aren't enough." He put his Tony down on the stage, placed his hands on his heart, and then threw open his arms.

"Okay, I'm going home," he said. "Bye!"

And then he twirled his way into the wings.

The next major award—Best Play—went to *The Life and Adventures of Nicholas Nickleby*, that joint production between the Shuberts and the Nederlanders. Schoenfeld, Jacobs, and Jimmy Nederlander accepted the award. Schoenfeld said it was "an honor to be producing with Jimmy Nederlander." Jacobs said nothing.

The tension in the Imperial was replaced by horror at the next musical interlude: Cher, sitting on an iceberg and wearing a white fur coat and boots, singing "My Heart Belongs to Daddy" to a bunch of chorus boys dressed as polar bears. Cher started to strip and said, "You guys are so butch!" There never was an explanation for why Cher sang and stripped with a bunch of gay polar bears at the Tony Awards in 1982.

Now it was time for choreography. Ben Vereen opened the envelope and said, "Yeah! Michael Bennett and Michael Peters for *Dreamgirls!*" Bennett and Peters bolted down the aisle. Holding the Tony aloft, Bennett, looking relieved, exclaimed, "We're very happy to be here!"

Dreamgirls picked up the next award: Ben Harney for Best Lead Actor in a Musical. He beat out Raul Julia.

Another musical interlude followed, this one featuring Ann Miller, pantless, performing "No Time at All" from *Pippin*. The lyrics were projected on the platform beneath her so that the audience could sing along. Surely Bennett was wincing. This kind of camp, hoary tap dancing routine was what the cinematic *Dreamgirls* was shoving into the showbiz graveyard.

The shove came soon after when Jennifer Holliday electrified the audience with "And I Am Telling You I'm Not Going." Her performance was so thrilling the *Dreamgirls* camp must have thought they had the Tony for Best Musical in the bag. But the tide shifted again with the next award for Best Featured Actress in a Musical. The nominees were Karen Akers, Liliane Montevecchi, and Anita Morris, all from *Nine*, and Laurie Beechman from *Joseph and the Amazing Technicolor Dreamcoat*. The award went to Montevecchi, clad in a white turban and and a dress with shoulder pads wider than Times Square.

But after cheers from the *Nine* side of the house subsided, cheers from the *Dreamgirls* side erupted when Cleavant Derricks, of *Dreamgirls*, picked up the award for Featured Actor in a Musical.

The final musical number was from *Nine*. The producers had wanted Anita Morris to perform the steamy "A Call from the Vatican," but CBS's office of Standards and Practices, in the form of two nice middle-aged ladies Jacksina dubbed "Miss Marmelstein and Aunt Pitty Pat," raised some objections. They saw *Nine* and met with Tune and Jacksina the next morning in the lobby of the 46th Street. Aunt Pitty Pat opened her spiral notebook. It was, she said, up to Tune to decide which number he would put on at the Tonys. But, consulting her notebook, she said that if he chose "A Call from the Vatican" there could be "no nipple rubbing, no self-fondling of breasts, no gyrating on the box after doing a split, no rubbing of the inner thigh, and no audible sounds of ecstasy." Aunt Pitty Pat closed her notebook and said, "Thank you very much for your time, and please let us know." Tune and Jacksina looked at each other and said, "Let's just do 'Be Italian.'"

During the performance of "Be Italian," Alex Cohen cut to Betty and Bernie Jacobs. They were not looking at the stage.

Victor Borge presented the Tony for Best Lead Actress in a Musical to Jennifer Holliday. "I want to thank the producers of the show, David Geffen, Bernie Jacobs—I call him Daddy!—and Jerry Schoenfield [*sic*]," she said. "And I especially want to thank my director, Michael Bennett. He is such a wonderful man, and he has taught me so much about life and the theater. Do you want to fight again?" she added, to laughter from the audience.

Heading into the final award of the night—Best Musical—the score was *Dreamgirls*, six; *Nine*, four.

Lena Horne, triumphant on Broadway with her show *Lena Horne: "The Lady and Her Music,"* presented the award. Backstage during the commercial break she said, "I hope they wrote the winner in big letters because I'm not going to put my glasses on on national TV." The winner, she was told, was typed in small letters. "That's not going to work," she said. One of the accountants who tallied the votes said he would open the envelope, write the winner in big letters, and put it in a fresh envelope. "Oh, never mind," Horne said. "Honey, I know how to read the word '*Dreamgirls*.'"

The Tonys were live again. Horne walked out from the wings, resplendent in a flowing gown. "This is a pretty theater," she said. "Full of all the sounds of this gorgeous music. I had a ball here in *Jamaica*. And now the award for Best Musical of the season. The nominees are: *Dreamgirls, Joseph and the Amazing Technicolor Dreamcoat, Nine*, and *Pump Boys and Dinettes*."

There wasn't a sound in the Imperial.

As she opened the envelope, she said, "I hope they printed this big enough to read without my glasses. The winner is"—she looked up, surprised—"*Nine*."

The left side of the theater erupted. As the *Nine* producers bounded down the aisle, Schoenfeld turned to his wife, Pat, and said, "I just can't believe it."

Michel Stuart thanked Sam Cohn, "our honorary producer." Alex Cohen cut to Bernie and Betty Jacobs. Bernie looked grim. He was not clapping. Betty clapped once, turned to her husband and shrugged.

CAT$

They day after *Nine* defeated *Dreamgirls* at the Tonys, Schoenfeld called Harvey Sabinson, the head of the League of New York Theatres and Producers, and demanded a recount. Sabinson had to stifle a laugh. The ballots, he told Schoenfeld, were destroyed by the accounting firm as soon as they were tallied precisely to discourage such disgruntled phone calls.

"Then we'll sift through the ashes!" Schoenfeld snarled.

The Shuberts were on the warpath, striking out at anyone they thought had a hand in toppling *Dreamgirls*. At the top of the list was Sam Cohn. For years, he dined regularly with Jacobs at the steakhouse Wally's & Joseph's. Even at the height of the Tony battle—when Cohn and Jacobs were screaming at each other over the phone—they continued to meet at Wally's to hash out business deals. But the day after the Tonys, Jacobs froze him out. He didn't return Cohn's calls for a year.

"In the aftermath of *Nine*—the rumors, the hostility—I was reluctant to deal with Sam Cohn," Jacobs later admitted to the *New York Times*.[1] "There's no doubt about that." Schoenfeld added: "Absent our personal friendship with Sam, we would not have been as affected by the *Nine* situation. But because we do have that friendship, it cut to the quick."

In the end, however, the Shuberts had to deal with an agent who represented Bob Fosse, Mike Nichols, Meryl Streep, Kevin Kline, and

Glenn Close. Producer Manny Azenberg brokered a lunch between Jacobs and Cohn in the spring of 1983. The lunch, though, had to be on neutral ground. Cohn's territory was the Russian Tea Room; Jacobs held court at Sardi's. And so the lunch took place at Joe Allen, a popular theater district restaurant. Jacobs told Cohn that "whatever my personal feelings, it's my job to deal with you."[2] By the end of the lunch, they hammered out a deal to bring Tom Stoppard's *The Real Thing* to Broadway, directed by Nichols.*

The other Cohen on Broadway—producer Alex Cohen—did not weather Shubert wrath as well. Cohen had defended Schoenfeld and Jacobs against Louis Lefkowitz's attacks in the 1970s. He and his wife, Hildy, vacationed with Betty and Bernie Jacobs in the south of France. Cohen's office was in the Shubert Theatre directly above the Shubert executive offices. He even had that most coveted of Broadway perks—parking privileges in Shubert Alley.

But his decision to switch sides in the battle to save the Hayes and Morosco infuriated Schoenfeld and Jacobs. He also seemed to revel in their defeat at the Tonys, allowing the cameras to linger a bit too long on their scowling faces. The friendship frayed. When his lease was up, the Shuberts threw him out.

"They punched a hole in the ceiling and put in a skylight where Alex's office used to be," producer Liz McCann said. "Nobody would ever be above them again."

Cohen had conceived and produced the first Tony Awards network telecast in 1967 and had presided over the event ever since. Every time his contract with the League of New York Theatres and Producers was up, it was renewed without negotiations. Though Cohen claimed the telecast made little money, Sabinson suspected otherwise. The League lost money on the Tonys, but Sabinson had been told Cohen had a "sweetheart deal" with CBS. "But you couldn't go into his books," said Sabinson. "He was unaccountable."

Before the theater battle, Schoenfeld and Jacobs let Cohen do what-

---

*   Jacobs had seen the play in London the previous year with his wife and a young producer they'd both grown fond of named Cameron Mackintosh. Betty and Mackintosh loved the play, but Jacobs nodded off during the second act. "It's good he had a sleep in the middle," Betty confided to Mackintosh. "I'm not sure he would have taken it if he'd sat through the whole thing."

ever he wanted with the Tonys. "They looked the other way," said Sabinson. But now they wanted to know just how much he was taking out of the awards. Sabinson, with the Shuberts' blessing, ordered a forensic accounting of the Tonys. The conclusion of the accountant: "You guys are really getting screwed." Cohen was getting $2 million from CBS to produce the show, a small portion of which he kicked back to the League. But the League was buying most of the tickets to the telecast and the Tony ball—with prices ranging from $250 to $500—and was losing anywhere from $50,000 to $100,000 on the event.[3] Cohen claimed he, too, lost money on the Tony ball. But the accounting revealed he was making money every year. Producers who had paid $500 for their gala tickets were irritated one year when Cohen served them kidney pie for dinner. "It's cheap but tasty!" Cohen said.

Cohen also pocketed advertising money from the Tony *Playbill*, estimated to be tens of thousands of dollars. Neither the League nor the American Theater Wing, a nonprofit organization that created and administers the Tony Awards, received a cut of the advertising revenue.

There was nothing the Shuberts or the League could do until Cohen's contract was up in 1986. But he was a condemned man, and during the 1985 Tony Awards he handed his enemies the rope to hang him with. At a rehearsal for the telecast in front of performers, stagehands, and chorus kids, Cohen suggested that the theme for that year's show be Fuck you, Frank Rich. Then, before the telecast began that night, he took a swipe at New York governor Mario Cuomo. The New York State Council on the Arts was to receive a special Tony that night and Cuomo had agreed to accept it. He backed out, however, at the last minute. Cohen told the Tony crowd: "The governor of New York hasn't been to the theater in twenty-five years, and he didn't want to break his record."

Theater people criticized Cohen for his attacks on Rich and the governor. The Shuberts told Sabinson, "Let him go." His contract was not renewed.

He was about to lose another perch as well. He was on the board of the Actors Fund, and produced the TV show *Night of 100 Stars* to benefit the charity, which looked after actors who had fallen on hard times. The Shuberts and Sabinson suspected Cohen was up to his old tricks with *Night of 100 Stars*. Another accounting was ordered up, revealing that Cohen made more money on the show than the Actors Fund did. Many of Cohen's "expenses"—including trips to the south of France—were paid for out of the Actors Fund endowment.

As Cohen himself was fond of saying, "I've had a million dollars and I've owed a million dollars, and my lifestyle has never changed."

"Alex was gracefully asked to leave the board of the Actors Fund," said Sabinson.

Once the closest of friends, Cohen seldom spoke to Schoenfeld or Jacobs again. He died in 2000 with little money in the bank. About the only asset he had was the copyright to the Tony Awards telecasts he had broadcast from 1967 to 1986.

Though there was acrimony in the air in Shubert Alley, it was time, after the Tonys, to get on with business. And Schoenfeld and Jacobs were about to make the biggest bet in the history of the company. They had secured the North American rights to a new musical from London and were getting it ready for New York in the summer of 1982. With a budget of $4.5 million, the show would be the most expensive in the history of Broadway. The Shuberts were putting up 40 percent of the investment. Their partners would be David Geffen, ABC Entertainment, and Metromedia. Two other partners would be the show's boyish producer in London, Cameron Mackintosh, and its composer, Andrew Lloyd Webber.

Jacobs first heard about the show—*Cats*—when it began previews at the New London Theatre in May 1981. Tyler Gatchell, a Broadway general manager who had worked on Andrew Lloyd Webber's *Jesus Christ Superstar* in New York, saw an early performance. He tracked Jacobs down in Argentina where he and Betty and their family were on vacation, and suggested they come to London to see a show that, Gatchell thought, had potential. Jacobs trusted Gatchell's judgment and booked a flight from Buenos Aires to London.

No one in London knew what to make of this new musical from Andrew Lloyd Webber. The idea of turning T. S. Eliot's *Old Possum's Book of Practical Cats* into a musical seemed, to use a British expression, barmy. Lloyd Webber, a cat lover, grew up with the poems. He reread them around the time he was writing *Evita* and thought they sounded like song lyrics. As he would later learn, Eliot had, in fact, written them while listening to the popular tunes of the day.

"Which explains a lot," Lloyd Webber said. "Because I remember one poem, 'Skimbleshanks: The Railway Cat,' and thinking, gosh—he must have written this to something. I could guess what, but I had to keep myself from thinking that way."

That Eliot's poems were like song lyrics was fortuitous, since Lloyd Webber was looking for a new lyricist. He'd written three musicals with Tim Rice—*Joseph and the Amazing Technicolor Dreamcoat, Jesus Christ Superstar*, and *Evita*—but the two men were drifting apart. Lloyd Webber was always eager to start a new show. Rice, enjoying royalties from *Superstar* and *Evita*, had developed other hobbies. He'd much rather be at a cricket match, his friends said, then at his desk writing lyrics. Rice, in turn, had little patience with Lloyd Webber's ever-expanding entourage. "I'd love to work with Andrew again, if I can get past his secretaries," he often quipped.

Lloyd Webber set some of Eliot's poems to music, thinking *Cats* might become a musical symphony for children along the lines of *Peter and the Wolf*.

In the summer of 1980, at a country house called Sydmonton he'd bought in 1973, Lloyd Webber played his songs for his friends. They had gathered for what Lloyd Webber called "my little festival," a weekend of music, games, food, and wine. Lloyd Webber shrewdly invited Eliot's widow, Valerie. He'd need her blessing, of course, to pursue *Cats*. She thought his tunes were delightful and told him her husband would have enjoyed them as well. She brought with her some unpublished material, including a long letter Eliot had written suggesting a way in which the poems might be put together for a theatrical evening. She also had a scrap of verse about Grizabella the Glamour Cat that had been left out of *Old Possum's* because Eliot thought it was too depressing for children.

"The letter contained basically a plot outline, including an event the cats attend once a year called the Jellicle Ball," Lloyd Webber recalled. "There was a long poem about cats and dogs, and how they all get in a balloon and fly over the Russell Hotel."

The poem, called "Pollicle Dogs and Jellicle Cats," did not appear in
Old Possum's, but Lloyd Webber set it to music (he can be heard singing
it on the bonus tracks of his CD anthology, *Now & Forever*). Eventually,
he "eliminated the dog bits," and the song became "The Jellicle Ball."

Now that he had his lyricist, albeit a dead one, Lloyd Webber
needed a producer. Robert Stigwood, a ruddy-faced Australian entertainment mogul who favored rum and Coke for breakfast over orange
juice, had produced *Joseph*, *Jesus Christ Superstar*, and *Evita*. He was also
Lloyd Webber and Tim Rice's agent and manager, taking an astounding 25 percent of their earnings.[4] But by 1980, his interest had shifted
to the movies. He'd already produced two big hits, *Saturday Night Fever* and *Grease*, and was spending more time in Hollywood. Stigwood
and Lloyd Webber, who was becoming as shrewd with the accounting
books as he was at the piano, also clashed over financial matters. Lloyd
Webber bristled at just how much money Stigwood had made off his
talent. As a result, the two parted ways in 1979. By then Lloyd Webber
had already set up his own production company, The Really Useful
Group. But he was not yet a producer himself, and so he was looking
for someone with producing experience to work on *Cats*.

His producer came in the form of a youthful, roly-poly would-be
impresario named Cameron Mackintosh. Their first encounter was
a disaster. Mackintosh produced the Society of West End Theater
awards—snickeringly referred to as SWET and today known as the
Laurence Olivier Awards—in 1978, the year *Evita* won for Best Musical.

"The ceremony was actually a shambles, the whole thing," Lloyd
Webber said. "And when Tim and I picked up our award, I said, 'It's a
shame that Hal Prince isn't around to direct this event.'"

Lloyd Webber had never heard of Cameron Mackintosh. He assumed he was some "sixty-five-year-old Scotsman" who'd been hanging around the fringes of show business for years. Mackintosh was
furious at Lloyd Webber's jab. He told friends he'd see to it that Lloyd
Webber would never work again in the West End. It was an absurd
threat, but the feud took hold. Theater people gossiped about it over
lunches at the Ivy restaurant. Lloyd Webber decided to make peace.
He invited Mackintosh to lunch at the Savile Club. "We met at twelve
thirty," Lloyd Webber said. "At six we were still having lunch."

The two biggest show queens in the West End (Lloyd Webber honorary—he's straight) had found each other.

They had similar backgrounds. Both men grew up immersed in music. Lloyd Webber's father was the director of the London College of Music. William Lloyd Webber dreamed of becoming a famous classical composer, but never did. An accomplished musician, he had to make a living taking academic jobs, which left him frustrated and bitter. "If you ever write a song as good as 'Some Enchanted Evening,' I'll tell you," Bill once said to Andrew. The approval never came.[5]

Mackintosh's father, Ian, was a jazz trumpeter who never made it, either. To raise his three sons (Cameron was the eldest), he took a job in his father's lumber business. But office work was not for him, and he could usually be found at the local pub drinking and playing his trumpet. "He liked to drink," Barry Burnett, one of Cameron Mackintosh's oldest friends, said of Ian. "But the boys loved him because he was fun."

Lloyd Webber and Mackintosh both had Mame-like aunts who hooked them on musical theater. Lloyd Webber's aunt Viola, a vivacious former actress, introduced her young nephew to the musicals of Richard Rodgers and Frederick Loewe. He saw the movie version of *South Pacific* twelve times. His first West End show was *My Fair Lady*. He was so enamored of musicals, he built a toy theater with which he spent hours re-creating *The King and I*, *Flower Drum Song*, and *Gigi*.

Mackintosh's aunt Jean took him, when he was eight, to see Julian Slade's popular British musical *Salad Days*, about a magic piano that makes anyone who hears it dance. He liked it so much he went back to see it a few days later. Slade was playing the piano in the orchestra and after the show, eight-year-old Cameron ran down to the pit and demanded to know how the magic piano worked. Slade gave the boy a backstage tour. At that moment Mackintosh determined to be in the theater.[6] He went home and built his own toy theater in which he staged puppet shows with his brother Robert.

When they met for lunch at the Savile Club after the shambolic SWET awards, Lloyd Webber was far more established than Mackintosh. The composer was rich and, at least in England, famous. Mackintosh was a second-tier producer with several flops to his credit and only one genuine success, *Side by Side by Sondheim*, a revue of Stephen Sondheim songs. But Mackintosh was irrepressible and ambitious. Nothing set him back. He landed his first professional job in the theater at eighteen as a stagehand for *Camelot* at the Drury Lane. By the time he was twenty, he'd set up an office as a producer, even though he was still earning his money polishing the brass rails of the Drury Lane after performances. Barry Burnett, a budding agent who represented a number of up-and-coming West End talents, got a call from a "Mr. Cameron Mackintosh" one day. He said he was producing a musical version of Oscar Wilde's *The Picture of Dorian Gray*. And wanted to audition one of Burnett's clients.

"Send over a script," Burnett said.

An hour later a pudgy kid arrived at the office with the script.

"Thank you very much," Burnett said. "Please tell Mr. Mackintosh I will be in touch when I've read it."

"I am Mr. Mackintosh," the pudgy kid said.

Mackintosh and Burnett spent the next five hours talking about musical theater, cementing an enduring friendship. Burnett liked Mackintosh so much, he offered him a desk and a phone in his office for five pounds a week. Mackintosh, who was just scraping by, accepted. He often took Burnett to lunch, but he never managed to come up with the rent. Burnett was surprised one morning when a middle-aged lady showed up at the office claiming to be "Mr. Mackintosh's new secretary." Where had Mackintosh gotten the money for a secretary? Mackintosh came bounding through the door. He smiled at the middle-aged lady and said, "Hi, mum!" *

Mackintosh's first West End production was a revival of *Anything Goes* in 1969. He threw the opening party at the Unicorn pub near the theater. Everybody got food poisoning. The show closed a few days later, losing $45,000. Mackintosh needed to earn money, so he took a job as a publicist for a touring production of *Hair*. He returned to

---

* Decades later, after Mackintosh had become the most successful producer in theater history, he bought several West End theaters, including the Prince of Wales. There was office space above the theater, which he let to Burnett. After six months, Burnett began to wonder why he never received a bill for the rent. He asked Mackintosh's secretary what he owed. She told him, "Cameron said, 'No rent for Barry for a year.'"

the West End with *Trelawny*, a musical version of Arthur Wing Pinero's play *Trelawny of the Wells*. It received good reviews, but did little business. His next show—*The Card*—was also well received, but didn't catch on. Though he was a producer without a hit, his backers remained loyal. They admired his ambition, and laughed at his bitchy sense of humor. Theater owners liked him, too. He became friendly with Toby Rowland and his assistant, Jack Barum. Rowland ran the Stoll Moss Theatres Group, essentially the Shuberts of the West End. Mackintosh learned firsthand their "brilliant" negotiating technique.

"When they were courting you for a show—or if you were courting them for a theater—they would invite you to the office around eleven thirty," he recalled. "Toby would be there on his own and say, 'How lovely to see you!' And about a quarter to twelve Jack came in—you could set your watch by it. There would be hugging and gossip, and then Toby would say, 'Oh, Jack, would you like a whiskey? Of course, Cameron, you'll join us.' There would be a little whiskey for Toby, a bigger one for Jack and a tumbler full for you. 'Cheers!' they'd say. 'How great to see you! Your show sounds marvelous!' By the time you finished your first drink, they were saying your show was one of the best shows ever and they would move heaven and earth to have it in one of their theaters. And then you'd get down to the nitty gritty of the terms, by which time you'd be on your third whiskey. When it came to the stuff that really mattered, you had no idea what you'd agreed to. You got whatever theater they wanted you to have, and on their terms. But you left euphoric because they loved your show and you had a theater. They were brilliant." [7]

It was through Toby Rowland that Cameron Mackintosh first met Bernie Jacobs. In 1975, Mackintosh had saved up enough money to buy a cheap ticket to New York, his first trip to America. Rowland told him he must meet the head of the Shuberts, and made a call to Jacobs by way of an introduction. Mackintosh presented himself at the Shubert executive offices and was ushered into Jacobs's office, where he also met Schoenfeld and Phil Smith.

"They couldn't have been nicer," he recalled. "They set me up with tickets to all the shows and they took me for lunch at Sardi's. And remember—there was nothing there for them but the possible promise of my having a career one day." In subsequent visits to New York, Bernie and Betty Jacobs put Mackintosh up in their guest room in their Upper East Side town house so he could save money on hotel rooms. "I used to call it my New York pad," Mackintosh said.

A little over a year after meeting the Shuberts, Mackintosh had his first hit with *Side by Side*, despite a warning from another New York friend, producer Arthur Cantor, that "Sondheim closes in previews!" *Side by Side* ran 781 performances in the West End. On an investment of six thousand pounds it returned a hundred thousand.[8] Emboldened by the success of the revue format, Mackintosh produced another one in 1977 called *After Shave*, with an all-female cast. "It was an almost-lesbian revue," he recalled. "Legendary that one was. Even I didn't want to go to the first night. Even I knew it was going to be a turkey."

After Shave would be the last of the Mackintosh flops for a long time to come. Midway through their six-hour lunch at the Savile, after a second bottle of good red wine, Andrew Lloyd Webber said, "Cameron, I have this daft idea of doing a musical based on a book of poems about cats."

Three hours later, they got up from the table and shook hands. Their deal for *Cats* was done.

Casting about for a director, Lloyd Webber and Mackintosh knew they wanted someone of stature—someone whose name would assure Valerie Eliot that her husband's poems would be in good hands. The director of the moment was Trevor Nunn, of the Royal Shakespeare Company. He'd never directed a musical before, but, as he'd demonstrated with *Nicholas Nickleby*, he knew how to move a large group of people around onstage. He'd also had another success at the RSC—a musical version of *Comedy of Errors*, which had dances by Gillian Lynne. Mackintosh knew Lynne from a production of *My Fair Lady* they'd done a few years earlier. He brought her on board, and she, in turn, convinced Nunn to direct *Cats*. John Napier, Nunn's collaborator on *Nicholas Nickleby*, signed up as set designer.

As they began planning their production, the creators of *Cats* realized they would need a lot of dancing as the story (such as it was) revolved around the Jellicle Ball. The show would be something new for the West End—a dance musical. "Which is another reason people thought we were stark-raving mad," Lloyd Webber said. "At the time, we didn't do dance musicals. We didn't have many choreographers in Britain."

Lloyd Webber and Mackintosh needed to raise five hundred thousand pounds. They had few takers. David Dein, a successful garment manufacturer who had backed all of Mackintosh's shows, said, "Cameron, I love you. But I'm not investing in this one. It will never work. England is a nation of dog lovers."

Mackintosh turned to other friends, including Burnett, who kicked in anywhere from five hundred to seven hundred and fifty pounds. But it was still a struggle. Eventually, Lloyd Webber came through with the money by mortgaging Sydmonton.

As *Cats* was coming together in rehearsals—though nobody in the cast really knew what it was about—Nunn told Lloyd Webber the show was missing an eleven o'clock number, the big tune that sends the audience out with the song ringing in their ears. He thought Grizabella should sing it. He wanted it to evoke memories of her "days in the sun," as Eliot had put it. As it so happened, Lloyd Webber had a song in his trunk of discarded tunes, a trunk that every composer has and riffles through in a pinch. Lloyd Webber once toyed with the idea of writing an opera about the rivalry between Puccini and Leoncavallo, who were both working on operas based on Henri Murger's novel *Scènes de la vie de bohème*. (Guess who won.) Lloyd Webber's opera never got anywhere, but he did manage to write a lush and haunting Puccini-esque tune, which he played for Nunn. It was exactly what Nunn was looking for. Lloyd Webber, however, was concerned. It sounded so much like Puccini that, he feared, it might be from a Puccini opera. He played it for his father, a Puccini expert, and asked, "Does this sound like anything?"

"It sounds like $10 million," his father replied, adding, "you've done a very clever pastiche, but it's not by Puccini." [9]

Soon after, Lloyd Webber met his friend Gary Moore, the singer and guitarist, for a drink in the West End. Moore had been the lead guitarist on Lloyd Webber's classical and rock fusion album, *Variations*. Lloyd Webber told Moore about what he thought of as his *Cats* theme.

"Fuck, I'd like to record that," Moore said. The recording wound up in the hands of a BBC radio host who played it one night on a popular music program.

Elaine Paige, who had triumphed in the West End as the star of *Evita*, was pulling up in front of her house in the suburbs when Moore's recording came on the radio.

"The tune gripped me somehow," she said, "and I remember jumping out of the car and running to the front door and fumbling through my bag for my keys because I wanted to try to tape-record it. I looked down and saw this black, rather feeble, pathetic looking cat at my feet. It rubbed up and down my ankles, and it followed me into the house as I ran to turn on the radio and the tape recorder. I gave the cat a saucer of milk and I went to bed with my Sony Walkman listening to Andrew's new tune over and over again. I vowed I'd ring Andrew up the next morning and tell him how touched I was by it."

The next morning her phone rang. It was Andrew. Judi Dench, who was playing Grizabella, had torn her Achilles tendon and was in the hospital. Previews were to start in less than a week. Dench would be off her feet for a month or more.

"We're in trouble," Lloyd Webber said. "Would you come down to the theater and have a chat with me and Trevor and Gilly about taking over the role of Grizabella?"

"What does it involve?" Paige asked. "I don't know anything about the show because you've kept it all under wraps."

"Well, it's not *Evita*," Lloyd Webber said. "You only have one song, but it's a great song."

"It wouldn't be the song I heard on the radio last night by any chance, would it?"

"That's it!"

Paige looked around the kitchen. Where is that damned cat? she thought. What was going on? This was spooky beyond belief.

As Paige entered the New London Theatre, she saw slender performers in beautifully painted body suits leaping about a stage strewn with rubble—giant cans of Heinz baked beans, the back end of an oversize junked car, an enormous tire. It was only then that she realized *Cats* was indeed about cats, that the actors were playing cats. "It was a well-kept secret until opening night. The idea of people cavorting around as cats seemed ridiculous to me, but the set was so unusual and clever," she recalled.

Nunn explained the show and Grizabella to her. Grizabella, the faded glamour cat, was the linchpin of the story. She'd fallen on hard times, but she would be chosen as the cat to go to the Heaviside Layer, the cat who would be redeemed. Andrew played her the *Cats* theme, and Nunn handed her a rough lyric he'd cobbled together from an Eliot poem called "Rhapsody on a Windy Night." The working title of the song was "Memory."

Paige showed the song to her lover, Tim Rice. He liked it and wanted to "have a go," as the British say, at the lyric. Lloyd Webber agreed, and Rice dashed off some verses. But he wasn't the only writer working on the song. Nunn asked Don Black, whose songs included "Born Free" and "Thunderball," to come up with something as well. When previews began, Paige sang Trevor Nunn's lyric at the matinee, Tim Rice's lyric in the evening, and Don Black's lyric the next day. "And sometimes they'd give me different bits of different people's lyrics," she said. "It was a nightmare. I didn't know if I was on foot or horseback."

In the end, Nunn decided to go with his lyric. They don't call him "Clever Trevor" for nothing. He realized Lloyd Webber's tune was beautiful and unforgettable, and if he wrote the lyrics to it, he would own one half of what, if the show worked, might become a standard. Rice was furious. He threatened legal action. Black didn't care. "It was no big deal," he said. "We're just lyric writers for hire." *

As this drama unfolded backstage, Bernie and Betty Jacobs took their seats at a preview of *Cats*. On the plane to London, Jacobs read Eliot's book and couldn't figure out how anyone could make a musical out of it. It was a children's book, so Jacobs brought his grandson Jared

---

* When it comes to "Memory," memories are hazy. Lloyd Webber says his friend Don Black never wrote any lyrics. Black differs: "I remember vividly having lunch with Trevor and Andrew at the Capital Hotel in Basil Street when I was asked to have a go at writing the lyrics to the now-familiar melody. I have been asked over the years to try and locate them and I've had a look through some old files to no avail. As this subject keeps coming up I am determined to dig a bit deeper and find them. I know 'Memory' did quite well, but can you imagine the impact it would have had if they had the sense to use my words!"

to the show. Afterward, in their suite at the Berkeley Hotel, Bernie and Betty discussed the show. It certainly was theatrical, but it didn't make much sense. There was no plot, just something to do with a bunch of cats in a junkyard getting ready for something called the Jellicle Ball. A haunted, mangy cat sang a pretty song and then went up to heaven on a tire. "We didn't know what to make of it," Betty Jacobs said. But their grandson liked it—so much so that he wanted to go back the next night. There weren't any tickets available—*Cats* was catching on and the final previews were sold out—so Jared, who was six, sat on the steps of the New London and watched it again. He was enchanted. Jacobs made his decision. "If the young ones like it, there must be something to it," he told Betty.

The first public performance of *Cats* was, as Lloyd Webber recalled, rocky. The first act played well, the second not so well. The next night, the first act died, but the second took off. The third night, a Friday, both acts worked. Relieved, Lloyd Webber and his wife thought they'd raise a glass at Annabel's, a private nightclub in Berkeley Square. When they arrived, the doorman asked Lloyd Webber if he could get tickets to *Cats*.

"That's when we knew it was a hit," Lloyd Webber said.

Cats opened at the New London on May 11, 1981. A few minutes before Paige sang "Memory," a note arrived at the stage door. It was a bomb scare. The stage doorman, knowing the show would be ruined without "Memory," delayed making an announcement. When the song was over, Brian Blessed, as Old Deuteronomy, stepped to the front of the stage and said, in his booming, theatrical voice, "Ladies and gentlemen, will you please move out of the theater in an orderly fashion." The audience, puzzled, began to laugh. "No, I'm quite serious. We have been asked to leave the theater."

The first-night crowd stood in front of the theater, while the actors lingered in the alleyway. Soon, the first-nighters were mingling with the actors. They wanted to see and touch the cat costumes.

"They were excited," Paige recalled. "I was terrified. There were police and dogs everywhere. But the audience didn't seem to care. They wanted to talk about our makeup. There was absolute excitement in the air. I knew then we were a hit. My only regret is that I didn't put any money in the show. It wasn't fully financed on opening night, and Cameron was asking us if we'd like to put a few pennies in. But Tim had said to me, 'Never invest in your own stuff.' So I told Cameron, 'I don't think so.' What an idiot!"

The reviews were mixed, their tone best caught in the *Observer*: "*Cats* isn't perfect. Don't miss it." The show opened with a small advance sale, but in a few weeks Lloyd Webber and Mackintosh realized they had more than a hit on their hands. They had a phenomenon. Articles about *Cats* began appearing in papers all over the world. Producers from other countries wanted it for their theaters. David Merrick offered them his smash *42nd Street* for London if they would give him *Cats* for New York.

The first place to go was, of course, Broadway—which, as Lloyd Webber knew from the success of *Evita*, was where the real money was made. That summer, Mackintosh and Lloyd Webber headed to New York to begin negotiations. They treated themselves to state rooms on the *Queen Elizabeth 2*. Lloyd Webber brought his wife and young daughter, Imogen.

"It was the first time I was allowed to stay up for dinner," Imogen recalled.

"Well, that was because the nanny went off with a member of the crew, which was a problem," her father said.

In New York, Lloyd Webber and Mackintosh started making the rounds of theater owners and producers. First they met Jimmy Nederlander in his ramshackle offices above the Palace Theatre. *Lena Horne: "The Lady and Her Music"* was the hottest show in town. Lloyd Webber and Mackintosh asked if they could have tickets. Jimmy jumped up and said to his staff, "These boys want tickets to *Lena Horne*! What have we got to do with Lena Horne?" Lloyd Webber and Mackintosh were baffled. The show was at the Nederlander Theatre, but Jimmy Nederlander didn't seem to know that.

Their next meeting was with Schoenfeld and Jacobs over lunch at Sardi's. Halfway through the meal, producer Manny Azenberg, a Shubert ally, walked over to the table and said, "See that brown roll? It was white before Bernie looked at it."

After lunch, Mackintosh and Lloyd Webber headed to a bar. They needed a drink. "These are the people who run Broadway?" they said to each other. "They're all mad."

In the end, they decided to go with the Shuberts. Mackintosh had grown close to Bernie and Betty, and neither he nor Lloyd Webber had any experience producing a show in New York. They needed Shubert resources and expertise.

Originally, they wanted to put *Cats* in an unconventional space. They traipsed around New York, examining Roseland, a concert hall, and the ballroom of the New Yorker Hotel, which was owned by the Moonies. They even scurried around backstage at the decrepit New Amsterdam Theatre with flashlights as a pornographic movie was being shown on a giant screen.

The Shuberts, of course, wanted the show for one of their theaters, but they indulged Lloyd Webber and Mackintosh's hunt for an unorthodox space. When the New Amsterdam Theatre entered the picture, Jacobs thought the Shuberts should buy it. He decided to inspect the property. As he and Phil Smith walked along Forty-Second Street from Eighth Avenue to Seventh, prostitutes and drug dealers propositioned them every step of the way. By the time they reached the theater, Jacobs had made up his mind. A show with family appeal could never be produced on this block.

With some prodding from Jacobs, Lloyd Webber and Mackintosh decided the best theater for *Cats* would be the Winter Garden, which had an unusual configuration since it had once been the American Horse Exchange. It was also in better shape than Jimmy Nederlander's houses. "Frankly, the Shubert theaters were the only ones that had ever seen a paintbrush," said Mackintosh. "The other theaters were scummy dumps. Awful. I just didn't want to put a show of mine into a hideous environment."

The Shuberts had spent several hundred thousand dollars gussying up the Winter Garden for *42nd Street*, which, at Merrick's urging, had moved to the Majestic. The theater was in beautiful shape, but it would have to be reconfigured to accommodate John Napier's junkyard set and giant hydraulic tire. So the tire could fly into the heavens, the Shuberts had to punch a hole through the roof. And that wasn't all. Napier and Nunn insisted the entire interior be painted black. The Shuberts would share the $4.5 million production cost of *Cats* with their partners. But the cost of renovating the theater—now approaching $1.5 million—would be borne by the Shubert Organization.

"This show had better work," Jacobs told Smith one day as they were going through the numbers. "We're laying out a lot of money here."

Mackintosh negotiated his and Lloyd Webber's deal with the Shubert Organization. He met Jacobs in his sumptuous office above the Shubert. They sat around a coffee table, where Jacobs liked to conduct business. He showed Mackintosh photographs of his family, and they gossiped about various shows in New York and London. And then he asked Phil Smith to come around. "He always wanted Phil there," said Mackintosh. Smith settled down on the couch by the coffee table, and the negotiation began.

"And that was the first time I saw Bernie the calculator," Mackintosh said. "He was absolutely brilliant at that little round table. As you talked numbers, you could almost hear the clicking going on in Bernie's mind. He could work out instantly the ramifications of shifting a goal post here or there. He knew to the dime what it actually meant, whether he was giving something away or, in a brilliant sleight of hand, gaining more than you knew. As soon as I clocked that with Bernie, I started taking my time in the negotiations."

The young producer had a few cards of his own to play. Mackintosh had worked in every area of the theater, including the box office. He knew that a popular show generated strong advance ticket sales. The theater owner controlled the advance so that a crooked producer couldn't make off with it in the night. The interest on the advance—called the "flow"—accrued to the theater owner. *Cats* would likely open on Broadway with the biggest advance in history, in the millions, no doubt. The prime rate in 1982 hovered around 15 percent. The flow on the advance for *Cats* would be significant.

"I knew how damn valuable the box office was on it, and so I said I want some of it or it's a deal breaker," Mackintosh said.

"No, no, no," Jacobs replied. "We will never do this for anyone."

"Well, I'm not anyone, and you're going to have to do this," Mackintosh shot back.

In the end, Jacobs agreed. He could not lose *Cats*. The Shuberts split the flow with Mackintosh and Lloyd Webber. From then on, Mackintosh always took a piece of the flow on his shows—*Les Misérables*, *The Phantom of the Opera*, and *Miss Saigon*, all of which opened with millions of dollars in the bank.

The deal done, Jacobs turned to artistic matters. "Cameron, *Cats* is a wonderful show," he said. "It is a work of genius. You know how much I love the show. And you know my friend Michael Bennett, who is also a genius?"

"Of course I do," said Mackintosh.

"Michael wants to come see the show, and I would love him to."

"We'd be honored to have Michael."

"Your show is magnificent," Jacobs continued. "It's genius. However, the choreography sucks."

Mackintosh was taken aback. *Cats* was a dance musical and much of its success was due to Gillian Lynne's choreography.

"I don't agree with you," Mackintosh said. "Gillian's done a brilliant job staging the show. It couldn't possibly exist if it wasn't for her, and that is what the audience is responding to—and that is why you bought the show."

"I know, I know," Jacobs said. "Gillian's a great choreographer. But Michael Bennett's a genius."

Bennett did fly to London to take a look at *Cats*. He met with Lloyd Webber and Mackintosh after the performance and told them the show would be a hit in New York.

Mackintosh responded: "Yes, but Bernie said the choreography isn't any good, and he wants you to become involved."

"I know what Bernie said," Bennett replied. "Sure, I might come up with a few better steps. But I'd never come up with a better show. And that's what Bernie doesn't understand."

In the spring of 1982, the Shuberts announced *Cats* would open at the Winter Garden in October. Now it was time to crank up the publicity machine. Turning the crank was a young publicist named Fred Nathan. He'd worked for David Merrick on *42nd Street*, but lost his job the day after the show opened. News of Gower Champion's death made headlines around the world. The *Daily News* quoted one of Nathan's assistants saying the party at the Waldorf that night felt more like a wake than a Broadway opening. Merrick hated the word "wake." He fired Nathan.[10]

Little on Broadway escaped Nathan's attention. He knew *Cats* was likely to be a winner. He also knew the Shuberts were producing it in New York. He began hanging around the Shubert offices, schmoozing the secretaries. He pressed Phil Smith for a meeting with Bernie Jacobs. The Shuberts favored conservative press agents who placed an article or two in the *Times* and then passed out tickets at critics' previews. Nathan was brash. He impressed Jacobs with his enthusiasm and creativity. *Cats* was an unusual show, he said (though he'd never seen it), and it needed an unusual publicity campaign.

Nathan also had a talent for something Jacobs enjoyed—gossip. He seemed to know everything that was going on backstage at every show and in the offices of producers, agents, and casting directors. He was, Jacobs thought, "a good piece of manpower." He got the job.

Growing up in Queens in the 1960s, Fred Nathan was obsessed with two things—Barbra Streisand and Broadway shows. "He did a wicked Barbra Streisand imitation, and he did it every day," said Rick Elice, Nathan's best friend at Francis Lewis High School in Queens.*

As for Broadway shows, Nathan's favorite was *Hello, Dolly!* starring Pearl Bailey leading an all-black cast. He went to the show at least once a week. Bailey had a habit of talking to the audience during the show. At one performance, thirteen-year-old Fred Nathan ran up to the stage and handed her an invitation to his bar mitzvah the following week. She opened the invitation and told the audience, "This boy down here has invited me to his bar mitzvah. Now he knows I can't do it because I got a show on Saturday!"

"She didn't come," said Elice. "I invited Soupy Sales to my bar mitzvah, but he didn't come, either."

Nathan was always dragging Elice into Manhattan to see Broad-

---

* Elice, after several years as a Broadway advertising executive, would go on to write the musicals *Jersey Boys* and *The Addams Family.*

way musicals. They saw a number of Hal Prince shows because Prince had a two-dollar obstructed view policy—which "was cheaper than a movie," Elice said. One Prince show they saw was *Company*, with a score by Stephen Sondheim. They hated it. "We couldn't understand what it was about," said Elice. "So we made fun of it." They saw *Follies* the next year—and became obsessed with Sondheim. "It was a real turning point for us," Elice recalled. "The way it looked, the way it sounded. It got under our skin."

For Hanukkah one year, Elice received a reel-to-reel tape recorder. Every Saturday, Nathan and Elice would catch a Broadway matinee and then buy the script and the cast album, assign each other parts and perform the entire show into Elice's recorder. "And then we would listen back to our wonderful talent over and over and over again. That's how I spent most of my teenage years. When I wasn't trying to kill myself."

Nathan went to Boston College so he could attend tryouts of Broadway shows at the Colonial Theatre. Elice attended Cornell. But every week Nathan would send him a letter containing that week's grosses from *Variety*. "He kept tabs on how well the shows were doing, especially the Sondheim shows," Elice said.

After college Nathan applied for a job with theater press agent Saul Richman. He wrapped his résumé around a Nathan's hot dog. Richman said anybody who does that to get a job "deserves to be a press agent." Nathan moved up the ranks. He opened his own office in the late 1970s, and by the time he landed *Cats*, he'd already handled publicity for Broadway revivals of *Oklahoma!* and *Brigadoon*.

For *Cats*, Nathan lined up stories in every magazine from *Esquire* to *Penthouse*.[11] Months before the show even went into rehearsal, he persuaded the Shuberts to lease the largest billboard in Times Square, paint it black, and put a pair of yellow eyes in its center. They splashed the same logo across the front of the Winter Garden, which stretched up Broadway from Fiftieth to Fifty-First Streets. Radio and TV spots ran with the tagline, "Isn't the curiosity killing you?"

Cats began rehearsals with an American cast led by Betty Buckley as Grizabella. She was not the first choice. David Geffen wanted his friend

Cher. Others wanted a Broadway star—Patti LuPone, Bernadette Peters, Liza Minnelli. Buckley was not in that league. A native of Texas, she only had two Broadway shows under her belt, *1776* and *Pippin*, before going off to Hollywood to appear as Abby in the television series *Eight Is Enough*. But her agent got her an audition for *Cats*, and she sang "Memory" for the casting department. She was wrong for the part, they told her. "You radiate health and well-being and we're looking for someone who radiates death and dying."

A few weeks later, however, she was called in to audition for Trevor Nunn at the Winter Garden.

Nunn directed her to sing "Memory" as if she wanted to commit suicide. She did it. "Do it again," Nunn said, "and be even more suicidal."

"I turned my insides out," she recalled. But Nunn just stood there, noncommittal. Buckley walked to the edge of the stage.

"Mr. Nunn, may I speak to you for a second?" she asked. "I know you've auditioned a lot of people for this part, and I know many of them can do it very well. But nobody can do it better than I can, and it's my turn. I just did a television series called *Eight Is Enough*. That probably doesn't mean anything to you, but I think there are some people who'd be curious to know that Abby can sing."

Nunn looked at her "as if I were nuts," she recalled.

She continued. "I'm a really good actress, Mr. Nunn. If you impart your vision, I can do it. If you want me to be smaller, I'll be smaller. If you want me to be thinner, I'll be thinner. If you want me to be older, I'll be older. You just have to tell me what it is you want, and I will deliver it for you."

Her speech finished, she turned and walked off the stage. As she was leaving, she saw the rehearsal pianist. He gave her the thumbs-up. In the wings, she ran into the stage manager. He gave her the thumbs-up as well.

But her agent did not.

"When are you going to learn to keep your mouth shut?" she asked Buckley over the phone. "He's a British director. He doesn't want some American actress who talks too much."

Dejected, Buckley took herself to lunch at her favorite restaurant,

Woods, on Madison Avenue. The maitre d' came up to her and said she was wanted on the phone. It was her agent. "You got the part."

Rehearsals for *Cats* began in the summer of 1982 at 890 Broadway, Michael Bennett's building. Nunn believed in research, and he liked to impart his research to his cast. On the first day of rehearsal, he lectured the cast on the life of T. S. Eliot and the history of modern British poetry.

"You would have thought he was teaching a seminar at Yale," recalled Geoffrey Johnson, the casting director. "And he went on a long time. The kids in the show—all the gypsies—had no idea what he was talking about. Watching their faces was fabulous. They were completely confused. And Trevor was oblivious. He just kept on talking."

The seminar over, Nunn and his cast spent the next three weeks doing improvisational theater games to bring the cast together as a "tribe," to use his word. One day he passed out pieces of paper on which he'd written an adjective describing each actor's cat. The actors had to incorporate that adjective into their theater games. Nunn instructed them to study cats and to begin behaving like cats from the moment they entered the rehearsal room.

"We did an improvisational exercise on our hands and knees, and that exercise went on forever," Buckley said. "I decided my cat was going to be a sleepy cat. So I found a sunny spot by a window, curled up and went to sleep. That's how I got through that improvisational exercise."

As rehearsals went on, Nunn began to ignore Buckley. He barely spoke to her and brushed off her questions. The company, picking up on Nunn's lead, shunned her, too. "It was torture," she recalled. "I felt like a buffoon. Then they started working on the dance numbers, but I only had one song, so they put me in a room for hours every day with a pianist going over the song again and again. I was completely cut off from everyone."

Slowly, Buckley began to understand Nunn's game. Grizabella is alone in the world, isolated from the tribe of cats. Nunn wanted the actors to feel that way about Buckley. The day of the first run-through, Buckley joined the company for the first time in weeks. When she sang

"Memory," people began crying. Nunn stopped the run-through and said to the company, "What everybody's feeling right now, you have to feel eight times a week. So figure out what that feeling is because this is what I want every time she sings this song."

In September, *Cats* began previews at the Winter Garden. The Shuberts hiked the top ticket price to forty-five dollars, the highest ever for a musical. But that didn't prevent the public—and the ticket brokers—from snapping them up. By the first preview, *Cats* had racked up an advance of $4 million. By opening night, the advance would hit a record-breaking $6 million.

But all was not well with the show. And Buckley was the problem. She had one assignment: stop the show with "Memory." But it wasn't happening. "I was only getting tepid applause," she said. Nunn started calling her in for special rehearsals during which he would tell her the story of *The Winter's Tale* and how she needed to incorporate the mood of that play into her performance. "I hung on his every word," she said, "but I had no idea what he was saying to me."

Other members of the creative team told her to think of Grizabella as the Marilyn Monroe of *Cats*, worn down by too much alcohol, too many drugs, too much sex, too many men.

A frustrated Lloyd Webber drilled her through the song again and again. "Placido Domingo was in last night and said, 'Just tell the girl to sing the song!'" he yelled.

"But I am just singing the song," Buckley said. She began to panic. Everybody was upset. Oh fuck, she thought. I'm going to be fired.

She asked her friend James Lapine, the director, to see the show. "You're doing everything nicely," he told her, "but I don't know what you feel."

"What I feel?" she said. "I feel what Trevor wants me to feel. I feel *The Winter's Tale*. I feel what Andrew wants me to feel. I feel what Placido Domingo wants me to feel!" Lapine put a hand on her shoulder. "Betty, calm down. You're playing a cat."

Frustrated, she turned to her vocal coach of thirteen years, Paul Gavert, for help. She went over to his studio and explained her predicament. He threw a pillow on the floor. "Get down on the floor and start hitting this pillow," he told her.

"I'm about to get fired from the biggest show on Broadway, and you want me to hit a pillow?" she asked.

"Do it," he said.

She started hitting the pillow, harder and harder. And then she began sobbing. "All these feelings started pouring out of me," she said. "And I suddenly realized the only person I hadn't consulted was myself, the kid who does the work, who sings the song. It sounds really New Age, but that's what happened."

A few days later, leaving her West End apartment, Buckley saw a "beautiful homeless woman, who was older, whose hair was exactly the same color as Grizabella's." The woman wore white pasty makeup and her face was marred by lipstick smears. And she floated down the street "like she was the most beautiful thing in the world," Buckley recalled. Their eyes met and Buckley had "this distinct feeling that she really took me in. It was like she was saying, 'There is so much I could share with you, but you don't have the time and neither do I.' And then she just floated off down the street."

That night in her dressing room, Buckley added a lipstick smear to her makeup. The next day—"as if I didn't get the message from the universe the first time"—another beautiful homeless woman with hair the moonlit color of Grizabella's and with white pasty makeup and a lipstick smear on her face floated across her path.

"There was a sense of beauty and dignity about her," Buckley said, "as if she, too, had something to share but couldn't because the world had turned its back on her."

Beauty. Dignity.

And a breakthrough.

Buckley realized what was wrong. She'd been directed to make the audience feel pathos toward Grizabella, so she played the part pathetically. But Grizabella wasn't pathetic. She was beautiful. She had dignity. She had lived, she had wisdom, she had much to share, and if the other cats didn't care, that was their problem, not hers.

The night before the critics came to see *Cats*, Buckley sang "Memory" and received a standing ovation. She had completed her assignment. She had stopped the show.

•   •   •

Cats opened in New York on October 7, 1982, to critics who approached this presold juggernaut skeptically. Their disdain for all the hype bled into their reviews. Douglas Watt, in the *Daily News*, said the razzle-dazzle of the production "may be enough to keep you in your seat for two and a half hours, if not exactly on the edge of it."

"It's quite a musical, but hardly purr-fect," said Clive Barnes of the *New York Post*.

Kevin Kelly of the *Boston Globe*, a big champion of Michael Bennett, wrote, simply, "*Cats* is a dog." And Michael Feingold, of the *Village Voice*, wrote, "To sit through [the show] is to realize that something has just peed on your pants leg."

As for the *New York Times*, Frank Rich waffled, though thoughtfully. He recognized that whatever the critics might say about the show "it is likely to lurk around Broadway for a long time." But not because it was brilliant or emotionally powerful or "has an idea in its head." Lloyd Webber's songs were "sweet," but the show was full of banalities and long, cat-nap inducing stretches of boredom. Its trump card, however, was its theatricality. "It's a musical that transports the audience into a complete fantasy world that could only exist in the theater and yet, these days, only rarely does. Whatever the other failings . . . of *Cats*, it believes in purely theatrical magic, and on that faith it unquestionably delivers."

The next morning, Nancy Coyne, who did the advertising for the show, walked into Bernie Jacobs's office to sort through the reviews and pick out the best lines for quote ads. But Jacobs was unhappy with the notices, especially Rich's giveth-on-the-one-hand-and-taketh-away-on-the-other assessment.

"I don't want to use any quotes," he told Coyne. "Just give me a copy line."

As it happened, Coyne had with her the script for a radio spot. It read, "When you walk into the Winter Garden Theatre, you will be transformed. From now on and forever, you will remember *Cats*."

Coyne had highlighted, in yellow, the phrase "from now on and forever." The phrase had been in her mind ever since she was a kid. It was the title of a 1934 Shirley Temple movie, *Now and Forever*.

When Jacobs read the line he said, "That's it."

Coyne dropped the "on" and Now and Forever became the slogan for *Cats*. For years, Jacobs refused to quote any critics in advertisements. He also wanted to keep the look of the production a secret. And so the ads for *Cats* were always black with a pair of yellow eyes and the words "Now and Forever."

Jacobs also wanted a television commercial. He would spend a lot of money to swamp the mixed reviews. But, as with the print ads, he did not want the TV commercial to give anything away. So Coyne simply animated the yellow eyes with a dancer in each. "*Cats*," an announcer said. "Now and Forever."

The mixed reviews did nothing to impede *Cats*. Within weeks, the $6.2 million advance hit $10 million. It would eventually reach $20 million. The show was doing the kind of business a successful movie does.

Everybody wanted tickets, many long before the show played its first preview. One morning in the summer of 1982, while *Cats* was still in rehearsal, producer Albert Poland walked into Jacobs's office to discuss a business matter. Jacobs was yelling into the phone. He had three pieces of toilet paper stuck to his face because he'd cut himself shaving.

"Mr. de Rothschild, I can't hear you!" he said. "Mr. de Rothschild, I'm in the business of *selling* tickets. I can't hear you. Mr. de Rothschild, I'm hanging up now."

"Was that the Baron de Rothschild?" Poland asked.

"Yes."

"What? He wants a free pair of tickets to *Cats*?"

"A free pair?" Jacobs snapped. "He wants the whole theater! He's giving a benefit and thinks I should donate all the tickets. Well," Jacobs grumbled, "what is he anyway? Just a Jew with a 'de' in front of his name."

The business matter Poland came to discuss that morning was the budget for an Off-Broadway musical the Shuberts were going to produce with David Geffen and Cameron Mackintosh at the Orpheum Theatre in the East Village. It was called *Little Shop of Horrors*. Poland was the general manager.

Based on Roger Corman's 1960 horror movie about a man-eating plant, the musical debuted in May 1982 at the tiny WPA Theatre. Poland first heard of it when he received a phone call from Kyle Renick, who ran the WPA. "I have this show down here, and twenty-five producers are chasing it and I would like you to come and see it and be our general manager if we move it to a larger theater," he told Poland.

Poland liked the show—it was funny and campy with a touch of menace—and he thought it would work commercially in an Off-Broadway theater. He rang up his friend Cameron Mackintosh, who was in town laying the groundwork that spring for *Cats*, to see if he'd like to invest. "OK," said Mackintosh, "but call Bernie."

Poland arranged for Jacobs and his wife to see the show that night. The next morning Jacobs delivered his verdict: "Well, it wasn't my cup of tea, and Betty didn't much care for it."

Poland could feel the show slipping away.

"The British would like it because it has a lot of whimsy, and the British like whimsy," Jacobs continued. "But if you want us to come along, we might consider it."

Poland called the agent who represented one of the creators and told her the Shuberts were ambivalent. She said David Geffen was coming to see the show that night. If he liked it, he might sway Jacobs. But Geffen never showed up. "Do you think Bernie said something negative?" she asked Poland. "No," he said, adding with a laugh, "he probably met someone on the way!" (Which, as Poland would later discover, was the case.)

A few days later Poland received a call from Jacobs. "Albert, I have David Geffen on the line with us," he said. "How much do you think *Little Shop of Horrors* will cost?"

Poland hadn't done a budget but blurted out, "Three hundred and fifty thousand."

"We'll take it," Jacobs said. "David, will you come in with us?"

"Whatever you say, Bernie," Geffen replied.

"We have to find room for Cameron," Poland said. "I called him first."

"All right, we'll give him ten percent," said Jacobs.

The deal was done. Poland could not figure out why Jacobs changed his mind about *Little Shop of Horrors*. He found out a few days later.

Broadway producer Alex Cohen went to see the show and told Jacobs he didn't like it.

"That's when I knew it would be a hit," Jacobs told Poland.

Little Shop was indeed a hit. By the fall of 1982, the show was turning a weekly profit of $4,000 to $6,000 in a theater with just three hundred and fifty seats. No show in Off-Broadway history had ever made such money. But the Shuberts weren't satisfied with the take. They wanted to raise ticket prices from seven dollars to ten so they could squeeze some more money out of what Schoenfeld referred to as "our little slot machine."

Poland resisted. He had spent his career Off Broadway. He knew the terrain better than the Shuberts. The audience would balk at a ten-dollar ticket and the show would suffer. "You will destroy Off Broadway with your greed," Poland protested. What, he wanted to know, was wrong with a profit of four to six thousand dollars a week?

Jacobs pulled out the accountant's statement for the first week of performances for *Cats* at the Winter Garden. The operating profit that week was $186,000.

"I almost fainted," Poland recalled.

Today, adjusted for inflation, that would be a weekly profit of $500,000. No show, in the history of Broadway, in the history of live theater, had ever made that much money. And it had the highest ticket price—forty-five dollars—ever for a Broadway musical. But that didn't stop people from wanting to see it. The Shuberts had a winner in *Little Shop*, and Jacobs believed that if people wanted to see it they would pay any price, as they did with *Cats*.

The price went up. *Little Shop* ran five years and became the highest-grossing musical in Off-Broadway history.

The impact of *Cats* on Broadway was enormous.

The Shuberts were already getting rich from the rent from such shows as *A Chorus Line* and *42nd Street* and their participation in *Dreamgirls*. But with *Cats*, they were getting money from all directions—their 40 percent stake, the rent from the Winter Garden, their slice of the merchandising. The profits would only swell. There would be North American tours, all of which the Shuberts would control. The show would make the Shuberts richer than anything even Sam, Lee, or J. J. Shubert could have imagined.

Since *Cats* was a hit with family audiences, the Shuberts had even more incentive to pressure city officials to clean up Times Square.

Cats would make Lloyd Webber the most famous Broadway composer since Irving Berlin. He could do whatever show he wanted because his name above the title meant a line at the box office. For Cameron Mackintosh, *Cats* ended a small-time hit-or-miss career and put him on the path to becoming the most successful producer in theatrical history. Together, Lloyd Webber and Mackintosh developed a new way of producing musicals, one that would introduce musical theater to the world. The Shuberts controlled *Cats* in North America, but Lloyd Webber and Mackintosh had the rights for every other market. At the time, producers of popular Broadway shows licensed those shows to local producers in other countries, believing that a local producer knew his audience better than a Broadway producer ever would. But there wasn't much demand for Broadway musicals outside of America, England, and Japan (the Japanese loved *Fiddler on the Roof* and *A Chorus Line*). The idea of a global hit did not exist. *Cats* would change that. And Lloyd Webber and Mackintosh knew it. They saw how popular the show was in New York and London with tourists who didn't speak English. *Cats* could probably play anywhere in the world, but to do so effectively it would have to be the same production that worked so well on Broadway. Lloyd Webber and Mackintosh would see to that.

"I remember having lunch with Cameron at that Movenpick restaurant around the corner from the Winter Garden Theatre on a very hot day," Lloyd Webber recalled. "And I told Cameron that we really should take a leaf out of what Robert Stigwood had told me. He said the key to a successful show was to replicate it quickly, and exactly, in other places. Cameron understood what Stigwood was on about, and he brilliantly got the bit between the teeth."

In short order there would be productions of *Cats* in Europe, Asia, Australia, and South America—each one a duplicate of the one at the Winter Garden.

The era of the global Broadway spectacle had arrived.

•   •   •

And yet down at the Orpheum Theatre on the Lower East Side, *Little Shop of Horrors* was planting the seeds of a phenomenon that, arguably, would alter Broadway—and New York City—even more profoundly than *Cats*, the Shuberts, or Andrew Lloyd Webber and Cameron Mackintosh.

Little Shop was written by Alan Menken and Howard Ashman. The company manager was Peter Schneider. In 1985 Schneider moved to Hollywood with the unenviable job of revitalizing Walt Disney Studio's moribund animation department. He got in touch with Ashman to see if he'd be interested in tackling some of the projects that were, quite literally, on Disney's drawing board.

One was *The Little Mermaid*.

The other was *Beauty and the Beast*.

Mesmerizing Temptation

Michael Bennett turned forty on April 9, 1983. Marvin Krauss, the wily general manager who tried to buy Henry Krieger's share of *Dreamgirls* during its Boston tryout, threw a party for Bennett at 890 Broadway. Everyone was asked to wear red, Bennett's favorite color. The vast rehearsal spaces of 890 were turned into a mini Coney Island, with a boardwalk, balloons, popcorn machines, an ice-cream parlor, and a hot dog stand. There were less family-friendly stands as well, some providing booze and another supplying "drugs of one's choice."[1]

Krauss, along with eight of Bennett's friends, paid for the party. Each also ponied up $4,000 for a red Porsche for Bennett, which was delivered to 890 wrapped in a giant red bow.

"As though Michael, who was making $90,000 a week, needed a Porsche from his friends," said John Breglio. "He didn't even drive. But Marvin wanted to show his love. I remember Michael called me up after the party and said, 'They bought me a sports car! I have no interest in it, but I'll act like I like it.' He never used it. He was scared of it."

Bernie and Betty Jacobs were invited. When Jacobs walked into 890, he realized he was a guest, not one of the hosts. Jacobs thought he knew everything that was going on in and around Bennett's life, but others close to Bennett—rivals for the director's affection and loyalty, in Jacobs's view—had produced this over-the-top birthday bash. He was furious, and the object of his wrath was Krauss. "Bernie hated Marvin's guts after that party," said Robin Wagner.

"If Bernie had thought of it, he would have thrown the party," said Breglio. "But it was too late. Marvin did it. But you didn't do things like that that would be perceived by Bernie as interfering with his direct link to Michael. He was the father, so who are you to give Michael a birthday party? But what Bernie didn't realize was that Michael was never going to turn on him. He was devoted to Bernie because he knew that Bernie was the power he needed to close the circle. Michael was the most powerful director on Broadway. He had the money, the talent, the actors. The only thing he didn't have was the theater. And Bernie could give him that. Whatever theater Michael wanted, Bernie gave him."

Soon after the party, Jacobs struck out at Krauss. The general manager was about to take over the national tour of *Dreamgirls*, a lucrative gig. Jacobs took the tour away from him. It was a swift and brutal way of cutting Krauss out of Bennett's affairs. After one bruising meeting with Jacobs, Krauss went to a bar and got so drunk he called his wife to come get him. He thought his career was over.

"Ninety percent of the time Bernie exercised his power with wisdom," said producer Robert Fox, a friend of Jacobs. "Ten percent of the time he could get ridiculously cranky—and that usually had something to do with Michael."

Krauss pleaded with Phil Smith and producer Manny Azenberg to intercede on his behalf. Eventually, they made Jacobs see he was overreacting. Or, as Azenberg put it, "Bernie, are you nuts?" Jacobs relented, but he never fully trusted Krauss again.*

As Jacobs seethed in a corner of 890 Broadway during Bennett's party, another drama was unfolding in the men's room. Tommy Tune and Bennett had begun to patch up their relationship after the battle between *Nine* and *Dreamgirls*. They'd run into each other at a party for

---

* And he was right. *Dreamgirls* played the Shubert Theatre in Philadelphia—and Krauss slipped in a booking fee for himself. He was, effectively, charging the Shuberts to play their own theater. When Jacobs discovered it, he "went apeshit," said Azenberg.

Broadway people on a cruise around Manhattan. Bennett had said to Tune, "Darling, it's a truce." So Tune accepted the invitation to the birthday party. He arrived from rehearsals for his next show, *My One and Only*, which featured songs by George and Ira Gershwin. Tune was starring in the show opposite Twiggy.

But *My One and Only* was in serious trouble.

The Boston tryout had been a disaster. The original director, Peter Sellars, who'd made his name directing avant-garde operas, wanted the show to be fluffy, silly fun—but also satirical and political. This musical comedy would deal with the colonization of the Third World, the rise of corporate culture, and the oppression of women.[2]

But *Guys and Dolls* does not meet *Mother Courage* easily, and a few days before previews began in Boston, an executive from Paramount Pictures, the lead producer, fired Sellars and his avant-garde collaborators. The show went on, but its incoherent plot baffled audiences. Tune took to giving curtain speeches. "Don't worry. The parts that don't make any sense to you don't make any sense to us, either. That's why we're in Boston." Paramount asked Tune to take over the direction and choreography—while continuing to star in the show. Tune sent out an all-points bulletin to his friends in the theater. Peter Stone, who wrote the musicals *1776* and *Woman of the Year* and had a reputation for fast rewrites, went to Boston. So, too, did Mike Nichols. Within weeks they performed major surgery on the show that "saved us from putting people to sleep," Tune told the *New York Times*.[3]

But the press, in the form of Bennett's friend Kevin Kelly of the *Boston Globe*, was out to get *My One and Only*. Kelly asked if he could write an article for the *Globe* on the out-of-town tryout. The producers gave him fly-on-the-wall access. He was there for the disastrous early previews, when audiences were leaving in droves, the firing of Sellars, and the arrival of Stone and Nichols. But the article never appeared in the *Globe*. Kelly sold it to *New York* magazine without telling anyone. His hatchet piece ran under the headline "Falling on Its Funny Face," with the helpful subhead, *"My One and Only* may well become a classic theater disaster."[4]

The Tony battle between *Nine* and *Dreamgirls* still irked Bennett's friends, including Kelly.

"We should have realized he wanted to murder us because of *Nine*," said Francine LeFrak, coproducer of both *Nine* and *My One and Only*.

My One and Only was back in rehearsals in New York at the time of Bennett's fortieth birthday party and was still undergoing extensive re-tooling. Bennett, of course, had heard the gossip. When Tune entered 890 Broadway with a few friends from the show, Bennett took them by the hand and pulled them into the men's room. He closed the door and said, "All right now, darlings, here's what's happening. I'm coming in to help you. I'm going to save your show."

Tune recalled, "We didn't ask him. And he was as high as a skunk. But most of us wouldn't be where we were in show business without him, and he's telling us, 'Don't worry. I'll save you. I'll pull this off for you.'"

The next morning, Bennett showed up at the St. James Theatre with his own team to fix *My One and Only*. But his approach, his energy, his whole demeanor were off. He seemed bent on taking a show aim-ing to be effervescent and turning it into something dark and brutal. He was giving orders like a general, demanding that Paramount come up with another $300,000 for new sets, including a giant suitcase on which he wanted Twiggy to make her entrance. "We were getting bills for money we didn't have," said LeFrak.

Bennett was working around the clock, keeping the cast in the the-ater until 2:00 a.m. drilling them in new and vulgar dance routines. He was running on booze and drugs. He stood on the stage, a vodka bottle in one hand, a bowl of cocaine in the other. Tune was so busy working on his performance—and helping Twiggy with hers (they were also having a fling)—that he didn't realize what Bennett was doing to *My One and Only*.

It took Mike Nichols to see that.

Nichols took Tune aside and said Bennett "is not doing good work. He may not be doing it consciously, but subconsciously he is ruining your show."

Bennett had to go—but nobody wanted to tell him. "I couldn't do it," said Tune. "And Nichols said, 'I can't do it.'" In the end, it fell to Don Sherkow, a junior Paramount executive, to fire Broadway's num-ber one director. He walked up to Bennett after a rehearsal one day and told him he was no longer wanted. Bennett put on his baseball cap and left the theater. He called Tune later and said, "Don't worry about me. But please write to my team and thank them for their work."

Tune did. And then he threw out everything they had done.

In the end, Tune, Nichols, and Stone managed to save *My One and Only*. It opened to enthusiastic reviews—"the only new or old musical that sends us home on air," wrote Frank Rich—and managed a decent run of nearly two years at the St. James. Tune won the Tony for his performance and his choreography. But the Shuberts, the producers of *Cats*, had nothing to fear that year from *My One and Only*.

Cats won seven Tonys, including Best Musical, Best Score, Best Direction, and Best Featured Actress—Betty Buckley. It even won Best Book, which was credited to T. S. Eliot, who had been dead for eighteen years. Peter Stone, whose fast, agile rewrite of *My One and Only* was up against Eliot's old poems, was pretty sure he was going to win that night. When he heard "And the winner is . . ." he got up out of his seat, only to sink back into it when the announcer said, "T. S. Eliot."

"In retrospect I should have realized what was going to happen," he said. "I saw Eliot's widow, Valerie, at the theater that night. The Shuberts would never have flown her over if they didn't think they were going to win."

Humiliated by his dismissal from *My One and Only*, Bennett turned his attention to staging the 3,389th performance of *A Chorus Line* at the Shubert Theatre on September 29, 1983. On that date, *A Chorus Line* would overtake *Grease* as the longest-running show in Broadway history. Bennett asked everyone who had ever been in the show, from the original cast, to Broadway replacements, to performers who toured America and the world, to take part in the performance. With just three days of rehearsal, he integrated over three hundred dancers into the production. Among the highlights: seven actresses who had played Cassie, including Donna McKechnie, performing "The Music and the Mirror"; Chikae Ishikawa, of the Japanese company, singing "Nothing" in Japanese; and an astonishing finale during which the dancers, clad in the by-now familiar gold top hats and tuxedos, filled the stage and the aisles of the orchestra and balcony and performed "One."

"The theater seemed to shake," Frank Rich wrote of the final number in the *Times* the next day. "The cast and the audience had become one, united in the at-least-momentary conviction that *A Chorus Line* was the best thing that had happened to any of us."

Bennett next turned his attention to a new show that, he believed, would push the Broadway musical into territory more controversial than anything he'd done with Stephen Sondheim and Hal Prince. It was a musical called *Scandal*, and it was about something never far from Bennett's mind—sex. The script was by Treva Silverman, who had been a story editor on *The Mary Tyler Moore Show*. Silverman and Bennett shared an intense curiosity about sex, Silverman admitting to Bennett (whom she met through their mutual friend, lyricist Ed Kleban) that, whenever she was in Europe, she would indulge in freewheeling sexual escapades. Bennett did the same in San Francisco, where he was having a fling with a clothing salesman. They frequented Golden Gate Park where they would have anonymous sex all night long.[5]

Scandal told the story of a woman who discovers her husband has been cheating on her. She then indulges in a series of sexual fantasies, which Bennett would choreograph. The score was by Jimmy Webb, who'd been hanging around 890 Broadway working on another Bennett project, *The Children's Crusade*, based on the (mostly) mythical story of a group of children in thirteenth-century France who travel to the Holy Land and try to stop wars by spreading their faith. John Heilpern, a critic for the *Times* of London, who became close to Bennett after he raved about *Dreamgirls*, was writing the script. Bennett wanted to stage the show at Madison Square Garden with a chorus of a hundred teenage boys—which led some around 890 to dub the show "Chicken Hawk Casserole."

Webb put aside *The Children's Crusade* and went to work with Silverman on *Scandal*. While they came up with songs such as "She's a Dyke," Bennett and Bob Avian choreographed a ménage à trois, blow jobs, and orgy ballets.[6]

Scandal began workshops in the spring of 1984 with a cast that included Swoosie Kurtz, Treat Williams, and Victor Garber. Bennett told the *Times*, "It's about sex. It's not *Oh, Calcutta!* It is about a marriage that is a scandal and about the divorce and about the sex."[7] He was cagey about the timetable, saying the workshop could take anywhere from six months to a year. But, he added, "I did start it, and someday it ends up on the stage."

But on what stage? It was true, as Breglio pointed out, Bennett could have any Shubert theater he wanted. Bernie Jacobs would see to that. But why not own a Broadway theater himself? As it happened, Jimmy Nederlander, feeling overextended with his theater empire, was looking for partners. One of his theaters was the Mark Hellinger, an art deco masterpiece, which he bought in 1970. Many theater people believed it was the best musical house on Broadway. It was Bennett's favorite theater, partly because of its wide stage but also because *Seesaw*, his calling-card musical, had played there at the end of its run.

In the fall of 1984, Bennett began negotiating with Nederlander for a 50 percent stake in the Hellinger. It would, Breglio told Bennett, cost him nothing. He would pay for his half of the theater from the proceeds of the shows he would stage there. For Nederlander, it meant filling a theater that often stood empty—and filling it with shows by Michael Bennett, the creator of *A Chorus Line* and *Dreamgirls*.

Bennett started making plans for the Hellinger. He would paint the interior red. He designed uniforms for the ushers. They would be red, too. Eventually, Bennett planned to buy out Nederlander. And with the last piece in place—a Broadway theater—his empire would be complete. He wouldn't need anyone anymore. He wouldn't need the Shuberts. He wouldn't need Bernie Jacobs.

Bennett tried to keep the negotiations secret from Jacobs, but the Broadway gossip vine began to hum. He had to tell Jacobs before he heard it on the street. He tracked Jacobs down in Sicily, where he was vacationing with his family, and told him over the phone. Jacobs was stunned, but said little.

The *Times* picked up the story. Asked how his deal with the Nederlanders would affect his relationship with the Shuberts and Bernie Jacobs, Bennett said they'd "been friends for too long" to let it get in the way.

Jacobs, ominously, declined to comment.

But he could not let the deal go through. He cut Marvin Krauss out of *Dreamgirls* because Krauss had thrown Bennett a birthday party, so how could he possibly stand by while Bennett went into business with his rival? Although he and Nederlander had gotten along during their joint production of *Nicholas Nickleby* in 1981, the rivalry, by 1984, had heated up again. The Shuberts produced Stephen Sondheim's *Sunday in the Park with George* that year at the Booth Theatre. The Nederlanders, meanwhile, were coproducers of Jerry Herman's *La Cage aux Folles*, which was at their flagship theater, the Palace. The competition between the two shows was almost as intense as that between *Dreamgirls* and *Nine*.

Sunday, about painter Georges Seurat and his devotion, at the exclusion of personal relationships, to his art, was hailed as a groundbreaking, intellectual musical. Frank Rich raved and, exercising his growing influence at the *Times*, put the paper behind the musical. The *Times* published story after story on *Sunday* to gin up ticket sales, which were never spectacular. Around Broadway the paper's relentless coverage was dubbed "Sunday in the *Times* with George."

As for *La Cage aux Folles*, Rich dismissed it as the "the schmaltziest, most old-fashioned major musical Broadway has seen since *Annie*, and is likely to be just as popular with children of all ages."

But *La Cage* had many champions. They thought *Sunday* was boring and pretentious. Once again, Broadway split between the Shubert camp and the Nederlander camp. At the Tonys that year, *Sunday* was up for ten awards, *La Cage* for nine. But the evening broke for *La Cage*, which picked up six major awards, including Best Musical. *Sunday* won just two. Accepting his award for Best Score, Herman said it was affirmation that "the simple, hummable show tune" was not dead—a remark widely interpreted as a jab at Sondheim's complex, not-so-hummable songs.

Without the Tony for Best Musical, *Sunday* began to sputter at the box office, and Jacobs took to calling a show he once thought was a work of brilliance "a piece of shit." [8]

The Shuberts were also battling the Nederlanders for control of the new theater being built inside the Marriott Marquis Hotel. Because the Shuberts had supported the building of the hotel, they assumed they would get the theater. (The consent decree preventing the company from owning any more theaters in New York was lifted in 1984.)

They had Michael Bennett, Robin Wagner, and lighting designer Jules Fisher draw up plans for a state-of-the-art theater. But John Portman, the architect of the Marriott, wasn't interested in designing a theater. He was building a hotel that happened to have a theater in it. He ignored the Shuberts and designed his own theater. The Shuberts were dismayed that he put the bathrooms in the adjoining hotel lobby and not the theater itself.

Jimmy Nederlander made a bid for the theater. "I don't care where the bathrooms are," he told Portman, "just so long as there's bathrooms."

In the end, Portman went with Nederlander, who opened the theater in the summer of 1986 with the smash hit *Me and My Girl*.

The Shuberts and the Nederlanders were fighting again—and Bennett was about to defect. Jacobs pressured Bennett to back out of the deal. The Nederlanders, he argued, could never take care of him or his shows the way the Shuberts did. Bennett resisted. "Don't you understand, Bernie?" he pleaded. "This is giving me my independence. I want this. Why don't you want this for me?"

The day came to sign the closing papers. Breglio set up a meeting between Bennett and Nederlander at his law office at 10:00 a.m. By 11:30, Nederlander and his lawyers were still waiting for Bennett. At last, he came through the door looking "ashen and exhausted," Breglio said, "obviously he had not slept all night."

Bennett took Breglio aside and whispered, "He will not let me do it."

"That's all he said to me," Breglio recalled. "And I knew what he meant. Something happened that night. Bernie got to him. I'll never know what he said or did. Michael wouldn't tell me."

The Godfather had spoken, and Bennett obeyed. But he resented it. He stopped speaking to Jacobs, even when they met for dinner. "Michael would only talk to me," Betty Jacobs said. "It was all very strange."

Bennett was losing ground on other fronts. *Scandal* was not going well, partly because, Bennett began to realize, it wasn't very good. "It was a complete sex show, and it was incoherent," said John Heilpern. "It was utterly incoherent. I said to Michael, 'Show me the beginning, the middle, and the end.'"

But there was another reason why *Scandal* stalled out. This celebration of promiscuous sex coincided with the start of the AIDS crisis. And few communities would be as devastated by the disease as the theater world. Already young men in the choruses of several Broadway shows were dying of pneumonia or a rare form of cancer nobody had ever heard of called Kaposi's sarcoma. Performers who appeared to be healthy would call in sick one day and never return. Around Broadway there were all sorts of theories as to what was going on. The "rare cancer," as the *Times* initially called the disease, was said to be caused by drugs gay men used to heighten sexual pleasure.[9]

Backstage at *La Cage* one day, a group of gay men were talking about the disease. Everybody knew someone who had died or was suffering from it. Arthur Laurents, the director of the show, claimed he knew what was going on. The previous summer there had been an outbreak of mosquitoes on Fire Island. Clearly they were carrying some sort of plague and had infected many gay men there, Laurents said.

Bennett and his circle of friends worried about the disease as well. During the run of *Dreamgirls* in Los Angeles in 1982, he took several gay men in the show, including Fritz Holt, the stage manager, to dinner at Joe Allen. They talked about friends who were dead or dying and they made a pact. They were all healthy, obviously, and so they vowed to sleep only with one another.*

Bennett abandoned *Scandal* the day Treva Silverman's agent sent over her contract to 890 Broadway. It contained a list of demands, including final script approval. It also stipulated that her name be equal to Bennett's on the billing. Bennett "exploded" when he read that demand, said Robin Wagner, who was with him when the contract arrived. The billing on a Michael Bennett show was inviolate. It was "conceived, directed, and choreographed by Michael Bennett." Everyone else came second. And now an unknown writer, whom Bennett was paying $1,000 a week out of his own pocket, wanted to be his equal.

"He tried to tear the contract in half, but it was too thick," Wagner

---

* Everyone at the table died of AIDS, said Jon Wilner.

said. "So he had his secretary cut the pages in half. He put them in an envelope and sent them over to Treva's agent. Then he told his secretary, 'Get me two tickets to St. Barts.' And he left. That was the end of *Scandal*."

Henry Krieger, the composer of *Dreamgirls*, happened to be at the airport in St. Barts the day Bennett arrived. Bennett looked tired and haunted, Krieger thought. Krieger had heard about the collapse of *Scandal*. He approached Bennett and said, "I know you've flown the coop. I know you don't want anyone to know where you are. I won't tell anyone I've seen you. You have my word on that."

Bennett put his arm around Krieger. "Of all the people I could have met here, I'm glad it was you," he said.

After he returned from St. Barts, Bennett turned his attention to *The Children's Crusade*. Robin Wagner designed a model set for Madison Square Garden, complete with a hundred little stick figure boys. Jimmy Webb had nearly completed the score, and John Heilpern had the book pretty well in hand. Bennett wanted to hear it read and sung. Webb banged out the score on the grand piano in Bennett's office, while Heilpern read all the parts. When they finished, two hours later, they were both exhausted and sweaty.

Bennett jumped up and said, "Well, there's good news and bad news. Which do you want first?"

"The good news," Heilpern said.

"The good news is, I am reconciled with Bernie."

"That's the good news?" Heilpern said. "I don't want to know the bad news."

"The bad news is, I can't do your musical because I have to go to London to direct *Chess* for him."

Heilpern was furious. "So how does it feel to be a gun for hire?" he snapped.

"Well, I have to do it," Bennett responded. "It's the right thing to do. But don't worry, when I'm done I will come back to your show."

Heilpern exploded, "We've been farting around on this thing for two years. All the promises you keep making about how I am going to be so fulfilled and so rich—and nothing is happening."

Bennett leaped to the chalkboard that ran the length of the wall in his office, grabbed a piece of chalk, and began scribbling. "Look," he said. "You're going to get two points of the show, right? It's going to gross $2 million a week. That's $200,000 a week for you." He wrote $200,000 on the blackboard. "Let's say the show runs four or five years." He wrote down more numbers trailed by more zeroes.

"He's dancing in front of the blackboard, and suddenly I'm making $400,000 a week," said Heilpern. "And then he looks at me and goes, 'And that's just one company.' I said, 'What do you mean?' He said, 'Well, there's the German company and the French company and the English company.' He drew more numbers with more zeroes. And then he put down the chalk and said, 'You're rich, John.'

"And thus enthused, I went back to my lonely flat and thought, I'm rich! And then I sat down and I thought, I am poor. I am poor. I am not rich! But that was the mesmerizing temptation of Michael Bennett."

End of the Line

Tim Rice had been toying with the idea of a musical about a grand-master chess tournament ever since the 1972 match between Bobby Fischer, of America, and Boris Spassky, of the Soviet Union. This bout was the Cold War played out on a chessboard in Reykjavik, Iceland. Rice began following chess tournaments, and in 1981 traveled to Merano, Italy, to watch Anatoly Karpov square off against Viktor Korchnoi, who had defected to the West in 1974, leaving his wife and son behind the Iron Curtain. It was said he had a mistress in the West and that when his wife and son were finally allowed to leave the Soviet Union, Korchnoi's lawyer greeted them with divorce papers.[1]

"Korchnoi had a confused private life," said Rice, "and I began to think there is more to this scenario than just two guys playing chess." Rice's life was, at the time, also "confused." He was having an open affair with Elaine Paige, though he remained married to his wife, Jane, and spent weekends with her and their children.

Rice wrote *Chess*, in part, for Paige, who would play Florence, an Englishwoman who has an affair with Anatoly, a Russian grand master and defector. Anatoly is torn between his love for Florence and his duties to his wife and family in the Soviet Union.

"There is certainly a bit of an autobiographical thing in *Chess*," Rice would tell *Vanity Fair*.[2] "A man with two women pulling in different directions—yes, well . . ."*

---

* The complicated love lives of British theater people always amused Bernie Jacobs. During *Cats*, Andrew Lloyd Webber, Trevor Nunn, and set designer John Napier all left their wives for younger women

Rice asked Lloyd Webber if he'd like to write a musical about chess, but Lloyd Webber preferred pub quizzes to chess. "I couldn't get my head 'round how to do it theatrically," he said. "It needed some sort of structure." Besides, he was already at the piano adapting T. S. Eliot's poems.

While he was working on *Chess*, Rice was also talking to the Nederlanders about writing a musical with Barry Manilow. One afternoon, Richard Vos, the Nederlanders' creative director, told him that ABBA wanted to do a musical. Rice thought that was a good idea. He loved their songs—"Waterloo," "Fernando," "Mamma Mia." A few months later, he traveled to Sweden to see a production of *Evita*. He arranged to meet Björn Ulvaeus and Benny Andersson. When he mentioned his idea for a show about chess, they jumped at it. Living next door to the Soviet Union, the Cold War was palpable. Within days, Rice and ABBA began drafting a story.

Over the next few years, Rice traveled back and forth to Sweden, writing songs with "the ABBA boys," as everyone called Ulvaeus and Andersson. He often brought Paige with him, and she'd perform the songs—"I Know Him So Well," "Pity the Child," "Heaven Help My Heart"—with singer Tommy Körberg in ABBA's recording studio, Polar.

"We mucked about," Paige recalled. "Tim mucked about with the lyrics, we changed keys, swapped parts. And Benny would sit at the piano and these gorgeous melodies of operatic proportions would pour out. We'd work all day, have dinner, and drink too much vodka. It was wonderful."

In 1984, they recorded the concept album of *Chess*, with Paige, Körberg, Murray Head, and Barbara Dickson backed up by a choir of fifty and the London Symphony Orchestra. "It was the eighties," says Paige, "everything was big and bold and brash." The album took off, reaching the Top Ten in Britain and Europe and climbing to #47 on *Billboard* in the United States. "One Night in Bangkok" became a number one hit all over the world. The record company produced a live concert version of the album, and Rice, Paige, ABBA, Körberg, Murray Head,

---

playing cats. In Lloyd Webber's case, the woman was Sarah Brightman. "The trouble with the English is that they have too many wives," Jacobs often said.

and Rice's personal assistant, a stylish blonde named Judy Craymer, toured Europe.

The album and the concert received terrific reviews. Rice was pleased one day to pick up *Time* magazine and see Bernard Jacobs, of the mighty Shubert Organization, quoted as saying *Chess* was "the best score I've heard since *My Fair Lady*."

The Shuberts wanted to produce the musical, but Rice's loyalties lay with Richard Vos. But Jacobs had a trump card: Michael Bennett. They'd patched up their relationship (with the gentle prodding of Betty Jacobs). Bernie gave Bennett the *Chess* album and asked him to direct the show. First in London, then New York.

"Bernie delivered Michael Bennett, which was portrayed to us as a coup," said Rice. "The Shuberts had moved in."

"Bernie was determined that *Chess* would be the show that returned Michael Bennett to Broadway," said Robert Fox, hired by Jacobs to manage the production in London. "Benny and Björn had no idea who Michael Bennett was, and Bernie was talking him up as the greatest director of all time. Michael would fly back and forth to meet with Tim and Benny and Björn and outline his vision for the show. The negotiations were endless as to who was going to do what, how much money it was going to cost, how much of the show everybody owned. Bernie was masterminding the whole thing. And he's absolutely loving it because he's manipulating lawyers in London and in New York and he's trying to fuck over Tim and Benny and Björn's lawyers, and they're trying to fuck him over and everyone's trying to fuck everybody—and the show isn't even in rehearsal."

Eventually, they reached a deal. The show would cost two million pounds, making it the most expensive production in West End history. Rice and ABBA would own 50 percent of it, the Shuberts 25 percent and Bennett 25 percent. *Chess* would be the first major musical the Shuberts would produce from scratch since the days of Sigmund Romberg.

Bennett invited Rice and ABBA to spend a weekend at his house in East Hampton, which he'd recently bought from David Geffen. They were going "to crack the story line," said Rice. "And crack turned out to be the appropriate word."

Rice was ferried in style by a Shubert limousine to East Hampton.

As he relaxed in the backseat, cocooned in black leather upholstery, the divider window slid down and Hank, the driver, said, "Oh, Mr. Rice—do you know where Mr. Bennett's house is?"

"Uh, no," Rice said. "I'll write the songs. You drive."

"Well, I'd better stop and make a call."

The limo glided into a rest stop along Montauk Highway where there was a pay phone. While Hank made a call, Rice hopped out of the limo to relieve himself. "I wandered over to this sign which indicated this was the first sighting of the Indians in 1643. It was very interesting stuff. When I finished, I began wandering back to the car and I saw Hank get in. I was twenty yards away and I was strolling and suddenly the car shot off. And I thought, Oh, my God. He thinks I'm in the back!"

Rice had left his jacket and wallet in the limo. He was stranded along Montauk Highway without even a quarter for the pay phone.

The Shubert limo rolled up to Bennett's house on James Lane. Bennett was standing in the driveway. He opened the back door and found Rice's jacket. "Where is he?" Bennett said. "Oh, my God," said Hank. "I know where he is!" He jumped in the car and sped off.

Bennett and Rice had a good, long laugh about the incident that night. It was, though, about the only laugh Rice would have that weekend. Bennett had exciting ideas for the show. The romantic triangle linking Florence to both the Russian and American chess champions would be played out along the lines of *Casablanca*. The production would have the elegance and pacing of a James Bond movie. Bennett envisioned a wall of video screens on which the chess match—and the media coverage of it—would be shown. *Chess*, he said, would not only be about the Cold War but also the media circus that descended on the two grand masters.

"All very interesting stuff," said Rice, "but I never had the feeling Michael really wanted to do the show. That may have been the beginning of our troubles."

Rice was also put off by the amount of drinking and coke sniffing Bennett was doing all weekend long. "I wasn't a hundred percent happy," Rice said. "I remember trying to find excuses to go into East Hampton and do a little shopping."

Bennett was usually high when he worked on *Chess*. At 890 Broadway, he, Bob Avian, and Robin Wagner would have lunch at a local Italian restaurant and down two or three martinis. Back at the office, Bennett would do lines of cocaine on his desk. Then he'd go to work on the show.[3]

Rice didn't think the weekend with Bennett had been that productive. But the show rolled on. Robin Wagner designed a giant computerized chessboard on which the action would take place. Hydraulically operated, the board could change shape, becoming a mountain range or the interior of a hotel. The production was going to be slick and spare. "Michael had seen some footage of a Stones concert I did [in 1967]," said Wagner. "He was starting to see *Chess* more and more like a rock concert."

Meanwhile, Robert Fox and other members of the production team went to Holland to see the giant video wall Bennett wanted. It had been designed by Philips, the technology company located in Amsterdam. "The viddy wall," as Fox called it, would cost several hundred thousand pounds—plus shipping to London.

In the fall of 1985, Bennett moved to London to conduct auditions. Elaine Paige, Murray Head, and Tommy Körberg were signed to play the leads but the ensemble had yet to be cast. Bennett rented John Le Carré's house along the Thames in Chelsea. He became friends with Judy Craymer, Rice's assistant. She was having a fling with Head. They often joined Bennett for dinner at the house. "He was vibrant and energetic—and wonderfully mischievous," she said. "And then one day he was gone and never came back."

Auditions for *Chess* were held on the second floor of an old rehearsal studio in the West End. One day Bennett was climbing the stairs and suddenly couldn't breathe. He struggled to the top of the stairs and collapsed. He knew something was wrong. He had noticed, before leaving for London, a purple spot on his right foot. He told friends—and himself—it was just a scab. But he'd also been losing weight. He flew back to New York and saw his doctor. The scab was Kaposi's. Bennett had AIDS. He told his best friend, Bob Avian, first. Then he told Robin Wagner at 890 Broadway. "I have bad news," he said. "You can't tell anyone. I have Kaposi's sarcoma." Wagner knew that meant AIDS. He ran into the gym and broke down in tears.

Bennett told Breglio over the phone late that night.

The one person Bennett could not bring himself to tell was Bernie Jacobs. After his diagnosis, he fled, once again, to St. Barts. He called Jacobs from there and told him he was pulling out of *Chess*. He said he didn't like working in London, he was unhappy with Elaine Paige, Tim Rice's script wasn't what he wanted—all sorts of excuses.[4] Jacobs wasn't buying it. When Bennett returned to New York, Jacobs pressured him to go back to London and the show. This time Bennett told Jacobs he had a heart condition and his doctor warned him against taking on the stress of a new musical. Jacobs still didn't believe him. He called Breglio and demanded to know what was going on. But Breglio had given Bennett his word he wouldn't say anything. "I told Bernie Michael wasn't feeling well," he said, "and Bernie went crazy."

Breglio told Bennett, "Michael, you can't keep this up. This is crazy. You see this man all the time. How can you not tell him?"

Bennett met Jacobs in his office above the Shubert Theatre. Jacobs was angry. "You can't walk away from the show like this," he said. "What is wrong with you?" Bennett stood up. "Come with me," he said and led Jacobs to the men's room. He closed the door and unbuttoned his shirt. He had Kaposi's sarcoma scars all over his chest. Jacobs fell into his arms. They held each other and cried.

"Once Bernie knew, we were on a mission to save Michael," said Breglio. "We knew it was fatal, but we just couldn't accept it." They contacted the National Institutes of Health and got hold of the experimental drug AZT. Bennett also had numerous blood transfusions. When he wasn't in the hospital, he retreated to his house in East Hampton.

The Broadway gossip mill began to churn. Why had Bennett withdrawn, so suddenly, from *Chess*? The *New York Times*, the *Post*'s Page Six, and *Daily News* gossip columnist Liz Smith were sniffing around the story. They had to be told something. Jacobs and Bennett decided on a cover story, "a fraud," as Breglio put it. Bennett had left the show, Jacobs told the *Times*, because he was suffering from angina pectoris, severe chest pains that cause shortness of breath and palpitations. Jacobs said a new director for *Chess* would be hired but that Bennett would continue to help with the show. "At times he's better, at times he's worse," Jacobs said.[5]

Jacobs told Robert Fox that Bennett had AIDS, but swore him to secrecy. "On a personal level, we were incredibly upset," said Fox. "On a professional level we were in shit. The show was nearly cast, the set was being built, we had a theater date, and we were selling tickets." Bennett was going to invest five hundred thousand pounds in *Chess*. Jacobs offered Fox the chance to raise Bennett's share.

"Even though there was no director, I thought, We'll get somebody and we're selling tickets," Fox said. "So I took it. Insane."

In London, the story was that Bennett left because he didn't get along with Elaine Paige.

"I was skiing in Courchevel, and it's white, white, white, and I see this black gentleman walking up the mountain," Paige said. "I looked and I thought, That's Baz Bamigboye [gossip columnist for the *Daily Mail*], and he's headed right toward me."

"Michael Bennett has pulled out of *Chess*, and I hear it's because you and he had a row," Bamigboye said.

"The story was all over the English press, and it was utter nonsense," said Paige.

Rice was kept out of the loop as well. He was simply told Bennett was leaving the project—no explanation given.

"And then there were these ludicrous arguments about his royalties," Rice said. "The Shuberts seemed more concerned about getting Michael paid for his work than getting the show on. I kept saying, but this guy has just dropped us in the cart. Finally, somebody said he was ill. I thought maybe Michael was using that as an excuse because he was never keen on the project. Somebody asked if there was any proof he was ill, and Robert Fox yelled, 'Don't ask anymore—shut up!' That's when I knew there was obviously something more going on here."

Though Jacobs was devastated to learn of Bennett's illness in January 1986, the Shuberts could not back out of *Chess*. The production was too far along to be scrapped. Over lunch at the restaurant Barbetta, Jacobs suggested to Bennett that Bob Avian take over the show. But Bennett dismissed the idea. "Bobby is a number two," he said. "That's what he wants to be. Leave him alone." The talk turned to Bennett's illness. He bent his head toward the table and parted his hair. The Kaposi's had spread to his scalp.

After kicking around a number of names—David Leveaux, a young director who'd come into the Shubert orbit with his acclaimed revival of *Anna Christie*, was on the list—the Shuberts turned to Trevor Nunn, the director of *Nicholas Nickleby* and *Cats*.

Nunn was in New York staying at the Sherry-Netherland when he got a call early one morning. Jacobs asked if he could see Nunn right away. Nunn knew it must be serious because instead of asking him to come over to the Shubert offices, Jacobs said he and Schoenfeld would come to the Sherry-Netherland. They entered his room looking, Nunn recalled, "very somber." They told him Bennett had AIDS. They also told him they had an enormous amount of money on the line with *Chess*.

"We're here, Trevor, to say, we need your help," Jacobs said.

Nunn was not going to say no to the Shuberts, but Clever Trevor had a price. A few months earlier, the Shuberts had agreed to produce a revival of *Nicholas Nickleby*, first on tour and then in New York. But they were having doubts about its viability. Nunn had cast the production—he'd promised jobs to a whole company of actors—when the Shuberts started to wobble. Nunn told them he'd do *Chess*, but only if they'd commit to his revival of *Nicholas Nickleby*.

The Shuberts informed their partners on *Chess*—Robert Fox, Tim Rice, ABBA—about the new arrangement. To get Nunn, they'd all have to invest in *Nicholas Nickleby*.

"Not only am I a producer of *Chess* for five hundred thousand pounds, which I have yet to raise," recalled Fox, "but I am also now a proud owner of 25 percent of the investment on *Nicholas Nickleby*, which I do not want. I am now drinking and taking anything I can get my hands on to stay afloat."

Jacobs privately told Fox, another young theater person to whom he felt paternal, not to worry. "You have to be seen to put up the money," he said, "but I'll underwrite you if it goes wrong."

He was not so paternal to Rice and ABBA. He told them they would have to become coproducers of *Nicholas Nickleby* if they wanted Nunn to direct *Chess*. They put $1 million of their own money into the revival.*

His price met, Nunn jumped into *Chess*. He inherited Bennett's production—Bennett's concept, his cast, much of his creative team, his "viddy wall"—but Nunn had his own ideas about how to stage the show. Bennett wanted a spare set—just the moving chessboard and the viddy wall. Nunn wanted realism. He wanted scenes set in hotel rooms to look like hotel rooms. He wanted furniture, in particular chairs—forty-seven chairs, to be exact. There were now so many chairs on stage the cast began calling the show *Chairs*, a cheeky reference to the absurdist play by Ionesco.

"Trevor started asking for adjustments here and adjustments there, and our budget is starting to balloon," said Fox. "We go from two million pounds, to three million pounds, and end up at four million pounds. Trevor is running amok with the budget because he knows we have to say yes. But we are taking in money at the box office. The show is selling extremely well. At this point, it's a megashow with a huge advance, and it's going to open in London and then New York and then California. And every time I tell Bernie about the budget he says, 'Fine.'"

If Jacobs was agreeing to all of Nunn's demands, it was because his mind was not on *Chess*. He wasn't even in London. He was in New York, trying to save Michael Bennett.

And then one afternoon his mind wasn't there at all.

"It was Rosh Hashanah, and we were having company for dinner," said Betty Jacobs. "Bernie had a nap and when he woke up, he didn't know where he was. He didn't remember anything. I took him to the doctor and the doctor said he had lost his memory—completely. All I remember now is the dinner, because I wasn't home to help the girl in the kitchen, so she put the gefilte fish in the chicken soup."

---

* The revival of *Nicholas Nickleby* opened in Los Angeles and did no business despite a strong plug from Johnny Carson on *The Tonight Show*. The production lost money everywhere it played. It opened in New York on August 24, 1986, at the Broadhurst Theatre and closed after just twenty-nine performances.

The immediate diagnosis was transient global amnesia, a neurological disorder that renders the victim incapable of remembering anything but the last few moments of consciousness. Bernie Jacobs, who only the day before could tell you what the stop clause was on David Merrick's production of *Promises, Promises* in 1968, could not remember where the bathroom was in his house.

Chess, the most expensive, the most anticipated musical in West End history, was now without a producer. It fell to Fox to steer the show to opening night. But Fox was not in good shape. He was drinking heavily and doing a great deal of cocaine. He was also leaving his wife for his lover, Natasha Richardson, Vanessa Redgrave's daughter. To make matters worse, Fox was fighting with Nunn, who, perhaps to show his disdain for the young producer, always called him "Roger."

There were problems with the set. The hydraulic chessboard, which weighed more than a ton, was operated with a joystick by a technician named Barry. But he was having trouble maneuvering the machinery. The board kept scratching the stage with an ear-piercing screech. Then, on a Saturday before the first week of public performances, Barry managed to work the board without a hitch. There were cheers—and relief—from the company.

But the chessboard still posed problems for the actors. When it became a mountain (some scenes in the show were set in the Italian Alps), the actors had to climb it. The trouble was, it was slippery. "Every time Murray tried to scale it, he ended up unceremoniously in a heap," said Paige. "But Murray was kind of Mr. Cool, anyway. He'd get back up, still singing, start climbing again—and tumble down. It was really very funny."

Finally, somebody had the idea of attaching thick rubber soles to the actors' shoes. It did the trick, though the entire company was now two inches taller.

In May 1986, with *Chess* about to begin previews at the Prince Edward Theatre, the Shuberts arrived in London. "Bernie was really not in good shape," said Fox. He was tired and depressed, often addled. Once, during a meeting in his suite at the Berkeley Hotel, he got up to use the bathroom and walked into the closet.

And he was drinking, which, aside from an occasional Scotch, he never used to do.

"We were in my office at midnight after one of the previews, and Bernie's drinking vodka practically out of the bottle," said Fox. "Everybody is saying to him, 'Bernie, you cannot drink! You must not drink!' But he was lost. He was really lost. And so were the rest of us. Because he was the strong guy, and the strong guy was no longer there."

And yet there were flashes of his quick wit. At a production meeting at the back of the theater after a preview, chubby Jerry Schoenfeld jumped up onto the bar. Jacobs scowled. "Get off there. You look like Humpty Dumpty!"

As for the show itself, Jacobs's verdict was simple—"Michael would have done it better."

Which was unfair to Nunn. He'd taken over a complex production at the last minute and brought it to opening night. "And it was not a catastrophe," said Fox.

The reviews were mixed, ranging from "gift-wrapped and gorgeous" (the *Telegraph*) to "inchoate mess" (the *Guardian*). But the show, largely on the strength of the popular concept album, did good business, managing to run nearly three years in London and break even.

Encouraged by its success in London, Schoenfeld and Jacobs decided to produce it on Broadway.

Back in New York rumors swirled around the unexpected news that Bennett was selling 890 Broadway. He was pouring $3 million a year into the place, subsidizing all his friends and colleagues who had sweetheart deals on their rent. Now that he was sick, he had to unload the money pit.

Editors at the *New York Times*, which thought it covered Broadway as aggressively as it covered the world, knew there was a story there. Jeremy Gerard joined the *Times* in September 1986 as the theater reporter. One of his first assignments was to find out what was going on with Michael Bennett. "The Broadway community was really shaken up," said Gerard. "Something must be seriously wrong for Michael to put that building up for sale."

Gerard was also hearing rumors that Bennett had AIDS.

He started calling Bennett, leaving messages for him at his apartment in New York and his house in East Hampton. Bennett always returned his calls—but to his answering machine at the *Times* late at night. "Oops! Sorry I missed you. Try me again!" he'd say.

Gerard started preparing his story, which would run with or without Bennett's cooperation. Close to deadline his phone rang. "This is Michael. What do you want to know?"

They spoke for two hours, about Bennett's life and career and the state of the Broadway musical. Gerard asked him if he was ill. "I have what my doctor is calling stress-related angina," Bennett told him.

"I never asked him if he had AIDS," Gerard said. "There is no question in my mind that other reporters would have pursued it more aggressively. But at the beginning of the epidemic we were trying to figure out where privacy ended and where the public's need to know began. I was not going to be the one to say to somebody, 'Are you dying of AIDS?' So I was tactful. Maybe too tactful."

Gerard's story ran on the front page of the Arts & Leisure section on November 2, 1986, under the headline WHY MICHAEL BENNETT HAS SAID GOODBYE, FOR NOW, TO BROADWAY. Bennett said he would soon undergo surgery for angina. "I've never been more scared in my life," he admitted. He discussed the collapse of *Scandal* and his withdrawal from *Chess*. He said he was being forced to sell 890 Broadway because it was a financial drain. At times he sounded philosophical, at other times bitter. "What Broadway community?" he said at one point. "There is no Broadway community. I went to the Shuberts and said, 'Buy the building, or you and the Nederlanders buy the building.' They weren't interested."

The interview ended on an optimistic note. All he needed, Bennett said, was six months to recover from surgery and a new show to work on.

"I think I'll be able to make my comeback at forty-four without a problem," he said.

"It was a great piece about Michael Bennett," said Gerard, "but it starts with his lie."

"Poor Jeremy Gerard," said Robin Wagner. "He got fucked."

• • •

A few weeks after the article appeared, an "intimate" of Bennett's phoned Gerard and requested a meeting. The friend brought along Bennett's hospital records. He showed them to Gerard. "I saw with my own eyes the incontrovertible proof that Michael Bennett had AIDS," said Gerard.

Gerard didn't know what to do with the information. And then in March 1987 another prominent theater figure, Charles Ludlam, founder of the Ridiculous Theatrical Company, withdrew from directing *Titus Andronicus* for Joseph Papp in Central Park. On a hunch, Gerard called St. Vincent's Hospital in Greenwich Village, which, he knew, was where many AIDS patients went. He asked for Charles Ludlam and was put through to his room. Ludlam would not say he had AIDS, but admitted he was suffering from pneumonia. "I'm going to beat it," he said.

"But his voice already sounded haunted," Gerard recalled.

A few months later the press agent for the Ridiculous Theatrical Company called Gerard to tell him Ludlam had died. The family wanted the *Times* to report he had died of pneumonia.

But Gerard could not knowingly put a lie in the *New York Times*. And he knew, as a cultural reporter, the toll AIDS was taking on the arts. He believed it was time to write about it. He made his case to Ludlam's grieving family. "The only way we can stop stigmatizing this disease is to be honest about how people whose names we know died. It will make it easier for the living to be able to deal with this—not in the closet, not in shame, not in private places where, in some cases, even their families don't know what is going on."

As Gerard was writing the obit on deadline, Ludlam's parents called to say that, yes, he could write that their son had died of AIDS. The obituary ran on the front page of the *New York Times*. "Charles Ludlam, one of the most prolific and flamboyant artists in the theater avant-garde, who seemed to be on the verge of breaking into the mainstream of American culture, died of pneumonia early yesterday," Gerard wrote. "He was forty-four years old and had been suffering from AIDS. Mr. Ludlam's death stunned a theater community that is struggling daily—mostly, until now, in private, personal ways—with the devastation of AIDS."

Ludlam's obit broke the dam. The *Times* had been reluctant to cover AIDS. The *Village Voice* and the *New York Native*, an openly gay newspaper, had been writing about it since the beginning of the 1980s. Activists like Larry Kramer, a founder of ACT UP, criticized the *Times* for ignoring what was now being called a plague. But the paper would make up for lost time. With Gerard as the lead reporter, the entire cultural staff set about writing a two-part series on AIDS and its impact on the arts in New York City. Gerard's assignment was the theater world, and he knew that Broadway's most celebrated director was dying of AIDS. He met with Arthur Gelb, the powerful managing editor of the *Times* who oversaw the paper's cultural coverage, and told him he'd seen Bennett's medical records.

"Arthur was very generous in allowing me to grapple with it," he said. "I felt we should print it because Michael used his access to the press not to say, 'It's none of your business,' but to put out a lie. And he certainly didn't care about my credibility—or the paper's—when he did that."

Gerard's story—CREATIVE ARTS BEING RESHAPED BY THE EPIDEMIC—appeared on the front page of the *New York Times* on June 9, 1987. Beverly Sills, the head of the New York City Opera, said in the article that within the past two months, two dozen members of City Opera—singers, musicians, administrators—had died of AIDS. She had delivered ten eulogies.

Joseph Papp said, "I have had so many people around me dying of this, I don't want to talk about it."

A few paragraphs later, Gerard noted AIDS was affecting artistic works still being created. "Michael Bennett, one of the most influential directors and choreographers of his generation, withdrew as the director of the musical *Chess* when, according to information confirmed by the *New York Times*, he was stricken with the illness. He has been in Tucson, Arizona, since December battling the disease that has prevented him from working for more than eighteen months."

Gerard never told Bennett—or his friends and representatives—that he was going to reveal that Bennett had AIDS. "I knew they would deny it," he said.

Blindsided by the revelation, the Bennett camp was furious.

"Michael went berserk and I went berserk," said Breglio. "I told Jeremy I would never speak to him again about anything having to do with Michael. As far as I was concerned, the *Times* had violated their policy by writing about Michael's illness and then not asking us for a comment. Yes, Jeremy was lied to. But it was Michael's option to tell people whether or not he had AIDS. It was his life. He didn't want to be a poster child for AIDS. He just didn't. It was a different time."

Bernie Jacobs called Gerard. "You didn't have to write that," he said as much in sorrow as in anger.

The reporter stood his ground. "With all due respect, Bernie, I did because I knew it to be true."

In Tucson, Bennett received regular blood transfusions at a clinic conducting experiments on AIDS patients. He bought a handsome adobe house, designed in the 1930s by Josias Thomas Joesler, at the foot of the Catalina Mountains. He lived with a nurse and a couple of close friends who had nothing to do with Broadway. He would only allow a few theater friends to visit him—Bob Avian, Robin Wagner, John Breglio. But not Bernie Jacobs. They spoke on the phone, but Bennett would not allow Jacobs to visit him in Arizona. He'd come to resent Jacobs for manipulating him out of buying the Mark Hellinger Theatre. And now that he was dying, he was determined to break free of Jacobs's control.

"It's all about business with Bernie," Bennett was now saying. "Don't kid yourself. It's about business."

"The relationship deteriorated," said Breglio. "By the end of his life, Michael didn't want to see Bernie. He cut him out."

Jacobs did not feel that way about Bennett. Distraught, he spiraled into a deep depression.

Michael Bennett died at his home in Tucson on Sunday, June 28, 1987.

For more than a year, whenever Jacobs spoke of him, he did so in the present tense.

The British Are Coming!
The British Are Coming!

Throughout the eighties and nineties, obituaries of theater people who had died of AIDS appeared almost daily in the *New York Times*—Wilford Leach, the Tony Award–winning director of *The Pirates of Penzance* and *The Mystery of Edwin Drood*; Tony Richardson, the director of *Look Back in Anger* and *The Entertainer*; Larry Kert, the original Tony in *West Side Story*; stage and screen star Anthony Perkins; Brad Davis, who gave a memorable performance in Larry Kramer's play about the AIDS crisis, *The Normal Heart*; Leonard Frey, the "ugly pockmarked Jew fairy" in *The Boys in the Band*; Ethyl Eichelberger, playwright and drag queen; A. J. Antoon, director of *That Championship Season*; Michael Peters, co-choreographer of *Dreamgirls*.

The most famous show business AIDS victim was Rock Hudson, who died in 1985. Shirley Herz, the press agent for *La Cage aux Folles*, said the box office plunged in the wake of the publicity surrounding Hudson's death. "People were afraid they'd get AIDS at the show because it was about homosexuals," she said. *La Cage* survived another two years, but it fell apart after the death, from AIDS, of its shrewd executive producer, Fritz Holt.

Jerry Herman, the composer of *La Cage*, was diagnosed with HIV in the mid-eighties. He moved to Los Angeles where, he said, he thought he would die. As it turned out, Herman became a longtime survivor of HIV. As of this writing, he's eighty-two and living in Miami Beach.

In addition to famous Broadway names, AIDS claimed countless chorus kids, some of whom, had they lived, would probably have become well-known performers, directors, and choreographers themselves. Michael Bennett stepped out of the chorus line to become the most important Broadway director of his generation. But he was cut down in the prime of his life. Who knows how many great shows he had left in him? Who knows how many young dancers he would have helped turn into first-rate directors and choreographers?

And, in fact, with Bennett's death the great tradition of the director-choreographer was coming to an end. Jerome Robbins, who began it with such shows as *West Side Story* and *Gypsy*, had abandoned Broadway for the ballet. Gower Champion, who staged *Hello, Dolly!* and *42nd Street*, was dead. And Joe Layton, director of *George M!* and *Barnum*, was suffering from AIDS (he would die in 1994).

Another giant—Bob Fosse—dropped dead of a heart attack on Pennsylvania Avenue in Washington, D.C., walking to the Willard Hotel from the National Theatre after the opening night of his revival of *Sweet Charity*.

The previous year, Fosse had tried to make a Broadway comeback with a show called *Big Deal*, which he wrote, choreographed, and directed. Based on the movie *Big Deal on Madonna Street*, the Shuberts produced it at the Broadway Theatre. It lasted just sixty-nine performances, and it ended the Shuberts' always-contentious relationship with Fosse. During tryouts in Boston, Fosse battled Schoenfeld and Jacobs. Every time they gave him a note on the production, Fosse would say, "I'm the director. You're the producer. Let me make my show, so shut the fuck up."[1]

Jacobs thought the physical production was too dark. But whenever he asked Fosse to lighten it up, Fosse would turn to Jules Fisher, the lighting designer, and say, "Jules, make it darker."

After the show opened to tepid reviews, Jacobs told the ad agency, Serino, Coyne & Nappi, "We're not going to support this show with advertising. But we have to do one thing. We have to make a TV commercial because it's in Bob's contract. So we're going to make the TV commercial, but we're not going to air it a lot."

"They hated him by that point," Rick Elice, who worked on the commercial, recalled.

When Fosse died, Jeremy Gerard called Jacobs for a comment for an obituary he was writing in the *Times*. "Within a short time, we've lost Gower Champion, Michael Bennett, and now Bobby," Jacobs said. "It's an enormous loss. And who's in sight to take their places?"

But then he added, "Bobby could be the nicest, most decent, politest, most considerate man you could ever hope to meet. He was thorough and he was hardworking, but he was not a very nice man. He was not just nasty to other people. He was nasty to himself." The comment enraged Fosse's widow, Gwen Verdon. She banned Jacobs from the funeral.*

But Jacobs had raised a serious point in Fosse's obituary. Who, indeed, would carry on the tradition of the American musical theater now that Bennett, Champion, and Fosse were gone? There was, of course, Tommy Tune. But he was touring in *My One and Only* and wouldn't come up with another musical until the spectacular *Grand Hotel* in 1989.

In the mid-eighties, Broadway looked a little thin. There were only thirty-one shows in the 1984–85 season, down from fifty just two years prior. And, for the first time since 1981, attendance began to drop, reaching a low of 6.5 million in 1985.[2]

But the downward trend would not last long. Two megahits were taking shape in London. Both shows were set in Paris, one in the streets during the 1832 Paris Uprising, the other at the Palais Garnier opera house. And neither was heavy on choreography, relying instead on special effects and soaring dramatic music. The dance-driven American musical was about to give way to the British pop opera.

In 1983, a friend of Cameron Mackintosh's gave the producer a tape of a concert version of Victor Hugo's *Les Misérables* that had been performed at the Palais des Sports. The songs were by Alain Boublil and Claude-Michel Schönberg, who had both been influenced by the 1970 recording of *Jesus Christ Superstar*. Mackintosh had little interest in a

---

* Jacobs would later claim, in Martin Gottfried's Fosse biography, *All His Jazz*, that his remarks to Gerard were off the record. "Bullshit," said Gerard. "Nobody knew better than Bernie when talking to a reporter what was on the record and what was off the record."

Hey, Mr. Producer! Gerald Schoenfeld (*left*), Bernard Jacobs (*center*), and Philip J. Smith (*right*), wearing Styrofoam hats, celebrate an American Express ad from the 1980s spotlighting Broadway producers. Smith was Jacobs's right-hand man for more than thirty years. Jacobs did not make a decision without consulting him. Producer Scott Rudin called Smith "the Tom Hagen of the Shuberts."

William Ivey Long's costume sketch for Anita Morris as Carla in *Nine*. After the first preview, every show queen in New York was on the phone talking about "the redhead in the cat suit," said Long. Tune wanted Morris to perform her sultry number "A Call from the Vatican" on the Tony Award telecast, but CBS censors forbid "nipple rubbing" and "audible sounds of ecstasy."

William Ivey Long's costume sketch for "The Grand Canal" in the second act of *Nine*. The number was an homage to rococo opéra bouffe, but "it was longer than *Aida*!" said press agent Judy Jacksina. The creators of *Nine* had barely finished the second act when the critics came to see the show. Clive Barnes wrote that he could smell the paint drying on the set.

Judy Jacksina, the press agent for *Nine,* knew the show had to make a splash if it stood a chance against the season's big hit, *Dreamgirls.* Her greatest weapons were the twenty-one striking women in the cast. She covered the front of the 46th Street Theatre with life-size photos of them in their black costumes. "I wanted to seductively represent what was going on inside the theater," she said. "I didn't want cute little tap-dancing photos. I wanted sex." The day the photos went up, traffic ground to a halt along the block.

Jerry Schoenfeld and Albert Poland at the opening of the Off-Broadway play *Modigliani* in 1978. As a young producer in the 1960s, Poland used Schoenfeld and Jacobs as his lawyers. He was in their office one day in 1972 and found Schoenfeld "impossible to deal with." A few days later he picked up the *New York Times* and read that Schoenfeld and Jacobs had staged a coup to take over the Shubert Organization.

Albert Poland with Bernie and Betty Jacobs at the opening of *Modigliani.* Poland was a frequent visitor to Jacobs's office above the Shubert Theatre. After Marsha Norman's play *'night, Mother,* about a lonely woman who kills herself, opened at the John Golden Theatre in 1983, he stopped by to ask Jacobs how it went. "It was fine," Jacobs replied. "But the depth of the suicide audience remains to be seen."

30

Emanuel Azenberg *(left)* with Neil Simon, Broadway's most successful playwright. Azenberg produced many of Simon's plays, including *Brighton Beach Memoirs, Biloxi Blues,* and *Broadway Bound.* He got his start in the theater as the company manager for the national tour of *I Can Get It for You Wholesale.* The first stop was Detroit, where he met D. T. Nederlander. Azenberg arrived at the theater the first night and found D. T. screaming at the show's star, Lillian Roth. She was entering the theater through the lobby. "Actors go in the stage door!" D. T. shouted.

Celebrating the 1983 Fred Astaire Awards are *(left to right)* Liliane Montevecchi, Michael Bennett, Vivian Reed, Charles "Honi" Coles, and critics Clive Barnes and Douglas Watt. Coles was appearing in Tommy Tune's hit musical *My One and Only* that year. Bennett tried to help Tune in rehearsals, but fueled by cocaine and vodka, he was turning a lighthearted romp into something dark and raunchy. He was asked to leave.

The men behind *Les Misérables*: *(left to right)* French writer Alain Boublil, producer Cameron Mackintosh, director Trevor Nunn, and Herbert Kretzmer, who did the English adaptation. They're celebrating their win for Best Musical at the 1987 Tony Awards. *Les Misérables* didn't look like a winner when it began performances at the Barbican Theatre in London in 1985. Kretzmer watched a run through and "my heart sank to my boots," he recalled. "Overplotted" and "interminable" were the words roiling in his head. "Disaster was staring us in the face," he said. "We'd really bought it this time."

33

Curtain call for the opening night of *The Phantom of the Opera*, January 26, 1988, with *(left to right)* Michael Crawford, Andrew Lloyd Webber, and Sarah Brightman. Lloyd Webber got the idea for the show when he picked up a secondhand copy of Gaston Leroux's 1910 thriller at the Strand bookstall on Fifth Avenue and Fifty-Ninth Street. "It was a sort of confused book, but the thing that struck me was this big love story going through it," he said.

34

David Merrick, after his stroke, attends the opening of *The Phantom of the Opera* with Etan Aronson, to whom he was twice married. Merrick had lost the use of his dagger-like tongue and could only grunt in approval or disapproval. But he knew a hit show when he saw one. He sent producer Cameron Mackintosh a telegram: "The torch has passed from me to you."

35

Andrew Lloyd Webber with his second wife, muse, and leading lady, Sarah Brightman, at the opening night party for *The Phantom of the Opera*. Lloyd Webber exploded that night when he read what Frank Rich wrote about Brightman in his *New York Times* review: "She simulates fear and affection alike by screwing her face into bug-eyed, chipmunk-cheek poses more appropriate to the Lon Chaney film version."

36

Broadway opening nights can be long, especially if you're a kid. Bernie Jacobs trades in his usual scowl for a smile as he gazes down on his sleeping grandson at the *Phantom* opening. He'd be smiling the next day, too, when the show broke box office records despite Frank Rich's tough review.

37

THE SHUBERT ORGANIZATION
3 KNIGHTS LTD · ROBERT FOX LTD

CORDIALLY INVITE YOU TO THE
OPENING NIGHT PARTY FOR

CHESS

AT THE UNITED NATIONS
46TH STREET AND FIRST AVENUE
VISITOR'S GATE

THURSDAY, APRIL 28TH
IMMEDIATELY FOLLOWING
THE PERFORMANCE

PLEASE PRESENT THIS CARD AT GATE
FOR SECURITY REASONS

EACH CARD ADMITS ONE   BLACK TIE

The opening night invitation for the *Chess* party at the United Nations. For the first time in years, the Shuberts were the lead producers of a major Broadway musical. Their partners were the show's creators: Benny Andersson, Björn Ulvaeus, and Tim Rice (3 Knights LTD); and British producer Robert Fox. Everybody lost a fortune.

38

The opening night marquee for *Chess* at the Imperial Theatre. The advertising agency struggled to create an image for the musical, which was about a chess tournament set against the backdrop of the Cold War. "We tried to build it around the U.S. vs. the U.S.S.R.—Gorbachev had just come in," said ad executive Rick Elice. "We tried to make it relevant. Nobody gave a fuck. We couldn't sell it."

39

Tim Rice (*left*), with Björn Ulvaeus, is defiant at the *Chess* opening. But in fact 1988 was the lowest point of his life. "My father died, and I was almost broke . . . because my outgoings were huge because of *Chess*, which hadn't really made any money in London," he said. Rice invested heavily in the New York production. "I took another hit there."

Producer Robert Fox, preparing himself for the reviews with several glasses of wine, at the *Chess* opening with his new wife, Natasha Richardson. As he left the party, the press agent handed him Frank Rich's blistering attack. "I read it, and laughed like a lunatic," he said, "because if you're going to get a bad review, this one is it.

The most powerful men in the American theater: Gerald Schoenfeld (*center*) and Bernard B. Jacobs (*right*) at an event with Mayor Ed Koch. Schoenfeld handled government relations for the Shuberts, often sparring with city officials who, he felt, were not committed to cleaning up Times Square. When he badgered Koch, the mayor responded: "Where's Broadway going to go? New Jersey?"

French musical based on a nineteenth-century doorstop of a novel, but out of courtesy to his friend he listened to the tape. The score was thrilling. By the fourth song, he knew he had to do the show.[3]

But there were problems. The concert was under two hours—sort of a collection of scenes from the novel rather than a proper musical—and it was in French. Mackintosh asked the critic and poet James Fenton to adapt Boublil and Schönberg's concert into a full-fledged, English stage musical. Fenton had never read the novel, so he took it with him on a two-month trip to Borneo. He read it as he was canoeing down the Kapuas River. To lighten his backpack, he ripped out the pages when he finished them, and tossed them to the crocodiles.

To direct the production, Mackintosh turned to Trevor Nunn and John Caird, codirectors of *Nicholas Nickleby*. Nunn was also the artistic director of the Royal Shakespeare Company (where Caird was a resident director), and was under fire in the British press for his lucrative outside work, mainly on *Cats*. He insisted that *Les Misérables* open at the Barbican, the RSC's theater in London, as a coproduction between the RSC and Mackintosh. It was, wrote critics Sheridan Morley and Ruth Leon, "his way of squaring his conscience with the RSC leadership."[4] Mackintosh would put up $450,000 for the show. The RSC would kick in $240,000, about the cost of a major Shakespeare production.[5] Mackintosh also had the right to move the production to a commercial West End theater if it was successful at the Barbican.

Les Misérables was scheduled to open in the fall of 1985, but Fenton, it turned out, was cavalier about deadlines. And though a fine poet, he was not a natural lyricist. He wrote evocative lines, but they were difficult to sing. "There's a frost in the air, there's a scare in the city," is striking on the page but, because there are too many *s*'s, would sound like hissing when sung by a cast of twenty-five.

In January 1985, six months before the show was to go into rehearsal, Mackintosh decided Fenton needed help from a proper lyricist. He invited Herbert Kretzmer to join the so-called *Les Miz* team. A TV critic for the *Daily Mail*, Kretzmer was also a songwriter who had adapted Charles Aznavour's French songs into English. Two—"She" and "Yesterday, When I Was Young"—were among Mackintosh's favorites. Kretzmer read what Fenton had written and knew it wouldn't work onstage.

"A poem is written to be absorbed at the reader's rhythm," he said. "You can absorb it into your being. A song doesn't allow that luxury. A song is tyrannical. It has its own thrust. It doesn't hang about for you to say, 'OK, I've got it.' A lyricist has to manufacture depth, so the listener gets an idea the song is offering profound thoughts when it may be doing nothing of the sort. It's a bluff, really, but it's an honorable bluff."

It was clear to Kretzmer that Fenton was writing poetry. With the deadline looming, Kretzmer needed to know if Fenton would take instruction in lyric writing because "we didn't have time to play around." He made some discreet inquiries and learned that Fenton was a writer "who will fight for every word." Kretzmer said to Mackintosh, "I am going to do it, but I am going to do it on my own. He who travels fast travels alone."

Mackintosh agreed. Fenton was out. Kretzmer was now the English lyricist of *Les Misérables*.*

In February 1985, Kretzmer took a leave of absence from the *Daily Mail* and holed up in his apartment in Basil Street near Harrods, an apartment he took over from his friend John Cleese. He went to work on *Les Misérables*.

"I would sleep the morning away, and start writing at noon and work to two or three in the morning," he recalled. "Time ceased to have any meaning. I had five months to write lyrics that rhymed and scanned. Important songs like 'I Dreamed a Dream' and 'Castle on a Cloud' needed English lyrics. Other songs, 'Bring Him Home,' for instance, hadn't even been conceived yet when the cast started rehearsals in August."

"Bring Him Home," protagonist Jean Valjean's eleven o'clock number in the second act, gave Kretzmer more trouble than anything else in the show. It was meant to be about the rage and sexual jealousy Val-

---

* Fenton had a good contract, and has made millions from the success of *Les Misérables*. Several years after the show opened, Fenton self-published a book of poems about the Philippines called *Manila Envelope*. He advertised it in the *Evening Standard*, offering it for twelve pounds. Kretzmer sent in the mail order. The book arrived with a handwritten note from Fenton: "Dear Herbert, Thanks for the moola!" "We were all making too much money by then," said Kretzmer. "More money than was good for us."

jean feels toward Marius, with whom Cosette has fallen in love. Kretzmer wanted an agitated melody to reflect Valjean's fractured state of mind. But Claude-Michel Schönberg turned in "a wistful stately little tune," Kretzmer recalled. It was wrong for that moment in the show, but it did show off the gorgeous Irish tenor of Colm Wilkinson, who was playing Valjean. The creators tried to figure out what to do with the stately tune late one night in Kretzmer's Basil Street flat. As he was leaving, John Caird remarked, "It sounds like a prayer to me."

"I thought, of course it is—it is a prayer!" Kretzmer said. "It doesn't have to be about sexual agitation. It's about the soul of the man, his altruism. He loves the girl, the girl has fallen in love with another man, so he will transfer his love, his protective love, to the other man. 'Bring Him Home.'"

Kretzmer wrote the lyrics—three-note phrases, "God on high/ Hear my prayer/In my need"—between one and three in the morning "after weeks and weeks of total anguish on my part," he said.

There was much more anguish to come.

Kretzmer sat through the first run-through of *Les Misérables* at the Barbican in August and "my heart sank to my boots," he said. The lumbering show lasted nearly four hours. "Overplotted" and "interminable" were the words roiling in Kretzmer's head. "Disaster was staring us in the face," he said. "We'd really bought it this time."

Kretzmer wasn't alone in thinking *Les Misérables* would never make it. The Shuberts arrived in London to check out an early performance of Mackintosh's latest musical. Everybody but Phil Smith hated it.

"I liked the music, and I thought it was very effective," Smith recalled. I told Bernie, and he said, 'Phil, have you lost your mind?'"

Mackintosh was surprised he did not hear from Jacobs after the Shuberts saw *Les Misérables*.

"They came on a Thursday, I heard nothing. The following Monday, I got through to their office in New York," Mackintosh said.

"Why didn't I hear from you in London?" Mackintosh asked.

"Cameron, you know I love you," Jacobs replied. "Obviously, you just have to move on."

"Pardon? So you didn't like *Les Misérables*."

"Cameron, we think it's a pile of shit."

Les Misérables opened at the Barbican on October 8, 1985, to blistering reviews—"witless and synthetic entertainment" (the *Observer*); "the reduction of a literary mountain to a dramatic molehill" (*Sunday Telegraph*); "Les Glums" (*Daily Mail*). A panel of literary critics on the BBC reviewed the show as well. "You'd have thought we'd stuffed a stinking fish up their noses," said Kretzmer. "They could barely contain their disgust."

The day the reviews came out, Mackintosh hosted a luncheon for the creators at the offices of his ad agency, Dewynters, in Mayfair. It was supposed to be celebratory—everyone was given a bottle of champagne with a *Les Misérables* label on it—but the mood was gloomy. Mackintosh had to make a crucial decision that afternoon. He'd secured the Palace Theatre, which was owned by Andrew Lloyd Webber, for a nonrefundable fee of fifty thousand pounds. If he didn't move the show, he was out the deposit, plus the $450,000 he'd already invested.

"I remember Cameron running from room to room, agitated, not knowing what to do," Kretzmer said. "And then he came into lunch covered in sunshine. He was beaming. 'We're coming in!' he said. 'We're coming in!'"

Before making his decision Mackintosh had called the Barbican box office to see what ticket sales were like.

"I don't know how you got through," the box office treasurer said. "We've never had a morning like this at the Barbican. We've sold five thousand tickets. Things are going crazy here."

The public had spoken—and Mackintosh had the public's taste.

Les Misérables opened in New York on March 12, 1987, after a sold-out run in Washington, D.C., at the Kennedy Center, which, because the Shuberts had passed on coproducing, became one of Mackintosh's American partners. But the Shuberts did secure it for one of their theaters, the Broadway, where it racked up the largest pre-opening night advance in Broadway history—$11 million, double that for *Cats*.

On his way into the theater on opening night, Mayor Koch said to Leslie Bennetts of the *New York Times*, "I expect it to be the best show I've ever seen."

Mackintosh threw a lavish party at the Park Avenue Armory. Schoenfeld came over to his table, beaming. "Cameron, you are a genius," he said. "What you have done to turn what you had in London into this glorious Broadway hit is phenomenal. The changes you've made are extraordinary!"

Mackintosh replied, "I've made no changes at all other than take ten minutes out of it. It's exactly the same show you both thought was a pile of shit."

In the summer of 1984 Andrew Lloyd Webber was walking down Fifth Avenue when he came to the Strand bookstalls at Fifty-Ninth Street. He browsed for a bit, picking up a worn copy of Gaston Leroux's 1910 thriller, *The Phantom of the Opera*. A year before, a producer had approached Lloyd Webber's new wife, Sarah Brightman, about appearing in a musical adaptation of the book. It was being staged at a small theater in London, and Lloyd Webber and Cameron Mackintosh went to check it out. They didn't think much of it. It was silly and a little camp. A friend, though, suggested that the story of the disfigured Phantom and his love for a beautiful young opera singer might make a musical romance, suitable to Lloyd Webber's gift for soaring melody. Lloyd Webber didn't think so, but the idea of writing a romantic musical began to take hold. He'd never read Leroux's novel but with an afternoon to kill, he bought the book and read it in his hotel room. "It was a very confused book," he said, "some of it sort of a detective story, some of it sort of a horror story. But the thing that struck me is this big love story going through it."

That night, at a dinner for Tony Award nominees at the Plaza Hotel, Lloyd Webber ran into Hal Prince, who had directed *Evita*. The dinner was dull and at one point Lloyd Webber said to Prince, "I think we ought to get out of here and go have a drink somewhere, don't you?" They ducked out, and over a glass of wine, Lloyd Webber said he'd just read *The Phantom of the Opera* and thought it might make a musical.

"Go on," said Prince.

"But Hal, it's not for you," Lloyd Webber said. "It's high romance. You don't do high romance."

Lloyd Webber was right: Prince was famous for his association with

Stephen Sondheim, whose musicals—*Company, Follies, A Little Night Music*—cast a cynical eye on relationships.

But Prince surprised Lloyd Webber. "I've been wanting to do a romantic musical for years," he said. "If you finish this thing, play it to me. I'm in." Many years later Prince would say, "There hadn't been a romantic musical in years. Everybody thinks musicals are romantic, but you had to go back to *South Pacific*. And Andrew and I both worship *South Pacific*. I wanted to do it right away."

Lloyd Webber returned to London and, working with lyricist Richard Stilgoe, with whom he had written *Starlight Express*, a musical about toy trains, started sketching in *The Phantom of the Opera*. He would write it for Sarah Brightman, who had a gorgeous soprano voice. Some of it was written in London, some of it at his house in the south of France on a white Yamaha piano.

In June 1985, Lloyd Webber, working with designer Maria S. Björnson, produced the first act of *Phantom* at his annual Sydmonton Festival. It was, as always, a jolly occasion, attended by the Shuberts and the Nederlanders. They were there to see what the man who had written *Cats* was up to next.

The premiere of the first act of *The Phantom of the Opera* took place at a church on the property that Lloyd Webber had converted to a theater. Björnson had rigged up a little chandelier that came down at the climactic moment. She also built a boat in which the Phantom, played there by Colm Wilkinson, ferried Christine, the woman he is obsessed with, to his underground lair.

The reaction to the presentation was mixed. Bernie Jacobs liked what he saw. He called Phil Smith in New York the next day and said, "This looks like a hell of a show." But Lloyd Webber was not pleased. The show lacked the high romance for which he was aiming. A retooling was necessary, probably with someone other than Stilgoe, who was fast and clever but, according to Lloyd Webber biographer Michael Walsh, had no feel for romance.[6]

Lloyd Webber invited Prince to Sydmonton, but the director was at his summer home in Majorca. He had the score and the script, neither of which impressed him. Later, Lloyd Webber sent him a tape of the Sydmonton presentation.

"Well, there was this little chandelier, and the audience had the time of its life laughing at it," he said. "That's not the point of what I thought we were going to do. I would not like to clock the laughs in *Phantom of the Opera*, if you know what I mean."

Prince decided to go to Paris and visit the Opéra itself for inspiration. "I knew a lot of people there, and they couldn't have been nicer," he said. "They took me all over the place. They took me to the roof, and I straddled [the sculptures] on a windy day." The opera house was built over a subterranean lake. Prince went down to take a look at it. "I dropped a coin through a grate and I heard a *tink*. That was wonderful."

Prince began researching the history of the opera house, its architecture, the kinds of operas that were performed there during Leroux's time, the scenic designs, the special effects. He wanted to use as many authentic Victorian stage special effects in the show as possible. He envisioned trapdoors, curtains, candelabras, and, of course, that mysterious lagoon beneath the opera house.

Back in New York that fall, Prince got a call from Cameron Mackintosh inviting him to breakfast. Prince arrived with a folder bulging with his research on the opera house. Before the coffee arrived Mackintosh said, "I'm sorry, but you can't direct the show. It must be an English director. We're going with Trevor."

Prince picked up his papers and said, "I'm not going to have any breakfast." Back at his office, he told his assistant, "Put all these in a file. They'll be back."

Trevor Nunn was, in the 1980s, the most sought-after director in the world. He had staged *Nicholas Nickleby*, *Cats*, and, London's newest sensation, *Les Misérables*. Prince, though a Broadway legend, had not had a hit since *Evita* in 1979. His track record of late was abysmal: *Merrily We Roll Along*, *A Doll's Life*, *Play Memory*, *End of the World*. All had closed soon after opening. Mackintosh wanted Nunn. Complicating matters, Nunn had started work on a new Lloyd Webber show—*Aspects of Love*—before Lloyd Webber shelved it to work on *Phantom*. Nunn was annoyed to hear some of the *Aspects* tunes recycled for *Phantom* at Sydmonton.[7]

A power game was now playing out. With the success in London of *Les Misérables*, Mackintosh had established himself independently of Lloyd Webber. But he knew *Phantom* was a good property, and he did not want to let it go. Lloyd Webber could produce *Phantom* himself, but he'd had his biggest success with Mackintosh, who was turning *Cats* into a worldwide sensation.

In the end, the composer defeated the producer. "I wanted Hal because I thought he had the showmanship to stage it," Lloyd Webber said. "Trevor would have intellectualized the whole thing."

Nunn was out, Prince back in. By this point, Lloyd Webber had a reputation for switching book writers, lyricists, and directors almost on a whim. Don Black, who was in and out of several Lloyd Webber shows, joked, "You have to admire Andrew. If you don't, you're fired."

Prince came back in with a price. He negotiated a royalty from the show of 2.55 percent, much higher than most directors receive.[8] And if the show moved to New York, Prince had theater approval.

On that little clause would turn tens of millions of dollars—for the Shuberts.

Lloyd Webber spent the better part of 1986 retooling *Phantom*. He found a young lyricist, Charles Hart, who could write romantic lyrics. They came up with "The Music of the Night," whose sensuous melody Lloyd Webber had used for a song called "Married Man" in his shelved *Aspects of Love*. Put to Hart's lyrics—"Turn your face away / from the garish light of day"—it became the most romantic song in the show, one of the most romantic songs in musical theater history.

Colm Wilkinson was unavailable to play the Phantom because he was committed to *Les Misérables*. Sarah Brightman suggested a friend, Michael Crawford. Best known in England as a comic actor, Crawford was a classically trained singer. He was also agile, charismatic, and handsome (though his face would be covered by a mask).

The early previews of *Phantom* at Her Majesty's Theatre in October 1986 were choppy. Technical issues, such as the falling chandelier, had to be worked out. But it was obvious from the first preview that the audience adored the show. Women especially were falling for Crawford's sensitive, childlike Phantom. At the box office, the show started off slowly—*Chess* was the big draw that season. But by opening night, with the town buzzing about the show, there was nearly $2 million in the till.

The Shuberts flew to London to attend the opening. That morning, Jacobs and Smith met Cameron Mackintosh for breakfast at a sidewalk café in Mayfair. Mackintosh wanted to know if the Majestic Theatre in New York was available.

"You have the theater," Jacobs told him. *42nd Street* was there, but Jacobs would move it out for *The Phantom of the Opera*.

Mackintosh knew about Jacobs's illness, that his memory was not what it once was. "Are you sure I have the Majestic, Bernie?" he repeated several times. Then he turned to Smith for confirmation. "You have the theater, Cameron," Smith said. "It's the perfect place for the show."

"Thank you," Mackintosh said. "I'd love to linger, but I have a lot to do today. See you tonight!"

The opening night audience adored the show, giving it a ten-minute standing ovation.[9] The reviews, as usual for a Lloyd Webber show, were mixed. But the reviews were irrelevant. *Phantom* already was on its way to becoming the most successful show in the West End.

Jacobs and Smith enjoyed the show tremendously. They knew the Shuberts stood to make a fortune from it at the Majestic. But something nagged at Smith. At the opening night performance he spotted James H. Binger in the audience. Binger, the head of the Honeywell Corporation, owned the five Broadway theaters not controlled by the Shuberts or the Nederlanders. They were bundled together in a company called Jujamcyn, an amalgam of the names of his children—Judith, James, and Cynthia. Except for the St. James on West Forty-Fourth Street, they were not the most desirable houses on Broadway. Jujamcyn never posed much of a threat to the Shuberts or the Nederlanders. Binger attended the opening with Dick Wolf, who ran Jujamcyn. Smith thought their presence was odd.

"I couldn't figure it out," he said. "They were not the type of guys you normally saw at these type of events in London."

He'd find out why soon enough.

• • •

Back in New York, construction began at the Majestic. The basement of the theater had to be dug out to accommodate the candelabras that rise from the stage as the Phantom ferries Christine to his lair. The construction cost would total more than $1 million, but it would be worth it. *The Phantom of the Opera* looked like it would run a long, long time.

And then Jacobs got a phone call from Jeremy Gerard at the *Times*. Gerard told him he had it on good authority that Mackintosh was taking *The Phantom of the Opera* to the Martin Beck Theatre (now the Al Hirschfeld), which was owned by Jujamcyn. Jacobs was shocked. "Don't write that story because it's not true. We have the show." Gerard did not back down. He had a quote from Mackintosh to the effect that as the Beck, at twelve hundred seats, was smaller than the Majestic (1,655 seats), it was more suitable to the intimacy of *Phantom*, which in London was still running at Her Majesty's Theatre, one of the West End's smallest houses.

Jacobs paused and then said to Gerard, "You know, Cameron is negotiating with me through you."

True enough, Gerard conceded. But the story was a good one, and he wanted a comment. "I disagree that the Majestic isn't right for the show" was all Jacobs would say.

Jacobs had an affectionate nickname for Mackintosh. He called him "the Wooden Spoon" because Mackintosh always liked to stir the pot. But this time the Wooden Spoon had stirred too much. Jacobs was furious. He summoned the producer to his office for a meeting with him and Phil Smith.

They sat around a coffee table, Mackintosh nervous, fiddling with the bric-a-brac on the table.

"What are you trying to do to us, Cameron?" Jacobs demanded.

"You have to understand, Bernie," he said, "this is a delicate show. It needs an intimate theater. The Majestic is too big."

Jacobs and Smith disagreed, but Mackintosh stood his ground. They went around and around until Jacobs, tired, said, "Enough. We'll talk to you later, Cameron." A few days later, they met with Mackintosh again in Washington, D.C., at the Willard Hotel for the pre-Broadway opening of *Les Misérables*. Again, they went around and around. This time Schoenfeld was with them, pressuring Mackintosh, too. But the producer would not budge. The Majestic was too big for *Phantom*, he insisted. Schoenfeld, furious, stormed out of the room. Phil Smith continued the debate until Jacobs said, "Enough, Phil. Forget it. Just forget it."

Talking about his decision to go to the Martin Beck many years later, Mackintosh said, "Maria [Björnson] and I were following an artistic impulse of the show. We were acutely aware that the intimacy of Her Majesty's Theatre in London was part and parcel to the original success of the show. I also remembered how well *Dracula* [starring Frank Langella] had worked at the Beck. The Majestic, at the time, looked like a sort of frumpy place where you'd hold a bar mitzvah. And it had a huge overhang from the balcony. About fifty percent of the audience in the orchestra would not be able to see the chandelier, which had become an icon. Maria and I were driven by art."

And money. As the Shuberts later found out, Jujamcyn offered Mackintosh a fantastic deal—he could have the Martin Beck rent-free until *Phantom* recouped.

Jimmy Nederlander also made a play for the show. He called up his old friend Hal Prince and asked him to take a look at the New Amsterdam Theatre on Forty-Second Street. Nederlander had picked it up in 1982 in a sweetheart deal with the city. As part of the deal, he agreed to restore it, but the theater was in such bad shape—there were mushrooms growing on seats—that the cost of restoration was beyond Nederlander's means. The theater sat empty for years, killing Nederlander in real estate taxes. He begged Prince to take a look at it for *Phantom*. If he could get the show, he could raise the money to refurbish the theater.

Prince did, and then sent Nederlander a note. The New Amsterdam would have been "ideal" for *Phantom*, he wrote. "But there's no way that I would go near Forty-Second Street or ask anyone else to. . . . While we were waiting in front of the theater . . . on one side of us a drug sale took place and on the other, a young girl had her hands in her boyfriend's pockets—need I tell you why?" [10]

•   •   •

Although Jacobs, tired and weakened from his illness, had given up on securing *Phantom*, Smith had not. He began plotting, without telling Jacobs, how to get the show back. Mackintosh did not have sole control over the show. Lloyd Webber and Prince had something to say about its fate in New York. Smith tracked down Brian Brolly, a chipper Englishman who ran Lloyd Webber's Really Useful Group. Brolly had organized RUG—and owned 15 percent of it.[11] Smith learned that Brolly had just arrived in New York that morning on the Concorde. He knew Brolly's favorite hotel was the Ritz-Carlton on Central Park South. He phoned the hotel and got through.

"Hello, Phil!" said a jolly Brolly. "I've just walked in. I haven't taken care of the boy who brought up my bags yet. Hold on!"

Smith waited a moment and when Brolly was back on the line said, "Brian, I've got a big story to tell you. So take off your coat, sit down, and relax."

Smith talked about Mackintosh's decision to move the show to the Martin Beck. If Brolly knew about it, he didn't let on. Then Smith went through the numbers. The Majestic had 455 more seats than the Martin Beck and so the show could gross nearly a third more a week at the Majestic. Everyone expected *Phantom* to play to sold-out houses for the foreseeable future. Lloyd Webber and Really Useful would pocket a substantial amount of the weekly gross. If *Phantom* played the smaller theater, Lloyd Webber was leaving millions of dollars on the table.

"We've got to act fast," Smith said.

Brolly agreed to meet with Smith and some members of the *Phantom* production team that afternoon at the Majestic. Smith asked Peter Feller, who was building the set for the show, to attend. He knew Feller was Prince's favorite carpenter on Broadway. The Shuberts had dispatched Feller to London to look at *Phantom*. He could make the case the show would fit into the Majestic. Jacobs jumped into the act as well. He called Prince's lawyer to find out if Prince had theater approval in his contract. He did. "Don't let him sign anything until you know that you have the Majestic," Jacobs said.

After the meeting at the Majestic, Brolly told Smith, "Don't worry, Phil. We'll work this out."

A few days later, Lloyd Webber phoned Smith. He was in town and wanted to know if Smith would show him and Sarah Brightman the Majestic.

"Anytime you want," Smith said.

"How about in half an hour?" asked Lloyd Webber.

Smith met them in the lobby of the theater. There were hugs and kisses and plenty of "darlings." Smith led them through the theater, explaining its history, the dimensions of its stage, how the Shuberts were going to excavate the basement to accommodate the special effects. Brightman wanted to see the balcony. Smith escorted her up the stairs and then to the back wall of the balcony, pointing out that, even up in the nether reaches of the theater, every seat had a full view of the stage. "It's the most beautifully designed theater in New York," said Smith, laying it on as thick as possible. "There isn't a bad seat in this theater."

"Isn't this beautiful, Sarah?" asked Lloyd Webber.

"Yes, darling, it is," she replied. "But, darling, do you think . . . I worry . . . well, do you think it might be too big?"

Smith's heart sank. He could have murdered the little porcelain diva right there on the spot.

"Oh no, dear," Lloyd Webber said. "It's not too big at all. It's perfect. And can you believe that eight times a week, 'Some Enchanted Evening' was sung from that stage." Richard Rodgers. One of Lloyd Webber's favorite composers. *South Pacific.* One of his favorite shows. It opened at the Majestic on April 7, 1949, running 1,925 performances there and, later, at the Broadway.

As they left the theater, Smith said, "Andrew, we're delighted to have you in this theater. In fact, it would be wonderful to have you in all our theaters." Turning to Brightman, he added, "And I'd like to have you starring in all those shows, if that was possible, Sarah."

"They tugged on Andrew's heartstrings with *South Pacific* and Richard Rodgers," said Mackintosh with a laugh. "But in the end I saw the sense of it, financially. I still think the Beck would have been better, artistically, for the show. But at that point I had to leave my artistic conscience at the stage door."

Phantom played its 11,319th performance on April 12, 2015. The

455-seat difference between the Majestic and the Beck has added up
not to tens of millions of dollars, but hundreds of millions of dollars.*

There was one more hitch on the way to the New York opening of
Phantom. In the summer of 1987, Actors' Equity turned down Sarah
Brightman's application to star in the show. That "galaxy of lunatics,"
as Jacobs called the union, ruled that in New York, the role of Christine must be played by an American. Lloyd Webber was furious. If his
wife couldn't come to Broadway, *Phantom* wouldn't either. He'd take
it to Toronto and Japan instead. Quietly, over the summer, Jacobs and
Prince brokered a deal with Alan Eisenberg, the executive director of
Equity. Eisenberg knew how many jobs, American jobs, were at stake
with *Phantom*. After a lengthy negotiation, a deal was reached. Lloyd
Webber agreed that his next show, *Aspects of Love*, would open in London with an American in the lead.

Equity's attempt to ban Brightman from Broadway was the beginning of what would come to be called the British backlash. Lloyd Webber had three shows running in New York—*Cats*, *Song and Dance*, and
Starlight Express. Mackintosh had *Les Misérables*. Homegrown hits were
rare. The British had colonized Broadway.

The *New York Times* played up the backlash. Frank Rich had, by the
end of the 1980s, emerged as the most powerful theater critic in the
history of the newspaper. He was dubbed the "Butcher of Broadway"
because he could close a show in one night with a devastating review.
In an essay called THE EMPIRE STRIKES BACK, Rich took on the British invasion, bemoaning the end of the traditional American Broadway musical. "For the New York theater, the rise of London as musical-theater
capital is as sobering a specter as the awakening of the Japanese auto-
mobile industry was for Detroit," he wrote.[12] He pointed out that with
the near extinction on Broadway of the independent producer such

---

* Dick Wolf, the head of Jujamcyn Theaters, left the company after losing *Phantom* to the Shuberts. His
replacement was Rocco Landesman, who produced the musical *Big River*. At Jujamcyn, Landesman went
on to coproduce *The Who's Tommy*, *Into the Woods*, *Guys and Dolls*, and *Angels in America*. In 2009, Barack
Obama appointed him chairman of the National Endowment for the Arts. Dick Wolf returned to the box
office as treasurer of the Shubert Theatre until his retirement in 2014.

as David Merrick (who hadn't produced anything since *42nd Street*), it was inevitable that "shrewd English impresarios would fill the vacuum by default." But he noted that British choreographers were nowhere near as sophisticated as Broadway's best—Robbins, Champion, Fosse, and Bennett. Nor, he said, were British songwriters. For all his success, Lloyd Webber's work "can't yet be compared seriously with Broadway's best of any period." Thrusting the knife in farther, he added, "His music has declined sharply since he lost the lyrics of his original collaborator Tim Rice." Ominously for Rice, Rich said that ABBA's "musical wallpaper" for *Chess* is "indistinguishable from Mr. Lloyd Webber's output."

Lloyd Webber was the most successful composer in theater history. And now the most powerful critic in theater history had him in his sights. It would not help *The Phantom of the Opera* that Rich's favorite songwriter, Stephen Sondheim, had a new show, *Into the Woods*, scheduled to go head-to-head with Lloyd Webber's musical in the 1987–88 theater season.

Phantom rode into New York on a wave of publicity, including a cover profile of Lloyd Webber in *Time*, a distinction he shared with Richard Rodgers, Larry Hart, Cole Porter, Oscar Hammerstein II, and Leonard Bernstein. The publicity helped boost advance ticket sales to nearly $18 million by the January 26 opening night—$7 million more than that for *Les Misérables*. (There were some who believed the reason Mackintosh tried to stick *Phantom* into a smaller theater was so that its box office could never rival that of *Les Misérables*—a charge Mackintosh always denied.) Among the opening night crowd were Barbara Walters, Bill Blass, Beverly Sills, and Mayor Koch, who cheered the effect the success of the show was having not only on Broadway but also on New York itself. "First *Les Miz* and now this!" he told the *New York Times*.

The opening night party was held at the Beacon Theatre, a historic landmark that, with its hodgepodge of Greek, Roman, Renaissance, and rococo grandeur felt, as one partygoer said, "very Belle Époque." [13] Mackintosh and Lloyd Webber spent $250,000 on the bash. The buffet table was laden with caviar, boneless stuffed quail, and leek chiffonade en barquette.

Fred Nathan, the publicist for the show, had an early copy of Rich's review, which he hesitated to show Lloyd Webber. But the composer wanted to read it. Rich did not dismiss the show outright as he had *Starlight Express*, which he called a "bore on wheels." He admitted *Phantom* "showered the audience with fantasy and fun," and he praised Prince's direction, Björnson's sets, and Michael Crawford's performance. But Lloyd Webber got it in the neck—"a characteristic Lloyd Webber project—long on pop professionalism and melody, impoverished of artistic personality and passion." By this point, Rich's liberal political leanings had begun to creep into his reviews, and to him Lloyd Webber represented the gauche excesses of the Reagan and Thatcher years—"our own Gilded Age," Rich wrote. He ended the review hoping that, perhaps, both Lloyd Webber and the Reagan-era boom were "poised to go bust."

Lloyd Webber could probably have withstood Rich's attacks. He was used to them by now. But what incensed him was the critic's attack on his wife. She "reveals little competence as an actress," Rich wrote. "She . . . simulates fear and affection alike by screwing her face into bug-eyed, chipmunk-cheeked poses more appropriate to the Lon Chaney film version." Lloyd Webber erupted. "This is a man who knows nothing about love," he shouted. He then gossiped with the London reporters at his table about Rich's private life and his impending divorce from his wife.[14]

In the end, the review amounted to nothing. There were lines outside the Majestic box office the next day, the advance clicked past $20 million, and scalpers were getting $250 for a $50 ticket. As the *New York Times* reported, "there is virtually no such thing as a $50 ticket to *Phantom of the Opera*."[15]

Mackintosh took time out from counting the money that day to read a telegram from David Merrick, who had been at the opening night performance. "The torch," Merrick wrote to Mackintosh, "has passed from me to you."

At the Tonys that year, *Into the Woods* picked up awards for its book, by James Lapine, and Sondheim's score. But Broadway could not turn its nose up at *Phantom*, which was contributing to a noticeable uptick in attendance. It won the top prize that year—Best Musical—despite all the carping about "the British invasion."

• • •

Soon after the Shuberts swiped *Phantom* back from Jujamcyn Theaters, Schoenfeld and Jacobs sat down for an interview with Jeremy Gerard of the *Times*. The story was headlined SHUBERT STAGES A DRAMATIC (AND MUSICAL) COMEBACK.[16] Gerard noted the success of *Les Misérables*, the impending success of *Phantom*, and the fact that all the Shubert theaters were booked. Attendance was back up, and business was booming. But Jacobs discussed, for the first time in public, the illness that had robbed him of his memory. "The truth is, I went through a very bad period," he said. Gerard introduced the touchy subject of who would succeed Schoenfeld and Jacobs at Shubert one day, pointing out their ages—Jacobs, seventy; Schoenfeld, sixty-two. The company would be fine, they said, adding that the board had a succession plan in place should anything happen to them. Still, as Schoenfeld said, "Because of our own talents we brought to this period a lot of different qualities than [the original Shubert brothers] had. So when people say, what will happen in the next generation, I don't know that you can say there are any criteria out there. There's no business like this. Shubert is sui generis."

Schoenfeld and Jacobs used the piece in the *Times* to dispel rumors they had lost faith in their next project, a Broadway production of *Chess*. It would arrive in New York, they insisted, in the spring of 1988, yet another megamusical from London, though with the Shuberts producing.

Nunn was now fully in charge of the show. But he wanted to do his show, not Michael Bennett's. He wanted a new script and a new set. He brought in Richard Nelson, an American playwright who had an association with the Royal Shakespeare Company. "He was smart, satiric, bright, and contemporary," said Nunn. "It was generally agreed that Richard and I should work at the show and see what we came up with."

Bennett had envisioned a slick, cool, James Bond–like roller coaster of a production. Nunn and Nelson wanted to explore the characters, giving the show emotional depth. They made a major change: Florence, a Hungarian-born British citizen in the London production, would be a Hungarian-born American citizen for the New York version. This meant Paige was out. Nunn replaced her with his friend

Judy Kuhn, who had appeared in the Broadway production of *Les Misérables*.

Rice was furious. He had written *Chess* for Paige, his lover. And now Nunn tossed her overboard for, Rice and Paige heard, one of his girlfriends. Rumors appeared in New York and London gossip columns that Nunn and Kuhn were having an affair. They denied it, and the papers reprinted retractions. Nunn has never wavered in his denial.

Because of Nunn's other commitments, *Chess* had to adhere to a tight timetable, rehearsing in New York in February 1988 for an April opening at the Imperial Theatre. But around Christmastime Nunn "slipped out of contact," as *Vanity Fair* would put it in a story about the saga of *Chess*.[17] Nunn had a reputation for mysteriously dropping out of sight. His nickname, in London, was "Macavity"—"for when they reach the scene of the crime, Macavity's not there!" as T. S. Eliot wrote. And now, on the eve of a $6 million Broadway musical, Nunn had pulled a Macavity. The Shuberts panicked, and announced yet another postponement. The announcement smoked Nunn out of his hideaway, and a conference call was arranged for all the major *Chess* players—the Shuberts, Robert Fox, Rice, the ABBA boys, and Nunn, whose whereabouts were still a mystery. He was supposed to be in New York right after the holidays to start work on the show. But there were rumors he was in Australia, checking up on a production of *Les Misérables*.[18]

Rice took pleasure in baiting him during the call.

"Trevor, where are you?" he asked at one point.

Nunn ignored the question.

A little later Rice asked, "Trevor, if you look out of your window, what do you see at the moment?"

Nunn turned to the subject of the show's set.

"Trevor," Rice persisted, "if you look out of your window, can you see a kangaroo?"

Nunn finally admitted he was in Australia, adding that his plane had been diverted from London to New York by way of Australia.

There were expressions of disbelief. Finally, Jacobs asked for a firm commitment from Nunn to open *Chess* on Broadway in April.

"I will absolutely do the show," Nunn said.

As *Chess* started to take shape, Fox noticed a change at the Shubert

Organization. Production meetings had always taken in place in Jacobs's office. They now took place in Schoenfeld's.

"Jerry was taking over more of the responsibility of the stuff that Bernie used to do," said Fox. "Bernie wasn't the vibrant and powerful leader that he had previously been. He was diminished. He was protected by everybody and loved by everybody, but the power had shifted. Jerry was in full control of his faculties, and *Chess* became very much Jerry's first artistic endeavor as the boss."

And the whole enterprise would turn out to be, in Fox's words, "a fucking disaster from beginning to end."

The infighting began over the poster art. Nobody could agree on a logo or a design. Nancy Coyne and her team presented ideas, the final image to be decided on by a majority vote. But people kept switching sides, almost, it seemed to Fox, just to annoy someone else in the room. In the end, they settled on the silhouette of a couple holding hands and running against the backdrop of the Soviet and American flags. Later that was changed to the lead actor, Philip Casnoff, draped in the American flag, with the words "Yes! Chess!"

"Yes! Chess!—we were roundly criticized for that," recalled Rick Elice, who worked on the campaign. "We tried to build it around US versus USSR. Gorbachev had just come in. We tried to make it relevant. Nobody gave a fuck. We couldn't sell it."

"We never got anything close to 'Now and Forever' on *Chess*," said Nancy Coyne. "There was never anything that was distillable. There was never any central message that was coming out of it."

Nelson and Nunn's script was, in its attempt to deal with the Cold War, love affairs, infidelities, and the game of chess itself, a muddle. Rice and the ABBA boys grew despondent as the show went into rehearsal, but they did manage to write some new songs, including the fine ballad "Someone Else's Story."

"We felt very encouraged by that song," said Fox. "We thought it would add a fantastic new element to the story and we kind of all convinced ourselves that somehow the miracle was gonna happen. And then the moment you walked into the Imperial Theatre and saw these towers and how ugly the fucking production was, it was perfectly clear that the miracle was not going to happen."

Nunn and Robin Wagner's new set featured several moving towers resembling chess pieces that were operated by computers when "computers were in the dark ages," said Fox. But they never worked. "We ended up putting men inside of them, but because they couldn't see, they kept bumping into each other."

"The set was a nightmare," said Rice. "It looked like an underground car park. And there was one scene in an underground car park, and that scene looked great. But the rest of it didn't quite work."

Schoenfeld watched the first long, tortured preview, the color draining from his face. The color returned at the end of the show, but it was an angry red.

"You schmucks!" he screamed, his wrath turning on Nunn. He started firing off notes about the production, most of which Nunn ignored. Rice, dejected, began to withdraw from the scene. "Nineteen eighty-eight," he said, "was the worst year of my life. My father died, and I was almost broke because of the money I'd lost on *Nicholas Nickleby*." Ulvaeus and Andersson, meanwhile, started hiding out in Nancy Coyne's conference room. They couldn't face what was onstage and vowed never to do another musical.

The Shuberts were pressuring Nunn to cut the show, which was running over three hours. Nunn ignored their entreaties, doing his best to shield his hard-working actors from the offstage strife. But at the critics' preview in April, Nunn sensed they were in for some rough treatment. "I stood at the back of the theater and watched Frank Rich and his girlfriend talking and giggling through 70 percent of the show. So the writing was on the wall."

The opening night party took place at the United Nations in an atmosphere that was "like a morgue," said Fox. As the producer climbed into a limousine to go home, a press agent handed him Rich's review. He read it in the car and "started laughing like a lunatic, because if you're going to get a bad review, this one is it."

"Anyone who associates the game of chess with quiet contemplation is in for a jolt at *Chess*," Rich began. "For over three hours, the characters onstage at the Imperial yell at one another to rock music. The show is a suite of temper tantrums. . . . If contentiousness were drama, *Chess* would be at least as riveting as *The Bickersons*. That the evening has the theatrical consistency of quicksand—and the drab color scheme to match—can be attributed to the fact that the show's book . . . and lyrics . . . are about nothing except the authors' own pompous pretentions." As for the music, Rich said it was "a sometimes tuneful but always a characterless smorgasbord of mainstream pop styles." Rich administered the coup de grâce in the final sentence: "War is hell, and for this . . . trapped audience, *Chess* sometimes comes remarkably close."

Looking back on the review almost twenty-five years later, Nunn said, "I think that Frank Rich's dismissal of the score as Europop should be quoted in fifty years' time the way that somebody came out of *Guys and Dolls* and said, 'Not a tune in it.' It should be their shame forever. It's a disgrace, an absolute disgrace. *Chess* has the most extraordinary musical theater score."

Faced with an onslaught of bad reviews (Rich was not alone), the Shuberts did what they could to save the show. Schoenfeld was reluctant to close a musical that had become "near and dear to him," said Fox. They made a TV commercial, they took out billboards in Times Square, they changed the ads. To save $25,000 a week in overtime, they wanted to take twenty minutes out of the show after it opened.

At yet another contentious meeting, Schoenfeld pressed Nunn, who always dressed in jeans, a T-shirt, and sneakers, to spend a few more days in town cutting the show. "I can't," said Nunn. "I'm leaving for London and I have to go home and pack."

"Pack?" Tim Rice exclaimed. "What do you have to pack, Trevor? A T-shirt and another pair of sneakers?"

Nunn cut the show, but it didn't matter. The box office was collapsing. The Shuberts closed the show on June 25, 1988, at a loss of $6.2 million.

"*Chess* is one of the few shows I have not gotten over," Schoenfeld wrote in his memoir, *Mr. Broadway*.[19] For the next twenty years, he nursed plans for a revival. He even flew to Stockholm in 2002 to see a revised version.

The reviews were excellent.

Unfortunately, they were in Swedish.

Pick-a-Little, Talk-a-Little

C*hess* was painful, but Schoenfeld and Jacobs could, in the summer of 1988, console themselves with numbers released by the League of New York Theatres and Producers. Broadway raked in $253 million in the 1987–88 theater season, the highest take in its history. Attendance was on the rise again, up to 8.1 million, a 16 percent increase over the previous season.

The majority of the revenue came from the megamusicals—*Cats, Les Misérables, The Phantom of the Opera, Starlight Express.* Which led to carping that the nonmusical, American play was in trouble on Broadway. Plays were no longer profitable on Broadway, and the theater audience was being conditioned to buy the musical spectacle, some producers complained.

There was some truth in the charge. Plays didn't generate nearly the return of musicals. But that was always the case. And, looking back, the 1980s were hardly a terrible time for the straight play on Broadway. David Mamet, Harvey Fierstein, Wendy Wasserstein, David Henry Hwang, Lanford Wilson—all emerged as Broadway names in the eighties. Neil Simon reached his artistic high point with a trilogy of successful plays—*Brighton Beach Memoirs, Biloxi Blues,* and *Broadway Bound.* And August Wilson became a major figure in American literature with plays such as *Ma Rainey's Black Bottom, Joe Turner's Come and Gone,* and *Fences,* which won the Tony Award and the Pulitzer Prize in 1987.

Off Broadway was thriving as well, with the rise of companies such as Playwrights Horizons, Second Stage, the Manhattan Theatre Club, and Circle Repertory Company Lincoln Center, under the direction of Gregory Mosher, was producing such works as *The House of Blue Leaves*, *Swimming to Cambodia*, a hit revival of *Anything Goes*, *Sarafina!*, and *Six Degrees of Separation*. And the Public Theater, flush with profits from *A Chorus Line* and led by the indefatigable Joe Papp, remained the leading nonprofit theater in the country with a roster of shows that included *Cuba and His Teddy Bear*, *The Normal Heart*, *Aunt Dan and Lemon*, *The Colored Museum*, *Talk Radio*, *Plenty*, and *Serious Money*.

The Shuberts did not take the lead in producing many straight plays, but the foundation gave enormous amounts of money to non-profit theaters in New York and throughout the country. And when an Off-Broadway or regional theater hit moved to Broadway, the Shuberts often put up a substantial chunk of the money. They helped finance *Glengarry Glen Ross*, *The Heidi Chronicles*, *Master Harold . . . and the Boys*, *'night, Mother*, *A Day in the Death of Joe Egg*, *The Gin Game*, and *As Is*—and usually booked them into their theaters.

The Shuberts were making money in other ways as well. A significant source of income came from air rights. New York City land-marked most of the theaters in Times Square after the Morosco and Helen Hayes were torn down. The Shuberts and the Nederlanders objected. Landmarking meant they could not alter their buildings in any way—or use them as anything but legitimate theaters. To compensate the theater owners for these constraints, the city granted them the right to sell the air above their buildings to real estate developers. That didn't amount to much at first, but in the late eighties and early nineties, skyscrapers began sprouting up in Times Square. Developers paid the Shuberts and the Nederlanders millions of dollars for the right to build higher and higher.*

At the close of the eighties, Schoenfeld and Jacobs could, from their offices above the Shubert Theatre, look down on a thriving theatrical

---

*   Air rights in Times Square are even more valuable today. Between 2008 and 2014, the Shuberts made $50 million in air rights transfers, according to public records.

empire, much of which they built. Well, Jacobs could. Schoenfeld's office had no windows. He'd hired a designer to block up the window in his office and install soft lighting.

"You had no fucking idea what time of day it was in there," said an old producer.

Across Times Square at the Palace Theatre, Jimmy Nederlander was not in such good shape. He'd missed out on the British invasion, landing only Lloyd Webber's *Starlight Express* for the Gershwin Theatre. It was not destined to be *Cats* or *Phantom of the Opera*. His big show of 1988 was *Legs Diamond*, written by and starring Peter Allen as the famous gangster. It was a disaster.

He acquired the show in typical Nederlander fashion. Flying home from London on the Concorde, he found himself sitting opposite John Breglio.

"What the hell are you up to, John?" Nederlander asked. "What show you got for me?"

As it happened, Breglio was representing Allen and *Legs Diamond*. The idea of Peter Allen, who had once been married to Liza Minnelli, wrote "I Go to Rio!," and performed in a skin-tight gold lamé pantsuit, playing a brutal womanizing gangster from the Prohibition Era may not have seemed ideal casting to many producers.

But it didn't bother Nederlander.

"I love Peter Allen!" he said. "He's great. I had him at the Greek Theatre in Los Angeles. Did great business. I want to do his show."

"But, Jimmy, you don't know the music," said Breglio.

"It'll be good. I'll do it," said Nederlander.

They sketched out the deal for *Legs Diamond* on a Concorde cocktail napkin. Nederlander put up most of the $4.5 million production cost (with a bit thrown in by his friend George Steinbrenner, the owner of the New York Yankees) and booked the show into his gorgeous art deco Mark Hellinger on West Fifty-First Street.

There was trouble from the start. The choreographer, Michael Shawn, became ill, another victim of AIDS. Marvin Krauss, the general manager, fired him. Shawn sued the producers. The incident, which was picked up by the papers, was an embarrassment to Allen, who was a tireless fund-raiser in the fight against AIDS.

The show played an early preview on November 4, 1988—the night of the presidential election. George Bush defeated Michael Dukakis.

Jon Wilner, who devised the show's ad campaign, was standing at the back of the theater during the preview. An assistant company manager came up to him and said, "George Bush just won the election."

"That's terrible," said Wilner.

"Not as terrible as what's going on in here," the manager said.

The curtain went up at 8:00—and didn't come down on the first act until 10:30. At the intermission, there was an exodus from the Hellinger. But the next night, Harvey Fierstein, who'd been brought in to rewrite the script, found reason for optimism. "We must be getting much better," he said. "Only a hundred and fifty people walked out tonight."

The opening number was a big problem. No matter how it was configured, Peter Allen could not get entrance applause. Finally, the production team decided to have him ride down from the rafters on a huge Legs Diamond sign and sing a new number, "When I Get My Name in Lights." Nederlander spent another $15,000 on the sign. Allen, perched on the L, came down beaming and waving, and belted out the number. No applause. Charlene Nederlander, Jimmy's wife, leaned over to Fierstein and said, "For that, I could have had a bracelet."

Legs Diamond opened December 26, 1988, to scathing reviews. The show still had a hefty advance sale, so Nederlander decided to fight for it. He told Allen, "You gotta sing 'I Go to Rio!' at the end of the show."

Allen looked at him as though he'd lost his mind.

"No, no," Nederlander protested. "They're coming to see Peter Allen. They don't like the show. Show's no good. Just do the show in the first act and come out in the second act and be Peter Allen and sing your songs. Make it a concert. It'll save the show!"

Allen demurred. After the show burned through its advance, Nederlander closed it in February 1989. Allen was devastated. He'd worked for years on *Legs Diamond* and he loved performing on Broadway.

Within a year, he was diagnosed with AIDS, dying in 1992 at forty-eight.*

The failure of *Legs Diamond* put Nederlander in a precarious position. He needed money. And so he leased the Hellinger to the Times Square Church, a nondenominational, fundamentalist church, for five years for $1 million a year. "There's no shows being produced," he told the *Times*.¹ "We have to keep the theaters filled. We don't have anything on the horizon to put in the theater."

That summer, while vacationing in Monaco, Nederlander had a stroke. His empire was adrift, its founder in a rehabilitation center, its finances shaky. "It was a difficult time," said Kathleen Raitt, who was in charge of investor relations for the Nederlander Organization. "We were loyal to Jimmy, but it was understood that if we found another job, we should take it."

The Hellinger Theatre never came back on the market. In 1991, after backing yet another flop, *Nick & Nora*, Nederlander sold the theater to the Times Square Church for $17 million.

The sale shored up his company, but outraged Broadway. How could Nederlander take the Hellinger—once home to *My Fair Lady*, *Jesus Christ Superstar*, *On a Clear Day You Can See Forever*, and *Sugar Babies*—off the market? And it wasn't as though he couldn't sell it to other theater people. Though Jacobs thwarted Michael Bennett's attempt to become part owner of the Hellinger, the Shuberts would have snapped up such a prime musical house. Cameron Mackintosh and Andrew Lloyd Webber might have bought it.

Years later, asked why he didn't make a deal with a theater person to keep the Hellinger as a legitimate theater, Nederlander said, "Why sell to a competitor?"

As Jimmy Nederlander struggled to recover from his stroke, Bernie Jacobs was battling his own health problems. He never fully recovered from the transient global amnesia he'd suffered in 1986. And though no

---

* Allen's reputation as a performer and songwriter was resurrected in 2003 in the Broadway musical *The Boy from Oz*, starring Hugh Jackman. The show opened to tepid reviews, but Jackman turned it into the Hugh Jackman show, making it the hottest ticket in town and launching his reputation as Broadway's most sought-after leading man.

one close to him would ever confirm it—and to this day deny it—many in the theater world suspected that the global amnesia was cover for a stroke.

"Bernie was never the same after his 'incident,' which is how everyone referred to it," said a veteran producer. "They [the Shuberts] tried to cover it up—they never discussed it—but it was obvious if you spent any time with him. He would repeat the same story three times. He could tell you all about J. J. Shubert and David Merrick, but he couldn't tell you what he had for lunch that day. He was a great man. He was just not the same."

Which is not to say he didn't have flashes of his old, cunning self. Nancy Coyne, the ad executive, had grown close to Jacobs over the years, seeing him as a father figure in a business dominated by tough men. (She keeps a picture of Jacobs on her desk.) In 1987, Dewynters, the London-based ad agency that had designed the marketing campaigns for *Cats*, *Les Misérables*, and *The Phantom of the Opera*, opened an office in New York. Coyne handled Cameron Mackintosh and Andrew Lloyd Webber shows in New York, but the founder of Dewynters, Anthony Pye-Jeary, was one of their closest friends. He could easily steal their shows away.

Jacobs called Coyne. "Do you know about this?" he asked.

Coyne was in the dark. "What should I do, Bernie? Anthony, Cameron, and Andrew are best friends. This is really bad for my agency."

"You're doing good work on *Les Miz*," Jacobs said. "Just keep giving Cameron ideas he can't live without because I'll tell you one thing about Cameron—he loves his shows more than he loves any person."

Coyne held off Dewynters for six months before they pulled up stakes and left New York.

Jacobs took a liking to another one of the few women in this male-dominated business. Bright, young, energetic, and pretty, Susan Lee landed a job at the League of New York Theatres and Producers looking after producers and presenters around the country, who collectively were known as "the road." The road had been in the doldrums throughout the seventies and early eighties but was starting to pick up again with demand for hits such as *Cats*, *Les Misérables*, and *The Phantom of the Opera*. Lee's title was Director of Road Resources, "which sounded like I was in construction," she said. She thought the term "road," used by New York producers, was patronizing. She believed her constituents should take a more active part in the League, which until then had been dominated by New York producers, mainly the Shuberts. She developed a list of proposals to build up the road, including changing "Road Resources" to "National Touring Council."

Whenever Jacobs was at the League, he dropped by to see Lee. One day, she outlined the proposals she planned to present at the next board meeting. "That's the dumbest idea I've ever heard," Jacobs said. Lee defended her case against Jacobs's lawyer-like interrogation. Phil Smith was in the room, laughing. She spent the next several days strengthening her arguments against Jacobs's objections. When she made her proposal to the League, nobody in the room responded. Then Jacobs spoke up and said, "I think we should agree to this." Everybody agreed. After the meeting, he took Lee aside and said, "I knew what you were going to say. Remember, always know where everybody stands when you walk into a room."

Lee noticed something else about the way Schoenfeld and Jacobs conducted themselves at League meetings. They always sat opposite each other at the conference table to "balance out the power," she said. "And the nonverbal communication between the two of them was a sign language unto itself."

Much of Jacobs's power stemmed from his vast industry grapevine. He had informants everywhere. He knew what was going on at every show, production office, and theatrical agency. One of his best sources was Fred Nathan, the powerful press agent. Nathan was also close to Frank Rich, a power on Broadway, of course, but also a power at the *Times*. Nathan and Rich both grew up devouring *Variety* and attending Broadway shows. And they shared a love, bordering on an obsession, with the musicals of Stephen Sondheim. As Rich's influence and celebrity increased in the eighties, he seldom socialized with theater people to avoid conflicts of interest. He acknowledged his friendship with Wendy Wasserstein but never reviewed her plays. His friendship with Nathan, not unusual since Nathan's job was to look after the press, was much discussed on Broadway.

"Fred bragged about it at the office," said one of Nathan's former employees.

"Fred fed on the fact that he was close to Frank," said Josh Ellis, one of Nathan's best friends.

"The first time I ever met Frank Rich was at Fred's apartment," said Rick Elice. "Fred called me up and said, 'I'm having a party!' And I went over to Fred's and I thought, Oh, my God, Frank Rich is at Fred Nathan's party! Oh my God! They were very close. Very."

Rich and Nathan often spoke at night on the phone, discussing shows and trading gossip. In the morning, at 8:30, Nathan would call Bernie Jacobs with the "morning report"—some of it from Rich. First, though, he'd call Josh Ellis at 7:30 and rehearse the items, selecting the best bits for Jacobs. Nathan and Ellis called their conversations "Mary in the Morning." The name derived from a story they'd both heard about Mary Martin. The Broadway star once had a woman fired from a show, though she left no fingerprints. The woman went to Martin and said, "I can't believe they're going to fire me." Martin said she would have a word with the producers, which of course she never did. She then told the woman, "They won't move, but I'm going to throw you a party!"

Every gossipy story in which someone got it in the neck usually ended with Ellis and Nathan saying, "We're just going to throw you a party!"

They developed a set of criteria for gossip. "First, it had to be the juiciest piece of gossip," Ellis said. "Second, it had to come from the best source. If it came from the horse's mouth—the person who was in the room—that was good. Third, it had to be up-to-date. God forbid that you told someone at 8:03 what had happened at 8:00 and there was a new wrinkle. Wrong! And how dare you spread old gossip? You had to be the first recipient of it. This was a big Shubert thing. They had to be first. And, finally, exclusivity. 'I'm glad you're telling me, but don't tell anyone else.' Now that's a really heavy burden for a piece of gossip."

Nathan, who had more than a touch of *Sweet Smell of Success*'s Sid-

ney Falco about him, skillfully deployed the information he gleaned
from his sources to become close to Jacobs and the Shuberts. Frank
Rich may not have known it at the time, but whatever he told Fred
Nathan went straight to Bernie Jacobs.*

As Jacobs once said of Nathan, "A terrific piece of manpower."

Until it all came crashing down.

There was, in 1990, plenty of theater gossip, and much of it was about
Frank Rich. A New York celebrity, he appeared regularly on Don Imus's
popular radio show. He even merited a *60 Minutes* profile. Theater people respected his talent but they came to resent his power. Few would
speak openly against him, but they whispered about him behind his
back. Much of the gossip was petty and wrong—and Rich was quick
to demand retractions.

But every now and then it hit the mark. When Rich collaborated
on a screenplay about Broadway with his friend Rafael Yglesias, the
novelist and screenwriter, copies of it circulated around Shubert Alley.
Now the reviewer was being reviewed. And the notices were not good.
The screenplay, *Opening Night*, was a feeble attempt to be a contemporary *All About Eve*.

But instead of such sparkling lines as "Fasten your seatbelts, it's
going to be a bumpy night," the best Rich and Yglesias could do was:

"I don't love you. It's just a sexual thing—"

"What a pity . . . and I only wanted to talk about Bernard Shaw."

Page Six and other gossip columns got hold of the screenplay and
poked fun at Rich's attempt to be Joseph L. Mankiewicz.†

The gossip items about *Opening Night* were fun, but they weren't
nearly as much fun as the talk swirling around Rich's love life. In
1990 he had taken up with a young, aggressive magazine columnist
named Alex Witchel. A graduate of the Yale School of Drama, Witchel
worked for the Shuberts when she first came to New York as the house

---

* The flow of gossip went both ways. Sometimes, when Nathan was on the phone with Jacobs, he would
conference in Rich without telling Jacobs. "He'd tell Frank not to make a sound," said one of Nathan's
associates. "Bernie had no idea Frank was on the line."

† *Opening Night* went into turnaround, which is Hollywood slang for limbo. It has never been seen again.
I still have my copy, however—which I will put on eBay when I'm broke.

manager of the Shubert Theatre, where *A Chorus Line* was playing. She also worked for Papp at the Public Theater. She then switched to journalism, landing junior editorial positions at *Elle* and *Mirabella*. In 1989, she started writing a theater column for *7 Days*, a stylish, gossipy magazine that covered New York. Its editor was Adam Moss, who would go on to edit the *New York Times Magazine* and *New York*. Witchel's column roiled Broadway. Having worked in the theater, she had excellent contacts and a killer's taste for juicy behind-the-scenes gossip. The *New York Times* had a Friday theater column, but it was genteel, most of its items spoon-fed by press agents.

Witchel dished. Her biggest exclusive was about Frank Rich. After he panned the Broadway production of David Hare's *The Secret Rapture*—which he'd raved about after seeing the London production—Hare requested to meet him. Rich turned him down, and Hare responded with a blistering letter. "Your moral position is, from the outside, that of Orson Welles in *The Third Man*," Hare wrote. "You are happy to stay up on the Ferris wheel and stop the little dots from moving. But nothing will persuade you to come down and look the little dots in the eye."

Whenever Rich was asked about his power, he would answer glibly, "I don't close plays, producers close plays." Hare found that dishonest. "No one," he wrote, "could write drama criticism for the *New York Times* without being aware that every word they wrote affected the livelihood of hundreds of people, and the vitality of the form from which they make their living." Rich's reviews, Hare wrote, had become "gratuitously abusive . . . a disfiguring note of personal cruelty has entered your writing." Rich's make-or-break power was driving serious writers away from Broadway, leaving only "insipid comedies and mindless musicals." Hare concluded, writing, "You're Emperor of all you survey. Only thing is, there isn't much left, except ashes."

Joe Papp, who produced *The Secret Rapture*, gave Hare's letter to Richard Hummler at *Variety*, which ran it under the immortal headline RUFFLED HARE AIRS RICH BITCH. (Rich never liked Hummler, sneeringly referring to him as "Charlie Brown.") Broadway was, as the gossip columns would say, "atwitter." Hare had taken on the most powerful drama critic in the world, and his letter spoke for many whose shows Rich had destroyed.

Some of Hare's criticisms could be batted away. The *New York Times'* drama critic, no matter who he was, would always be powerful. And a critic should never hedge his opinions because of that power. Rich was the most powerful critic in the paper's history. But that was because he was a lively writer, had the taste of his readers, and was generally on the mark with his judgments. But Hare had hit on something. Rich's writing had become brutal. Bad reviews gave him a chance to show off. As one of his colleagues said, "When Frank wrote a killer review, you could practically see the blood dripping from his mouth." *

Rich responded with a pointed letter of his own—which he gave to Witchel. She ran Hare's and Rich's letters side by side in *7 Days*. Broadway was gripped by the Rich-Hare feud. Not long after, Witchel began attending shows with Rich. When *7 Days* folded in the spring of 1990, she was hired by the *Times* as a theater reporter. That's when rumors of a relationship began to swirl. By fall, Witchel had taken over the Friday theater column, muscling aside veteran *Times* writer Enid Nemy. Al Hirschfeld, who for years had illustrated the column with his drawings, was pushed out as well. Photographs replaced his caricatures, much to the dismay of readers who enjoyed hunting for the Ninas (the name of his daughter) he hid in his drawings.

The changes made clear to Broadway that there was now only one star of the Friday theater column—Alex Witchel. She clawed her mark quickly. There were no more nice little items about casting. No more sweet interviews with up-and-coming performers. Witchel offered delicious—and vicious—backstage gossip, written with a sting. If Amanda Plummer threw a fit about her wig, it became the lead item in Witchel's column. Broadway was riveted, and appalled. Witchel had basketfuls of its dirty laundry, and she was airing it in the most powerful newspaper in the world.

---

* Hare thinks his letter had an effect on Rich's writing. He says, "Producers used to ring me up and say, 'You've made Frank sentimental. All he talks about now is his love of the theater. I think we preferred him mean.'"

She wielded her power with Walter Winchell–like tactics. Press agents who fed her juicy items were awarded plugs for their shows. Those who didn't were frozen out of the column. The veteran producer Arthur Cantor once called her up with news of a new show he was producing Off Broadway. The item didn't interest her. "Take out an ad!" she snapped. A press agent phoned to tell her that Sid Caesar and Imogene Coca were going to re-create their old *Your Show of Shows* routines at Michael's Pub. "Well, I'm glad they're still walking, but it isn't news," she responded.

Above all, she demanded exclusives. When José Ferrer had to pull out of the play *Conversations with My Father* because he had been diagnosed with cancer, he gave the news to his old friend Army Archerd at *Variety*. The day the story appeared, Witchel called the show's press agent, Jeffrey Richards, and left a message on his answering machine. "If you ever do that again, Jeffrey, you are dead fucking meat," she said.[2]

Witchel's budding relationship with Rich began to seep into her column. If Rich liked a show, Witchel wrote glowing items about how well the box office was doing. If he panned it, she wrote about its problems backstage. Rich favorites—George C. Wolfe, William Finn, and, above all, Stephen Sondheim—were heralded as theater gods in her column. Those he didn't like got it in the neck. When Joe Papp was diagnosed with cancer in 1991, he handed over the reins of the Public Theater to avant-garde director JoAnne Akalaitis. Rich panned most of Akalaitis's productions, and she became Witchel's favorite target. The columnist hounded the director for her lack of administrative skills, her brusqueness with the Public's staff, and her selection of plays. Akalaitis had other detractors—and her tenure at the Public was rocky—but even theater people who didn't like her work were taken aback by the one-two punch she was getting from Rich and Witchel.*

The theater world whispered incessantly about the *Times'* new power couple, dubbing them the "Ceaușescus of Broadway." But no-

---

* The Public's board of directors fired Akalaitis in 1993. Her replacement, George C. Wofle, was a Rich-Witchel favorite.

body dared speak openly about the relationship and its effect on Broadway. If you crossed them, they'd hand you your head.

And then, in a final burst of diabolical genius, came David Merrick.

In November 1990, Merrick attempted a Broadway comeback with a revival, imported from the Goodspeed Opera House in Connecticut, of George and Ira Gershwin's *Oh, Kay!* Rich panned it, gleefully, as "a chintzy, innocuous slab of stock that is likely to leave more than a few theatergoers shrugging their shoulders and asking, 'Didn't I doze through that a couple of summers ago in a barn?'"

Witchel took a shot at the show in her column the same day. "Things are not as O.K. at *Oh, Kay!* as at least one cast member would like," she began an item about an actor who'd filed a complaint with Equity because Merrick refused to let him take his curtain call. (The actor was playing the villain, and Merrick didn't want the villain onstage at the end of the show.)

It was another Rich-Witchel attack. But this time, the target struck back.

Merrick sent a letter to Arthur Sulzberger, publisher of the *Times*. Merrick wrote that he had sat near Rich and Witchel at the performance they'd attended and noticed that Witchel whispered to Rich throughout the performance. "At one point the whispering must have gotten loud because the woman sitting in front of them had to turn around to hush them," he wrote. Merrick "violently" objected to Witchel's "unsuitable behavior," adding that he "will always wonder how her shockingly unprofessional behavior in the theatre influenced Frank Rich's judgment of my show."

He dispatched the letter, by hand, to Sulzberger's office at the *Times* on West Forty-Third Street. Copies of it also landed on gossip columnists' desks all over the city.

Merrick then met with his press agent, Josh Ellis; his ad man, Jon Wilner; and his general manager, Leo Cohen. "What are we going to do about Frank Rich's review?" Wilner asked. Merrick, whose speech was impaired by his stroke, made the sign of a gun with his fingers. Ellis began scribbling on a yellow legal pad. He wrote down two quotes, one from Rich's pan, the other from Witchel's gossip column. Then he drew a cupid's heart around them. Cohen picked up a pen and above the heart wrote, "At last, people are holding hands in the theater again!"

Ellis pushed the mock ad around the table and everyone laughed. It was a good joke.

Merrick didn't laugh. He looked at Ellis and said, "Run it."

His voice was clear as a bell.

Everyone laughed again.

"Run it," he said again. Everyone fell silent. Then, at the bottom of the heart, Ellis wrote, "To Frank and Alex, All My Love." He handed the pen to Merrick who signed his name.

"You won't get that through the *Times*, Mr. Merrick," Cohen said.

Merrick looked at Wilner.

"I have been waiting twenty years to do this," Wilner said. "Every time I take an ad to the *New York Times* late, the people in advertising just want to go home. I've always said you could write 'fuck you' and get it in the paper if you turn it in late, because nobody looks at it. If you want to run that ad, Mr. Merrick, I'll get it in."

Merrick chuckled.

Wilner created the ad, and, fifteen minutes before midnight on Friday, November 9, 1990, dropped it off at the *Times* for publication the following Monday. "I'm sorry, it's late," he told the staffers in the advertising department. "They're keeping me so late at the office, it's horrible. Here's the ad."

On Sunday night, Wilner hung around his local newsstand waiting for the early edition of Monday's paper to hit the streets. As soon as the first stack of papers came off the truck, he grabbed a copy and ripped it open. The ad was there, in the Metro section. He raced back to his apartment and called Merrick. "It's in!" he exclaimed. "It's in!"

Rich picked up an early edition of the paper as well and saw the ad. Years later, he would pass it off as a fun Merrick stunt. "And by Merrick standards, the treatment I got was mild," he wrote.[3] But at the time he was furious. He called Paul Goldberger, the paper's culture editor, and demanded the ad be pulled from the next edition. Witchel, meanwhile, berated Goldberger for letting the ad slip through.[4]

The heart-shaped ad was effaced from the *Times*, but for the next week papers and magazines from the *New York Post* to *Time* reprinted it. The publicity couldn't save *Oh, Kay!*, which soon closed, ensnaring Merrick in financial battles with his associates. But it told the world—well, that part of the world that cared—that Frank Rich and Alex Witchel were a couple.

Some of those involved in the stunt felt Rich and Witchel's fury. A top producer friendly with Rich said to Ellis, "Get out. You'll never get another job in the theater again."

"I felt repercussions all the time," said Ellis. "My relationship with Frank was strained to begin with, so this made it more strained. Shortly after *Oh, Kay!* I did leave the business and New York. And not just because of Frank. It wasn't fun anymore. The party was over in a lot of ways, and I'm not big on staying at a party longer than the party's fun." *

Wilner was also in the line of fire. He was up for the ad job on a revival of *Guys and Dolls*, to be produced by Jujamcyn Theaters and Dodger Theatricals. An executive with the Dodgers called him to his office and said, "I have very bad news for you. You're not gonna get it. We can't hire you. It's horrible, but that's the way it is."

"I had done *Into the Woods* and *Prelude to a Kiss* for them," said Wilner. "They loved us. But now they couldn't hire us."

Dan Jinks was Wilner's assistant at the time (he would go on to be a Hollywood producer whose credits include *American Beauty*). Rich was friendly with Jinks, but after the Merrick stunt, he called him and said, "You cannot be my friend anymore. You work for Jon Wilner."[5]

Wilner, fearing that his livelihood was being cut off, asked his friend press agent Shirley Herz to intercede. Rich liked and admired Herz. She went over to his office and told the critic, "It's David Merrick. What do you want Jon to do? He was just doing his job." She reported back to Wilner, "Frank threw me out of his office."

Why did Rich and Witchel seem so infuriated by what was, as Rich would later call it, a mild stunt? For one thing, there was no shortage of self-importance at the *Times*, and David Merrick had made it—and

---

* Ellis eventually moved back to New York. He occasionally finds himself in a room with Rich and Witchel. "We avoid each other," he says.

Rich and Witchel—a laughingstock. But there may have been another reason. At the time, theater people whispered Rich was so angry because Alex was a man's name and the public might conclude Rich was gay.

Asked if that angle occurred to Merrick and his team, Ellis chuckled and said, "We might have been aware it would leave that impression."

The same week the stunt captured headlines, two go-go boys were appearing at the Gaiety Burlesque, a male strip club on West Forty-Sixth Street, sandwiched between the Lunt-Fontanne Theatre and a Howard Johnson's. The couple were billed as Frank and Alex. All that week, Jacques le Sourd, the critic for Gannett Newspapers and a Gaiety regular, would announce to his table at Joe Allen, "Hey, everybody! Frank and Alex are at the Gaiety!"

Nobody enjoyed Merrick's stunt more than his old adversary—and friend—Bernie Jacobs. "He's still got it," Jacobs said.

Eventually, Rich and Witchel decided to marry. They kept the news under wraps at first, telling only a few close friends. One Saturday morning in the spring of 1991, Rich called Fred Nathan and said, "I'm calling to let you know that I'm going to marry Alex." Nathan's next call was to Bernie Jacobs, who then called Schoenfeld with the news. Schoenfeld was not pleased. He called Arthur Sulzberger and said, "Don't you have a policy that your people can't be married to each other and cover the same beat?"

Sulzberger was surprised. Apparently, he hadn't heard the news.

Rich phoned Nathan. "Don't ever call me again," he said.

"So that was the end of that," said Albert Poland, one of Nathan's closest friends.*

Nathan was showing poor judgment on other fronts. He regularly came home to his San Remo apartment with hustlers, some of them rough looking. There were times when the doormen would not let him bring his "friends" into the building. He was also drinking heavily

---

* Frank Rich married Alex Witchel on June 9, 1991. She gave up the theater column later that year; Rich left the theater beat in 1994, becoming an op-ed writer for the paper.

and doing enormous amounts of cocaine. And he'd been diagnosed with HIV.

Sometimes late at night he'd call friends he knew were in Alcoholics Anonymous and say, in slurred speech, "I just got back from an AA meeting. AA is fantastic. I love AA."

"It was a real mind fuck," said Poland, who was in AA. "It really made me angry. And then he called one night and he said, 'I need you to come over now.' And I said, 'Look, I will do this once. If this is the time you want it, I will come, but I am doing it once.' He said, 'I want it now.'"

Poland went over and found Nathan "falling all over the fucking apartment."

"See these draperies? Seventy thousand dollars!" he said, stumbling. "See this lamp? Forty thousand!"

"He was like Dorothy Malone in *Written on the Wind*," Poland said years later.

Colleagues in Cameron Mackintosh's office noticed how much money Nathan was spending on his lamps—and his cocaine. They also knew what he was making. It was a nice paycheck, but it wasn't enough to support his spending habits. Mackintosh himself went over to Nathan's apartment one day, looked at the furnishings and later said to friends, "I know what I pay him. There's something wrong." He asked his business managers to look into Nathan's financial affairs.

Once again, Nathan called his friend Albert Poland. "I stole one million dollars," he admitted.

He'd been stealing it from Mackintosh. He submitted fake invoices for expenses on touring productions of *Les Misérables* and *The Phantom of the Opera*. He didn't just claim the odd expense. He sought reimbursement for two or three thousand dollars' worth of phony expenses at a time.

Mackintosh threw him out of the kingdom. Jacobs and Phil Smith examined the books on *Cats* to see if Nathan had been stealing from them. They concluded he had not.

Nathan got himself sober, but he was now without an income—and he was dying of AIDS. But because he'd been a valuable ally,

Jacobs decided to keep him on *Cats*. The union job came with health benefits.

"Bernie and Phil were loyal to him to the end, which just touches my heart because Fred had no friends left in the world," said Poland.

Nathan died on June 28, 1994, at thirty-eight. For more than a decade he had been the most powerful press agent on Broadway. His obituary in the *Times* ran a scant 168 words.

Nothing Matters

The debacle of *Chess* notwithstanding, the Shuberts plunged into another major Broadway musical in 1989—the $10 million *Jerome Robbins' Broadway*, a revue of musical numbers from shows staged by the legendary director including *High Button Shoes, On the Town, West Side Story, A Funny Thing Happened on the Way to the Forum, Gypsy,* and *Fiddler on the Roof* among others.

Jacobs was not up to the job of overseeing the show. Schoenfeld took the lead, coproducing with Manny Azenberg. Schoenfeld loved playing Mr. Producer, but he had a weakness. He was susceptible to flattery, especially when poured on by someone of Robbins's stature. Schoenfeld gave the difficult director everything he wanted, including an unheard of (and expensive) six-month rehearsal period.

As a director Robbins, seventy at the time, was a tyrant, notorious for his tantrums. During a rehearsal of the original *West Side Story*, he gathered the cast on stage and screamed at them. He slowly walked backward toward the orchestra pit pounding his fist into his palm. Nobody warned him as he approached the edge, and he tumbled into the pit. One of Azenberg's jobs on *Jerome Robbins' Broadway* was to run interference between the director and his dancers. "If you gained a pound, he'd send you to the back of the line," said Azenberg. "He'd scream and shout and humiliate you. He was a horrible man."

Robbins had no interest in budgets. The Shuberts spent several hundred thousand dollars on costumes, and then one day Robbins decided he wanted the actors in nothing but leotards. Azenberg was furious and nearly quit the show. Robbins eventually realized that an evening of leotards was not what a Broadway audience expected from a big-budget musical.

The only person Robbins didn't "piss all over," said Azenberg, was Leonard Bernstein, the composer of *Fancy Free*, *On the Town*, and *West Side Story*. Since Robbins's show was running long—more than three hours at one point—he thought he would cut a number from *On the Town*. But he wanted Bernstein's approval. Bernstein came to a preview at the Imperial Theatre. He was not in good shape, battling emphysema from years of smoking. He was wizened and hooked up to oxygen—but still smoking. Azenberg was leaning up against the back wall of the theater. Bernstein looked up at him and said, "You don't look so bad." Azenberg responded, "Lenny, I used to be six foot three."

"Look at me," the hunched-over Bernstein said. "I did three shows with him!"

(Bernstein didn't think the *On the Town* material should be cut. Leaving the theater, he said to Azenberg, "The show's too long. Cut *Fiddler*.")

Jerome Robbins' Broadway opened to glowing reviews on February 26, 1989. In a pathetically thin season for musicals—*Starmites*, *Legs Diamond*, *Kenny Loggins on Broadway!*—it swept the Tonys, winning six awards including Best Musical. It ran nearly seven hundred performances, but because it was so expensive it only returned 40 percent of its $10 million capitalization. It would be the last musical the Shuberts would take the lead in producing until 1994, when the company backed Stephen Sondheim's *Passion*, about an ugly woman who falls in love with a stud.

By 1990, the Broadway landscape was beginning to change. Schoenfeld and Jacobs were being overshadowed, at least publicly, by younger producers. Rocco Landesman, the charismatic head of Jujamcyn Theaters, was, in the estimation of the *New York Times* and the *New Yorker*, the future of Broadway—a man with impeccable taste and good breeding.[1] He went to Yale! And he was colorful. He wore cowboy boots and bet on the horses. Landesman teamed up with some other, younger producers—Michael David, Ed Strong, director Des McAnuff—to form

Dodger Theatricals, which in the early nineties produced acclaimed revivals of *Guys and Dolls*, making a star of Nathan Lane, *The Who's Tommy*, and *How to Succeed in Business Without Really Trying*, starring Matthew Broderick.

Landesman also coproduced Tony Kushner's two-part *Angels in America: A Gay Fantasia on National Themes*, which Frank Rich slobbered over—"miraculous," "revolutionary," "mind-exploding." Rich's last review as chief drama critic for the *New York Times* was for *Perestroika*, the second part of *Angels in America*. Rich was so enamored of the play, he celebrated its opening night over dinner at Orso with Landesman.[2]

Schoenfeld and Jacobs admired and respected Landesman. Schoenfeld, quoted in a glowing profile of Landesman, said, "I think he's a very welcome addition to our business."[3] Privately, Schoenfeld would sometimes chafe at all the attention being showered on Landesman. The implication, especially from the *Times*, was that Landesman was young and vibrant—Broadway's future—while the Shuberts, old and unimaginative, were its past.

Another new producer in town was Garth Drabinsky, an impresario from Toronto who arrived on Broadway in 1993 with the John Kander-Fred Ebb musical *Kiss of the Spider Woman*, starring Chita Rivera. Drabinsky was the founder of Cineplex Odeon, the movie chain. A man of unbridled ambition, he expanded the company past the breaking point by taking on a huge amount of debt. He was forced out in 1989 by his partner, MCA. As part of his golden parachute he acquired the Canadian rights to *The Phantom of the Opera*, which he produced in Toronto. He parlayed the success of *Phantom* into Livent, a publically traded company that produced Broadway shows and acquired theaters throughout North America, including, in 1998, the Ford Center for the Performing Arts on Forty-Second Street, a new theater that combined restored elements of the old Lyric and Apollo theaters.

Schoenfeld and Jacobs watched Drabinsky from the sidelines, marveling at his drive but questioning his finances. He produced shows—*Kiss of the Spider Woman*, *Show Boat*, *Candide*—with no thought of the bottom line. He claimed they were all hits, no matter what they cost. But the Shuberts, and a few other veteran producers, had their doubts.

They knew how Broadway financing worked, and they could not figure out where Drabinsky's profits were coming from. In the end, their hunch was correct. Drabinsky was a fraud. Like Max Bialystock in *The Producers*, he kept two sets of books—one for shareholders that showed enormous profits, the other for himself and his cohorts that revealed staggering losses. Livent went bankrupt, and Drabinsky went to jail in Canada on several counts of fraud and forgery.

At the same time Rocco Landesman, the Dodgers, and Garth Drabinsky were coming up in the world, the Shuberts' closest allies, Andrew Lloyd Webber and Cameron Mackintosh, were winding down. After *Phantom*, Lloyd Webber wrote *Aspects of Love*, which had a fine score but, in a bloated production directed by Trevor Nunn, died an expensive death at the Shuberts' Broadhurst Theatre. One of Lloyd Webber's best shows, *Sunset Boulevard*, opened on Broadway at the Minskoff (a Nederlander theater) in 1994. It received strong reviews—especially for its leading lady, Glenn Close—and ran over two years. But it was so expensive that it closed without recouping its $13 million production cost.

Mackintosh produced *Miss Saigon* in 1991 at the Shuberts' Broadway Theatre, and it was a smash. But it was the last of the British pop-operas to succeed in New York. Mackintosh's next show, *Five Guys Named Moe*, was a modest, forgettable revue. In London he produced flop after flop—*Martin Guerre*, *The Witches of Eastwick*, *Moby Dick*, *The Fix*.

None made it to New York.

The British invasion, which had made the Shuberts immensely rich, was over.

If the Shuberts were not as aggressive on the producing front in the early nineties, they were still, led by Schoenfeld, fighting for a better Times Square. The Marriott Marquis, though despised by many on Broadway, did prove a boon to the area. It became a draw for business conferences and tourists, who braved the still sketchy neighborhood so they could see the now world-famous musicals *Cats*, *Les Misérables*, *The Phantom of the Opera*, and *Miss Saigon*.

Other construction projects were beginning to lift the fortunes of Times Square as well. To its west, in the block between Forty-Second and Forty-Third Streets and Ninth and Tenth Avenues, sits Manhattan Plaza, with 1,689 apartments in two towers and town houses, a playground, fitness center, basketball and tennis courts.[4] Apartments were originally conceived to be offered at market rate, but through a confluence of events—the oil crisis, the city approaching default—and the realities of the neighborhood, the developers went bankrupt, and the buildings sat vacant. An idea developed to make the complex available to people in the performing arts, low-income people, and the elderly living in the area displaced by the construction. A number of the apartments would be covered by federal US Housing and Urban Development Section 8 subsidies, while others would fall under New York State's Mitchell-Lama program. The Shuberts backed this idea. Schoenfeld and producer Alex Cohen promoted it in the press and with city officials. Opening in 1977, Manhattan Plaza became a vast colony of artists in what had been one of the most dangerous blocks in New York. Herb Sturz, deputy mayor for criminal justice under Ed Koch, said Manhattan Plaza was "part and parcel of stabilizing a part of the city that was no man's land."

Along Forty-Second Street between Ninth and Tenth Avenues is Theatre Row, a collection of Off-Broadway theaters including Playwrights Horizons, put together by real estate developer Fred Papert and Bob Moss, a director and producer. They spent more than a decade getting the project off the ground, but by the 1990s the theaters were full of productions and the block was "hurtling toward respectability."[5]

But Times Square was hardly free of crime. And the crack cocaine epidemic of the 1980s and early nineties only made matters worse. One morning, over breakfast at the Pierre Hotel on Fifth Avenue, Schoenfeld, Herb Sturz, and Carl Weisbrod, then running the New York City Economic Development Corporation for Mayor David Dinkins, discussed the issue. Schoenfeld complained that Broadway theatergoers were under assault from petty thieves, prostitutes, drug dealers, and hustlers. But these low-level, so-called quality of life crimes were of little interest to law enforcement, which channeled its resources toward violent felonies. Prostitutes and other petty criminals, if and when they were arrested, were sent downtown to the criminal court at 100 Centre Street, where they were fined and released, only to ply their trades again in Times Square.

In 1982, social scientists James Q. Wilson and George L. Kelling argued in an essay in *The Atlantic* that petty crime and low-level anti-social behavior created an atmosphere in which more serious crimes thrived. They urged law enforcement to crack down on small crimes as an important step in deterring major crimes. Their argument became known as the "broken windows" theory, after their contention that if broken windows were not repaired, vandals would return to break more windows, eventually destroying the entire building. Wilson and Kelling believed broken windows—and petty crimes—should be addressed before they mushroomed into something more serious.

William J. Bratton, then the head of the New York City Transit Police, was an early proponent of the broken windows theory. He implemented it by cracking down on fare beaters in the subway system. It turned out that people who jump turnstiles often commit more serious crimes. Sturz and Weisbrod thought the theory could be applied to the hundreds of petty crimes in Times Square. Their idea was to create a community court in Midtown where people who pleaded guilty to minor offenses would be sentenced quickly, fined, sent to rehabilitation facilities, or ordered to perform community service.

Schoenfeld offered the city rent-free use of the Longacre Theatre, which had been dark for more than a year. The Shuberts would refurbish the theater and set up an actual court on stage. Coincidently, the first show to play the Longacre in 1913 was *Are You a Crook?*[6] The Shubert Foundation provided early funding for the court, and Schoenfeld raised money from other charitable organizations committed to improving quality of life in the city, including, crucially, the *New York Times* Foundation.

The court was not without detractors, especially civil rights advocates who feared a rush to judgment that might violate the rights of the accused. Proponents countered that there would be a battery of public defenders on hand to represent those who came before the court. Another skeptic was District Attorney Robert M. Morgenthau, who questioned, rather oddly given the amount of crime in Times Square, whether there were enough cases to justify the court. Morgenthau, in the view of Herb Sturz, also thought it would cut into his control over a centralized legal system.

Without Morgenthau's support, the Midtown Community Court, as it was to be called, was unlikely to get off the ground. Schoenfeld stepped in and arranged a lunch with Morgenthau, Sturz, and Arthur Sulzberger, the publisher of the *New York Times* and an advocate of the court.

"That lunch was pivotal," said Sturz. "It was all about getting the *Times* to swing the district attorney, and it did."

In the end, the court was not housed at the Longacre. Owners of office and residential buildings near the theater fretted the court would bring more criminals to the area. Theater groups and preservationists objected to taking another legitimate theater off the market. But Mayor Dinkins was behind the idea. The court was moved to a city-owned building on West Fifty-Fourth Street next to a police station where it continues to operate today.

The court became "the best show in town," said Phil Smith, who, when he had some free time before or after lunch, would wander into the court to watch the parade of Times Square eccentrics.

Entertainment value aside, the court also proved effective. It brought a sense of law and order to a neighborhood that appeared to be sliding into chaos. By the end of the decade, there were community courts in Harlem, Red Hook, and other parts of the city. Located in low-income neighborhoods, the courts helped "restore trust" in the criminal justice system, "a bond that many legal experts feel has frayed over time." [7]

Looking back on the success of the Midtown Community Court twenty years later, Sturz said, "Without Jerry, I don't think the court would have happened. I give him the lion's share of the credit. The Shuberts had a huge vested interest that coincided with the public interest. Not that everything that is good for Shubert is good for the city. But in this instance, it turned out to be good policy for the Shuberts and the city."

As Times Square began its resurgence in the early nineties, one block remained mired in the muck—Forty-Second Street between Broad-

way and Eighth Avenue. The Shubert brothers built their first Times
Square theater on the street—the Lyric in 1903—but eventually moved
their empire north to Forty-Fourth Street, leaving the block in control
of their mortal enemy, Abe Erlanger and the Syndicate, which operated out of the New Amsterdam Theatre. The Shuberts lost the Lyric
during the Depression, and it became a movie house. Schoenfeld and
Jacobs never showed much interest in the block, thinking it could never
be reclaimed for legitimate purposes. They concentrated their cleanup
efforts between Forty-Fourth and Fifty-Second Streets.

Attempts to salvage the Deuce went nowhere in the seventies and
eighties, especially after Ed Koch nixed the City at 42nd Street project
early in his first term. Developers planned massive office buildings on
the block in the 1980s, but those plans became entangled in a blizzard
of lawsuits with the city, preservationists, and small-business owners.
For-profit development plans were scuttled when New York plunged
into a recession after the stock market crash of 1987. The Deuce looked
like it would forever be New York's street of sleaze.

But by 1990, plans were coming together that would, in the end,
reverse decades of decline.

For years, the idea of reviving Forty-Second Street hinged on con-
structing office buildings to attract high-end tenants. The plan that
came to the fore was called the Times Square Center, which consisted
of four office towers that would be built at Forty-Second Street and
Broadway. Architectural plans were drawn up, models made. City officials announced that the resurgence of Times Square was underway.
But the project moved slowly, and critics said there would never be
enough demand to fill the office towers.

An urban planner named Rebecca Robertson, president of the
42nd Street Development Project, had another idea. Instead of fo-
cusing on office buildings, why not refurbish what had always been
the lifeblood of Forty-Second Street—its theaters, including the
Lyric, the Apollo, the Selwyn, and the New Amsterdam? Robertson
formed the New 42nd Street, Inc., a city and state venture dedicated
to restoring the theaters.[8] Robertson brought two key figures into
her camp—Marian Heiskell, older sister of Arthur Sulzberger, and
Cora Cahan, cofounder of the Joyce Theater, a dance company, and

a capable arts administrator. Heiskell rallied the *Times* to the cause; Cahan, who is married to Bernard Gersten, marshalled the Broadway community.

Once again, the theater was there for Times Square when so much else had deserted it.

Another, and more controversial, development set things in motion—the government intervened. On April 18, 1990, the New York State Supreme Court issued a sweeping ruling. It granted the 42nd Street Development Project title to most of the block, including the theaters. Real estate moguls were furious, especially the Durst Organization, which owned several of the theaters. "They stole those theaters from us," a bitter Douglas Durst complained.[9] Durst had been restoring some of the theaters and renting them out to theater companies. But it was a piecemeal effort. The city argued before the court that the only way to clean up Forty-Second Street would be to give condemnation power to the 42nd Street Development Project. That power in hand, Robertson wasted no time condemning buildings along the Deuce, forcing out nearly three hundred tenants, some of whom had been in their seedy cubbyhole offices for years.

But redevelopment stalled once again when Governor Mario Cuomo shelved the Times Square Center in 1992. The critics were right. There simply were not enough tenants to fill the towers, Cuomo conceded. With its theaters and buildings empty, Forty-Second Street looked like a ghost town. A block that once thronged with pedestrians was now "as still as a tomb."[10]

What Robertson needed was at least one major tenant for one of her empty theaters, a tenant who would put on popular shows that would attract the throngs—civilized, well-behaved, law-abiding throngs—back to the Deuce.

As it so happened, Mickey Mouse was eyeing Times Square.

Riding high from the success of *Little Shop of Horrors*, Howard Ashman, who wrote and directed the Shuberts' little "slot machine," decided to try his hand at a Broadway show. He teamed up with Marvin Hamlisch to a write a musical based on *Smile*, the 1975 movie satirizing beauty pageants. The Shuberts and David Geffen funded a $250,000 workshop in 1985. But they didn't care for the show, which was sharp and cynical, so they withdrew. But they never bothered to tell Ashman, who heard about it from gossip. Not long after, Ashman was at a party with Schoenfeld at *Little Shop* general manager Albert Poland's apartment.

Schoenfeld went over to say hello.

"Don't come near me!" Ashman snarled. "I don't want to hear anything you have to say!"

Schoenfeld was furious. He pulled Poland aside and said, "Does Howard want a career in the theater?"

"Listen," Poland replied. "You did a workshop of his show and then you did not have the decency to tell him that you were not continuing."

"Should I apologize?" Schoenfeld asked.

"Well, that would be a start."

Another set of producers eventually picked up *Smile*, which opened November 24, 1986, at the Lunt-Fontanne Theatre. But the Shuberts were right. The show was too cynical and cold to have much appeal for Broadway audiences. The reviews were tepid, and *Smile* closed after just forty-eight performances.

Hamlisch and Ashman, who also directed the show, were devastated. Hamlisch, who helped save the theater industry with *A Chorus Line*, turned his back on Broadway and resumed his Hollywood career. Ashman, in demand after *Little Shop*, now experienced firsthand how fickle the theater world could be. As writer and director of the season's biggest flop, nobody would hire him.

And then he got a phone call from Peter Schneider, who'd been a company manager on *Little Shop*. Schneider had moved to Los Angeles, where he'd been hired by Disney to help salvage its moribund animation department. Long gone were the days of *Snow White and the Seven Dwarfs*, *Bambi*, and *Dumbo*. The animation department was producing such second- and third-tier titles as *The Great Mouse Detective*, *The Black Cauldron*, and *Oliver & Company*.

The score to *Oliver & Company* was a grab bag of songs by Barry Manilow, Dean Pitchford, and Charlie Midnight. Ashman and Barry Mann had a song in it as well—"Once Upon a Time in New York City." Schneider, who joined the animation department just as *Oliver & Company* was about to be released, felt the score lacked a consistent tone.

He was not afraid to express his displeasure to the staff.

"You guys don't know jack shit," he said. "You can't have a musical written by five people!"

But Schneider liked Ashman's song. For Disney's next movie, *The Little Mermaid*, he wanted Ashman to write all the songs. Eager to get out of New York after the failure of *Smile*, Ashman said yes, provided he could work with his *Little Shop* collaborator Alan Menken.

An initial draft of *The Little Mermaid* was, according to Schneider, "very white, very nonurban, and, dare I say it, very non-homosexual." Ashman brought a New Yorker's showbiz savvy to the material. For the voice of Ursula, the villainess octopus, Ashman wanted the gravelly-voiced transvestite Divine, who had a cult following from John Waters movies such as *Pink Flamingos* and *Hairspray*. The crab that looked out for Ariel became Jamaican, and was played by Samuel E. Wright, who auditioned for the part as if he were up for a stage musical.

Ashman and Menken tackled *The Little Mermaid* as if they were writing a Broadway show, which suited Schneider and his second-in-command, Thomas Schumacher, as both had theater backgrounds. (Schumacher spent several years at the Mark Taper Forum and the Los Angeles Festival of Arts. While working in the nonprofit theater, he became friendly with a young, ambitious director named Julie Taymor.)

Disney executives Michael Eisner, Jeffrey Katzenberg, and Roy Disney gathered in a small studio on the Disney lot to hear the score to *The Little Mermaid*. Menken played the songs on a synthesizer, and he and Ashman played all the characters. But for the Hollywood setting, the whole afternoon could have been a backers' audition in New York for a new Broadway musical.

The movie was to be released on November 15, 1989. That summer, Ashman went to New York but told Schneider he'd be back in California for the final polish.

"Howard was all over *Little Mermaid*," said Schneider. "It was his show. But Howard doesn't show up for the scoring sessions. And Howard doesn't show up for the final editing. I get on the phone with Howard and I say, 'What the fuck is going on? Get your ass out here!'"

"I can't come," said Ashman. But he refused to say why.

"For days it puzzled me," said Schneider. I couldn't figure out what the fuck was going on. And then I got a call from Jeffrey Katzenberg and he said, 'I have some disturbing news. Howard has AIDS. The Walt Disney Company will do anything to support Howard. You're in charge.'"

Ashman, Schneider learned, was "scared to death" that Disney would cut him loose because he had AIDS. "He thought you can't have someone who is homosexual, who has AIDS, and has the word 'Disney' next to his name," Schneider said. "But we would have done anything for him. I look back on it, and I wish Howard had told us earlier because I would have moved the whole fucking production to New York—the scoring, the editing. I think the movie cost us $18 million. For $50,000, we could all have gotten to New York and finished it there with Howard."

The Little Mermaid was an immediate hit with critics and audiences, becoming the first animated movie to gross more than $100 million. It won two Oscars, for Best Score and Song ("Under the Sea"). Though Ashman was reluctant to travel—with no immune system, an airplane ride could bring on a life-threatening illness—he wasn't going to miss out on the Academy Awards. Before the ceremony, he told Menken, "I'm really happy, but when we get back to New York, we have to have a serious talk."

"What? What? Tell me now!" Menken said.

"No, not tonight."

Menken suspected Ashman was sick, but, when he'd confronted him a few months earlier, Ashman denied he had AIDS.

Back in New York, Ashman told him the truth. They had already started writing *Beauty and the Beast*, and all Ashman wanted to do "was bury himself in his work," said Menken. Disney held the recording sessions in New York, so Ashman could attend. "He looked painfully thin at those sessions," said Schneider.

In March 1991, Disney unveiled sketches, songs, and bits of the unfinished film for a select group of influential members of the New York media. Menken was there, but Ashman, now gravely ill, was at St. Vincent's Hospital in Greenwich Village. After the presentation, Schneider, Jeffrey Katzenberg, Don Hahn (a Disney producer), and David Geffen rushed down to St. Vincent's to tell Ashman how well it had gone. His mother and his sister were by his bedside. He was wearing a *Beauty and the Beast* T-shirt.

"We were all sitting around saying platitudes because what do you say to someone who's dying?" Schneider recalled. "And then David Geffen—and I will never forget this—kneels at Howard's bedside and, as if there's no one else in the room, takes Howard's hand and says, 'You are important. And we will find a cure for this disease.' I thought, This is how you deal with death. You give up any fear you have of being embarrassed around someone who is dying. David knelt there a good ten minutes talking to Howard, and only to Howard."

Four days later, on March 14, 1991, Howard Ashman died of complications from AIDS. He was forty.

Beauty and the Beast was released that November, and went on to shatter all box office records set by *The Little Mermaid*. The critics were ecstatic. In a year-end wrap up, Frank Rich, in the *New York Times*, wrote, "The best Broadway musical score of 1991 was that written by Alan Menken and Howard Ashman for the Disney animated movie *Beauty and the Beast*."

Michael Eisner read the story and thought, Why not? Born and raised in New York, Eisner loved Broadway. If the most influential drama critic in the world thought so highly of the score to *Beauty and the Beast*, why shouldn't it be a Broadway show? Eisner and others at Disney were also aware of the multimillion-dollar grosses being posted by *Cats*, *Les Misérables*, and *The Phantom of the Opera*. Not bad returns for shows that cost less than $10 million to produce on Broadway, an insignificant amount of money for a company the size of Disney.

At an early production meeting for a *Beauty and the Beast* stage musical, Katzenberg asked his team what they thought it should cost. Nobody knew. "We said $12 million," said Schneider. "And Jeffrey said fine. Little did he know he had just made it the most expensive show in Broadway history. And it turned out to be even more than advertised!" (Disney never discussed costs but the unofficial figure put on *Beauty* was $18 to $20 million.)

Beauty and the Beast opened at the Palace Theatre on April 18, 1994, and the critics, for the most part, were unimpressed. The new critic at the *Times*, David Richards, compared it to FAO Schwarz and the Circle Line boat tour of Manhattan—a middlebrow tourist attraction. Culture critics fretted about the Disneyfication of Broadway. And the theater community snickered at "Team Disney." The musical was nominated for nine Tony Awards that year, but won only one, for costumes. Stephen Sondheim and James Lapine's *Passion*, produced by the Shuberts, beat it out for Best Musical, Best Score, Best Book, and Best Actress (Donna Murphy).

But *Beauty and the Beast* was unstoppable. It broke box office records at the Palace, reviving the fortunes of Jimmy Nederlander, who owned the theater. It would go on to run 5,461 performances and gross nearly $2 billion worldwide.

Passion, meanwhile, ran less than a year, and lost most of its $3.5 million production cost.

Even before he put *Beauty and the Beast* in the Palace, Eisner had explored the possibility of acquiring a theater for Disney. Cora Cahan, of the 42nd Street Development Project, took him on a tour of the decrepit New Amsterdam Theatre in the spring of 1993. Eisner saw the holes in the ceiling, water dripping into the auditorium, birds flying above the stage, rubble strewn about the lobby. But he also noticed the art nouveau details, the friezes depicting scenes from Shakespeare and *Faust*, the remains of the Irish marble fireplace in the lounge, what was left of the porcelain vines and flowers snaking up the walls of the auditorium. He looked passed the decay and saw the former grandeur. He left the New Amsterdam knowing that this was where Disney would plant its flag in Times Square.[11]

It took nearly two years to work out the arrangements, but on July 20, 1995, at a press conference in front of the theater, Mayor Rudolph Giuliani and New York governor George Pataki announced that Disney would take a forty-nine-year lease from the city on the New Amsterdam. It was a good deal for Disney. New York State kicked in $26 million, in the form of a loan to Disney, to renovate the theater. Disney put up $8 million. But as Anthony Bianco points out in *Ghosts of 42nd Street*, the company also received a 20 percent federal tax credit, which reduced its exposure in the New Amsterdam to just $3 million.[12]

With Disney on board, two other entertainment companies—AMC, the movie chain, and Madame Tussauds—struck deals with the 42nd Street Development Project to plant their flags on the Deuce as well.

The rehabilitation of Forty-Second Street was underway.

After years of battling to save Times Square, the Shuberts, one might think, would have welcomed Disney. But Schoenfeld and Jacobs were not pleased. They'd never received the tax breaks and loans the city and state showered on Disney. And now there would be another theater in the neighborhood they did not control. Jujamcyn and the Nederlanders objected to the Disney deal as well.* The three theater owners wanted the Broadway unions to stand with them against the deal.

Alan Eisenberg, the head of Actors' Equity, had a "polite" conversation with the disgruntled theater owners, but made it clear that his union applauded the arrival of Disney on Broadway. The theater owners didn't make any headway with the other unions, either. From the unions' perspective, Disney meant employment, for actors, stagehands, musicians, ushers, and box office treasurers.

The theater owners' rebellion never got off the ground. Schoenfeld grumbled to the *New York Times* about Disney's "unfair advantage," but nobody paid much attention, especially since the complaints were coming from a man who sat atop a multimillion-dollar empire himself.[13]

Disney opened the refurbished New Amsterdam on May 18, 1997, with a concert version of *King David*, a musical by Alan Menken and Tim Rice. It had some pleasant songs, but it was dull. Wags called it a "boratoria." The eighteen hundred guests, however, weren't paying much attention to the show. They were dazzled by the return to glory of an architectural treasure. Before the curtain went up, they wandered through the theater, marveling at the restored murals and friezes, porcelain statues and ivy-covered boxes, terra-cotta staircases and lower-level grand bar. After the show, they gathered behind the New Amsterdam on West Forty-First Street, once one of the scariest

---

* The Nederlanders were making money from *Beauty and the Beast* at the Palace, but they wanted Disney to be a tenant, not a rival landlord.

streets in all New York. Disney put a tent over the entire block and threw a lavish black-tie gala.

That fall Disney opened *The Lion King*, directed by Julie Taymor, at the New Amsterdam. It was a smash. A theater that Hal Prince, inspecting it for *The Phantom of the Opera* in 1987, said he "would not go near" was now being mobbed nightly by parents and their children.

The new *42nd Street* had arrived.

With the arrival of Disney and Livent and a raft of young, hungry producers, the Shuberts' grip on the theater industry was being challenged. In the fall of 1995, the newcomers staged a coup of their own against the Shuberts.

As long as anyone could remember, Schoenfeld and Jacobs negotiated every theater contract. Jacobs handled the stagehands and the actors; Schoenfeld dealt with the musicians, the ushers, the press agents, and the company managers. Their reign was remarkably free of labor strife, and they were liked and respected by their adversaries across the table. When Jacobs suffered his bout of transient global amnesia, Phil Smith took Alan Eisenberg aside and told him, "Bernie is still Bernie, but he's going to need a little help" in the upcoming negotiations. Eisenberg understood. He met privately with Jacobs to coach him through the talks so he wouldn't embarrass himself in front of the other producers.

"Phil and I walked him through that negotiation, practically holding his hand," Eisenberg recalled.

Producers had grumbled for years, mostly off the record for fear of retribution, that Schoenfeld and Jacobs were "giving away the store" to avoid work stoppages. Generous contracts with the unions, the producers complained, were driving up production costs. Schoenfeld and Jacobs negotiated the deals—but the producers shouldered the costs. And they had little to say at the table.

There was some truth to the charge.

"Bernie didn't have much use for a lot of the producers," said Eisenberg. "He didn't give a shit what they wanted from him or what they wanted from us. He knew where the deal was going to be from his perspective and that was it."

Schoenfeld and Jacobs always countered that they were producers as well as theater owners, so they paid their share of the production costs. But they also believed, having suffered under J. J. Shubert, that theater people deserved a living wage. And they valued labor peace. Strikes meant dark theaters and, with Broadway now earning hundreds of millions of dollars every year, an enormous loss of revenue.

But the new group of producers—the "Young Turks" as the Shuberts called them—were tired of those arguments. They wanted a say in the negotiations, and they were not afraid of a showdown with the unions. Taking advantage of Jacobs's diminished capacity, they banded together and at a contentious meeting of the League of New York Theatres and Producers sidelined Schoenfeld and Jacobs from upcoming union negotiations.

Schoenfeld was furious. Smith was stunned. "I couldn't believe what they were doing to Bernie."

But Jacobs was resigned. He was tired and not up for another battle. It hurt his pride, Smith said, but he let the Young Turks have their way.

As negotiations with the stagehands approached in the fall of 1995, the Young Turks asserted themselves. We are "absolutely prepared to put up the barriers," Barry Weissler, the producer of a revival of *Grease*, told the *Daily News*. "It will certainly be injurious to my business, and believe me no one wants it, but we must not be afraid of it." Another producer, Stewart Lane, added, "We will hang together if there's a showdown."

Schoenfeld watched the posturing with contempt. "The only producers eager to close shows are those who do not have shows to close," he told the *News*.[14]

The negotiations that year with both stagehands and actors were torturous. Labor leaders were amused at how baffled some of the producers were by their own contracts. "They had no idea what was going on," said a source at the stagehands union. As he monitored the negotiations, Phil Smith often had to hide his frustration. Points that Jacobs could have hashed out in minutes took hours, sometimes days. And in the end, the Young Turks did not, as some would later concede, get much more than producers had gotten in the past. But they made their point. They had a seat at the table. The Shuberts would never again be allowed to negotiate for them—and then stick them with the bill.

Schoenfeld and Jacobs were still powerful—they controlled seventeen Broadway theaters—but their domination was on the wane.

In June of 1996, Bernie and Betty Jacobs celebrated their fiftieth wedding anniversary by taking their two children, Sally and Steven, and their three grandchildren on a two-week cruise to Alaska. It was a happy trip, with Bernie enjoying the role of family patriarch. Later that summer, he began complaining of fatigue. His doctor diagnosed heart trouble. On August 23, he underwent bypass surgery at St. Francis Hospital in Roslyn, Long Island.

His old friend Albert Poland had a bad feeling. That Monday, Poland went to see Phil Smith and started crying. "I just know this is the end," he said. The next morning, August 27, at 11:30 a.m., he received a call from Schoenfeld. He was sobbing.

"Albert," he said, "Bernie died."

Jacobs, eighty years old, died of complications from heart surgery.

Schoenfeld and Jacobs had fought their way to the top of the American theater. They survived J. J. Shubert and his drunken successor, Lawrence. They endured attacks on their character and integrity by powerful public officials. They stood by their neighborhood, Times Square, when it was a symbol of America's urban crisis. They bet on creative people who had strange ideas for shows—a boy who blinds horses, a bunch of chorus kids, a man-eating plant, a show about cats.

Their partnership, forged in friendship and business, never broke up. They had an agreement, never written down, that they would stand by each other no matter what came their way. If one felt strongly about something, the other would yield. Whatever disagreements they had never became public. The Shubert empire endured in part because nothing ever came between its two leaders.

Lee and J. J. Shubert, even when they weren't speaking to each other, always presented a united front.

So, too, did Lee and J. J.'s real heirs—Gerald Schoenfeld and Bernard B. Jacobs.

As soon as he learned Jacobs had died, Poland rushed over to the Shubert offices to be with Schoenfeld. He was in his office with two longtime Shubert employees. Everyone was crying. Poland and Schoenfeld embraced. Schoenfeld turned toward his large, impressive desk from which he ran his part of the Shubert empire. He gestured at the contracts, the photographs of theater stars, the awards and citations for his work in helping to revive Broadway and Times Square.

And then, echoing the last words of another entertainment mogul, Louis B. Mayer, he told Poland, "None of this really matters. None of this matters at all."

Exit Music

Not long after Jacobs died, the Shubert Foundation's board of directors raised a touchy subject with Schoenfeld—succession. Schoenfeld and Jacobs never gave much thought to the matter, at least publicly. When asked who would run Shubert when he was gone, Jacobs would say, "Dead is dead. I won't care."

Their partnership worked so well, the board never pressed them on the issue. "There was never a sense of urgency," said Michael Sovern, a board member and the former president of Columbia University. But now one of the partners was dead, and the other, at seventy-one, was "no spring chicken," said Sovern.

The board appointed Phil Smith president of the company. He moved into Jacobs's old office above the Shubert Theatre. "I know of no one who has more knowledge of the theater business than Phil," Schoenfeld said. But Schoenfeld resisted any discussion of long-term plans for succession. Finally, Sovern said, "Look, Jerry, if you don't want to have a conversation with the board about what you think should happen if something happens to you, write it down and put it in your safe so we can find it."

Schoenfeld began discussing with the board potential candidates who could run the company when he was gone. A few names from outside Shubert were mentioned—Rocco Landesman, of Jujamcyn Theaters, as well as Peter Schneider and Tom Schumacher, who ran Disney Theatrical Productions. But in the end, the board decided to promote from within. Schoenfeld believed his successor as chairman of the Shubert empire should be Jacobs's loyal lieutenant, Phil Smith. The board agreed. It also elevated Robert Wankel, another long-time Shubert employee who was close to Schoenfeld. In the event of Schoenfeld's death, Wankel would become cochairman of the company with Smith.

Schoenfeld still did not like to speak publicly about what would happen when he was gone. And he hated talking about his age—or death. Over an off-the-record lunch at Frankie & Johnnie's Steakhouse, a reporter dared to bring up the sensitive topic. "What do you mean, 'When I die?'" Schoenfeld replied. "*If* I die," he amended. "And *if* I die, I will die behind my desk!"

In 2005, when a reporter for the *Times* wanted to do an article on Schoenfeld and who would succeed him at Shubert, Schoenfeld resisted. "All they're going to do is say how old I am," he grumbled. But he relented and the story ran under the headline THE MAN BEHIND THE CURTAIN.[1]

"I want you to describe me as an aspiring forty-seven-year-old with a bit in his teeth and ready to jump from the starting gate," he told the reporter. "That's me."

And the truth was, Schoenfeld's energy never flagged. He was at the office every day, attended nearly every Broadway opening and remained a powerful advocate for the theater industry in its relations with city and state governments. He led the charge in 2004 to thwart Mayor Michael Bloomberg's plan to build a $1.4 billion football stadium for the New York Jets on the West Side rail yards, arguing it would cause traffic jams that would hurt the theater business.

He kept an eye on labor negotiations, though he was no longer a force at the table. When the musicians went on strike in 2003, he watched, with a mixture of amusement and disdain, from the sidelines. He had far more contempt for the producers and their tactics than he did for the musicians. He spoke frequently with Bill Moriarty, the head of the musicians union, during the strike. "Jerry and I could have ended the strike in a minute, if I'd been negotiating with him," Moriarty said.

Though he no longer wielded the kind of power he and Jacobs enjoyed in the 1980s, Schoenfeld could be, when provoked, a dangerous enemy. The Shuberts produced Arthur Miller's *The Ride Down Mt. Morgan* in 2000 on Broadway. It starred one of Schoenfeld's close friends, Patrick Stewart. But Stewart and Miller thought the Shuberts weren't doing enough to promote the play. After a Saturday matinee performance, Stewart gave a curtain speech, denouncing the Shuberts for their lack of attention to the production. Furious, Schoenfeld hauled him up on charges of unprofessional conduct before Actors' Equity. With the flourish of Henry Drummond in *Inherit the Wind*, Schoenfeld obliterated Stewart's defense during a hearing. Stewart's own union forced him to apologize to Schoenfeld and the Shuberts. But Schoenfeld, always one to hold a grudge, never forgave the actor. Years later, both were lunching at Michael's restaurant on West Fifty-Fifth Street. As Stewart passed Schoenfeld on the way to the door, he extended his hand. Schoenfeld refused to take it.

Schoenfeld wanted to be seen as a producer in his own right, but that was never his strength. He took the lead in producing *Amour*, a musical by Michel Legrand, in 2002, but it closed after just two weeks. He loved *Passing Strange*, a rock musical by the musician Stew that the Shuberts moved to Broadway from the Public Theater. It received rave reviews but lost the 2008 Tony for Best Musical to *In the Heights*, and Schoenfeld had to close it.

In 2005, the Shubert board voted to change the name of the Royale Theatre to the Bernard B. Jacobs. Behind the scenes, Schoenfeld's wife, Pat, lobbied the board to name a theater after her husband as well. "Instead of doing something to honor Jerry after he dies, do something now," she insisted.[2] The board agreed, renaming the Plymouth the Gerald Schoenfeld. Many on Broadway grumbled, albeit off the record, about the unseemliness of naming theaters after "lawyers," especially when there were no theaters named Arthur Miller or Tennessee Williams or Irving Berlin. But others, like Rocco Landesman, knew what Schoenfeld and Jacobs had done for their industry, and spoke out in favor of the honor. Privately, Schoenfeld had a name for those who snickered at the renaming of the theaters. "Schmucks!" he called them. But at the ceremony hosted by Hugh Jackman to light the new marquees, Schoenfeld drew laughs when, visibly moved, he said,

"Thank you all for coming and being part of this unforgivable—er, unforgettable—moment." *

On November 24, 2008, Schoenfeld and his wife attended the premiere of *Australia*, starring Hugh Jackman and Nicole Kidman. He was his usual, ebullient self, shaking hands and hugging old friends. He was trying to convince Jackman to play Little Chap in a Shubert-produced revival of *Stop the World—I Want to Get Off!*. As he walked up the aisle after the movie was over, he ran into Jackman. "*You*," he shouted at the star ("He always left the *H* off my name," Jackman recalled), "enough of this Hollywood shit. It's time to come back home to Broadway!" In his Madison Avenue apartment after the screening, he was feeling peckish. He went into the kitchen for a slice of herring. His wife heard him gasp. She rushed into the kitchen and found him on the floor. He died, in his apartment, of a heart attack. He was eighty-four.

The theater industry was shocked to learn of his death, the *New York Post* reported. The Shuberts without Schoenfeld—indeed an opening night without Schoenfeld—"hardly seemed possible."[3]

"People didn't actually call him Mr. Broadway. But they could have," the *Times* noted, describing him as a "Runyonesque figure" who left an indelible stamp on America by bringing dozens of hit shows to Broadway.[4]

His memorial service at the Majestic was packed with celebrities—Liam Neeson, Vanessa Redgrave, Andrew Lloyd Webber, Hugh Jackman, Barbara Walters, Henry Kissinger, Whoopi Goldberg, Helen Mirren, Jeremy Irons.

Mayor Bloomberg spoke, recalling how Schoenfeld loved to harangue him about traffic in Times Square.

"Jerry's already arguing with God about air rights," Bloomberg said. "And God knows he will never hear the end of it."

"I'm the last of the Mohicans," Jimmy Nederlander declared a few weeks after Schoenfeld's death. He was sitting in his office in Times

---

* That was not nearly as embarrassing as an event at the Pierre Hotel a year later honoring Schoenfeld. He was called up to the stage, sat in a throne, and donned an ermine cape and a crown. A parade of leading ladies, including Marin Mazzie and Betty Buckley, serenaded him. Longtime Shubert employees winced, but King Jerry loved it.

Square talking to a reporter from the *New York Post* about his sixty-plus years in show business.[5] At eighty-six, he was, indeed, the last of the theater owners who had transformed Broadway from a "crumbling cottage industry into a multibillion-dollar global empire."[*]

Nederlander considered Schoenfeld a "good friend." Their fierce rivalry in the seventies and eighties had long abated and, throughout the 2000s, they spoke on the phone almost every day. Nederlander was the first to extend a hand. Over lunch at Andrew Lloyd Webber's Sydmonton Festival in 1992, where the composer unveiled his new show, *Sunset Boulevard*, Nederlander said to Jacobs, "Bernie, when are we going to stop all this? We're getting too old to keep doing this." Jacobs replied, "Why don't we get together for lunch when we're back in New York?"

The following week, Nederlander's assistant, Nick Scandalios, received a call from Schoenfeld. If Jimmy was serious about ending the feud, he and Jacobs would be happy to join him for lunch, Schoenfeld said. The peace talks took place in the garden of Barbetta, the restaurant on West Forty-Sixth Street. Schoenfeld, Jacobs, and Phil Smith were on one side of the table, Nederlander, his son, Jimmy, and Scandalios on the other. The lunch lasted three hours. Schoenfeld, Jacobs, and Nederlander regaled one another with war stories.

"They each told the story of an incident from their perspective," Scandalios recalled. "It was cathartic. I don't think they changed their opinion of anything, but there was a lot of laughter."

During the lunch, a few theater producers walked into the garden, but as soon as they saw the Shuberts and the Nederlanders breaking bread they "immediately turned on their heels and left," said Scandalios. "They were stunned."

Nederlander weathered his rough patch in the late eighties and nineties, emerging in the 2000s with his theaters home to such shows as *Beauty and the Beast*, *Wicked*, *Hairspray*, and *The Lion King* (which moved from Disney's New Amsterdam to Nederlander's Minskoff

---

[*] Broadway's third landlord, James H. Binger, founder of Jujamcyn Theaters and the chairman of the Honeywell Corporation, died in 2004. Though Binger was not immersed in Broadway the way the Shuberts and the Nederlanders were, his acquisition of five Broadway theaters undoubtedly saved them from the wrecking ball.

Theatre in 2006). Touring productions of those and other megahits filled his theaters in Los Angeles, San Francisco, and Chicago. Real estate bets he made long ago paid off. He bought the four corners of Hollywood and Vine in the early eighties, when that part of Los Angeles was seedy and crime ridden. Every time a small business went belly up, he'd buy the building and tear it down to make more parking space for his Pantages Theatre. He still owns most of Hollywood and Vine, a parcel of land worth tens of millions of dollars today.

Over the last ten years, companies from Clear Channel to Disney have tried to buy Nederlander's empire. Nobody knows how much it's worth, but it's likely billions. Nederlander, ninety-three as of this writing, isn't selling. He runs the empire today with his son, Jimmy, and his former assistant, Scandalios, now vice president of the company. It was and will always be, Nederlander says, a family business.

In his office next to his big desk are a small plastic table and two little chairs. On the back of the chairs are the names of his grandchildren, James and Kathleen.

"They're my board of directors," he says.

Andrew Lloyd Webber and Cameron Mackintosh continue to be active in the theater.

Mackintosh owns and operates eight West End theaters, including the Victoria Palace, the Prince of Wales, the Novello, and the Prince Edward. He turned to the movies in 2012, producing *Les Misérables*, starring Hugh Jackman and Anne Hathaway (who won an Oscar). In 2014, he produced successful revivals of *Les Misérables* (in New York) and *Miss Saigon* (in London). That same year, the *Sunday Times* of London anointed him the most successful producer in theater history, with a net worth of $1.6 billion.

Lloyd Webber's Really Useful Group owns and operates six West End theaters, including the Drury Lane and the Palladium. *The Phantom of the Opera* is in its twenty-seventh year in London and its twenty-sixth in New York. On any given day, productions of *Evita*, *Cats*, *Jesus Christ Superstar*, and *Joseph and the Amazing Technicolor Dreamcoat* are running somewhere in the world. Queen Elizabeth II made Lloyd Webber a life peer in 1997. He sits on the Conservative side of the

House of Lords. In 2006, he became a reality TV star as the producer and lead judge of *How Do You Solve a Problem Like Maria?*—a BBC series about the search for an actress to play Maria in a West End revival of *The Sound of Music*. He continues to write new musicals, but without the success he once had. Two recent shows, *Love Never Dies*, the sequel to *Phantom*, and *Stephen Ward*, about the Profumo affair, were flops. In 2015 he was working on a musical version of *School of Rock* for Broadway.

After *Beauty and the Beast*, Disney produced *The Lion King*, which is still running on Broadway today and has grossed, worldwide, $6.2 billion, making it the most successful theatrical production of all time. (*The Phantom of the Opera* is number two.) Not every Disney show has been a success, however. *Tarzan* and *The Little Mermaid* flopped on Broadway, though they've proved popular in Europe and Asia. But *Mary Poppins*, *Newsies*, and *Aladdin* were hits, and the Disney Store is among the most popular tourist destinations in Times Square.

Disney's success lured other entertainment companies to Broadway. Warner Bros., Clear Channel, 20th Century Fox, and Dreamworks have all produced shows on Broadway, though with mixed results. Nearly every movie studio today has a theater division seeking to turn back catalogues of popular movies into stage shows.

After Disney, Universal Studios has had the most success on Broadway. The company owns a large stake in *Mamma Mia!* whose producer, Judy Craymer, had been Tim Rice's assistant on *Chess*. Craymer worked for several years as a freelance television producer after *Chess* closed. But she wanted to put together a stage show using the songs of ABBA. Scarred by their experience on *Chess*, Benny Andersson and Björn Ulvaeus vowed never to do another musical. But liking and trusting Craymer, they agreed to let her give it a try. She fashioned a show around their catalogue of hit songs. She was forty thousand pounds in debt and renting a friend's apartment when she finally got *Mamma Mia!* on stage in the West End in 1999. As of 2014, it was still running in London and New York, and has been performed all over the world, with grosses totalling nearly $3 billion. The 2008 movie remains the most successful movie musical of all time. Craymer owns 18.5 percent of *Mamma Mia!*. She is thought to be the third richest woman in England, after the queen and J. K. Rowling.

Universal also owns more than 50 percent of *Wicked*, which opened on Broadway at a cost of $14 million in 2003. It has become a global hit, breaking box office records from London to Auckland, and posting grosses of more than $3 billion. In 2014, the Broadway production alone was grossing $1.6 million a week.

Throughout the 1990s, Broadway attendance increased dramatically. Seven million people saw a Broadway show in the 1990–91 season. Ten years later, the figure had risen to nearly 12 million. In the 2000–01 theater season, Broadway grossed an all-time high of $666 million.

By the fall of 2001, Broadway had become such a crucial part of the cultural and economic fabric of the city that the day after the attack on the World Trade Center, Mayor Giuliani called the League of New York Theatres and Producers and requested that Broadway shows resume performances on September 13. The marquee lights were dimmed that night in memory of the victims of the attacks and their families. But when the lights went back on, the symbolism was unmistakable—New York was open for business. No act of terrorism, however horrific, could still this great city for long. At the hottest show in town—*The Producers*—Mel Brooks, Matthew Broderick, and Nathan Lane led the audience, standing and weeping, in singing "God Bless America" during the curtain call.

Broadway—and New York—rebounded quickly from the September 11 attacks. Attendance and revenue continued to climb. By the end of the decade, average yearly attendance on Broadway was 12 million. And the annual box office gross regularly exceeded $1 billion. The Times Square of *Midnight Cowboy*, of drugs, crime, and prostitution, of crumbling theaters and seedy peep shows, is now one of the world's leading tourist attractions. A 2011 economic report by the city noted that 10 percent of all the jobs in New York City were located in Times Square. The neighborhood contributed 11 percent of the entire economic output of the city.

One of Times Square's anchors, the Shubert Organization, founded in 1900, continues to thrive. All of its seventeen theaters were booked in the spring of 2015 with hits such as *Mamma Mia!*, *The Phantom of the Opera*, *Matilda*, *It's Only a Play* with Nathan Lane and Matthew Broderick, *The Elephant Man* with Bradley Cooper, *Fish in the Dark* with Larry David, and *The Audience* with Helen Mirren. The seventeen theaters post gross receipts of more than $6 million every week.

Back in 1972, when the Shubert Organization was on the verge of insolvency, Bernard Jacobs went to Morgan Quarterly to secure a $1 million line of credit. He used as collateral those seventeen theaters. J. P. Morgan turned him down.

In 2015, the Shuberts were exploring the possibility of building a fifteen-hundred-seat theater on land the company owns between Forty-Fifth and Forty-Sixth Streets along Eighth Avenue.

The estimated cost was $150 million.

For one theater.

ACKNOWLEDGMENTS

As with so much in life, timing—especially for a book like this—is everything. I was lucky enough to stumble on a story that could be put together from interviews with people who lived it. They had vivid, often hilarious, memories of Broadway and its personalities in the 1960s, '70s, and '80s. But enough time had gone by so that they could also be candid and reflective about some of the more painful parts of the story I have tried to tell. This book could not have been written without their help.

The first person I interviewed was Albert Poland. I spent several hours with him at his house in Dutchess County as he regaled me with tales of Gerald Schoenfeld, Bernard Jacobs, and the world of the Shubert Organization. Albert loved Bernie and Jerry, and they loved him. He understood what I was trying to accomplish with this book, and encouraged me throughout the reporting and writing. He read every chapter, providing thoughtful comments and correcting grievous errors. A writer could not have a better source or friend.

I have nearly twenty hours of interviews with Philip J. Smith, the chairman of the Shubert Organization. He was a participant in, or had a ringside seat at, almost every event that takes place in *Razzle Dazzle*. As Scott Rudin likes to say, "Phil Smith is the Tom Hagen of the Shuberts." Phil remembers everything and tells it with flair. He is also a wise and generous friend. I hope this book gives him the credit he deserves for his part in saving the Shuberts and Broadway in the 1970s.

I had many fun lunches with James M. Nederlander, who like Phil Smith has an astonishing memory. He can tell you how much he paid, to the dime, for every theater he owns. I would also like to thank James L. Nederlander ("Jimmy Jr.") and his wife, Margo, for their friendship and support.

Three other friends were great sources. Elizabeth I. McCann, also possessed of a sharp memory, poked fun at all the characters in this story, but never minimized their accomplishments. Emanuel Azenberg understood better than anyone the complex and often ridiculous rivalry between the Shuberts and the Nederlanders. And John Breglio, over the course of three long interviews, helped me grasp the brilliance, charisma, and tragedy of Michael Bennett.

I would also like to thank the following people for their time and their memories: John Barlow, Clive Barnes, Sidney Baumgarten, Joseph Berger, Ira Bernstein, Arthur Birsh, Don Black, Mark Bramble, Betty Buckley, Barry Burnett, David Clurman, Lawrence Cohen, Robert Cole, Nancy Coyne, Judy Craymer, Alan Eisenberg, Rick Elice, Josh Ellis, Dasha Epstein, Robert Fox, Merle Frimark, Jeremy Gerard, Bernard Gersten, Roberta Gratz, John Heilpern, Shirley Herz, William Ivey Long, Judy Jacksina, Betty Jacobs, Geoffrey Johnson, Robert Kamlot, Ed Koch, Herbert Kretzmer, Henry Krieger, Lionel Larner, Susan Lee, Francine LeFrak, Jerry Leichtling, William Liberman, Paul Libin, Andrew Lloyd Webber, Cameron Mackintosh, Richard Maltby Jr., Robert McDonald, Thomas Meehan, Alan Menken, Trevor Nunn, Elaine Paige, Harold Prince, Kathleen Raitt, Lee Roy Reams, Tim Rice, Arthur Rubin, Harvey Sabinson, Nick Scandalios, Peter Schneider, Richard Seff, Peter Shaffer, Michael Sovern, Herbert Sturz, Joseph Traina, Tommy Tune, Norman Twain, Edward Foley Vaughan, George Wachtel, Robin Wagner, Carl Weisbrod, Franklin Weissberg, Barry Weissler, Jon Wilner, and Bobby Zarem.

Although much of this book is drawn from interviews, I have also relied on several secondary sources. Foster Hirsch's *The Boys from Syracuse* is the best book about the Shubert brothers and their rise to power. It is scholarly but readable, and it was by my side as I wrote the early chapters of *Razzle Dazzle*. Jerry Stagg's *The Brothers Shubert* is fun and gossipy, but its sourcing is vague, so I only took from it what

I could confirm elsewhere. Brooks Atkinson's *Broadway* is an excellent overview of the Great White Way from 1900 to 1970. My friend Ken Mandelbaum's *A Chorus Line and the Musicals of Michael Bennett* is indispensable when writing about Bennett. And Michael Walsh's *Andrew Lloyd Webber: His Life and Works* is a well-written and insightful biography of the composer.

For background on Times Square, New York City, and the financial crisis of 1975, I am indebted to Lynne B. Sagalyn's *Times Square Roulette,* Anthony Bianco's *Ghosts of 42nd Street: A History of America's Most Infamous Block*, Vincent J. Cannato's *The Ungovernable City: John Lindsay and His Struggle to Save New York*, Ken Auletta's *The Streets Were Paved with Gold*, and Roger Starr's *The Rise and Fall of New York City.*

I am grateful to Christopher Bonanos, a senior editor at *New York*, for digging out several articles from his magazine that I could not find on my own.

Many friends supported and encouraged me throughout the three years it took to write this book. Eric Fettman, a member of the *New York Post*'s editorial board, talked me off the ledge when I felt overwhelmed by the project. He was also an excellent guide to the history and politics of New York City. Scott Rudin read early drafts of chapters and kept my spirits up with his enthusiastic responses. Barbara Hoffman, my editor at the *New York Post* for more than fifteen years, was always patient when I was up against a deadline. Clive Hirschhorn, a friend of twenty-five years, put me up at his apartment and country house while I conducted interviews in London. He was also an invaluable source about the musicals that appear in these pages. Wendy Kidd always made sure I had a quiet place to write when I was her guest at Holders House in Barbados. And Tita Cahn looked after me in Los Angeles. It was a great thrill to work in the garden where her husband, Sammy, wrote many of his incomparable songs.

My thanks also to Col Allan, Rob Bartlett, Stefanie Cohen, Stewart Collins, Margi Conklin, Clive Davis, Steven Doloff, Jonathan Foreman, Amanda Foreman, Susan Haskins, Katie and Peter Hermant, Charles Isherwood, Hugh Jackman, Linda Kline, George Lane, Imogen Lloyd Webber, Dagen McDowell, Patrick Pacheco, John Simon, Kevin Spacey, David Stone, Jan Stuart, Robert Wankel, and Fran Weissler.

Michael Kuchwara was one of the kindest people I have ever known. He was also a great reporter and critic. Jacques le Sourd made me laugh every day for twenty years. And Martin Gottfried gave me the best advice about writing a book: "Take your time. Do the research, and you'll find the story." I wish they could have stuck around to attend the book party.

David Kuhn invited me for a drink and changed my life. He asked if I'd ever thought of writing a book. I hadn't, but after a couple of glasses of Sauvignon blanc, I threw out a vague idea. "That's a book," he said. He is a great agent, editor, and friend. Thanks also to his associate Becky Sweren, who kept on top of things that had slipped my mind.

I am grateful to Jonathan Karp at Simon & Schuster for taking a chance on a newspaperman who had never written anything longer than 1,200 words. He has been a champion of *Razzle Dazzle* from the moment he read the proposal. Ben Loehnen was my editor and became my friend as I worked on this book. "You have a mountain to climb," he told me over drinks at the Lambs Club after I signed the contract. I would have fallen off that mountain long ago without his help. His red pen made me a better writer than I ever imagined I could be. I am also indebted to Jonathan Evans and Anthony Newfield, copyeditors who asked all the right questions.

Christina Amoroso came into my life the day I started working on *Razzle Dazzle*. God knows why, but she stuck with me the whole time, never complaining when weekends that might have been devoted to bike riding or wine tasting on the North Fork of Long Island were consumed with work. She is more than I deserve.

My sister, Leslie Riedel, and her husband, Scott Friend, took care of me when I had doubts about my ability to write *Razzle Dazzle*. I sat on their porch in West Newton, Massachusetts, for a week in the summer of 2011, read some short stories by F. Scott Fitzgerald, cleared my head, and went to work. Their love and support was, and always will be, essential to this book and anything else I try to do.

Most of all, I thank my parents, who let me scurry down to Florida, turn their lanai into a writer's colony, and work for hours undisturbed. Without them, there would be no book, no writer, no life.

NOTES

Chapter One: The Ice Age

1. William Goldman, *The Season: A Candid Look at Broadway* (New York: Limelight Editions, 1984), 340.
2. Stuart W. Little and Arthur Cantor, *The Playmakers* (New York: W. W. Norton, 1970), 228.
3. Jerry Stagg, *The Brothers Shubert* (New York: Random House, 1968), 356.
4. Milton Esterow, "Scalpers' Profit on Shows in a Year Put at $10 Million," *New York Times*, December 11, 1963.
5. Esterow, "Scalpers' Profit on Shows."
6. Ibid.

Chapter Two: The Phantom

1. Foster Hirsch, *The Boys from Syracuse: The Shuberts' Theatrical Empire* (New York: Cooper Square Press, 2000), 231.
2. Philip J. Smith, interview with author.
3. Foster Hirsch, *The Boys from Syracuse*, 15.
4. Brooks Atkinson, *Broadway* (New York: Limelight Editions, 1985), 14.
5. Hirsch, *The Boys from Syracuse*, 45.
6. *Syracuse Journal*, May 12, 1905.

Chapter Three: Mr. Lee and Mr. J. J.

1. Stagg, *The Brothers Shubert*, 70.
2. A. J. Liebling, *The Telephone Booth Indian* (New York: Broadway Books, 2004), 118.
3. Hirsch, *The Boys from Syracuse*, 167.
4. Hirsch, quoting U.S. Representative Emanuel Cellar, *The Boys from Syracuse*, 217.

Chapter Four: While There Is Death There Is Hope

1. Gerald Schoenfeld, *Mr. Broadway: The Inside Story of the Shuberts, the Shows, and the Stars* (Milwaukee, Wisc.: Applause Theatre & Cinema Books, 2012), 32.
2. Hirsch, *The Boys from Syracuse,* 226.
3. Schoenfeld, *Mr. Broadway,* 46.
4. Richard Crossman, *The Diaries of a Cabinet Minister* (New York: Holt, Rinehart and Winston), 11.
5. Schoenfeld, *Mr. Broadway,* 55.
6. Hirsch, *The Boys from Syracuse,* 269.
7. Schoenfeld, *Mr. Broadway,* 86.

Chapter Five: Bastards, Criminals, and Drunks

1. Hirsch, *The Boys from Syracuse,* 254.
2. Joseph Berger, "Goldman & the Shubert Estate Settlement," *New York Post,* May 3, 1974.
3. Edith Evans Asbury, "First Wife Gets Shubert Estate; Children of 2nd Held Legitimate," *New York Times,* August 9, 1963.
4. Nora Ephron, "Shubert Sent Love Letters to Wife He Was Shedding," *New York Post,* August 7, 1963.
5. Berger, "Goldman & the Shubert Estate Settlement."
6. Hirsch, *The Boys from Syracuse,* 269.
7. Berger, "Goldman & the Shubert Estate Settlement."
8. Hirsch, *The Boys from Syracuse,* 258.
9. N. R. Kleinfield, "How a Shubert Fund Produces and Directs," *New York Times,* July 10, 1994.

Chapter Six: Changing of the Guard

1. Richard Rodgers, *Musical Stages: An Autobiography* (New York: Da Capo Press, 1995), 302.
2. Laurence Bergreen, *As Thousands Cheer: The Life of Irving Berlin* (New York: Viking, 1990), 547.
3. Michael Riedel, "One Day Put a Tune in My Life," *New York Post,* July 2, 2010.
4. Al Kasha and Joel Hirschhorn, *Notes on Broadway: Conversations with the Great Songwriters* (Chicago: Contemporary Books, 1985), 98.
5. Martin Gottfried, *All His Jazz: The Life and Death of Bob Fosse* (New York: Bantam Books 1990), 150.

Chapter Seven: New York, New York, a Helluva Mess

1. Ken Mandelbaum, *Not Since Carrie: Forty Years of Broadway Musical Flops* (New York: St. Martin's Press, 1991), 153.

2. Fred Siegel, *The Prince of the City: Giuliani, New York and the Genius of American Life* (San Francisco: Encounter Books, 2005), 4.

3. Greg David, *Modern New York: The Life and Economics of a City* (New York: Palgrave Macmillan, 2012), 10.

4. George J. Lankevich, *New York City: A Short History* (New York: New York University Press 1998), 197.

5. Lankevich, *New York City,* 197.

6. David, *Modern New York,* 11.

7. Vincent J. Cannato, *The Ungovernable City: John Lindsay and His Struggle to Save New York* (New York: Basic Books 2002), 526.

8. Carl Weisbrod, interview with author.

9. Sidney J. Baumgarten, interview with author.

10. Anthony Bianco, *Ghosts of 42nd Street: A History of America's Most Infamous Block* (New York: Harper Paperbacks, 2005), 26.

11. Lynne B. Sagalyn, *Times Square Roulette: Remaking the City Icon* (Cambridge: MIT Press, 2001), 42.

12. George Chauncey, *Gay New York: Gender, Urban Culture, and the Making of the Gay Male World, 1890–1940,* (New York: Basic Books, 1994), 339.

13. Cannato, *The Ungovernable City,* 537.

Chapter Eight: The Coup

1. Murray Schumach, "Shubert Empire Fighting a Financial Crisis," *New York Times,* December 11, 1972.

2. Kleinfield, "How a Shubert Fund Produces and Directs."

3. Abel Green, "Shuberts' 3 New 'Exec Directors'; Show Biz Ponders Power Struggle," *Variety,* July 12, 1972.

4. Hirsh, *The Boys from Syracuse,* 272.

Chapter Nine: Rotten to the Core

1. Stuart Ostrow, *Present at the Creation, Leaping in the Dark, and Going Against the Grain: 1776, Pippin, M. Butterfly, La Bête, and Other Broadway Adventures* (New York: Applause Theatre & Cinema Books, 2006), 65.

2. Gottfried, *All His Jazz,* 253.

3. Murray Schumach, "State Investigating Charge By Deposed Shubert Heir," *New York Times,* December 21, 1972.

4.   Hirsh, *The Boys from Syracuse,* 272.

5.   Murray Schumach, "Deposed Head of Shubert Empire Seeks to Oust 3 Successors," *New York Times,* January 8, 1973.

6.   Robert D. McFadden, "Shubert Figure Loses Court Bid to Regain Empire," *New York Times,* April 10, 1973.

7.   Gary Pearlman, "Give My Regards to Broadway: Guts, Greed, and Betrayal," *Palm Beach Times,* November 20, 2012.

Chapter Ten: Horsing Around

1.   John Dexter, *The Honourable Beast: A Posthumous Autobiography* (New York: Routledge/Theatre Arts, 1993), 45.

2.   Dexter, *The Honourable Beast,* 84.

Chapter Eleven: The Paintman Cometh

1.   Ralph Blumenthal, "Shubert Grants in Drama Linked to Buying of Paint," *New York Times,* April 16, 1974.

2.   Joseph Berger, "The Paint Truck That Carries Cash," *New York Post,* July 17, 1974.

3.   Joseph Berger, "Goldman and His Charities," *New York Post,* April 17, 1974.

4.   Joseph Berger, "Shubert Pair Deny Conflict," *New York Post,* March 30, 1974.

5.   Berger, "Shubert Pair Deny Conflict."

6.   Ralph Blumenthal, "Shubert Fund Directors Refuse Lefkowitz Request to Step Aside," *New York Times,* May 10, 1974.

7.   Jack Newfield, "Nadjari: In His Heart He Knows You're Guilty," *Village Voice,* October 17, 1977.

8.   Richard F. Shepard, "Producers Define Shubert Support," *New York Times,* May 15, 1974.

9.   Shepard, "Producers Define Shubert Support."

10. Ibid.

11. Joe Nicholson, "Lefky Hails $2M Shubert Decision," *New York Post,* April 14, 1977.

12. Lawrence Van Gelder, "Goldman Is Taking Leave of Absence from Shubert Post," *New York Times,* March 20, 1975.

Chapter Twelve: The Jockey

1.   "Backstage with A Chorus Line," *Ideastream,* May 20, 2008, http://wclv.idea stream.org/programs/backstage-with/chorus-line-0.

2.   Michael Bennett, tape-recorded interview heard in *Every Little Step,* 2008.

3. Bennett, interview heard in *Every Little Step.*

4. Jeremy Gerard, "Michael Bennett, Theater Innovator, Dies at 44," *New York Times,* July 3, 1987.

5. Ken Mandelbaum, *A Chorus Line and the Musicals of Michael Bennett* (New York: St. Martin's Press, 1989), 60.

6. Gerard, "Michael Bennett."

7. Tommy Tune, interview with author.

8. Lawrence Cohen, interview with author.

Chapter Thirteen: The One

1. Mandelbaum, *A Chorus Line,* 100.

2. Ibid., 117.

3. Ibid., 144.

Chapter Fourteen: The Interloper

1. Michiko Kakutani, "The Great Theater Duel and How It Affects Broadway Theaters," *New York Times,* September 14, 1980.

2. Vincent Canby, "Nederlander Family Building a Theater Empire," *New York Times,* July 18, 1967.

3. *New York Newsday,* January 20, 1971.

Chapter Fifteen: I Love New York, Especially in the Evening

1. Lankevich, *New York City,* 219.

2. Ibid.

3. R. Thomas Collins, *NewsWalker: A Story for Sweeney* (Virginia: RavensYard Publishing, 2002), 96.

4. Harvey Sabinson, interview with author.

5. Francis X. Clines, "Mayor Plans New Times Square Cleanup," *New York Times,* October 28, 1975.

6. Bianco, *Ghosts of 42nd Street,* 207.

7. Collins, *NewsWalker: A Story for Sweeney,* 92.

8. Selwyn Raab, "Screeners Block Baumgarten Bid for a Criminal Court Judgeship," *New York Times,* December 22, 1977.

9. Philip H. Dougherty, "Letting the Theater Spotlight New York," *New York Times,* January 25, 1978.

10. James P. Sterba, " 'I Love New York' Campaign Going National," *New York Times,* July 7, 1978.

Chapter Sixteen: The Coiled Cobra

1. Howard Kissel, *David Merrick: The Abominable Showman* (New York: Applause Theatre & Cinema Books, 1993), 324.

2. Leslie Bennetts, "Scrooged: David Merrick Faces His Final Curtain," *Vanity Fair,* December 1989.

3. Bennetts, "Scrooged."

4. Frank Rich, "Confessions of the Butcher of Broadway," *New York Times Magazine,* February 13, 1994.

5. Rich, "Confessions of the Butcher of Broadway."

6. Kissel, *The Abominable Showman,* 452.

Chapter Seventeen: The Bernie and Jerry Show

1. Martin Gottfried, *All His Jazz,* 365.

2. Clive Barnes, "Cleaning Up the Great White Way," *New York Post,* April 6, 1978.

3. Kakutani, "The Great Theater Duel."

4. Ibid.

5. Ibid.

6. N. R. Kleinfield, "I.R.S. Ruling Wrote Script for the Shubert Tax Break," *New York Times,* July 11, 1994.

7. Kleinfield, "I.R.S. Ruling Wrote Script."

8. Ibid.

9. Ibid.

10. Richard Corliss, "A Dickens of a Show," *Time,* October 5, 1981.

Chapter Eighteen: The Jockey and the Godfather

1. Kevin Kelly, *One Singular Sensation: The Michael Bennett Story* (New York: Zebra Books, 1991), 239.

2. Kenneth Turan and Joseph Papp, *Free for All: Joe Papp, The Public, and the Greatest Theater Story Ever Told* (New York: Doubleday, 2009), 465.

3. Robert Fox, interview with author.

4. Kevin Kelly, "The Next 'Chorus Line'?" *New York,* December 24, 1981.

Chapter Nineteen: Civil War

1. "A Times Sq. Youth Shelter Seeks Evictions to Expand," *New York Times,* January 28, 1979.

2. Bianco, *Ghosts of 42nd Street,* 248.

3. "A Times Sq. Youth Shelter Seeks Evictions to Expand."

4. Sagalyn, *Times Square Roulette,* 58.

5. Ibid., 61.

6. Ibid.

7. Ibid., 65.

8. William E. Geist, "New Broadway Hotel Gets the Once Over," *New York Times,* October 12, 1985.

9. Sydney H. Schanberg, "Portman's Progress," *New York Times,* March 13, 1982.

10. Nicholas Van Hoogstraten, *Lost Broadway Theaters* (New York: Princeton Architectural Press), 137.

11. Bernard Hughes, "On With the Show, Not the Hotel," *New York Times,* February 10, 1980.

12. Roberta Brandes Gratz, *The Living City: How America's Cities Are Being Revitalized By Thinking Small in a Big Way* (New York: Simon & Schuster, 1989), 358.

13. Michiko Kakutani, "Broadway Is a House Divided," *New York Times,* January 24, 1982.

14. Kakutani, "Broadway Is a House Divided."

Chapter Twenty: And the Winner Is . . .

1. Ethan Mordden, *Ziegfeld: The Man Who Invented Show Business* (New York: St. Martin's Press 2008), 142.

2. Maury Yeston, interviewed by Speakeasystage.com, January 2011.

3. Gratz, *The Living City,* 355.

4. Gratz, *The Living City,* 365.

5. William Ivey Long, interview with author.

6. Samuel G. Freedman, "How an Uneasy Alliance Helps Shape Broadway," *New York Times,* April 1, 1984.

Chapter Twenty-One: CAT$

1. Freedman, "How an Uneasy Alliance Helps Shape Broadway."

2. Ibid.

3. Samuel G. Freedman, "Cohen Resigns From Theater League: Producers Criticize Remarks at Tonys," *New York Times,* June 5, 1985.

4. Michael Walsh, *Andrew Lloyd Webber: His Life and Works* (New York: Abrams, 1989), 112.

5. Walsh, *Andrew Lloyd Webber,* 16.

6. Sheridan Morley and Ruth Leon, *Hey, Mr. Producer! The Musical World of Cameron Mackintosh* (New York: Back Stage Books, 1998), 16.

7. Cameron Mackintosh, interview with author.

8. Walsh, *Andrew Lloyd Webber,* 118.

9.   Andrew Lloyd Webber, interview with author.

10. Josh Ellis, interview with author.

11. Walsh, *Andrew Lloyd Webber*, 126.

Chapter Twenty-Two: Mesmerizing Temptation

1.   Kelly, *One Singular Sensation*, 358.

2.   Kevin Kelly, "Falling on Its Funny Face," *New York*, February 28, 1983.

3.   Don Shewey, "How 'My One and Only' Came to Broadway," *New York Times*, May 1, 1983.

4.   Kelly, "Falling on Its Funny Face."

5.   John Breglio, interview with author.

6.   Kelly, *One Singular Sensation*, 374.

7.   Carol Lawson, "Broadway; Scott to direct 'Design for Living' at Circle in the Square," *New York Times*, May 4, 1984.

8.   Cameron Mackintosh, interview with author.

9.   Lawrence K. Altman, "Rare Cancer Seen in 41 Homosexuals," *New York Times*, July 3, 1981.

Chapter Twenty-Three: End of the Line

1.   "Anti-hero?" *Chess in Translation*, March 24, 2011.

2.   Leslie Bennetts, "Backstage Drama," *Vanity Fair*, May 1988.

3.   Robin Wagner, interview with author.

4.   Kelly, *One Singular Sensation*, 401.

5.   Nan Robertson, "Michael Bennett Leaves Musical," *New York Times*, January 23, 1986.

Chapter Twenty-Four: The British Are Coming! The British Are Coming!

1.   Rick Elice, interview with author.

2.   Harold L. Vogel, *Entertainment Industry Economics: A Guide for Financial Analysis* (New York: Cambridge University Press, 2014), 390.

3.   Morley and Leon, *Hey, Mr. Producer!*, 91.

4.   Ibid., 92.

5.   Benedict Nightingale, " 'Les Miserables' Is Reborn as a Lavish Rock Opera," *New York Times*, March 30, 1986.

6.   Walsh, *Andrew Lloyd Webber*, 176.

7.   Ibid., 178.

8.   Ibid., 218.

9.   Ibid., 203.

10. Sagalyn, *Times Square Roulette*, 278.

11. Walsh, *Andrew Lloyd Webber*, 179.

12. Frank Rich, "Broadway: The Empire Strikes Back," *New York Times*, March 29, 1987.

13. Ron Alexander, "After Opening at the Majestic, Gala at the Beacon," *New York Times*, January 27, 1988.

14. Walsh, *Andrew Lloyd Webber*, 219.

15. Jeremy Gerard, " 'Phantom': Scalpers' Bonanza," *New York Times*, January 20, 1988.

16. Jeremy Gerard, "Shubert Stages a Dramatic (and Musical) Comeback," *New York Times*, April 8, 1987.

17. Bennetts, "Backstage Drama."

18. Robert Fox and Tim Rice, interviews with author.

19. Schoenfeld, *Mr. Broadway*, 186.

Chapter Twenty-Five: Pick-a-Little, Talk-a-Little

1. Mervyn Rothstein, "The Hellinger Theater Is Leased to a Church," *New York Times*, February 8, 1989.

2. Michael Riedel, "What the Butcher Forgot to Tell You," *New York Daily News*, February 20, 1994.

3. Rich, "Confessions of the Butcher of Broadway."

4. Riedel, "What the Butcher Forgot to Tell You."

5. Jon Wilner, interview with author.

Chapter Twenty-Six: Nothing Matters

1. Mervyn Rothstein, "How a High Roller Bets on Broadway," *New York Times*, June 3, 1990; David Owen, "Betting on Broadway," *New Yorker*, June 13, 1994.

2. "Curtain Call," Page Six, *New York Post*, November 29, 1993.

3. Rothstein, "How a High Roller Bets on Broadway."

4. Sagalyn, *Times Square Roulette*, 53.

5. Bianco, *Ghosts of 42nd Street*, 215.

6. Ralph Blumenthal, "Real-Life Courtroom Drama May Play on Broadway Stage," *New York Times*, November 15, 1991.

7. Susan Saulny, "A Dignitary Examines Community Court," *New York Times*, December 16, 2003.

8. Bianco, *Ghosts of 42nd Street*, 246.

9. Ibid., 271.

10. Ibid., 273.

11. Ibid., 279.

12. Ibid., 284.

13. David W. Dunlap, "Theater Owners Battle Planned Disney Leap into 42nd Street," *New York Times,* November 17, 1993.

14. Michael Riedel, "Showdown on the Great White Way," *New York Daily News,* March 12, 1995.

Epilogue: Exit Music

1. Jesse McKinley, "The Man Behind the Curtain," *New York Times,* November 27, 2005.

2. Michael I. Sovern, *An Improbable Life: My 60 Years at Columbia and Other Adventures* (New York: Columbia University Press, 2014), 235.

3. Michael Riedel, "Chairman of the Boards," *New York Post,* November 26, 2008.

4. Bruce Weber, "He Relit Broadway: Gerald Schoenfeld Dies at 84," *New York Times,* November 26, 2008.

5. Michael Riedel, "The Last of the B'Way Titans," *New York Post,* December 4, 2008.

BIBLIOGRAPHY

Atkinson, Brooks. *Broadway*. New York: Limelight Editions, 1985.

Auletta, Ken. *The Streets Were Paved with Gold*. New York: Random House, 1979.

Behr, Edward. *Les Misérables: History in the Making*. London: Pavilion Books Limited, 1989.

Bergreen, Laurence. *As Thousands Cheer: The Life of Irving Berlin*. New York: Viking, 1990.

Berman, Marshall. *On the Town: One Hundred Years of Spectacle in Times Square*. London: Verso, 2009.

Bianco, Anthony. *Ghosts of 42nd Street: A History of America's Most Infamous Block*. New York: Harper Paperbacks, 2005.

Bloom, Ken. *Broadway: An Encyclopedic Guide to the History, People and Places of Times Square*. New York: Facts on File, 1991.

Botto, Louis. *At This Theatre: An Informal History of New York's Legitimate Theatres*. New York: Dodd Mead, 1984.

Bram, Christopher. *Eminent Outlaws: The Gay Writers Who Changed America*. New York: Twelve, 2012.

Cannato, Vincent J. *The Ungovernable City: John Lindsay and His Struggle to Save New York*. New York: Basic Books, 2002.

Caro, Robert A. *The Power Broker: Robert Moses and the Fall of New York*. New York: Vintage Books, 1975.

Chauncey, George. *Gay New York: Gender, Urban Culture, and the Making of the Gay Male World, 1890–1940*. New York: Basic Books, 1994.

Collins, R. Thomas. *NewsWalker: A Story for Sweeney*. Virginia: RavensYard Publishing, 2002.

Crossman, Richard. *The Diaries of a Cabinet Minister*. New York: Holt, Rinehart and Winston, 1976.

David, Greg. *Modern New York: The Life and Economics of a City*. New York: Palgrave Macmillan, 2012.

Delany, Samuel R. *Times Square Red, Times Square Blue*. New York: New York University Press, 1999.

Dexter, John. *The Honourable Beast: A Posthumous Autobiography*. New York: Routledge/Theatre Arts, 1993.

Epstein, Helen. *Joe Papp: An American Life*. New York: Little, Brown, 1994.

Gelb, Arthur. *City Room*. New York: A Marian Wood Book/Putnam, 2003.

Goldman, William. *The Season: A Candid Look at Broadway*. New York: Limelight Editions, 1984.

Gottfried, Martin. *All His Jazz: The Life and Death of Bob Fosse*. New York: Bantam Books, 1990.

———. *Broadway Musicals*. New York: Abrams, 1979.

Gratz, Roberta Brandes. *The Living City: How America's Cities Are Being Revitalized By Thinking Small in a Big Way*. New York: Simon & Schuster, 1989.

———, with Norman Mintz. *Cities Back from the Edge: New Life for Downtown*. New York: John Wiley & Sons, 1989.

Green, Stanley. *The World of Musical Comedy*. New York: Da Capo Press, 1984.

Hirsch, Foster. *The Boys from Syracuse: The Shuberts' Theatrical Empire*. New York: Cooper Square Press, 2000.

———. *Harold Prince and the American Musical Theatre*. New York: Applause Theatre & Cinema Books, 2005.

Jackson, Kenneth T. *The Encyclopedia of New York City*. New Haven: Yale University Press, 1995.

Kasha, Al, and Joel Hirschhorn. *Notes on Broadway: Conversations with the Great Songwriters*. Chicago: Contemporary Books, 1985.

Kelly, Kevin. *One Singular Sensation: The Michael Bennett Story*. New York: Zebra Books, 1991.

King, Tom. *The Operator: David Geffen Builds, Buys, and Sells the New Hollywood*. New York: Random House, 2000.

Kissel, Howard. *David Merrick, The Abominable Showman: The Unauthorized Biography*. New York: Applause Theatre & Cinema Books, 1993.

Lankevich, George J. *New York City: A Short History*. New York: New York University Press, 1998.

Lerner, Alan Jay. *The Musical Theatre: A Celebration*. New York: McGraw-Hill, 1986.

Liebling, A. J. *The Telephone Booth Indian*. New York: Broadway Books, 2004.

Little, Stuart W., and Arthur Cantor. *The Playmakers*. New York: W. W. Norton, 1970.

Loesser, Susan. *A Most Remarkable Fella: Frank Loesser and the Guys and Dolls in His Life*. New York: Donald I. Fine, 1993.

Mandelbaum, Ken. *A Chorus Line and the Musicals of Michael Bennett*. New York: St. Martin's Press, 1989.

———. *Not Since Carrie: Forty Years of Broadway Musical Flops*. New York: St. Martin's Press, 1991.

McNamara, Brooks. *The Shuberts of Broadway: A History Drawn from the Collections of the Shubert Archive*. New York: Oxford University Press, 1990.

Mordden, Ethan. *Ziegfeld: The Man Who Invented Show Business*. New York: St. Martin's Press, 2008.

———. *Open a New Window: The Broadway Musical in the 1960s*. New York: St. Martin's Press, 2001.

———. *Anything Goes: A History of American Musical Theatre*. New York: Oxford University Press, 2013.

Morley, Sheridan, and Ruth Leon. *Hey, Mr. Producer! The Musical World of Cameron Mackintosh*. New York: Back Stage Books, 1998.

Morris, Charles R. *The Cost of Good Intentions: New York City and the Liberal Experiment*. New York: W. W. Norton, 1980.

Morton, Ray. *Amadeus*. Milwaukee, Wisc.: Limelight Editions, 2011.

Ostrow, Stuart. *Present at the Creation, Leaping in the Dark, and Going Against the Grain: 1776, Pippin, M. Butterfly, La Bête and Other Broadway Adventures*. New York: Applause Theatre & Cinema Books, 2006.

Rodgers, Richard. *Musical Stages: An Autobiography*. New York: Da Capo Press, 1995.

Sagalyn, Lynne B. *Times Square Roulette: Remaking the City Icon*. Cambridge: MIT Press, 2001.

Schoenfeld, Gerald. *Mr. Broadway: The Inside Story of the Shuberts, the Shows, and the Stars*. Milwaukee, Wisc.: Applause Theatre & Cinema Books, 2012.

Siegel, Fred. *The Prince of the City: Giuliani, New York, and the Genius of American Life*. San Francisco: Encounter Books, 2005.

Simon, Neil. *Rewrites: A Memoir*. New York: Simon & Schuster, 1996.

Simonson, Robert. *The Gentleman Press Agent: Fifty Years in the Theatrical Trenches with Merle Debuskey*. Milwaukee, Wisc.: Applause Theatre & Cinema Books, 2010.

Sovern, Michael I. *An Improbable Life: My 60 Years at Columbia and Other Adventures*. New York: Columbia University Press, 2014.

Stagg, Jerry. *The Brothers Shubert*. New York: Random House, 1968.

Starr, Roger. *The Rise and Fall of New York City*. New York: Basic Books, 1985.

Steyn, Mark. *Broadway Babies Say Goodnight: Musicals Then and Now*. London: Faber and Faber, 1997.

Taylor, William R., ed. *Inventing Times Square: Commerce and Culture at the Crossroads of the World*. Baltimore: The Johns Hopkins University Press, 1991.

Thorndike, Joseph J., Jr. *The Very Rich: A History of Wealth*. New York: American Heritage, 1976.

Traub, James. *The Devil's Playground: A Century of Pleasure and Profit in Times Square.* New York: Random House, 2004.

Turan, Kenneth, and Joseph Papp. *Free for All: Joe Papp, The Public, and the Greatest Theater Story Ever Told.* New York: Doubleday, 2009.

Van Hoogstraten, Nicholas. *Lost Broadway Theatres.* New York: Princeton Architectural Press, 1991.

Vogel, Harold L. *Entertainment Industry Economics: A Guide for Financial Analysis.* New York: Cambridge University Press, 2014.

Wallace, David. *Capital of the World: A Portrait of New York City in the Roaring Twenties.* Guilford, Conn.: Lyons Press, 2011.

Walsh, Michael. *Andrew Lloyd Webber: His Life and Works.* New York: Abrams, 1989.

Wharton, John F. *Life among the Playwrights: Being Mostly the Story of The Playwrights Producing Company.* New York: Quadrangle/The New York Times Book Company, 1974.

White, Norval, and Elliot Willensky with Fran Leadon. *AIA Guide to New York City.* New York: Oxford University Press, 2010.

INDEX